The Educational Role
of the Museum

Edited by
Eilean Hooper-Greenhill

ROUTLEDGE

London and New York

First published 1994
by Routledge
11 New Fetter Lane, London EC4P 4EE

Simultaneously published in the USA and Canada
by Routledge
29 West 35th Street, New York, NY 10001

Reprinted 1996

Routledge is an International Thomson Publishing company

© 1994 Eilean Hooper-Greenhill

Typeset in Sabon by Florencetype Ltd, Stoodleigh, Devon

Printed and bound in Great Britain by T.J.Press Ltd, Padstow, Cornwall

British Library Cataloguing in Publication Data
A catalogue record for this book is available from the British Library

Library of Congress Cataloguing in Publication Data
A catalogue record for this book is available from the Library of Congress

ISBN 0–415–11286–9 (hbk)
ISBN 0–415–11287–7 (pbk)

Contents

Contents

Figures

Tables

Series preface

Museums are established institutions, but they exist in a changing world. The modern notion of a museum and its collections runs back into the sixteenth or even fifteenth centuries, and the origins of the earliest surviving museums belong to the period soon after. Museums have subsequently been and continue to be founded along these well-understood lines. But the end of the second millennium AD and the advent of the third one points up the new needs and preoccupations of contemporary society. These are many, but some can be picked out as particularly significant here. Access is crucially important: access to information, the decision-making process and resources like gallery space, and access by children, ethnic minorities, women and the disadvantaged and underprivileged. Similarly, the nature of museum work itself needs to be examined, so that we can come to a clearer idea of the nature of the institution and its material, of what museum professionalism means, and how the issues of management and collection management affect outcomes. Running across all these debates is the recurrent theme of the relationship between theory and practice in what is, at the end of the day, an important area of work.

New needs mean fresh efforts at information-gathering and understanding, and the best possible access to important literature for teaching and study. It is this need which the *Leicester Sources in Museum Studies* series addresses. The series as a whole breaks new ground by bringing together, for the first time, an important body of published work, much of it very recent, much of it taken from journals which few libraries carry, and all of it representing fresh approaches to the study of the museum operation.

The series has been divided into six volumes each of which covers a significant aspect of museum studies. These six topics bear a generic relationship to the modular arrangement of the Leicester Department of Museum Studies post-graduate course in Museum Studies, but, more fundamentally, they reflect current thinking about museums and their study. Within each volume, each editor has been responsible for his or her choice of papers. Each volume reflects the approach of its own editor, and the different feel of the various traditions and discourses upon which it draws. The range of individual emphases and the diversity of points of view is as important as the over-arching theme in which each volume finds its place.

It is our intention to produce a new edition of the volumes in the series every three years, so that the selection of papers for inclusion is a continuing process and the contemporary stance of the series is maintained. All the editors of the series are happy to receive suggestions for inclusions (or exclusions), and details of newly published material.

Acknowledgements

The publishers and editors would like to thank the following people and organizations for permission to reproduce copyright material:

Eilean Hooper-Greenhill, 'Museum communication: an introductory essay', reprinted from Eilean Hooper-Greenhill (ed.) (1994) *Museum, Media, Message*, London: Routledge. Eilean Hooper-Greenhill, 'A new communications model for museums', reprinted from Gaynor Kavanagh (ed.) (1991) *Museum Languages: Objects and Texts*, by permission of Leicester University Press (a division of Pinter Publishers Ltd), London. All rights reserved. J. Morgan and P. Welton, 'The process of communication', reprinted from J. Morgan and P. Welton (eds) (1986) *See What I Mean: An Introduction to Visual Communication*, Edward Arnold, by permission of Hodder & Stoughton Ltd. Robert Hodge and Wilfred D'Souza, 'The museum as a communicator: a semiotic analysis of the Western Australian Gallery, Perth', *Museum* 31(4) (1979), © UNESCO 1979, reproduced by permission of UNESCO. Eilean Hooper-Greenhill, 'Who goes to museums', reprinted from Eilean Hooper-Greenhill (1993) *Museums and their Visitors*, London: Routledge. Tanya Du Bery, 'Why don't people go to museums?', reprinted from *Museum Development* (March 1991) by permission of the Museum Development Company. Stephen Bitgood, 'Problems in visitor orientation and circulation', reprinted from S. Bitgood, S. Roper and A. Benfield (eds) (1988) *Visitor Studies 1988: Theory, Practice and Research, Proceedings of the First Annual Visitor Studies Conference*, Jacksonville, Alabama: Center for Social Design, pp. 155–70. Anita Rui Olds, 'Sending them home alive': this article is reproduced with the permission of Museum Education Roundtable. It first appeared in the *Journal of Museum Education* 15(1) (1990). Marista Leishman, 'Image and self-image', reprinted from *Museums Journal* 93(6) (1993) by permission of the Museums Association. R. S. Miles and A. F. Tout, 'Outline of a technology for effective science exhibits', reprinted from *Curation of Palaeontological Collections: Special Papers in Palaeontology* 22 (1979) by permission of the authors. R. S. Miles and A. F. Tout, 'Impact of research on the approach to the visiting public at the Natural History Museum, London', reproduced from *International Journal of Science Education* 13(5) (1991) by permission of Taylor and Francis publishers and the authors. Sam H. Ham, 'Cognitive psychology and interpretation: synthesis and application', reproduced from *Journal of Interpretation* 8(1) (1983). Hank Grasso and Howard Morrison, 'Collaboration: towards a more holistic design process', reprinted by permission of the publisher from *History News* 47(3) (May/June 1992): 12–15. Copyright © by the American Association for State and Local History. Pat

Rabbitt with an introduction by Andy Millward, 'Learning to make an exhibition of ourselves', *Museum Design* 1 (1990) reprinted by permission. Mark O'Neill, 'Cheap and cheerful: techniques for temporary displays', *Scottish Museum News*, the magazine of the Scottish Museums Council (Spring 1990) reprinted by permission of the Scottish Museums Council. Helen Coxall, 'Museum text as mediated message', *Women, Heritage and Museums (WHAM)* 14 (1990) reprinted by permission. Margareta Ekarv, 'Combating redundancy: writing texts for exhibitions', *Exhibitions in Sweden* 27/8 (1986/7) reprinted by permission of Riksutställningar. Translated from 'PÅ GÅNG i utställningssverige' 27/28 (1986/7), quarterly magazine published by Riksutställningar (Swedish Travelling Exhibitions). James Carter, 'How old is this text?', reproduced from 'A Way with Words', *Environmental Interpretation, the Bulletin of the Centre for Environmental Interpretation* (February 1993) by permission of the Centre for Environmental Interpretation; J. Carter and D. Hillier, 'A writing checklist', reproduced from 'A Way with Words', *Environmental Interpretation, the Bulletin of the Centre for Environmental Interpretation* (February 1993) by permission of the Centre for Environmental Interpretation. *Environmental Interpretation, the Bulletin of the Centre for Environmental Interpretation* is available from CEI at Manchester Metropolitan University, Manchester, UK, tel.: 061 247 1067, fax: 061 236 7383. Elizabeth Frostick, 'Worth a Hull lot more', *Museums Journal* 91(2) (1991) reprinted by permission of the Museums Association. John Millard (with David Phillips), 'Art history for all the family', *Museums Journal* 92(2) (1992) reprinted by permission of the Museums Association. Jane Peirson-Jones (with Anandi Ramamurthy), 'Multiculturalism incarnate', *Museums Journal* 92(1) (1992) reprinted by permission of the Museums Association. Gaby Porter, 'Alternative perspectives', *Museums Journal* 93(11) (1993) reprinted by permission of the Museums Association. Patrick Sudbury, 'Science by stealth', *Museums Journal* 93(11) (1993) reprinted by permission of the Museums Association. Nick Winterbotham, 'Happy hands-on', *Museums Journal* 93(2) (1993) reprinted by permission of the Museums Association. Harriet Purkis, 'History: in hand, low-tech and cheap', *Museums Journal* 93(2) (1993) reprinted by permission of the Museums Association. Betty Davidson, Candace Heald and George Hein, 'Increased exhibit accessibility through multisensory interaction', reprinted from *Curator* 34(4), pp. 273–90. Copyright © The American Museum of Natural History 1991. Sandra Bicknell and Peter Mann, 'A picture of visitors for exhibition developers', forthcoming in D. Thompson, A. Benefield, S. Bitgood, H. Shettel and R. Williams (eds) (1992) *Visitor Studies: Theory, Research and Practice, Volume 5, Collected Papers from the 1992 Visitor Studies Conference (St. Louis, Missouri)*, Jacksonville, Alabama: Visitor Studies Association. Paul Alter and Rita Ward (formerly Rita Alter), 'Exhibit evaluation: taking account of human factors', reprinted from *Curator* 31(3), pp. 167–77. Copyright © The American Museum of Natural History 1988. Phil Bull, 'A beginner's guide to evaluation', reproduced from 'A Way with Words', *Environmental Interpretation, the Bulletin of the Centre for Environmental Interpretation* (July 1989) by permission of the Centre for Environmental Interpretation, Manchester Metropolitan University, Manchester, UK. Benjamin E. Braverman, 'Empowering visitors: focus group interviews for art museums', reprinted from *Curator* 31(1), pp. 43–52. Copyright © The American Museum of Natural History 1988. G. Binks and D. Uzzell, 'Monitoring and evaluation: the techniques', reproduced from 'Evaluation Interpretation', *Environmental Interpretation, the Bulletin of the Centre for Environmental Interpretation* (July 1990) by permission of the Centre for Environmental Interpretation, Manchester Metropolitan University, Manchester, UK. Eilean Hooper-Greenhill, 'Museum education', reprinted with permission from J. M. A. Thompson (ed.) (1992) *Manual of Curatorship*, second edition, Butterworth-Heinemann Ltd, Oxford, UK. Eilean Hooper-Greenhill, 'The past, the present and the future: museum education from the 1790s to the 1990s', *Journal of Education in Museums* 12 (1991). Joseph H. Suina, 'Museum multicultural education for young learners': this article is reproduced with the permission of Museum Education Roundtable. It first appeared in the *Journal of Museum Education* 15(1) (1990). Nina Jensen, 'Children, teenagers and adults in museums: a developmental perspective', reprinted, with permission, from *Museum News*, May/June 1982. Copyright © the American Association of Museums. All rights reserved. Lynn Plourde, 'Teaching with collections', from *Young Children* 44(3) (1989), pp. 78–80. Copyright © 1989 by the National Association for the Education of Young Children. Reprinted by permission. Gail Durbin, 'Improving worksheets', reprinted from the *Journal of Education in Museums* 10 (1989). Charles F. Gunther, 'Museumgoers: life-styles and learning characteristics', reprinted from *Museums and Universities: New Paths for Continuing Education,* edited by Janet W. Solinger (1989). Used by permission of the American Council on Education and The Oryx Press, 4041 N. Central at Indian School Rd, Phoenix, AZ 85012. Luke Baldwin, Sharlene Cochrane, Constance Counts, John Dolomore, Martha McKenna and Barbara Vacarr, 'Passionate and purposeful: adult learning communities': this article is reproduced with the permission of Museum Education Roundtable. It first appeared in the *Journal of Museum Education* 15(1) (1990). Jocelyn Dodd, 'Whose museum is it anyway? Museum education and the community', *Journal of Education in Museums* 13 (1992). George Hein, 'Evaluation of museum programmes and exhibits', *Museum Education*, Danish ICOM/CECA, Copenhagen. Reproduced by kind permission of the author. Tim Badman, 'Small-scale evaluation', reproduced from 'Evaluating Interpretation', *Environmental Interpretation, the Bulletin of the Centre for Environmental Interpretation* (July 1990) by permission of the Centre for Environmental Interpretation, Manchester Metropolitan University, Manchester, UK. Marilyn Ingle, 'Pupils' perceptions of museum education sessions', *Journal for Education in Museum* 11 (1990). Eilean Hooper-Greenhill, 'Education: at the heart of museums', keynote paper to the conference *Pathways to Partnerships*, organized by the Museum Education Association of Australia and Museum Education Association of New Zealand, Melbourne, September 1993. Reproduced by kind permission of the author.

Every attempt has been made to obtain permission to reproduce copyright material. If any proper acknowledgement has not been made, we would invite copyright holders to inform us of the oversight.

Introduction

One of the main functions of museums and galleries is education. What do we mean by 'education' in a museum context? In the past, 'museum education' was understood to mean provision for school children. Nowadays 'museum education' includes services for a much broader range of audiences both in the museum and in the community.

Museum education is generally concerned with the provision of services including training and guidance for teachers and others, programmes, objects for loan, teaching kits and packs based on exhibitions and the collections. The educational role of the museum is a much broader concept, and really goes to the heart of the mission of a museum. All museums and galleries have an educational role, which can be defined as the development of responsive relationships with visitors and other users such that increased enjoyment, motivation, and knowledge result.

Education in this context is life-long. It is not tied to certain age-groups, or to particular ways of teaching, or to institutional contexts. Life-long learning relates to the natural curiosity people have about their lives and environments, and it builds on the problem-solving skills that we all possess. Museum collections of all sorts can be linked to many of the questions that arise in the pursuit of making sense of the world we live in. Thus the examination of, for example, a nineteenth century Maori carved stone pendant (*hel tiki*) raises initial questions about jewellery and personal decoration, aesthetics, sculptural techniques, uses of materials, memory, affiliations, trade and travel, and subsequent questions about the politics of collecting, imperialism, and cultural identity.

For some people, 'education' means the accumulation of facts and information. This is a very narrow view, and it is not appropriate in museums and galleries. Alternative meanings for 'education' stress the process of learning rather than the outcomes, and include affective as well as cognitive elements. The emotions and feeling-responses which give rise to attitudes, values and perceptions are understood to underpin the acquisition of knowledge. It is well understood that at all stages it is the need to learn, the motivation to find out, that is critical for success in learning. It is here that museums and galleries can play their part best. Although it is of course possible to acquire information in museums, museums are no better at imparting information than other places. What museums can do extremely effectively and perhaps in a unique way, is give people an experience of the real thing such that a desire to know more ensues. Museums can be phenomenally successful in terms of increasing motivation to learn, in enabling people to discover and develop new passions, in making a previously mundane set of facts suddenly come alive and become meaningful.

How can this be done and how can we develop our understanding of the processes involved?

The educational role of the museum can be achieved in a number of ways, but the two methods which are the most familiar are exhibitions and educational programmes. Each of these methods involves complex procedures and processes and each of these methods can be seen as specific types of communication. Exhibitions can be described as a form of mass communication, while educational programmes involving face-to-face teaching can be described as a form of interpersonal communication. Communication theory enables us to examine the individual characteristics of each of these forms of communication. In doing so we can make a relationship between two museum processes which have in the past frequently been held apart, and we can begin to understand why many museum exhibitions in the past failed to communicate. As exhibitions take on more of the characteristics of interpersonal communication, we can see how the integration of education and communication theory can improve the communicative effectiveness of exhibitions.

Given that not all museums are able to employ education staff, and that even if they do, not all visitors are able to benefit from educational services, for a great deal of the time, museums rely on their exhibitions to carry out their educational function. It is critical therefore that exhibitions are planned with clear communicative goals, and produced with a knowledge of communication theory.

MASS COMMUNICATION AND INTERPERSONAL COMMUNICATION IN MUSEUMS

In 1979 Hodge and D'Souza wrote an article in *Museum* reviewing a gallery of Aboriginal art in the Western Australian Museum, Perth (Hodge and D'Souza 1979). The article was interesting in many ways, but one was because it drew attention to the fact that museum displays shared many of the classic characteristics of the mass media.

Museums, the authors asserted, are one branch of the mass media and operate through processes of mass communication.

What are the characteristics of mass communication (see Fig. 0.1)?

---

1. The audience

* large
* undifferentiated
* unknown to itself
* unable to act as a whole
* acted upon/passive

2. The process

* one way assertive communication
* communicator defines the message
* communicator is the power-base
* receiver not considered
* no automatic feedback

Fig. 0.1 Features of mass communication

First, let us consider the way audiences are understood. The mass audience is very large and dispersed, with members of the audience unknown to each other. Because this mass audience lacks self-awareness and self-identity it is incapable of acting to secure its objectives. It is acted upon, it does not act for itself. The audience is therefore understood to be passive.

In a mass communication situation, the basic model for conceptualizing the communication process is extremely simple. A communicator originates a message that is passed through a channel to a receiver. In this model the message is defined by the originator, (the curator in the museum), and the message is one-way only, imposed upon the passive audience. In communication theory this model is called the 'magic bullet' or 'hypodermic needle' theory of communication.

Do we see these 'magic bullets' and/or 'hypodermic needles' in museums? Certainly in museums, we do have very large audiences (more than 6m is the latest figure for the British Museum, for example). Very often they are referred to as the 'general public', and understood as a mass with no specific individual features; and displays as they have traditionally been mounted allow for little except a one-way assertion of meaning. Museums are in fact full of curatorial 'hypodermics'. We could certainly argue that museums share some of the features and some of the problems of the mass media.

However, museums are more flexible and varied than this. Along with the mass communication process, typified by exhibitions, we also find interpersonal communication. Museums are systems of both mass and interpersonal communication.

What are the features of interpersonal communication (see Fig. 0.2)? This can be represented by a face-to-face conversation between two people with a shared background. The meaning of the communication is evolved through a two-way process where the message can be checked and restated, and is supported by non-verbal channels of communication, such as hand and body gestures. In museums, we can see this with educational sessions, with gallery assistants and with many other instances of face-to-face interaction.

Until recently, museums have been content to maintain the distinction between exhibitions (mass communication) and education (interpersonal communication). Exhibitions

---

1. The audience

* small groups/individuals
* differentiated
* aware of each other and in contact
* active

2. The process

* two-way reactive communication
* multiple methods possible
* meaning made between the parties
* power shared more equally
* possibility of feedback

Fig. 0.2 Features of interpersonal communications

have generally been designed for the general public, and in some cases, for example with 'blockbuster' exhibitions, very large numbers of the general public who have been valued because of their contribution to the statistics rather than anything else. Education staff have worked with the exhibition once it was opened, very often operating a programme of damage limitation – finding ways to make the exhibition interesting and accessible to various groups who had not been considered as part of the exhibition planning.

AUDIENCE STUDIES AND THE DEVELOPMENT OF THE 'ACTIVE AUDIENCE'

There has been little analysis of the museum as mass media, but for other types of mass media, there has been a great deal of work done on audiences and their responses, and the conclusions have been very interesting. In studies of the television audience, for example, considerable gender differences in the mode of consumption have been found, which is not surprising, perhaps, in view of the domestic site for most television viewing. Television is viewed in the context of 'the politics of the living room' (Cubitt 1985, quoted in Morley 1992: 139–40). We know very little of how the politics of the living room is transferred to museums, as transferred or renegotiated it certainly must be.

In analysing the meanings made out of news broadcasting, it has been found that a range of meanings are made and that people do not slavishly follow the interpretations that they are offered. Although TV News sets an agenda for thinking, not everyone reacts to the agenda in the same way. From a great range of research studies it is clear that people actively decode media messages according to their personal backgrounds, life-experience, personalities and values. In addition to these interpretations, race, class and gender have structuring effects. Although there is still much work to be done to develop this work, it has become clear that audiences are very far from 'passive'.

The early notion in mass communication theory of the passive audience was rejected some twenty to thirty years ago, to be replaced by the idea of the 'active audience'. Audiences are now understood to be active, decisive, working from their own agendas, and well able to refuse to be communicated to if they do not want to be. Genuine communication is a shared process. It is now understood that audiences are not large and undifferentiated but made up of a great many individuals that can be grouped into specific groups with specific needs.

As ideas about the active audience have developed, mass communication theory has abandoned the notion of the mass audience. The mass audience has fragmented. New concepts have emerged, of audience segments, target audiences, and niche marketing: in other words, differentiated products for specific groups of people. In relation to this, new concepts in mass communication theory offer us the 'addressable users of micro-multimedia' (Heath and Bryant 1992: 295–6).

Interactivity and de-massification are two key concepts in the new theory of communication. Models of communication are no longer linear and one way, but take account of the exchange of messages and the transaction and negotiation of meaning (Fig. 0.3). These features, of message exchange, negotiation and transaction bring the mass media process much closer to the processes of inter-personal communication.

We can see this happening in museum exhibitions where individuals can pick and choose their own experience from a menu of opportunities. Using interactive exhibits and videos, handling tables and books of information, people can shape their own interpretation

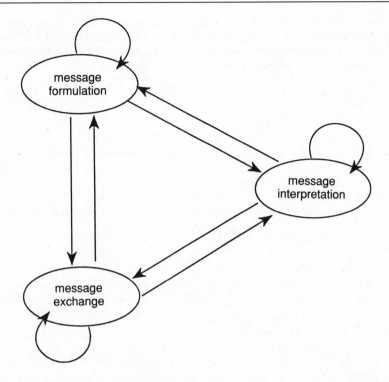

Fig. 0.3 Communication = the process by which messages are formulated, exchanged and interpreted (from Heath and Bryant, 1992: 300)

of the exhibition content. The old-style linear narrative exhibition is being replaced by a modular format that enables personal choice, the exercise of individual learning styles and selection of unique points of interest from the whole.

The processes of mass communication are moving closer to the processes of interpersonal communication in communication fields as a whole, and we see this reflected in museums. In order to take advantage of this shift in communication method, museums must develop a knowledge of learning processes. When exhibitions were understood as acts of one-way communication, a concentration on producing an exhibition that was scholarly and aesthetically pleasing was enough. Now that communication is conceptualized as a much more active event, we need to know much more about learning styles, how people respond and learn at different ages, how people process information, what makes people interested and what social, cultural or political factors might aid or inhibit learning. In other words, the psychology and sociology of learning become of enormous importance.

At the present time in many parts of the world, museums and galleries are being asked to justify their funding through adopting new and more overt social roles. This places the educational role of the museum at the forefront.

THE STRUCTURE OF THIS VOLUME

This volume has been assembled to explore and analyse the educational role of museums. It is organized in two parts.

Part one – *Communication theory and museum exhibitions* – relates some basic ideas from mass communication studies to the museum context, considers the audience for museums and galleries, and discusses how to increase the communicative competence of museums with a particular emphasis on exhibitions.

Part two – *Learning theory and educational practice in museums* – looks at how educational services are organized, what we know about how children and adults learn, teaching with collections, and evaluation of educational programmes.

Inevitably hard choices have had to be made about what to include and what to omit. Space has been at a premium in such an enormous subject area. However, I have not found it necessary to edit the individual articles a great deal. Most of them say exactly what I want them to and have therefore been included in their entirety. In making decisions about footnotes and bibliographies, each article has been treated separately and is reproduced using whichever style of referencing was used in the original published version.

Further information on the themes addressed here will be found in my other books: *Museums and their Visitors* and *Museum and Gallery Education*. There are also relevant papers in the volume of conference papers *Museum: Media: Message*.

Many of the papers in this volume already carry, for me, affectionate memories of discussions about their content, approach and value with past students. I look forward to many more with future students and hope that all readers will find this collection stimulating, interesting and useful.

REFERENCES

Hall, S. (1993) 'Encoding, decoding', in S. During (ed.) *The Cultural Studies Reader*, London: Routledge, 90–103.
Heath, R. L. and Bryant, J. (1992) *Human Communication Theory and Research: concepts, contexts and challenges*, Hillsdale, New Jersey, Hove and London: Lawrence Erlbaum Associates.
Hodge, R. and D'Souza, W. (1979) 'The museum as a communicator: a semiotic analysis of the Western Australian Museum Aboriginal Gallery, Perth', *Museum* 31(4): 251–6.
Hooper-Greenhill, E. (1991) *Museum and Gallery Education*, Leicester: Leicester University Press.
Hooper-Greenhill, E. (1994) *Museums and Their Visitors*, London: Routledge.
Hooper-Greenhill, E. (ed.) (1995) *Museum: Media: Message*, London: Routledge.
Lewis, J. (1991) *The Ideological Octopus – an Exploration of Television and its Audience*, London: Routledge.
MacDonald, S. (1995) 'Changing our minds – planning a responsive service', in E. Hooper-Greenhill (ed.) *Museum: Media: Message*, London: Routledge.
McQuail, D. (1992) *Mass Communication Theory: an introduction*, London: Sage Publications.
Morley, D. (1992) *Television Audiences and Cultural Studies*, London: Routledge.
The Susie Fisher Group, (1990) *Bringing History and the Arts to a New Audience – qualitative research for the London Borough of Croydon*, London: Susie Fisher Group.
Walsh, A. (1991) *Insights – museums, visitors, attitudes, expectations: a focus group experiment*, Malibu, CA: The Getty Center for Education in the Arts and The J. Paul Getty Museum.

Part 1
Communication theory and museum exhibitions

1

Museum communication: an introductory essay

Eilean Hooper-Greenhill

This paper introduced the conference Museum: Media: Message *held at the University of Leicester in April 1993. It briefly discusses the changes in the political environment of museums and galleries in Britain that have demanded a development of the communicative function, and goes on to consider the theoretical background, looking at audience studies and the introduction of market research in museums.*

The work done in museums is placed in the context of audience studies in non-museum fields such as television. Museums are exposed as being very much behind other parts of the mass media in terms of understanding their own communicative processes.

The paper and the accompanying bibliography act as an introduction to the fields of cultural and media studies.

MUSEUM COMMUNICATION IN BRITAIN

If the future for museums lies in the development of the communicative competence of the museum, what can the past offer us to help? I want to focus particularly here on what we know about museum audiences, because if we want to become better communicators we have to become very aware of our partners in the communication process.

What do we know about our audiences? I will discuss this mainly in the British context, as not only is this the one with which I am most familiar, but also because the nature of the field in Britain demonstrates some important points rather well.

Let us consider audience studies in British museums.

Surveys of visitors to museums began in the 1960s. On the whole they were very small scale, and concentrated mainly on the demographic details of visitors such as age, sex, geographical location and so on. Mostly these small studies were carried out by museum staff, sometimes with the help of the local university or college. They were generally done with very limited resources, tended towards amateurism in methodology, and contented themselves with measuring a limited range of visitor characteristics. As public accountability increased, so the pace and the professionalism of visitor surveys has accelerated, with a particular urgency in the last eight years. It has been discovered that, with some exceptions, visitors to museums tend to be better educated and of a higher social class than the population in general. On the whole, it is the white population that sees museums as relevant, although specific exhibitions will attract specific audiences: in Leicester for example, an exhibition of Afro-Caribbean history and art was visited by the

Afro-Caribbean community, and an exhibition called 'Vasna – an Indian village', was very popular with Leicester's large Asian population. This has taught us that museums attract the audiences for whom they provide.

Very few museum visitor studies looked at the museum visitor profile in the context of the profile of the local population, but gradually this too has become more frequent. Now, most museums know who their visitors are, how they reflect population patterns within a specific geographical area, how they relate to tourist movements and so on. Surveys in both local and national museums are carried out over time to monitor change and the effects of major policy shifts. Gathering basic data about visitors has become a necessary management tool.

During the 1980s a second type of analysis, which can be called participation studies, began. Government statistics such as Social Trends or Cultural Trends had already built up a small amount of not very helpful data on museum visitor patterns. During the 1980s, more specific studies commissioned by the tourist organisations (English Tourist Board 1982) central government agencies (Myerscough 1988) and some arts and museum bodies (Middleton 1990; Touche Ross 1989; RSGB 1991) began to look in more detail at what proportion of British adults visited museums, who they were, and, in outline, why they visited, generally looking at the previous twelve (sometimes twenty-four) months.

These studies were necessarily more broadly based than the museum visitor survey. They accelerated towards the end of the 1980s and the early 1990s. Their conclusions are difficult to analyse as they variously report that 24 per cent, 33 per cent, 45 per cent and 56 per cent of the general population of Britain visits museums (Merriman 1991). Clearly we have to examine this data very carefully and ask questions about what definition of a museum has been used – whether, for example this includes or excludes art galleries, or the built heritage. The time frame is also vital. The longer the time span, the greater the number of people who respond positively. In other words, if people are asked if they have visited a museum during the last two years, they are more likely to say yes than if they are asked about the last twelve months. The data suggests that a small proportion of people visit fairly frequently, but that a great many people visit rather irregularly over a longish period of time.

The most encouraging of these studies is one carried out for the Arts Council in 1991 (RSGB 1991) which used the time-frame 'nowadays', which generally means 'in the last four weeks'. This showed that 48 per cent of the British population visited art galleries, museums and exhibitions, combined as a joint category, 'nowadays'. If 'nowadays' is a fairly short time span, and positive responses increase with longer time spans, a very large proportion of the British population is interested in museums and related institutions.

What do we know about what visitors do once they arrive in a museum or gallery? Research here is lamentably thin in Britain, although, under the title of evaluation, some work is beginning and some of the work that has been done is discussed in the conference volume. The pioneer in this area is, of course, the Natural History Museum in London.

The work that has been carried out at the Natural History Museum under the direction of Roger Miles is familiar to many. It is interesting that this work was carried out in a science museum, rather than in an art gallery. Science museums are often more aware of a specifically didactic purpose than other types of museum, and therefore have felt more strongly that therefore they need to know what their visitors have learnt.

During the 1970s the Natural History Museum began to develop a series of new exhibitions. This was done as a very self-conscious process that was continuously monitored and documented. It was virtually unique at the time, although there was a glimmer of interest in exhibition theory at Liverpool Museum by the early 1980s, and further interesting evaluation work has been carried out there since.

Roger Miles and his colleagues concentrated on building an effective exhibition technology, using communication models from information technology, learning models from behaviourist psychology and sociological models from positivist American mass communication theory (Miles and Tout 1979). The assumption of this research was that by perfecting the medium of communication (the exhibition), a successful transfer of messages would take place. It was assumed that if the exhibition was sufficiently expertly designed, visitors would automatically respond; in other words that the media itself was all-powerful and that the visitors were open to manipulation through the effects of the media. Visitors were treated as a mass, a 'population'. After much trial and error and nearly two decades of work, it was admitted that this approach was not entirely successful, and that more attention need to be paid to the visitors and to their reasons for being in the museum in the first place (Miles and Tout 1991).

Other research into museum visitors at this time was virtually non-existent. Exhibitions were designed for 'the general public'. In the education department, with face-to-face teaching for identifiable groups with specific learning needs, the attention to audience was much more sharply focused, but this approach was not perceived as relevant to any other aspect of museum work. Now in the early 1990s, we are becoming more aware of the importance of the social context of museum visits, and of the fact that museum visitors do not become new-born beings as they enter the museum. People come to museums carrying with them the rest of their lives, with their own reasons for visiting, and their specific prior experience.

During the late 1980s and early 1990s the introduction of marketing methods to museums coincided with the rise to power within museums of younger staff who frequently held strong convictions that museums should be more open and more democratic. These two forces both focused on audiences and their needs, and this resulted in the opening up of the issue of what people *felt* about about museums, for the first time. The combination of marketing and the move to democratize museums led to a pioneering study in London of the attitudes towards museums of people who were not regular visitors. A mass communications research firm, Mass Observation, was commissioned to do the work by the London Museums Service (which is a London-based museum advisory body, part of the Area Museum Service for South Eastern England). Earlier demographic surveys which had identified the main characteristics of typical museum visitors were used to construct a picture of those who were unlikely to visit. Discussion groups were then formed with, for example, men over 60, Asian women, and women with pre-school children. Together with an experienced and appropriate moderator, perceptions of museums were explored. For the first time in Britain, market research techniques were applied in the museum context to build a picture of perceptions and attitudes (Trevelyan 1991).

In museums in North America, this approach to the collection of qualitative data is one aspect of what is know as naturalistic evaluation but in Britain this is still very unfamiliar. Marketing methods in British museums have, therefore, established the value of regular research into demographic profiles of visitors, and research such as the London studies are demonstrating how valuable qualitative work can be.

A further concept from marketing is that of 'target groups'. We now no longer design exhibitions for 'the general public'. We understand that different sections of the audience have different expectations and approach the museum for different reasons. We consider the needs of children, families, tourists, the elderly, schools, and people with a range of disabilities. This is becoming almost routine. However, our concept of 'need' is still at a very primitive and underdeveloped stage.

We have just about got to the point in museums in Britain now where we are asking what we can do to behave in a more sensitive way towards our audiences. We are beginning to wonder what 'evaluation' is and whether it can help us to do our job better. Finding very little qualitative work with audiences in museums, we are beginning to look outside museums to see what other people are doing. In the National Museums of Scotland, for example, an assessment of visitor responses to their Discovery Room in the summer of 1990 was organized jointly with the Open University in Scotland, and video techniques generally used for evaluating lecturers were adapted (Stevenson and Bryden 1991).

If we do look outside museums for helpful methods, where should we look? We can argue that museums work with two distinct modes of communication. On the one hand, we can use interpersonal, face-to-face communication, and we see this in action in inquiry services for example, where the curator and an inquirer meet each other directly. Other examples might be found in some aspects of the educational work of museums, where museum teachers work directly with groups. On the other hand, museums can also be categorized as mass communicators, as, in addition to dealing with some people face-to-face, they also deal with a great number of people in a less personal way.

Many exhibitions share the major characteristics of most forms of mass communication. Most forms of mass communication involve a one-way process of communication, a single message source with a large group of receivers, and the messages themselves are in the public domain. Museums, when they communicate through exhibitions, publications, advertisements and other methods such as videos, can be characterized as mass communication media.

So museums can be seen as both mass communicators and interpersonal communicators. This means that there are a broad range of methods in other fields that might be relevant. Clearly work in the educational field is useful, and many papers in parts 2 and 3 of the conference volume discuss examples of relevant educational theory and practice. I want, therefore, to go on to try to make some sense out of the great body of material that can be found in mass communication studies, and in the related fields of media studies and cultural studies.

AUDIENCE RESEARCH IN NON-MUSEUM FIELDS

The mass media have been studied since the beginning of the century, mainly but not exclusively in America. By the 1990s we are at a point in Britain where there are great numbers of courses in communication studies and in media studies. There are now many overviews of approaches to the subject (for example, Gurevitch, Bennett, Curran and Woollacott 1982; Curran and Gurevitch 1991; McQuail 1987; Heath and Bryant 1992) and many accounts of specific projects which examine topics ranging from the political effects to the gender specific uses made of the mass media. Museums are rarely, if ever, to be found in these accounts.

Early mass communication theorists assumed the media audience to be an undifferentiated mass, widely dispersed, lacking in both self-awareness and self-identity, and incapable of acting together to secure objectives (McQuail 1987: 31). The mass audience did not act for itself, it was acted upon.

Media at the beginning of the century included the press, radio, cinema and advertising. During the 1920s and 1930s there was a broad consensus that the mass media exercised a powerful and persuasive influence on audiences susceptible to manipulation. This 'magic bullet', or 'hypodermic needle' theory proposed that the media 'worked' on the passive public and that the effects of this could be measured through the use of scientific techniques (Curran, Gurevitch and Woollacott 1982). Studies of 'audience effects' proliferated.

During the 1950s and 1960s, following these 'effects' studies, it became clear that the audience was not in fact as passive as had originally been thought and that people in many ways made their own use of media messages. People manipulated the media, rather than were manipulated by the media. It was found that people expose themselves to, understand, and remember communications selectively according to prior dispositions. The manipulative and persuasive effects of the media were therefore likely to be negated by the interpretations of the 'active audience'. Studies of 'uses and gratifications' were carried out.

The late 1960s saw the development of cultural studies in Britain, and the decisive rejection of the simplistic communications model and consensual model of society that American mass communication theorists had used (Turner 1990; McGuigan 1992). British cultural studies employed Marxist models of society, and saw the mass media as a site for ideological reproduction in the maintenance of social, economic and cultural power relations. Ideological 'work' was studied through semiotic analyses of texts; first the literary text, and then later, other cultural artefacts such as film, or rarely, exhibitions.

Semiotic analysis studies the implicit ideological messages of texts achieved through representation and mediation; how for example are women portrayed in Bond movies, in coffee advertisements, or in social history exhibitions? The analysis of the text is carried out at a theoretical level by the theorist and rarely tested. Where empirical studies were done, it was frequently shown that the theorist's analysis was mere assumption, and was not borne out by audience responses. Ideology did not in fact 'interpellate the subject' (to use Althusser's words), 'preferred readings' (Stuart Hall's terminology) (Hall 1982) were not achieved: in contrast, the audience was actively deconstructing the message according to a whole range of complex factors that left the media message with a role little short of that of setting the agenda for thought. Media messages (and much of this work has been done in relation to television) could not tell people how to think, but could set the agenda as to what to think about. This in itself is not insignificant, but it swings the focus back again to the audience, away from the text. A focus on the text alone does not tell us how audiences use the text.

In the new focus on audiences that is developing, both mass communication studies and cultural studies theorists are united in their interest in the development of ethnographic methods. The older 'uses and gratifications' studies have been rejected, criticized for remaining at the level of individual psychology and failing to take account of larger social divisions and structures that in large part shape individual psychologies and responses. Ethnographic audience studies have used and adapted methods from anthropological fieldwork, where the researcher works very closely with the people she is studying, and the research is carried out in an open and reflexive way.

Recent TV audience studies are particularly interesting. It has been shown that gender, race and class have specific structuring effects in the reception of TV messages. To take just one example, which I found especially fascinating: *The Cosby Show* is an American comedy soap, which concerns, uniquely, an upper-middle-class black family and their daily doings (Lewis 1991). Unlike other black American TV shows, it has, in

America, a very broad audience of both black and white middle- and lower-class viewers. Detailed ethnographic audience research was carried out in America through home-based discussions with different types of people, using class and race as structuring categories. It emerged that different categories of people interpreted the programme according to their own aspirations and understanding of self and that they failed to see those aspects of the programme that did not support their own world view. The interpretations were personal, but also depended strongly on race and class.

Middle-class white viewers, for example, saw the upper-middle-class American life-style and failed to accord any importance to the fact that the family was black. The family was perceived as so 'normal', so much in line with the everyday middle-class American as seen on TV that their blackness 'just sort of drifted out of' the minds of viewers. (Lewis 1991: 174). Working-class black people, on the other hand, were very aware of the blackness of the actors and found the positive black images all-important. They celebrated the small references to black culture that middle-class whites had failed to see, such as the naming of the grandchildren as Nelson and Winnie. Other groups responded in other ways.

The show is constructed around ambiguity. The family is both black, and through their life-style, like whites. The show presents a view of blacks that is both radical, in that most American blacks do not live as they do, and every-day, in that many American soap families do. This ambiguity allows people with radically different political views and social perceptions to accept the programme as appropriate and to find it sufficiently undisturbing to enjoy it.

The analysis of *The Cosby Show* focused on the nature of the text (the TV message) and also analysed, using ethnographic methods, the ways in which several different audience categories used the message to create pleasure for themselves. The way forward for communication studies and cultural studies is seen as the combination of textual and audience studies, with a sophisticated and complex model of both text and audience in place. This combination of models remains to be developed.

What can we in museums learn from this brief overview of audience studies in mass communications and cultural studies?

Firstly we can see that in terms of concept development, museums have not been at the forefront. Media studies in the 1950s proposed the active audience and the importance of social context in the reception of the message long before we had even begun to study our audiences in museums. Our methodology in museums has not paid attention to methods used by communication and cultural theorists, and an over-reliance on behaviourist, positivist methods has failed to reveal the importance of audience decoding. Up till now, we have had, in Britain, no ethnographic studies of museum visitors, and some of the papers in the conference volume describe new work in this field. We do need to begin to work in a more reflexive and more open way with audiences, to allow their descriptions of what museums mean to them to emerge during the research process.

A very important lesson from *The Cosby Show* example is the importance of the notion of polysemia, of plurality of meanings, what has been called in other contexts – semiotic excess. *The Cosby Show* is carefully constructed to contain a range of meanings that are designed to appeal to the known different audience segments. The balance of appeal is carefully reviewed, in the knowledge that some people will see one thing and focus on one aspect, while others will pick up other messages. How much potential in museums is there for exactly this semiotic excess, this range of meanings, many of which will be invisible to many audiences, but which exist to be activated when someone with the experience to perceive and decode the message is present. I think the potential here is enormous and very exciting.

Mass communication research has thrown up other useful ideas, such as the rejection of the linear communications model in favour of a transactional model where messages are formulated, exchanged and interpreted in a continuous process.

We have, in Britain, learnt a great deal about audiences during the last decade. We know, for example, that we can to quite a large extent, manipulate our audiences, by designing a product for a specific market. If we put on an exhibition about football, and market it appropriately, people who are interested in football will come to see it. We know also that people appear to respond very positively to the opportunity to handle objects and exhibits at discovery and interactive centres. At the National Museum of Scotland, for example, large numbers of people queue down the stairs and in front of the glass cased exhibits in order to visit the Discovery Room.

What we don't really know is why people like to handle things, or why football (or other) memorabilia is important. Our learning has taken the form of trial and error. We observe large numbers of people queueing for the Discovery Room in Scotland and decide that we must have one too. The danger of learning in this way is that we adopt the practices without understanding the principles. We go away and replicate the Scottish Discovery Room, and pretty soon, there are little Scottish discovery rooms all over the place and everyone is bored to tears with them. Meanwhile the glass cases are just as boring as ever.

In order to truly develop we must look more deeply behind the successes and try to identify the principles of learning and of engagement that lie behind the success. We need to know from the individual visitor's viewpoint what is meaningful to them, and we need to target individuals for our research according to specific structuring categories which include gender, race and class. Mass communications and cultural studies offer examples of work carried out in relation to other cultural fields. We can usefully learn from them.

This paper is forthcoming in E. Hooper-Greenhill (ed.) Museum, Media, Message, *London: Routledge.*

REFERENCES

Boyd-Barret, O. and Braham, P. (1987) *Media, Knowledge and Power*, London and Sydney: Croom Helm and the Open University.

Certeau, M. (1984) *The Practice of Everyday Life*, Berkeley: University of California Press.

Curran, J., Gurevitch, M. and Woollacott, J. (1982) 'The study of the media: theoretical approaches', in M. Gurevitch, T. Bennett and J. Woollacott, *Culture, Society and the Media*, London: Routledge, 11–29.

Curran, J. and Gurevitch, M. (1991) *Mass Media and Society*, London and New York: Edward Arnold.

English Tourist Board (1982) *Visitors to Museums Survey 1982*, report by the English Tourist Board and NOP Market Research Limited, England.

Gurevitch, M., Bennett, T., Curran, J. and Woollacott, J. (eds) (1982) *Culture, Society and the Media*, London: Methuen.

Hall, S. (1982) 'The rediscovery of "ideology": the return of the "repressed" in media studies', in M. Gurevitch, T. Bennett, J. Curran and J. Woollacott (eds) *Culture, Society and the Media*, London: Methuen, 56–90.

Heath, R. and Bryant, J. (1992) *Human Communication Theory and Research: Concepts, Contexts and Challenges*, Hove and London: Lawrence Erlbaum and Associates.

Lewis, J. (1991) *The Ideological Octopus: an Exploration of Television and its Audience*, London and New York: Routledge.

McGuigan, J. (1992) *Cultural Populism*, London and New York: Routledge.

McQuail, D. (1987) *Mass Communication Theory: an Introduction*, London: Sage Publications.

McQuail, D. (1992) *Media Performance – Mass Communication and the Public Interest*, London and New Delhi: Sage Publications.

Merriman, N. (1991) *Beyond the Glass Case: the Past, the Heritage and the Public in Britain*, London and New York: Leicester University Press.

Middleton, V. (1990) *New Visions for Independent Museums in the UK*, West Sussex: Association of Independent Museums.

Miles, R. and Tout, A. (1979) 'Outline of a technology for effective science exhibits', *Special Papers in Paleontology* 22: 209–24.

Miles, R. and Tout, A. (1991) 'Impact of research on the approach to the visiting public at the Natural History Museum', *International Journal of Science Education* 13(5): 534–49.

Morley, D. (1992) *Television Audiences and Cultural Studies*, London and New York: Routledge.

Museums & Galleries Commission (1992) *Guidelines on Disability for Museums and Galleries in the United Kingdom*, London: Museums and Galleries Commission.

Museums and Galleries Commission (1993) *Quality of Service in Museums and Galleries: Customer Care in Museums – Guidelines on Implementation*, London: Museums & Galleries Commission.

Myerscough, J. (1988) *The Economic Importance of the Arts in Britain*, London: Policy Studies Institute.

National Audit Office (1993) *Department of National Heritage, National Museums and Galleries: quality of service to the public*, Report by the Comptroller and Auditor General, National Audit Office, London: HMSO.

Office of Arts and Libraries (1991) *Report on the Development of Performance Indicators for the National Museums and Galleries*, London: Office of Arts and Libraries.

RSGB Omnibus Arts Survey (1991) *Report on a Survey on Arts and Cultural Activities in G.B.*, Arts Council of Great Britain.

Stevenson and Bryden (1991) 'The National Museums of Scotland's 1990 Discovery Room: an evaluation', *Museum Management and Curatorship* 10: 24–36.

Susie Fisher Group (1990) *Bringing History and the Arts to a New Audience: Qualitative Research for the London Borough of Croydon*, London: The Susie Fisher Group.

Touche Ross (1989) *Museum Funding and Services: the Visitor's Perspective*, Touche Ross Management Consultants.

Trevelyan, V. (1991) *'Dingy Places with Different Kinds of Bits': an Attitudes Survey of London Museums Amongst Non-visitors*, London Museums Service.

Turner, G. (1990) *British Cultural Studies: an Introduction*, Boston: Unwin Hyman.

2

A *new communication model for museums*

Eilean Hooper-Greenhill

How can we understand the communicative process, in museums or elsewhere? Semiotic analysis has become popular in order to deconstruct existing message systems, and some few studies have been carried out in museums. The semiology of signification, however, has its limitations for people who are constructing message systems. The semiology of communication and the concept of 'pertinence' is discussed in the context of recent communication models as used in museum work. A new communication model is proposed, with both museum communicators and audiences construed as active meaning-makers with the field of meaning being in permanent flux.

HOW MEANING IS STUDIED: SEMIOTICS AND ITS RELEVANCE

In recent years, studies of meanings within cultural contexts have been carried out under the broad umbrella of 'semiotics'. Semiotics has been defined as 'the doctrine of general theory of signs . . . (which) . . . deals with meanings and messages in all their forms and all their contexts' (Innis 1985: vii) and as 'the systematic and "scientific" study of all those factors that enter into semiosis, that is, the production and interpretation of signs' (Innis 1985: viii).

Semiotics, then, according to this definition looks at signs and signifying practices and analyses them. All observable socio-cultural phenomena are studied as signifying systems that constitute and are constituted through hidden social logics. These hidden agendas might be kinship systems, myths, ritualized behaviours and so on. In many, if not most, instances, the analyses of sign systems and signifying practices seek to uncover the (often hidden) ideological messages that are carried.

What studies can be found that analyse museums, or museum practices such as exhibitions, from this standpoint? How useful are such studies? I want to look very briefly at one such analysis, of an exhibition.

One chapter in Roland Barthes' well-known *Mythologies* is called 'The great family of man' (Barthes 1973: 100–2). Barthes analysed a photographic exhibition held in Paris during the 1970s, in which he discussed the way in which the objects (the photographs) were put together, the choice of content, division and section subtitles, and the stylistic manner in which the exhibition texts were written. In doing this, he demonstrated how myths may be constructed through exhibitions. The exhibition sought to establish a mythical 'human community'. Universal values were constructed through such subtitles as 'birth', 'death', 'work', 'play'. An essential humanism was posited. The photographs were accompanied by texts in the introductory leaflet and the catalogue (statements such as 'the Earth is a Mother that never dies'). Together the objects and the texts established a discourse which celebrated a timeless ahistorical harmonious 'human condition'.

'What is the use of this essentialism?', asks Barthes. An eternal lyricism about birth masks the true social facts that reveal whether a child was born with ease or with difficulty, whether the mother was caused harm by the birth, whether it was in an area of high mortality, and so on. The meaning of the photographs, Barthes is telling us, is constituted through ideology, and taken as a whole the meanings of the objects and the exhibition construct an essentialist myth of human harmony, as opposed to the social reality of conflict and competition. This myth serves to maintain the *status quo*, and preserve the definitions of the world made by existing power groups.

The analysis reveals how exhibitions construct values and how these values are construed through a hidden ideological agenda. Barthes analyses a meaning hidden in the way in which the objects (photographs) are assembled, contextualized, and presented.

Other analyses of museums and museum practices tend to operate in a similar way. Hodge and D'Souza (1979), for example, used a semiotic analysis to analyse the Western Australian Museum's Aboriginal gallery. Where the display purported to celebrate the culture of the aborigines, the researchers discovered quite another message, that of the power of curators to define the world on their own terms. A similar analysis of the exhibition at the Natural History Museum 'Man's Place in Evolution' (dubbed 'Adam's ancestors: Eve's in-laws'), discovered that the three-dimensional images and the texts used in the displays revealed very Victorian assumptions about the social roles of men and women (Anon 1980). Duncan and Wallach (1980) state that the museum's primary function is ideological, and that its task is to impress on its visitors society's most revered beliefs and values. They analysed the Louvre as a ritual experiential agenda that incorporates the unaware visitor as an ideal citizen of the state. Earlier, Duncan and Wallach (1978) had analysed the Museum of Modern Art in New York. They described the architectural script and the iconographic programme established by the arrangement of the collections and showed how the experience of the museum as a labyrinth is a metaphor for spiritual enlightenment and apparently universal values which act to reconcile us to the world outside the museum, as it is.

USES AND PROBLEMS OF SEMIOTIC ANALYSIS FOR MUSEUMS

These analyses of museums and their meanings work from the outside in: that is, they analyse the experience and significance of the museum from the point of view of the consumer of the museum as a cultural artefact, rather than from the point of view of the producers of such an artefact. The researchers claim to speak as though for the visitor, rather than on behalf of the museum worker.

The studies I have discussed also work with analyses which are theoretical rather than practical, by which I mean that the researcher has built a theoretical model which he or she then seeks to prove through a personal analysis which, as we have seen, can include the museum building, the arrangement of the collections, the labels and other texts, and so on. A hypothesis is proposed, and an examination of the visible aspects of a museum or gallery is then carried out to prove the hypothesis. Most of the hypotheses concern the hidden curriculum, or the underlying ideological agenda of museums and galleries.

It is quite clear from the various studies that have emerged, that it is extremely easy to discover and document the ideological functions of museums. It is all too easy to prove that museums as a whole, and separate aspects of museum practices, act to construct values, to represent images, all of which have class, gender, and ethnic biases. In a sense, what else would one expect?

However, this is not to deny the validity of these studies. On the contrary, the studies demonstrate that museums and galleries have a role in representation in exactly the same way as other social and cultural institutions and that the representations of museums have political and ideological functions. This is something which cannot be disputed and it is useful that we, as museum professionals, know and acknowledge it. Without these studies, it would be difficult to begin to understand and work with these complex functions of museums. They illuminate the various alternative and sometimes fragmented meanings that may be construed from the experience of the museum.

But how does this help the museum professional in the production of cultural meanings? For a practising museum worker, these studies can make very discouraging reading. In relation to actually doing museum work, they help by alerting us to areas of difficulty, and enable us to analyse the finished product, but they don't help too much in the design of exhibitions, or museum posters, or in the rearrangement of the building.

There are critiques that can be made of the analyses that I have discussed. In terms of the meaning that is made of the museums and the displays, meaning is posited rather than demonstrated. Visitors to the exhibition were not interviewed. The 'meanings' of the photographs (for example) are those that Barthes found supported his own viewpoint. These meanings certainly present an alternative way of reading the exhibition from that intended by the curator, but we don't know how many other people read the exhibition as Barthes did, nor how many other ways of interpreting the exhibition there were, nor even if anyone went. Theoretically, the idea is beautifully constructed. Practically, it tells us very little.

These analyses have a further problem, in my view. The studies imply that individual subjects (individuals) do not construct their own messages, but are themselves constructed by the messages implicit in the experience of the museum. Barthes, for example, assumes, in so far as he is interested, that visitors are automatically deceived by the messages of the exhibition. Duncan and Wallach assume that visitors to MOMA are carried away by the ceremonial agenda and the iconic programme and are not themselves actively constructing and reconstructing the experience to suit their own needs. Visitors are assumed to be passive and uncritical, incapable of making their own meanings, and manipulated by the hidden social and ideological functions of the museum.

A further aspect of these studies is useful to bear in mind. These analyses set out to analyse the unintended rather than the intended effects of signifying systems. The researchers are interested in the revelatory power of their hypothesis, in showing how museums and galleries, unwittingly, make certain social statements, or represent certain beliefs and values. These analyses of communicative acts as signifying systems do not help in the *production* of cultural meaning. This is not their intention. We, as museum workers, and as those who are charged with the production of systems in which meanings are made, are not offered guidelines to produce, for example, exhibitions that work with non-essentialist values, nor are we assisted in working out new forms of museums that relate to the conflictual fragmented world in modes other than those of reconciliation.

How can we analyse cultural meaning in such a way as to illuminate and develop actual work practices in museums? How is meaning construed by individuals from the continually shifting flux of experiences of the world? How do these two questions relate?

Museum professionals work in a number of different ways, according to their functions (as designers, curators, educators, outreach workers, public relations people and so on), to communicate messages. These messages relate to the museum, the collections, and the interrelationship of people with the museum and its practices. These messages are intentioned messages. Exhibitions are evolved with specific teaching points or ideas that they intend to convey. Museum posters or leaflets deliberately present particular bits of information and specific images. Yes, they will also have hidden ideological messages, as we live within and are constructed through ideologies. It is not possible to live in a social world without partaking of that social world, and there is no finite truth 'beneath' an ideological 'distortion'.

The semiological studies that we looked at earlier do not offer any analytical method for the analysis of intended messages. However, I know a man who does!

SEMIOLOGY OF SIGNIFICATION, SEMIOLOGY OF COMMUNICATION

I have recently come across the work of George Mounin, a French semiotician and linguistic theorist. His work has been little known in England, but recently a book of collected essays appeared under the title *Semiotic Praxis: Studies in Pertinence and in the Means of Expression and Communication* (1985). Mounin has developed some ideas that may be useful to us.

Mounin proposes that Saussure, the founding father of present-day semiotics, opened up two theoretical avenues (Mounin 1985: 21). One of these avenues, which Mounin calls the semiology of signification, has been followed by such writers as Barthes and Kristeva, and has been particularly influential in American developments. This avenue has led to the exploration of the hidden or unintended logics of signifying systems. The studies we looked at above fall into this category.

The other avenue, followed by writers such as Prieto, Martinet and Mounin himself, follows the lines of a semiology of communication. The semiology of communication deals with purposeful and conventional communicational systems. Mounin identifies two important characteristics of systems of communication: first, that they involve a conventional code that is acquired through social learning; second, that there is an intention to communicate which is recognized by at least two people.

The semiology of communication studies, therefore, intended messages, and the semiology of signification studies unintended messages. Methodologically, the difference in the two semiologies lies in their different understanding of signs and indices.

The semiologists of communication make a sharp differentiation between an indice and a sign (or signal). The translators had a problem over the word 'indice' and have used this expression as it enables a clarity of distinction. An indice is an observable fact (an indicator) which carries information about another fact which is not observable (something which is indicated). For example, the presence of a particular type of distant smoke indicates the presence of a fire. On the other hand, a sign or signal is an artificial indice, produced and expressed by a sender with the intention to send information about another non-observable fact. Thus the smoke from a forest fire is an indice, but the smoke from a fire lit by an Indian to announce an enemy approach is a sign or signal. The semiology of communication studies communication systems that are known and understood as such through social learning. One of Mounin's papers, for example is called 'An analysis of Indian sign language'.

In contrast the semiology of signification posits, without explicitly proving, that all socio-cultural phenomena that can function as indices can also function as signs and are therefore communication facts. This is justified by stating that all aspects of all socio-cultural phenomena have signification, and analyses have been undertaken which show how this works. The task is to decode the sign systems, or signifying systems, using the general structural-linguistic model (Mounin 1985: 24). The studies we looked at above adopt this approach, by insisting, for example, as Duncan and Wallach do, that the architectural code of the Louvre or of MOMA had a signifying effect, even though we do not know and are not told, which visitors noticed which parts of it.

From the point of view of the analysis of intended communication, the distinction between indices and signs is crucial, because it enables the observation of the selection of indices. In other words, it enables the making of a methodological distinction between that which is intended by the communicator to be meaningful (a sign) and that which may become meaningful to the viewer because of some relationship that they perceive between themselves and the phenomenon (an index). Mounin points out that indices are not in themselves necessarily signifying (*signifiant*) but that they do have the potential to signify if selected to do so by someone. Indices are 'signicative' (*signicatif*). They may come to mean something to the observer through a process of interpretation. All socio-cultural phenomena, including museums, exhibitions, posters, and objects, are saturated by indices, which are 'signicative': they may become 'signifying' if relevant to and selected by the observer through a personal process of interpretation.

For example, recently I went to the British Museum and walked, without any partic-ular intention, into a display entitled 'Archaic Greece'. The display contained a series of *signs* that patently made up an intended communication system. This consisted of introductory text panels, headlines, object labels, photographs, maps, diagrams, objects of various sorts, and so on, all admirably consistent and intentionally designed to convey information about some aspects of Archaic Greece. Alongside this system of intended messages, there were also many *indices* which had the potential to interest observers, or which might have remained virtually invisible. I ignored the intended messages (the signs) about the cultural and historical context of the objects, and looked instead at the form of some large pots. I observed how they stood up, if they had legs or feet, where their handles were, and how big they were. A secondary inter-est was how they were decorated and which materials had been used. The indices relating to the sculptural aspects of the objects (form, size, texture, decoration) became, for me, signifying indices through the relationship I made with my own inter-ests in making sculpture. I interpreted a gallery with pots from Crete in it, in the same way, for the same reasons.

Museums and exhibitions are saturated with indices, but are also constructed through an assemblage of signs and signals, which in Mounin's terminology means that they carry intentioned messages. I think we could legitimately claim that museum exhibitions and posters, for example, operate within a system of communication that can be socially learnt. There is certainly an argument to be made about who has access to such social learning, and how effective this social learning is, but at the moment I want to put this to one side. If we accept Mounin's approach to the semiology of communication, and if we can for the moment accept that museum communicative practices fall within a communicative system that can be socially learnt, then we can proceed to say that all com-municative acts in museums will consist of: first, signs and signals, which carry intended messages: and second, signicative indices, which may or may not become signifying through a process of interpretation.

21

Mounin points out that it is sometimes difficult to differentiate between the two semiologies, that is between the semiology of signification and the semiology of communication, because some socio-cultural phenomena can participate in both. His examples of such social-cultural phenomena are literature, film and theatre, but I think we can definitely add museums to the list. Museums clearly can be part of both the semiology of signification, as we have seen from the analyses I have cited, and I propose to demonstrate how museums can be approached through, and can usefully use, the semiology of communication.

However, before we go on to consider the semiology of communication, we should first ask how communication as a process is understood in museums at the present time.

COMMUNICATION MODELS IN MUSEUMS TODAY

I am not at all sure that we can in fact be very clear about how communication as a process is understood in museums today. If we look back a few years we can discover quite a debate about how museum communication should be understood. Thus Duncan Cameron in 1968 in an article entitled 'A viewpoint: the museum as a communications system and implications for museum education', posited a communications model which was drawn from the then contemporary information theory.

He dismissed a simple communications model of transmitter, medium and receiver in favour of one with a variety of transmitters, many media and many varying receivers. However, a schematic diagram of this model will reveal its basic structure (Fig. 2.1).

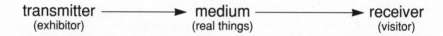

Fig. 2.1 Basic communications model from Cameron (1968)

It is of course based on the original Shannon and Weaver model of communication, one of the most influential models of communication, developed to assist in the construction of a mathematical theory of communication which would apply to any situation of information transfer, whether by people, machines or other systems (Fig. 2.2; McQuail 1975: 21).

Cameron added the notion of the feedback loop. 'The addition of feedback to the museum communications system is the basis of exhibit effectiveness research', he wrote. This will enable the transmitter to modify the transmission. Alternatively, feedback loops allow the visitor to compare his or her understanding with the intended message, that is to see if the message has been received correctly (Fig. 2.3).

This model has been relatively influential in museum thinking. Borun (1977) states, for example, that 'the museum visitor can be seen as part of a special communications system in which he is the recipient of messages from the staff through the medium of the exhibit. In order to know whether or not the message has been received and understood, the museum must complete the communication process by providing feedback channels for visitor response'. Steven Griggs points out that one of the most often-cited reasons for evaluation in museums is to provide feedback to the process of developing exhibits (Griggs 1984: 413). This suggests that where people are thinking about how useful their exhibitions are, they are taking this basic communication model as a given.

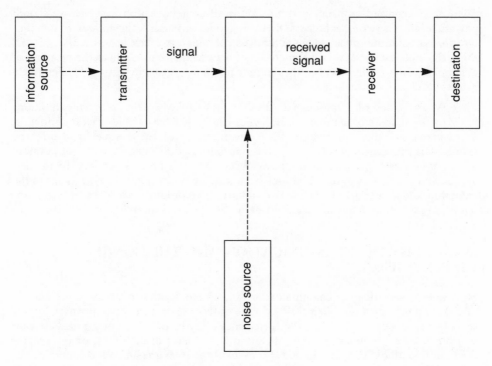

Fig. 2.2 Shannon and Weaver model from Duffy (1989)

It is, in fact, extremely difficult today to find out what, if any, model of communication underpins the communicative efforts of museum professionals. I am not sure how far people are thinking about it in this way. However, I think it is fair to say that most museum workers are thinking in terms of the messages of the display, and thinking in terms of how messages may be transmitted effectively, which suggests that the model I have cited is still in operation.

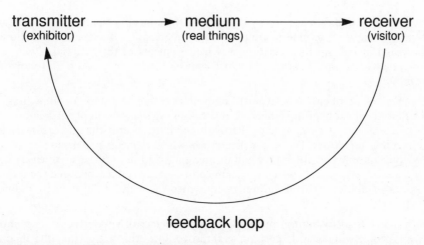

Fig. 2.3 Cameron's model with feedback loop

There are recognized problems with this model of communication to which we should pay attention. These are as follows: first, the model proposes a linear view of communication; second, the model suggests that the communicative act begins with a sender; third, the model suggests that the intention of the communicator defines the meaning of a communicative event; and fourth, the model assumes that the receiver is cognitively passive (McQuail 1975: 1–3).

Roger Miles has described museums as 'disabling systems' where they produce exhibitions based on this model of communications (Miles 1985: 31). One of Miles' major critiques is that where communication is seen as a linear process, with the message defined by the transmitter, this generally means that the transmitter is the curator, and that curators therefore become what he calls the power-brokers in this process defining the themes, approaches and processes of exhibitions from their own viewpoint. The meanings of the exhibition and its artefacts are defined by the curator according to his or her agenda, without paying attention to the interests, desires, needs of visitors, or indeed non-visitors.

SEMIOLOGY OF COMMUNICATION AND THE CONCEPT OF 'PERTINENCE'

How can the semiology of communication help to modify the communications model, or help to moderate a disabling process? One of the most fruitful concepts used by this school of semiotics is the concept of 'pertinence'. 'Pertinence' is a fairly broad concept which can cover the point of view, the approach, the set of questions, or the general theoretical outlook that guides either observation or expression of communication systems (Mounin 1985: xvi).

In linguistics, for example, communicational pertinence both determines that structural function of the elements of language and leads to an identification of these elements. Mounin suggests that this concept can be borrowed by other fields of semiotics. 'By determining which elements in a given phenomenon will become indices, the concept of pertinence allows for an interplay between a point of view on the one hand and the specificity of a given phenomenon studied on the other, because indices are at the same time materially part of the phenomenon and abstracted from it into a conceptual scheme' (Mounin 1985).

We might apply this to museums by saying that the concept of pertinence allows us to study how a given set of objects are related for the purposes of, say, an exhibition; the study would include an identification of which elements of the material phenomenon (the object) had become indices, and which approach to display had been followed for what reason.

The concept of pertinence is relevant to both observation (the study of something) and expression (the making of something). Thus we can use the concept of pertinence to help make relationships with audiences. Pertinence implies that although reality is inexhaustible, it is not elusive. Pertinence determines which elements of a given phenomenon will become meaningful. Relevance and meaning in relation to objects will ensue with a congruence of pertinence between communicator and interpreter, between the messages of a given exhibition and the meanings construed from this exhibition by individual visitors.

From a material socio-cultural phenomenon (an artefact or specimen, an exhibition, a museum) people will select (imperceptively) those indices that are pertinent to their own agendas at that time. Things will become of meaning if relevance if found between the phenomenon and the viewer. When Mounin was asked 'What makes a linguistic statement a poem?', his answer was the effect on the readers. The moment of reading is as important as the moment of creation. Thus for the success of any communicative act, both the expression and the interpretation need to be in a dynamic relation. For an exhibition to be a success, the effect on the viewer is as important as the work of the museum workers in setting it up.

A new communication model for museums must be proposed which would look something like Figure 2.4. The 'communicator' is replaced by a team which would include the interests of the curator, the designer, the conservator, the audience. The 'receiver' is recognized as an active maker of his or her own meanings for experiences, an interpreter with previous knowledge, attitudes and values which will inform any interpretation; and the 'medium' is reconceptualized as the middle ground between the communicators and the interpreters where many, varied, and possibly conflictual meanings will constantly be made and remade. This middle ground is never still, but always in flux. Each new interpreter brings a new interpretation to both the intended communication and the potential indices. The middle ground includes all the communicative media of the museum; the building, the people, the exhibitions, the objects, the café the toilets and so on. Museum meaning is not confined merely to an interpretation of the exhibitions or displays. A good experience in the café or at the information desk, will influence the meaning of the artefacts, as we all know.

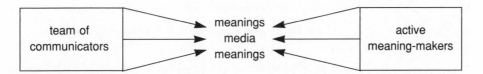

Fig. 2.4 A new communication model for museums

Mounin's distinction between the semiology of signification and the semiology of communication enables us, as museum workers, to make several distinctions. We can understand that museums as cultural and ideological artefacts may be analysed as signifying systems, as Barthes and others have done, and we can grasp the strengths and weaknesses of this analysis. We can also understand, through the semiology of communication, that museums can be analysed as intentional communication systems, with a use of intended signs and signals that may be both socially learnt and socially taught. The semiology of communication also enables us to understand what we always knew, that people will make their own sense of experiences, in other words that indices will become signifying according to personal meaning systems. We can also realize that indices can be manipulated as part of the system of intended meanings.

There are several tools here that are of use to museum workers. Clearly if museums do operate as systems of intended communication which can be socially learnt, this system can be studied, analysed, improved, modified, taught and so on. Museum workers would benefit from such studies.

Maybe we should assume that museum audiences have not in general been taught the communicative system of museums, and we should develop ways of enabling people to grasp the system quickly. Some museums are finding ways of working together with audiences to produce communicative systems. This acts as training for both museum worker and audience member.

How can we make the museum pertinent to the lives of audiences? Can we interest new audiences by finding new ways of approaching the collections, new questions to ask, new indices to become significant? How do we know when an indice has shifted from being 'potentially signifying' to 'significant' if we don't ask? How would the answers change the intended communication systems?

I feel that many museums are already beginning to explore these avenues and are beginning to find ways to develop the dynamic relation between expression and interpretation. This dynamic relation is the way forward for museum communication.

This paper first appeared in G. Kavanagh (ed.) (1991) Museum Languages: Objects and Texts, Leicester: Leicester University Press, pp. 49–61.

REFERENCES

Anon (1980) 'Adam's ancestors: Eve's in-laws', *Schooling and Culture* 8: 57–62.

Barthes, R. (1973) 'The great family of man', in *Mythologies*, London: Paladin.

Borun, M. (1977) *Measuring the Immeasurable: A Pilot Study of Museum Effectiveness*, Philadelphia, PA: The Franklin Institute.

Cameron, D. (1968) 'A viewpoint: the museum as a communications system and implications for museum education', *Curator* 11: 33–40.

Duffy, C. (1989) 'Museum visitors – a suitable case for treatment', unpublished paper for the Museum Education Association of Australia conference, 1989.

Duncan, C. and Wallach, A. (1978) 'The Museum of Modern Art as late capitalist ritual: an iconographic analysis', *Marxist Perspectives* Winter: 28–51

Duncan, C. and Wallach, A. (1980) 'The universal survey museum', *Art History* 3(4): 448–69.

Griggs, S. (1984) 'Evaluating exhibitions', in J. M. A. Thompson (ed.) *Manual of Curatorship*, London: Butterworth.

Hodge, R. and D'Souza, W. (1979) 'The museum as a communicator: a semiotic analysis of the Western Australian Museum Aboriginal Gallery, Perth', *Museum* 31(4): 251–66.

Innis, E. (1985) *Semiotics: An Introductory Reader*, London: Hutchinson.

McQuail, D. (1975) *Communication*, London and New York: Longman.

Miles, R. (1985) 'Exhibitions: management for a change', in N. Cossons (ed.) *The Management of Change in Museums*, London: National Maritime Museum.

Mounin, G. (1985) *Semiotic Praxis: Studies in Pertinence and in the Means and Expression of Communication*, New York and London: Plenum Press.

3

The process of communication
J. Morgan and P. Welton

An act of communication is one which aims to produce an effect in another person. If this intention is absent, the process becomes one of expression. Communicative acts can be improved through an understanding of the communicative process.

The process of communication is explained using the 'bull's eye' or 'hypodermic needle' model of communication, with the various elements of the model discussed. This is developed with a consideration of the skills necessary for communication, in the context of shared experience.

Useful references are given for further study, and some exercises are suggested to sharpen communication skills.

EXPRESSION AND COMMUNICATION

You get up in the morning, go over to your wardrobe, and wonder what to wear. Is it a jeans-and-tee-shirt day, a sober-suit day, or a leather-jacket-and-boots day? If you have such a range of clothes, your selection will depend upon two things: the way you feel and the version of yourself that you wish to send out to other people. The suit is a sign of conformity to the organization which employs you. Choosing a tee shirt and jeans may tell other people that you are adopting an informal role: 'I'm not on duty – it's the weekend.' For you, it may also be a part of the pleasure of being away from work: 'Hurray! Thank goodness I can relax today.' By contrast the leather jacket and boots for some people may be a way of announcing: 'I'm tough and energetic; watch me go!' and may also serve to build up their self-confidence to face a social encounter in which they feel a need to compete.

Every time we communicate, these two different forces are in operation: on the one hand, the need to influence the other person, and on the other, the need to remind ourselves who we are or who we want to be. The relative strength of the impulses will vary from minute to minute, and there are many occasions when we simply wish to express ourselves for the inherent pleasure of the act; I may, for instance, spend a morning cleaning my motor-bike for the sheer pleasure I know I will get from polishing the chrome parts and achieving a real mirror finish in the paintwork. It may well be that in doing this simple but satisfying job I will have time to think about other problems I have and I may be able to come to terms with conflicting emotions. I could use this task as a kind of therapy. The chances are, however, that in the back of my mind is the awareness that I am likely to meet some friends who will inevitably comment on the state of the bike and possibly draw conclusions about my attitude to this valued possession.

Here we will concentrate on acts where the need to influence is paramount; not because we underrate the subjective importance of the visual arts as expression, but because we are concerned that both practitioners and consumers of the visual arts should be able to use them to the best effect.

The most intensely personal and expressive piece of work will produce an effect on a few of the people who see it, either because of their understanding of the circumstances which produced it or because of their broad experience and sensitivity. But if you are aiming at a wider audience than these few perceptive individuals, an awareness of the mechanics and psychology of the communication process can help to sharpen your presentation. The choice of a target remains in your hands – or in those of the client who is employing you.

CRITICAL SKILLS AND VISUAL COMMUNICATION

Professionals in any field need a vocabulary and a set of systems for analysing their work. This is as true in the visual field as in any other. The art-director in an advertising agency needs to be able to explain what is required to the photographer, the account director and the copywriter who form part of the team working on an advertising campaign. Each of them will discuss a particular proposal and go away with a precise idea of what has been agreed and how their tasks complement each other. Their discussions will have covered not only obvious questions such as the subject of the advertisement, camera angles and possible layout, but also more abstract questions of style, approach and potential audience. A measure of the effectiveness of the team is the precision with which each member can communicate the concepts required.

A wide range of occupations depends, as advertisers do, upon the visual skills of other people, occupations as diverse as railway guard, football coach, architect, or stage designer, all of whom rely for their success on conveying information to selected target groups in order that a desired response should be produced. As target groups or consumers of visual information become more skilled in receiving, understanding and reacting to such information, so the quality or effectiveness of the communication is improved and the subtlety of the messages can be developed. More than that, however, it is also possible that as we expand the visual awareness of consumers, they become more sophisticated in their awareness of the techniques deployed against them, which in turn provides a defence against unwanted blandishments from skilled communicators. The development of visual skills also opens up a range of pleasurable experiences which are denied to those who perceive visual media in simple, narrow terms.

Lasswell (1948) claimed that an act of communication was adequately explained only when every aspect of his famous question had been answered:

who	says what	in which channel	to whom	with what effect?

As a starting-point for the analysis of a communication, this cannot be bettered, although as we shall see the discussion can go very much further. For example, the message 'Come up and see me some time' means something very different when spoken by Mae West than it would in the mouth of Ronald Reagan; even from her, it has a different significance when she speaks it at a party than when she writes it in a letter; when addressed to a woman it clearly means something different from when a man is on the receiving end. And, of course, without a description of the effect which it produces, the story is incomplete.

LEARNING TO COMMUNICATE

The processes by which children learn to speak and, much later, to write are well documented; those by which we learn to make and decipher visual messages are just as complex but much less well studied. Our society places a high value on the word, both written and spoken, but new technology has helped to emphasize the importance of other means of communication: film and television depend primarily on picture rather than sound, and modern printing technology extends the range of colours, textures and shapes available to the advertiser and book designer. International trade puts a premium on any method of communication which can reduce dependence on expensive and sometimes confusing translations of the written word. We need greater awareness of the means by which we understand what we see, not simply because any study of humanity is fascinating, but because without it we shall be unable to take advantage of the technical, commercial and social possibilities of the latter years of the twentieth century. Others may take control of the channels and seek to manipulate us; only by understanding the techniques at their disposal will we be placed to defend our own interests.

Visual education today is too often an erratic and spasmodic affair of which the greater part takes place outside the classroom. The art class is an embattled tower of self-expression in a school which has been occupied by armies of facts. In defending this role, art teachers have had little time or energy to impart the analytic tools which would enable their students to discuss pictures, advertisements or exhibitions with the same precision that, say, an English teacher would give to the techniques displayed in a written text.

Children watch advertisements on television, read comics and magazines, discuss each other's clothes, play electronic games, observe road signs, browse through record sleeves, collect badges. Each of these activities has effects on the images they produce. The thoughtful art teacher will, if sufficient time can be squeezed in, use these images as the starting point for discussion of the processes which generated them and the effects they produce in others. These discussions will need to be supported by a clear awareness on the part of the teacher of the theories on which they depend, not in order to turn the lesson into another marshalling of 'facts', but because any teacher needs to have both an analytic and an intuitive understanding of the skills and perceptions which are being developed. If the students, too, acquire an analytical understanding of what they are doing, then this is a bonus.

In schools, there is a case for replacing the traditional expressive function of art education with one in which the 'language' of the visual world is taught. Such elements as colour, line, tone, shape, and so on are the building-blocks of visual communication yet, with some notable exceptions, most people leave school with only the haziest notion of them, to say nothing of the more abstract concepts which will be developed in this book. Yet the constant bombardment of visual images from many quarters is already shaping their lives, influencing their attitudes, tuning their responses. A well-developed critical capacity applicable to the visual world should be the normal equipment of every school leaver, in the same way as an English teacher aims to form adults who are critics as well as receivers of the spoken and written word. This approach need not stifle the expressive needs of children but would better equip them positively to realize their purposes.

The first requirement of any field of study is to establish an overall framework within which discussion can take place. We need to consider a number of models of the communication process: each of these representations can only be a partial description, but each throws light on a particular aspect of the complexities of human interaction, and can help us to produce more effective messages.

THE 'BULL'S-EYE' MODEL OF COMMUNICATION

The simplest way of regarding communication is to see the sender of a message as an archer and the recipient as the bull's-eye in the middle of the target. The sender chooses a message, calculates the best way to send it and fires it off at the intended audience.

Take a simple situation: I wish to stop you smoking in my room. I have several choices to produce this effect; I could simply say to you, 'Would you mind very much not smoking in here?' or I could point out a notice which I have drawn and which lies on the table between us.

If for some reason I reject both of these, I can break into loud coughs and rush to open the window.

It is immediately apparent that in considering sender and receiver as archer and target, we have seriously oversimplified the nature of the transaction: the message has not only to be sent, it has to be understood and accepted, and each of the messages I have described could fail on this account. You may fail to recognize my pantomime as a message at all; you may be unfamiliar with the dialect which I speak; you may be unaware of the convention which produced the 'No Smoking' sign. There may be some distraction or interruption which prevents you from noticing my message: an attractive stranger may walk into the room, my table may be cluttered with other objects or a noisy lorry may pass the window. Finally, my choice of a way to convey my feelings may irritate, amuse or embarrass you.

This situation presents each of the elements in one of the earliest and most influential models of human communication, elaborated by Shannon and Weaver (1949) as an aid to improving the efficiency of telecommunications systems (see Fig. 3.1):

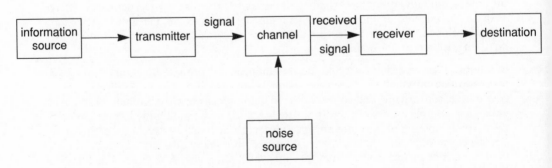

Fig. 3.1 Shannon and Weaver communications model

The most useful wider application of this model is to clarify potential causes of communication breakdown: each of the elements can contribute to misunderstanding and even conflict:

(a) *Noise*: any event which shares the same channel as a message and interferes with the receiver's ability to perceive it. In the example above, the attractive stranger, the other objects on the table and the passing lorry are all, in this sense, *noise*. A boldly coloured poster next to your delicate pastel may be noise; a nauseating scene of horror preceding your television advertisement can also be noise.

(b) *Information source*: The actual message may be confused in the mind of the sender: do I really wish to stop you smoking, or do I simply wish to exercise my authority? If I am unsure which is my real message. I may fail to transmit either.

(c) *Transmitter*. A message is said to be encoded when a conscious decision has been made by the sender to attempt to put the message across in a particular way and when the appropriate signs have been chosen – words, gestures, shapes, images. Of course, the signs chosen may fail to convey a message to you at all, or only a message which is so garbled that you completely misunderstand my intentions.

(d) *Channel*: The channel is the physical means by which the message is sent – the sound-waves or electromagnetic impulses which pass between sender and receiver. Related to this is the term *medium*, a broader term which includes all the types of equipment which extend the range of our communication: posters, radio and magnetic tape are all media. Each medium has its own peculiarities, advantages and disadvantages: the attributes of photography are quite distinct from those of pen and ink drawing, yet each is ideal for certain purposes.

(e) *Receiver*: We talk of decoding a message when the signs received are turned into meanings: if the communication has been successful, the meaning produced is close to that which the sender encoded. This does not, of course, always happen. The message may use unfamiliar signs and conventions: the 'No Smoking' sign may mean little to a person unfamiliar with the road signs which it resembles. Each group within a society has its own dialect, its own distinct variation on a more general language, and this is as true of visual as it is of verbal communication.

(f) *Destination*: The person or group at whom the sender has directed the message. The receiver may have no concepts equivalent to those included in the sender's message, although the words may appear to have been in some way decoded. The inhabitant of an oasis may have some trouble with the feelings implicit in the words 'sleet' and 'slush' when used by a Scottish Highlander. Furthermore, although the individual concepts may be shared by both parties, the complexity with which they are organized may be beyond the receiver's grasp.

We have so far discussed this model as a description of two people communicating face to face. It is even more useful when applied to more remote methods of communication: 'transmitter' could be interpreted as a telephone mouthpiece or as a modem (the electronic device which connects a computer to a telephone line), in which case the channel becomes the telephone cable and the receiver, a telephone earpiece or another modem.

The model can also be used to describe the relationship between a number of organizations working on the same message – say, a television advertisement. An advertising agency, as information source, devises an advertising campaign and hires a film unit (transmitter) to produce an advertisement which is broadcast by a satellite television company (channel) to a cable company (receiver) which passes the transmission to the home (destination).

COMMUNICATION AS A SKILL

The last section began by describing communication as like an archer taking aim at a target: if the arrow hits the bull's-eye, it is because of the skill of the archer. A little consideration of the more detailed description, however, makes clear that the process is in fact interactive: both sender and receiver have a part to play in a successful transaction.

Both parties to a transaction must be active: as the sender struggles to find a way of encoding the message, the receiver must focus attention on it, interpret it, and if necessary seek clarification. Both parties are exercising knowledge, experience and skill. Successful communication depends on this, so that failure can rarely be blamed unhesitatingly on just one party.

Who is to blame if I fail to show you that, although I wish you to stop smoking, I do not wish you to interpret this as a simple assertion of my authority over you? It may be my fault for failing to give sufficient thought to the complexity of the problem. It may be your fault for failing to study my message attentively. Our relationship may make such delicacy impossible: our previous rivalries and mistrust may prevent this kind of message from being offered or accepted at face value – we see and hear what we expect, rather than what takes place. Both of us can improve our effectiveness with greater experience, discussion and practice: this is what is meant when communication is described as a skill.

A notice goes up to announce an important meeting of those involved in organizing and using the services of a creche. Only half of those expected actually come to the meeting. What can have gone wrong?

The poster may have failed to include vital information, like the time and place of the meeting. Because it used the same format as routine announcements, it may have failed to distinguish this meeting as important. The paper on which it was printed may have been of a colour normally used only by a small, specialized department. It may have been indistinguishable from a mass of other notices around it on the notice-board, so that the members of the group failed to pick it out in their routine scanning of the notice-board as they came to work.

Every one of these failures can be described as ultimately a failure of skill, and therefore as something which can be remedied. Once the problem has been analysed, we can set about improving our chances of success next time. We need to look at the message, the interpretation and the receiver so that we can identify at which point confusion crept in.

COMMUNICATION AS SHARED EXPERIENCE

Communication does not involve the transmission of thoughts. This statement may seem perverse, but it is more than a quibble to say that what we exchange are messages, not thoughts. In listening to me, or in looking at the picture which I have drawn, you may have the illusion of being in direct touch with what is going on in my head. This is not so. You are trying to decode my message in order to infer the state of mind which produced it. In showing you my drawing, I am trying to produce in you a particular effect, which may or may not be the same as my state of mind in making the drawing.

My aim in communicating is always to do something – to make you like me, to stop you smoking, to get you to come to a meeting, to park your car here or to buy my house. Without such an aim, communication becomes purely expression. With such an aim, both parties must start from what they share: language, experience, knowledge and values.

Someone once remarked that, even if a miracle enabled us to talk to an ant, communication would be impossible because there would be nothing to talk about. The world of the ant is so totally dissimilar from our world that every word we exchanged would evoke a totally different range of experience in the two minds. In human discourse, this problem is reflected by the use of such expressions as 'They were speaking different languages' to describe people whose ideas are so far apart that communication between them seems all but impossible.

Wilbur Schramm (1973) devised a model of communication which expressed this restriction in graphic terms (see Fig. 3.2):

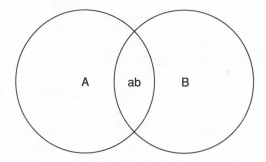

Fig. 3.2 Schramm's model of communication

'The area ab where A's life-space overlaps that of B is the setting for their communication'.

In other words, we have to identify those parts of our experience which we share with our audience, and use this common pool of experience and ideas to provide equivalents for any novel ideas from beyond these limits. For example, I keep bees, but you are allergic to bee-stings and avoid the slightest contact with them. I want you to understand the pleasure which I take in going to my hives and in handling and caring for the bees. How can I do this? One solution might be to build upon our shared pleasure in gardening and in driving fast cars. Thus, handling bees without getting stung is something you might understand in terms of your pleasure in driving fast but safely; watching the development of a colony and keeping it in good condition to encourage a heavy honey crop can be felt as similar to your enjoyment of cultivating, watching plants grow and harvesting crops of vegetables or flowers.

In this example, the idea of the bee produces a different effect in both of us, this difference being the result of differences in our mental worlds. The study of communication is beset by examples of failure produced by such ambiguity. A camel means daily transport to a bedouin of the desert, an embarrassing sign of technological backwardness to the sophisticated Arab townsman, and an exciting novelty to the London child who rode a camel on a visit to the zoo last summer. Each person will interpret a picture of a camel in terms of their own experience, and may incorrectly assume that the picture means the same to others. We are easily misled into thinking that our shared use of a language implies a shared pool of experience.

A MODEL OF COMMUNICATION SKILL

Starting from Shannon and Weaver's model, Berlo (1960) developed a framework which demonstrates the complex web of skills and knowledge which two parties need if they are to communicate successfully: a more analytical version of the 'overlapping life space' which Schramm said was the setting for their communication. This model is a graphic representation of the factors which distinguish awkward, embarrassing or laborious transactions from those which give us pleasure and permit the apparently effortless cooperation on which so much of our daily life depends.

This is a summary: in its layout, it implies a number of definitions and explanations.

(a) Sender and receiver have to share the same set of *skills*: they have to use the same language or code, and they have to use words or signs in the same way. For this to happen, they must have experience of the same *social system* and *culture* (the values, rules and beliefs through which people live).

Furthermore, they must share at least some *attitudes* to the subject of their conversation. Absolute disagreement on all aspects of the topic means that discussion is impossible: even an argument has to grow out of a fundamental level of agreement on some issues.

(b) The two parties must be linked by a *channel* or medium of communication.

(c) The message consists of a number of inseparable components which may be discussed individually but which work together to produce their effects. Their interdependence is implied by Berlo's 'M' framework which binds them together.

  (i) *Content*: the information or emotion which is the subject of the message.

  (ii) *Elements*: the individual items (words, sounds, brushstrokes, gestures, colours, pictures) which are assembled to form the message.

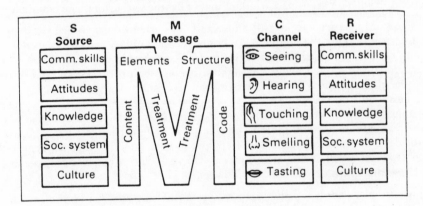

Fig. 3.3 Berlo's SMCR model of communication

  (iii) *Structure*: the way in which the elements of the message are assembled. The same elements can produce different messages when combined in a different way: 'Dog bites man' is not the same as 'Man bites dog', and Chagall's lovers floating at the top of the painting would convey a different message if they lay along the bottom edge of the picture.

(iv) *Treatment*: elements and structure may be combined in the same essential way, but a skilled communicator can introduce subtle variations to vary the impact of the final message: like the word 'style', this concept depends on the subjective contribution of the individual communicator.

(v) *Code*: the rules and conventions on which the message is built, such as the alphabet used for writing, the grammar of a language, or the 'Highway Code' used to establish the meaning of a road-sign.

SUMMARY

An act of communication is one which aims to produce an effect in another person. If this intention is absent, we refer to the act as expression rather than communication. It is possible to improve the effectiveness of visual communicators by analysing the means which they use and by extending their range of concepts and the vocabulary which they use to discuss or explain their work. In so doing, they may deepen the quality of their response to visual media and be more sensitive to techniques which may be marshalled against them. The transmission of a message can be analysed into five components: selecting an idea to be conveyed, encoding it, transmitting it through a channel, decoding and interpretation by the receiver. Problems may occur at any one of these stages; in particular, noise may operate on the channel to prevent accurate transmission of the message itself. Communication depends upon a range of shared experiences, attitudes and knowledge.

WHERE DO WE GO FROM HERE?

A most thorough view of communication theory is provided by C.D. Mortensen's *Communication: the study of human interaction* (McGraw-Hill, 1972); it is, however, demanding and expensive. D.K. Berlo's *The Process of Communication* (Holt, Rinehart & Winston, 1960) is more accessible and gives a broad introduction to the philosophy of communication. D. McQuail and S. Windahl's *Communication Models* for the study of mass communications (Longman, 1982) concentrates on mass media models but is clear and concise. Slightly more demanding, but nevertheless quite accessible, is John Fiske's *Introduction to Communication Studies* (Methuen, 1982).

A useful exercise to sharpen one's critical vocabulary is to choose an artist, photographer or designer with whose work one is familiar and express in words what makes that work distinctive. A successful definition would permit someone who had never before encountered this work to identify samples of it in a folder of similar pictures. The similarity may be one of theme, subject, technique or historical context; indeed, as you gain confidence in this analysis, you may wish to increase the number of areas of similarity in order to sharpen the precision of your distinctions.

Many people are disturbed by the implications of such analysis, feeling that it in some sense inhibits or distorts imagination and creativity. What are the potential advantages of an analytical approach to the communication process?

Any model or statement concerning communication must of necessity simplify the complex process which it describes. In describing your own field of study, what modifications would you wish to make to the models discussed in this chapter?

Berlo's model (p. 34) presents a number of features which source and receiver must share for successful communication to be possible: communication skills, attitudes, knowledge, social system and culture. Test this with the work of a skilled communicator (photographer, designer, painter, film-maker) which you know well. Is it possible to understand the work without all of these elements? Are there any additional elements which need to be added?

This paper first appeared in J. Morgan and P. Welton (eds) (1986) See What I Mean: An Introduction to Visual Communication, *London: Edward Arnold, pp. 1–12.*

REFERENCES

Berlo, D.K. (1960) *The Process of Communication*, London: Holt, Rinehart & Winston.

Schramm, W. (ed.) (1954) *The Process and Effects of Mass Communication*, Chicago: University of Illinois Press.

Shannon, C.E. and Weaver, W. (1949) *Mathematical Theory of Communication*, Chicago: University of Illinois Press.

4

The museum as a communicator: a semiotic analysis of the Western Australian Gallery, Perth

Robert Hodge and Wilfred D'Souza

Written by two lecturers in communication studies, the article examines the sign systems of an exhibition such as space, language, photographs and objects. The potentials and problems of the various signifying elements are discussed in detail and the capacity for deeply held attitudes to be revealed through the choices made by the writers and designers producing the exhibition is described.

The problems discovered in the case-study are identified as inherent in any act of communication. The communicative process is positioned within social, cultural and political contexts, and cannot therefore be considered outside of these contexts which shape our daily lives in very specific ways.

Museums exist for a variety of purposes, Mohammed Aziz Lahbabi, in his article 'The Museum and the Protection of the Cultural Heritage of the Maghreb', says 'It is the function of museums . . . to be the living memory of the people and for the people.' Museums are not only protectors but also communicators of this living memory. A museum display is an exercise in one branch of the mass media, requiring a special kind of understanding of the processes of communication, namely the nature of mass communication systems. The essential thing to understand here is that mass communication is in some important ways an unnatural form of communication. We are all experts in natural communication, more expert than we are aware. We perform complex acts of communication with the confidence and unconsciousness born of long habit. So everyone is likely to adjust insufficiently to the major differences involved in a mass communication situation.

In a natural communication, typified by face-to-face conversation between two people of similar background, the main message of any one speaker is interpreted through this common background. It is backed up by innumerable supporting channels of communication (intonation patterns, gestures, expressions, etc.). It can be repeated, or parts of it emphasized, in the light of the hearer's response. The exposure-time of the message is controlled by the speaker, and is the same for speaker and hearer. Mass communication systems generally depart from all these conditions, and a museum display is no exception. This divergence from natural communication gives rise to characteristic kinds of communication failure or inappropriate communication in mass communications systems, which will be the main focus of attention in the present study.

Inappropriate communication here includes two basic kinds of breakdown: saying things you did not mean to say, as well as not quite getting across whatever it was you wanted to say. The first of these is very common and more insidious than the second, since for obvious reasons the communicator is less likely to be aware of its happening. Most of us realize that not all of our message is likely to reach target so we are inclined to react by raising the volume – like the well-known tourist strategy of speaking loudly to uncomprehending foreigners. But what if a 10-per-cent increase in message *A* (the intended meaning) can only be achieved at the cost of 40-per-cent increase in message *B*, the meaning of which the speaker was not conscious?

In a traditional kind of museum, where exhibits are carefully organized into galleries and individual displays, there are certain features of the communication situation that make inappropriate communication more likely. One is the potential difference between communicator and communicatees. Visitors to a museum gallery may be different in age, class, sex, language, and cultural background from the communicator and from each other. All these differences can be regarded as differences of language, and their effect is to stratify the whole display, so that the communicator's single message is received as a large number of different messages, some of them contrary to the original intended message.

This tendency of the single message to fragment is likely to be intensified by the existence of multiple channels of communication used in a display, which are required to substitute for the multiple channels of communication available in everyday conversation. The task for the communicator is a massive piece of translation, from a language he does not realize he knows into an artificial language system that neither he nor anyone else is thoroughly familiar with. Between conception and communication, then, there is likely to be many a slip. Communicators and public may seem at times as though they had seen entirely different exhibitions. Some diversity of response, of course, is natural and desirable, but it is well for the planner of a display to have some notion of the likely responses, and some responsibility for what his display is doing.

IDEOLOGY AND AIMS

As an example of a museum as communicator, we have taken one gallery, the Aboriginal Gallery of the Western Australian Museum, Perth which is administered by the local Western Australian state government. We are grateful for the generous assistance of the museum in compiling this study. Serving a population of 1,197,000, the museum is situated in Perth, the capital city, which has a population of 820,100. The Western Australian population is predominiantly of European stock, with the Aborigines, the original inhabitants, now a dwindling minority.

In the past there has been open hostility between Aborigines and the newcomers, and there is continuing conflict over the role of Aboriginal culture in the Eurocentric dominant culture. An exhibition of this kind, therefore, necessarily has an ideological problem that interacts with the aims and effect of any possible display. The result is that the planners of the display show a characteristic kind of uncertainty about aims and unawareness of effects. This is only a particular instance of the general problem faced by museums that attempt to do justice to a minority culture or the culture of an oppressed or expropriated group within the society. However, any analysis of communication success has to know the answer to the question: Successful at communicating what? And it often happens that such a question asked very precisely brings out uncertainties or even contradictions in the general aims that affect the overall structure of a display.

Headings and introductory statements are clearly one place to start in determining the overall intention of a display, since this is where the member of the public will start. The title of this exhibition is *Patterns of Life in a Vast Land*. This suggests a concern with the relation between man and his environment. 'Patterns' suggests a harmonious, aesthetically pleasing object of study, the plural indicating a diversity that adds to the aesthetic pleasure. The explanatory subheading narrows down the scope of this title. The 'Vast Land' becomes 'Western Australia', which is only one part of the 'Vast Land' covered. 'Patterns of Life' becomes 'The Story of The Aboriginal People'. Where ' patterns' suggests an arrangement of elements perceived at one time, 'story' suggests a narrative taking place through time, a kind of history. The explanatory description of the exhibition runs as follows:

> Europeans have inhabited Western Australia for a century and a half. But for tens of thousands of years this land has been the home of the aboriginal people and their ancestors. This exhibition is planned as a tribute to them, and as a record of the ways of life that served them so well, for so long.

The first two sentences discreetly mention the two races that have competed for possession of this country, and hint at claims of the Aborigines. 'Tens of thousands' is longer than a century and a half 'and home' is stronger than 'inhabited'. The tense 'has been the home' implies that it still is their 'home', which makes the Europeans who also 'inhabit' it seem like squatters. The impression that the exhibition has sympathy for the Aboriginal cause comes over clearly in the word 'tribute', which connotes a celebration or commemoration of the Aborigines by those conscious of a debt.

However, the display is both 'tribute' and 'record'. This dual function contains a potential contradiction. A record is a factual historical document, whereas a tribute is concerned to create an attitude that is favourable. What if the historical record is unflattering? What if facts are not enough to create the desired attitude? We have in fact four different though overlapping descriptions of the form of the exhibition: patterns, story, tribute, record. Two of these are concerned with pleasing, harmonious effects, two with factual, historical materials. The potential conflict here corresponds to the problematic dual function of the museum as educator: to correct prejudices, which are firmly rooted attitudes, and to overcome ignorance.

This preliminary analysis brings out the problems facing this display. The major messages we expect will concern key relationships, between man and his environment, European and Aboriginal, present and past, each of these relationships being blurred: and the thrust of the exhibition will be divided between scientific and educative, concerned with history and facts or with attitudes and values, as it presents Aboriginal life for a European and Eurocentred public.

SIGNS OF IMPORTANCE

One very general but very important message the display is designed to communicate is that an understanding of Aboriginal life is important. There are a number of resources, or sign-systems, that can be drawn on to indicate this meaning, for a display as a whole and for components of a display.

The location of notices and the size of the lettering on them comprise the two dimensions of one system of signs. The rule with size is, of course, that the larger the notice the more important the exhibit, 'larger' being relative to the norms for such notices. Other general signals of status include forms of conspicuous expenditure, lavish use of space being one important indicator of this. The Aboriginal gallery has a whole floor assigned to it, a sign of high status. Within the gallery there is free floor space, and room to move about the individual exhibits. This principle also indicates the relative importance of particular exhibits. In general, the more space and the fewer the items in a given space, the more important the item or exhibit. In this gallery, top status is accorded to one component entitled 'The Aboriginal Way of Life', which is what the visitor sees first on entering the gallery (a sign of status), and which has the largest area in front of it, in absolute terms (a visitor can stand up to 40 feet back from it) and because the opposite side has no competing exhibits for that large space.

Two other indicators of expense, and therefore status, in a museum display are the presumed cost of an exhibit and the deployment of technology. The difficulty of obtaining an exhibit is not usually made evident, though it could be. All that the members of the public have to go on is the distinction between artefacts, simulations and photographs. Of these, photographs are likely to be the low-prestige form, especially recent photographs, however much enlarged. Simulations if well done are high-prestige forms. Artefacts will tend to be intermediate in prestige, on their own. Technology will tend to add prestige. So a series of slides on a screen activated by a button will add prestige to the contents of the slides. Even simple technology, like lighting effects or machines that make things move, add to the status of the item, and cumulatively to the status of the gallery itself.

Indicators of status usually have the effect of drawing the attention of visitors to the item or exhibit concerned, and making it more likely to be remembered. However, there are two potential dangers with signs of status. One is that they make a kind of claim on the members of the public that has to be justified. That is, the public must feel that the items which the museum is signalling as important are important. Otherwise, they will at a subconscious level feel alienated from the museum's values, and the museum will have failed badly in its aim of changing the attitudes of the general public. The gallery section 'The Aboriginal Way of Life' illustrates the difficulties here. It has signals of importance due to position and space, as noted above, but it contains no rare objects, no recondite knowledge, nothing that seems special or difficult to obtain or worthy of close attention. This is because it is precisely the ordinariness and typicality of it that are important. However, the planner of an exhibition has to take care, with a potentially self-contradictory meaning like this, that he does not produce a display whose message cancels itself out: an important kind of unimportance.

A second danger inherent in the use of status signals is that they represent an intrusion by their user. They claim importance, but they are generally indeterminate as to the further questions: important to whom, and for what? Important to the museum, of course, but to the museum as representing the public, responding to demand, or the museum as teacher, educating the public, imposing more or less subtly its values on the public? Hugues de Varine-Bohan, in his article 'The Modern Museum: Requirements and Problems of a New Approach', says:

> We would further plead that the museum should be selective and 'client-centred'. All too often present-day museums are regarded by their curators as providing 'lessons' for a homogeneous but perhaps non-existent public, a public which exists mainly in the curator's mind: a group of well-bred, culture-hungry, beauty-loving, logically minded people with plenty of time to spare, inexhaustible physical stamina and, above all, at least an arts degree.
>
> (de Varine-Bohan 1976: 139)

With such a gallery, which is designed as a 'tribute' to people who are themselves citizens of Western Australia, it is proper to ask the questions: important to whom, and for what? Against this pervasive evaluation by others of their culture, the value-judgements of the indigenous culture, which are so important a part of that culture, need to be prominent. The absence of Aboriginal signs of importance in this exhibition is a general though unconscious sign of the unimportance of Aboriginal values for the exhibitors. This kind of unintentional slight is probably widespread. Mohammed Aziz Lahbabi observes something similar in his article when he says:

> Out of an alleged respect for tradition, the tendency was to see the indigenous culture in terms of fixed tastes and structures. Forms devoid of living substance. The structures of a vanished past cannot, however, help to overcome underdevelopment. Colonial domination took objectivity away from science and dispossessed the people of its authenticity.
>
> (Lahbabi 1976: 148–9)

Some indications of status, such as the amount of space assigned to an item, are neutral between Aboriginal and European values, but others are not. In particular the use of technology and the products of the white man's technology carries an ambivalent evaluation. It magnifies by association, but disparages by comparison. The signal transmitted can be 'We, the museum staff, are very skilful' rather than 'the Aboriginals are very interesting'. One example would be the display of spears, carefully arranged and labelled, superimposed on a picture of Aborigines holding spears. The photograph competes with the artefacts as though they were not interesting enough. The spears themselves form a set of parallel lines, losing their individuality and function in this rigid non-Aboriginal patterning. Similarly, the pattern of boomerangs is created by museum staff, which distracts attention from the patterns created by Aborigines on the boomerangs themselves.

CODES AND THEIR CAPACITY

The messages transmitted by a museum display come via many channels or media, each of which has a different communication potential. Kinds of message are often tied to a particular medium. For instance, messages about large numbers, or events over different times or places, cannot easily be communicated through pictures, and conversely messages about qualities cannot easily be communicated by numbers.

The Aboriginal display uses the following main media: (a) objects and artefacts; (b) simulated environments; (c) photographs and slides; (d) diagrams; (e) labels and (f) writing. These media differ along a continuum with respect to their closeness to reality or their closeness to language. Artefacts are selected examples of reality, while language refers to reality but at some remove. We can generalize about this list of media, and say that the greater the predominance of earlier media the stronger will be the sense of reality being directly experienced. The distinctive mode of communication for museums is through objects. Hugues de Varine-Bohan in his article expands on this emphasis and its value as follows:

> The obtrusive image, the all powerful influence of words, bureaucracy, etc., must be counterbalanced. It is objects, real things, which will provide this antidote: the growing success, in every country, of nature reserves, the well-known popularity of zoos and botanical gardens and even the universal taste for tourism and for escaping to countries which are still 'authentic' show that such things meet a genuine need. What we said earlier also applies here: the man in the street is inundated with second-hand information which has been processed, arranged and commercialized: he wants not to be given but to be left free to choose for himself the first-hand information that he wants for its knowledge content.
>
> (de Varine-Bohan 1976: 134)

Communication through objects and artefacts is generally less well understood than more developed forms. An artefact communicates by being what it is. It therefore communicates or signifies that perfectly. Potentially it is accessible to every sense. It can be seen, tapped, touched, handled, smelt and even tasted. This multisensual experience could communicate a complex and open set of messages with an incomparable vividness and immediacy. For instance, someone handling a *woomera* perceives directly what could be put in a large number of sentences: 'A *woomera* is made of wood, a hard wood with a distinctive resonance, hollowed out in the middle, between 1 and 2 feet long, the point of balance near the middle, etc.' The strength of artefactual communication is this immediacy and openness. The weakness is that these meanings are only potential, and are liable to disappear unless they are coded and retained in language. If a museum displayed only artefacts, without explanatory labels, neither museum nor public would know what had been communicated, which of course is bad communication. However, the strength of communication by objects and artefacts should not be underestimated. Precisely because it is pre-linguistic it is a kind of universal language, which can mediate between Aborigines and European and communicate to all ages and classes of the public.

In a traditional kind of museum display, items tend to be kept behind glass cases. In Lahbabi's words:

> Museums seem to set a barrier between life and culture, appearing as places of contemplative silence. In North African museums, as things stand at present, a culture which enjoys official approval and prestige (because it is hermetic and above the general level) tends to co-exist with a culture which belongs more or less to the people. The co-existence is peaceful and neutral and there is neither complementarity nor interaction between the cultures.

> (Lahbabi 1976: 146)

The glass barrier severely restricts the communication potential of objects and artefacts. They communicate only through one sense, the visual, that sense itself operating under certain restrictions, limited to a specific distance, angle of vision, etc. The eye with its high powers of resolution is the master sense, and visual cues can convey information to the other senses. However, this works abstractly, by inference, drawing on previous experience, and is inferior to direct experience by other senses. With rare or fragile items it would obviously be impracticable to allow items out of the display cases, but with some items that are common and robust, it ought to be possible to allow visitors to handle them, with suitable safeguards against theft or damage. A child who has picked up and handled a boomerang, for instance, tested its point of balance and felt its edge, will know more about boomerangs than if he had gazed at one pinned down behind a glass plate. An exhibition intended to be accessible to the blind has to adapt in this way (Favière, *et al.* 1976), and museums for the sighted should strive to incorporate such strategies. Simulated environments or reproduced objects have similar advantages over photographs. They are three-dimensional, which allows spatial information to be more fully coded. They have an advantage over reality in that scale can be controlled. This means, however, that scale is not communicated unequivocally in this medium. A *wiltja* shelter's size could not be deduced from the model shown.

Photographs have similar disadvantages, as a result of their greater flexibility. Their great strength as a communicating medium is that they can represent people and landscapes with something of the immediacy of artefactual communication. In a display concerned with the relations of man and his environment this is a crucial kind of message. Like an artefact, though, a photograph on its own cannot communicate abstract meanings. If we see a photo of five Aborigines, for instance, we do not know what is meant to be interesting or important about them, nor whether all Aborigines have the qualities claimed, or whether it is only particular individuals at a particular time.

Diagrams differ from photographs in that they contain only what is coded in them. Their strength is that they can contain in a visual form elements and relationships that are not simultaneous in space and time within a single perceptual frame. They can, therefore, communicate abstract meanings that are language like, with something of the directness and immediacy of artefactual communication.

There are two kinds of use of language attached to museum displays: labels and full sentences. Full sentences have only the limitations of human language; which with all its imperfections is the best system of communication known to man. Labels, however, are very restricted in the kinds of meaning that they can communicate. Essentially they can communicate only two kinds of message: this is an *X*, or these are kinds of/parts of a *Y*. Labels are frequent in museum displays, including the one under review. It should be pointed out that labels give only a vocabulary, not a message. Labels on their own, therefore, cannot communicate any message about man or his relation to the environment, the major theme of the display.

Language itself can be categorized in a number of ways. Relevant here are two distinctions: between written and spoken language and between indigenous languages and the dominant language (in this case English). Spoken language (not written language read aloud, but language produced by and for oral communication) tends to have a different structure, and the majority of people even in a literate culture find it easier to process fully oral language. The language of the indigenous culture is another matter. One problem with using any single Aborigine language for such an exhibition is that there are so many distinct forms. However, if the aim of the exhibition is to convey an understanding of Aboriginal ways of life and attitudes to life, and their ways of thinking, some thought must be given to a way of conveying the qualities of their language: the sound of it, and more important, some of its syntactic and semantic resources, and the ways language functions in such a society, for example, how do Aborigines of the Bardi tribe say 'I am/he is stalking a kangaroo'? Such material could be presented attractively and it would help to correct the Eurocentric impression given by the display at present.

Lahbabi's description of the North African situation applies to all such cultures:

> A major part of the North African cultural heritage has come down to us by way of oral tradition. Music, song and poetry, for instance, are to a great extent anonymous and are passed in oral form during family or seasonal celebrations. It would be desirable for university research to be set up which, with the help of the regional museums, would be responsible for all oral arts and oral literature. A healthy and militant North African culture cannot be envisaged unless the ground work is laid in this way.
>
> (Lahbabi 1976: 146)

Given this aspect of museum communication, there are obvious advantages in the concept of the ecomuseum over more traditionally organized forms of display, if the concern is for total communication to a universal public.

COMBINING CODES AND MESSAGES

Language is the only medium that can communicate self-sufficient messages about the themes of the display; the patterns of life of the Aborigine people, their history and the relation between their way of life and the environment. The other media only communicate such messages in combination with language and each other. However, a museum must use more than language and photographs. Otherwise it will be no more than a walk-through book.

Objects and artefacts typically form the basis of a museum display, but on their own they contain none of the desired meanings. The aim of the display is to give the public access to a way of life through a collection of objects. The meanings that must be communicated concern relationships, involving one or more of the following: (a) origins, (b) manufacture, (c) use and (d) place in a system of values or meanings. Photographs plus artefacts and objects or texts can be used very effectively for (b) and (c). For instance, one photograph shows two women making a hair girdle, and wearing one, above a case that contains examples of them.

Photographs are used extensively in the display, one reason no doubt is that they are so cheap. Another justification is that they can represent many things that cannot be presented directly, and in particular they can show relationships between people and things, people and people, and people and the landscape. However, to communicate, photographs must be carefully chosen, and they must be supplemented by an appropriate text.

In general, photographs are an effective way of showing people making and using things. The relations between people and people present more problems for photographic communication. People in photographs can relate either to each other or to the viewer. In the latter case, the result is a posed photograph, which primarily communicates messages about the relation between photographer and photographee. This can be an interesting and significant message. Such a photo also communicates messages about the social relations of the people concerned, but this is likely to be only the official version of these relationships. Unposed photographs can represent far more complex relationships.

The limitations of a photograph are that it shows only the disposition of bodies in space, whereas social relations are coded in many other ways, and even the language of spatial relations (who stands in front of whom, what distance expresses regret, or intimacy, etc.) is a code, relying on conventions that need to be translated for a viewer from a different culture. This difficult kind of meaning requires focusing sharply enough to pick up expressions and gestures, plus explanations of what these mean, as a key to interpretation.

Similar observations apply to the attempts to convey the relation between man and his environment. A photograph of a bare terrain is not enough, since this terrain constitutes both a set of problems and a resource for the Aboriginal people, having both positive and negative aspects. Careful selection and focusing plus verbal explanation are necessary to help the visitor to see the meaning of this landscape for Aborigines, and its relation to his life.

Labels are always used in conjunction with something else, usually artefacts. Labels characteristically assign names and organize perception. These two functions can work together, or in opposition. The main heading of a showcase or sequence can help the viewer to grasp the separate items as part of a larger whole. However, a label attached to an item gives two things to attend to, and loads the memory, adding the name of the object as something to remember. This diverts attention from the rest of the display. The adverse effects are intensified if the label is a long way from the item, especially if it is attached via a number, through a numerical key. The only justification for this latter method occurs when the items make up a strong visual whole whose unity would be disturbed by prominence being given to labels. Otherwise, from a communication point of view it is unsatisfactory. In general, labels make exhibits easier to talk about, if they are learnt, but interfere with the strength and immediacy of response. But the messages conveyed by labels are only taxonomic; they cannot convey messages about the theme of the display, which is concerned with relationships, functions and living.

Label size also affects the possibilities for coherence of a display. In general, if label and item are to be perceived as a single perceptual whole, then both must be decipherable from the same point in space. If the writing on the label is so small that a viewer cannot see the relevant item or exhibit even in peripheral vision, then the possibilities of meaning connecting with perception are reduced. Where letter size is so different that two adjacent messages cannot be read at the same time, the effect is again to fragment the whole. To illustrate with the opening words of the exhibition: the huge writing of *Patterns of Life in a Vast Land* can be read at the same time as the smaller but still large writing of *The Story of the Aboriginal People of Western Australia*, and the large theme-picture of a group of Aborigines can also be seen within the same frame. However, the text beginning 'Europeans have inhabited . . .' is in smaller lettering that requires the viewer to stand so close to it that he cannot read the larger writing or take in the picture: so this is related only in an abstract way to these other components. The letter-size is influenced by the amount of text felt to be necessary, which is, of course, a decision to be made by the communicator, but the cost of a decision in favour of more text leads to fragmentation of the perceptual unity of a display.

STRATIFICATION OF THE MUSEUM PUBLIC

Visitors to the museum clearly have differences of age, class, educational background, sex and nationality, as well as differences of interest and intelligence. This creates problems for a mass communicator, since these differences all affect communication. They have an effect equivalent to differences in language. This stratificational effect is liable to interact with the differences in the media used in a display. In particular there is likely to be a polarization between communication through objects and communication through extended written prose. Communication that is strongly concrete and particular is known to be correlated with the young, and with the working class. It is reasonable to assume that communication through objects will be much more accessible to Aborigines than written elaborated language. So messages, and kinds of message, communicated through objects, or what could be called more generally the restricted codes, will be the main content of the display for at least three important groups of museum users. Such users will hardly be aware of the messages transmitted by what could be called the more elaborated codes or channels. Since, as we have seen, the majority of the messages concerned with the theme of the display are communicated mainly through elaborated-code media, this raises the worrying possibility that these messages are not reaching large numbers who would most need to receive them. A substantial proportion of visitors to this display are students, some very young, who would come into the category of restricted-code media users.

This suggests two areas for attention. One is to strengthen artefactual communication so that it can communicate the more abstract meaning and relationships desired. The other is to be more careful about the clarity and level of the explanatory material. Written language too can be a relatively more restricted form of elaborated-code. The following text illustrates the difficulties of some of the language used:

Life's Sacred Meaning

In a time called the Dreaming, creative beings shaped the plants, animals, and landscapes; and established rules for Aboriginals to follow. The Dreaming is eternal, explaining the Aboriginal past, directing their present, and shaping their future.

Elaborated-code words here include 'creative beings', 'established', 'eternal' and 'directing', but the difficulty is not simply one of vocabulary. The syntax is difficult, more difficult than it appears on the surface because of a number of elisions. For instance, 'called' – who 'called' or 'calls' it this? Who is the subject of 'established'? We have to go right back to the mysterious 'creative beings'. And how can 'the Dreaming', which in the previous sentence was a time in the past, become 'eternal'? Even if it does, how can a time rather than a person 'explain' anything or direct or shape a present or future?

The result is a very difficult utterance, which would strain the capacity even of a university-trained elite to understand. The concept being conveyed is itself difficult, but this difficulty is concealed by the translation, which replaces interesting and important difficulties with extrinsic puzzles. Aboriginal ways of representing the concept might need supplementary explanations, they might need effort and imagination on the part of a European public even to be partially understood, but that effort and imagination are what a museum exists to foster. The language the museum has used is not deliberately difficult, and not untypical of the language used in this and other museums. It is natural that descriptions giving ideas or information from academic sources will be communicated in language that retains traces of that origin. The modern museum relies on a dedicated community of scholars to provide it with its intellectual basis. Inevitably exhibitions will make most sense in terms of the language and modes of thought of that community.

Leaving aside particular successes and failures of the exhibition we have looked at, the analysis brings out a number of points of fundamental importance in any museum display. The communication process is so pervasive and so unconscious that communication breakdown will be the rule, not the exception, and this breakdown will typically be invisible to communicators and public alike. The problems stem from the essential nature and functions of a museum, as an institution that must mediate between different communities and different cultures, offering its own physical and temporal unity as a guarantee that resolution of differences has occurred. A museum cannot suppress differences and antagonisms in the society it serves, however persuasive and sincere the image of reconciliation it offers may be. If it refuses to acknowledge these social realities in what it shows, they will silently determine what is seen. What is at issue is in some respects a failure to understand the complexities of the communication process, but this should not be regarded simply as ignorance of a set of communication techniques. Communication is inseparably bound up with habitual ways of thinking, feeling and seeing, which give definition to a culture and a community. Communication breakdown, then is a consequence of the failure to mediate between the communities involved at the level of cultural differences. But total communication is an unattainable ideal for the modern museum, until all social differences have been eliminated and made all communication redundant.

REFERENCES

de Varine-Bohan, H. (1976) 'The modern museum: requirements and problems of a new approach', *Museum* 28(3).

Favière, J., Duczmal-Pacowska, H. and Delevoy-Otlet, S. (1976) 'The museum and the blind', *Museum* 28(3): 176–80.

Lahbabi, M. A. (1976) 'The museum and the protection of the cultural heritage of the Maghreb', *Museum* 28(3).

5

Who goes to museums?

Eilean Hooper-Greenhill

What kind of people visit museums? How many? What research has been done on this aspect of the museum experience? This chapter from Museums and their visitors *draws together and discusses what is known about who goes to museums in Britain. There is some reference to research from Europe and North America. The need for information in this area is seen as an essential management tool for the modern museum.*

Museums and galleries have been concerned to know who their visitors are for some years. But why do we need to know who visits museums? And is it enough to know who visitors are? What else is there to know? Why bother anyway? How can we find out?

There are a number of reasons why museum workers need to be aware of the patterns of use of museums and galleries. These include the continued justification of a public service, the demonstration of a professional approach to management, the development of knowledge and expertise and the improvement of performance.

First, museums are a public service, and it is important to be aware of how the service is taken up. A public service will not be maintained if it is not used. How are museums used? Which sections of the public benefit from museums and which do not? Why, and what are the implications? Visiting the displays is an obvious use of museums, but there are others that should also be considered, monitored and documented and encouraged. The numbers of enquiries about objects received and answered, the numbers of photographs of items from the collection supplied, the range of researchers and scholars that use the collections and the expertise of the staff for information, the extent of corporate hire and so on. All these are also indications of the use and value of museums and galleries as a public service. They are on the whole, much broader and more varied than most of the public, or the governors and funders of museums, would think.

Second, information about the uses of the institution in relation to resources is vital to demonstrate managerial competence. Museum staff will not be perceived as professionals by government, colleagues in other areas of leisure or educational work or other business colleagues, unless detailed knowledge of the operation of the museum can be called upon when required. No business can succeed if its managers do not know who wants its products or services.

Third, in the present climate of accountability, it is sensible for museums and galleries to begin to develop some in-house knowledge and expertise by carrying out research, even if on a small scale, into the perceived use and value of the institution. This experience will be useful as standards for museums are developed. One example is in relation to the development of standards of visitor satisfaction and customer care, where the existence in museums of an understanding of how to measure the experiences of visitors would aid the development of realistic and useful performance indicators. Ignorance on the part of museum workers of the procedures of discovering what visitors enjoy, how they respond to the museum, why they have come and so on, may lead to the imposition of unrealistic and unhelpful demands.

In addition, in using the concepts of 'visitor satisfaction' and 'customer care' (Museums and Galleries Commission 1993), the measurement of the use of the museum tends to become limited to the activities and perceptions of visitors, whereas the use of museums is in fact much wider than this. If judgements are to be made about the public effectiveness of the museum following the measurement of 'visitor' satisfaction (and it is possible that levels of funding may be determined by this), then it will become vital to be alert to 'use' as a broad category, rather than 'visit', which although extremely important, is a narrower concept.

Finally, it is important for all staff to know what level of success is being achieved. Both quantitative and qualitative information should be used by managers on a regular basis to monitor successes and failures and to improve targeting of provision.

What do we need to know? We have discussed the idea of the 'use' of the museum as a broad category. It is of great importance to gather information about 'use', which would include details of a whole range of public functions that are generally not very visible, such as the use of the museum for work-experience for school and college students, the use of the museum as a place to volunteer, the museum as a location for film, the provision of archive material for the press and so on. The invisible and behind-the-scenes character of much of this public provision makes it all the more important to monitor and document.

In this chapter, however we will concentrate on the idea of the 'visit'. Knowledge about patterns of museum and gallery visiting operates both at a general level, in relation to the museum's role in society, and at a specific level, in relation to particular institutions. Both types of information are necessary.

It is important for museum professionals to have a broad understanding of the social functions of museums and galleries. What proportion, and which sections, of the population visit museums? Does this vary in relation to different types of museum? What image do people have of museums, and what expectations do they have when visiting? Why do some people feel that museums are not for them? Knowledge of the general level and structure of patterns of museum and gallery visiting will give a measure against which to assess achievements in individual institutions.

At a specific level, museum workers need to know who comes to their own institution. How does this pattern relate to the broad general pattern of museum visits? Do we attract a more or less élite public; more or fewer school groups; are visitors more or less pleased with their visits to my institution than to others? Although these kinds of comparisons are extremely difficult to make as we shall see, the questions deserve to be asked.

The pattern of visitors to any museum or gallery should be compared with the pattern of the population in its catchment area. This geographical area can be identified and elaborated in relation to obvious geographical characteristics; so, for example, with museums in a city with approximately 250,000 inhabitants, we might have a first-level catchment area to include the city, a second-level area to include the immediate region, and then a third-level very diffuse area outside this region. The demographic pattern of visitors to the city-centre museums could be usefully compared to the demographic composition of the population of the city and the county. The match with a local population is particularly necessary for a community museum; perhaps of less immediate need for a national museum.

HOW CAN WE FIND OUT?

There is now considerable information available about the patterns of use of museums and galleries by visitors. From this we can assemble a sketchy outline, but it is not easy to build up a reliable composite picture of a national or international pattern of visiting. Some of the work which has been done is contradictory, and much of it addresses specific issues related to the objectives of a particular piece of research. There are several approaches to research which may be used, each of which tends to yield specific types of data, which can make comparison difficult. Sources of information on museum visiting include academic research, government statistics, research from the leisure industry and research generated from within the museum, gallery and arts community.

A great deal of research on visitor patterns has been carried out in the United States. Much of this is most usefully collated and discussed by Falk and Dierking in their book *The Museum Experience* (1992) which discusses museums from the point of view of visitors, and draws on a large reservoir of research studies that have mainly been produced in the last twenty years. The funding arrangements of American museums, which tend to rely heavily on grants for specific projects, have encouraged attention to the evaluation of these projects. The responses of participants in educational programmes, the attention paid to exhibits, perceptions of a range of types of museum and memories of museum visits have been comprehensively analysed. Some of these studies have been published in journals such as *Curator*, *Journal of Museum Education* (originally called *Roundtable Reports* and renamed in 1985) or the more recent *International Laboratory of Visitor Studies (ILVS) Review: A Journal of Visitor Behaviour*; some of the research has a more tenuous existence as conference papers. *The Art Museum as Educator* (Newsom and Silver 1978) and *Museum Visitor Evaluation: New Tool for Management* (Loomis 1987) are key texts with relevance for all museums. The two anthologies drawn from the Journal of Museum Education, *Museum Education Anthology*, *Perspectives on Informal Learning: a Decade of Roundtable Reports 1973–1983* (Museum Education Roundtable 1984) and *Patterns in Practice* (Museum Education Roundtable, 1992), are also essential reading. Harris (1990) offers a review of the history of visitor research in America.

In Canada, the development of a national museums policy in 1971 led to a very interesting and comprehensive survey on museum use published as *The Museum and the Canadian Public* (Dixon, Courtney and Bailey 1974). The exemplary methods used, including questionnaires and focus groups, are discussed in the appendices. Attention to the needs of visitors once in the museum is discussed in the Royal Ontario Museum's *Communicating with the Museum Visitor: Guidelines for Planning* (Royal Ontario Museum 1976) and in subsequent publications.

There has been considerable research into the patterns of museum and gallery use in some parts of Europe, notably in Holland, and some centres for study, such as Paris, France and Karlsruhe, Germany, can be identified. Little of this work is available in English. The Swedish travelling exhibitions, Riksutställningar, carried out a fascinating study of visitors to their exhibitions in the 1970s which is still of value (Arnell, Hammer and Nylof 1980).

In Britain, some interesting pieces of academic research have been carried out in recent years. Two will be introduced here to illustrate the breadth of different approaches that may be adopted when considering the use of museums and galleries. Placed within different theoretical perspectives, both have been published and are easily available. Each yields useful material.

Merriman's approach is drawn from sociological paradigms (Merriman 1989, 1991): it tackles some first principles relating to the social functions of museums. Merriman's basic contention is that although museums are seen and see themselves as educational institutions, access for all has not been achieved. This idea in itself is not revolutionary, but the value of Merriman's work is that he wishes to go further than mere documentation of this fact. He seeks to explain it by analysing the symbolic power of museums, using the work of Pierre Bourdieu. A large-scale survey was carried out in 1985 to examine attitudes to the past, to archaeology and history and to museums. Attitudes and perceptions were then analysed in relation to status, education and other social variables. Bourdieu's work has been concerned with the reproduction of social relations, and specifically, the reproduction of power and domination. Through the analysis of social phenomena such as education systems and cultural systems (including museums) he demonstrates the interrelationships of economic and symbolic power. Merriman uses Bourdieu's work as a starting point for the construction of an explanation for the patterns of museum visiting, analysed in the context of hierarchical social structures.

McManus takes a different approach. In some ways her focus is narrower, limited to the investigation of how people learn in science museums. Her research is based on psychological methods and approaches, with an attention to the way individuals behave within particular environments. McManus observed and documented the reactions of groups and individuals in the displays of the Natural History Museum, London (previously known as the British Museum (Natural History) or BM(NH)) and in other science museums (Lucas, McManus and Thomas 1986; McManus 1987, 1988, 1989, 1990, 1991).

In Britain, the work of government departments and bodies is sometimes very useful in tracking down information. Although much of the data is too general to be of use, some is vital, and often forms the basis for reporting in the national media. For example, the *General Household Survey* is produced annually: in the 1979 edition, the subject of Chapter 7 was leisure. Of more use in recent years has been *Cultural Trends* produced four times per year. In *Cultural Trends*, 8, 1990, the first twenty-four pages were concerned with museums, and gave useful information on funding, costs and other management issues. In *Cultural Trends*, 12, 1991 (Eckstein and Feist 1992) one section focused on attendance at museums and galleries.

The Office of Public Censuses and Surveys has carried out a number of surveys on behalf of specific national institutions during the last ten years (for example Heady 1984; Harvey 1987). These vary in interest and quality. The Policy Studies Institute, a government think-tank, published *The Economic Importance of the Arts in Britain* in 1989 (Myerscough 1988). The aim of this report was to demonstrate how the arts, in a changing policy framework, contributed to the economic life of the nation. Research was conducted in three contrasting areas of Britain, and this included the investigation of audiences for the arts, including museums and galleries.

The leisure industry in Britain regularly produces information which is useful, but mainly limited to tourist statistics, such as numbers of visitors to specific sites. Now and then more detailed work is produced, such as the English Tourist Board's *Visitors to Museums Survey 1982* (English Tourist Board 1982). *Sightseeing in the UK, 1990* places the statistics for museums and galleries in the context of visits to other places (British Tourist Authority 1991). The Henley Centre for Leisure Forecasting, a private business supported by subscribers, produces a time-use survey for the leisure industry four times per year. These look at what people do in their leisure time, and generally include a few details about museums and galleries.

Two detailed reports have emerged recently. *Museum Funding and Services – the Visitor's Perspective* (Touche Ross 1989) reports the results of a national opinion poll of 2,800 museum visitors and their attitudes towards museum funding, including entry fees. Details include information on visiting patterns and visitor perceptions. *New Visions for Independent Museums* (Middleton 1990), a comprehensive review of the issues faced by Independent museums in the UK, is based on the best available information on museum visiting including references to many of the sources listed above.

A final source of information is the research that is carried out by or on behalf of the museum or arts community. The major arts community bodies in Britain, including the Arts Council and the Regional Arts Boards, are all to a greater or lesser extent generators of research. Although most of it is concerned with the arts in general, this includes art galleries and sometimes museums.

The Arts Council commissions research for their clients on a regular basis, with recent reports including *Target Group Index 1990/1* (Arts Council 1991a), *Galleries and Museums Research Digest* (Millward Brown/Arts Council 1991) and *RSGB Omnibus Arts Survey, Report on a Survey on Arts and Cultural Activities in GB* (Arts Council 1991b) prepared by Research Surveys of Great Britain (RSGB).

Greater London Arts produced two useful reports in 1990: *Arts in London: a Survey of Attitudes of Users and Non-users* (Greater London Arts 1990a) and *Arts in London: a Qualitative Research Study* (Greater London Arts 1990b). Both of these were carried out by Mass Observation, and used market research methods to talk to people to ascertain how they felt and what participation in the arts meant to them.

Museums UK: the Findings of the Museums Data-base Project (Prince and Higgins-McLoughlin 1987) gathered useful data about museums and their collections, but was less concerned about their use. However, *Museums UK* pointed out that museum visitor surveys have been increasing in frequency since the early 1980s, and were likely to become a basic tool for planning.

Museums in Great Britain began to survey their visitors during the 1960s, rather later than museums in North America (Merriman 1991: 42). Merriman lists and discusses some of the early British surveys, many of which were published in the *Museums Journal*. Many of the early surveys were limited to one-off studies. An important suite of surveys were those carried out at the Natural History Museum, listed in Miles and Tout (1991).

Interesting recent approaches include large-scale detailed surveys of the use of museums by the population of a defined area, such as *The Findings of the 1991–1992 Study of the Perception and Use of Leicestershire Museums, Arts and Records Service*, recently carried out by Prince Research Consultants Limited (Prince and Higgins 1992), and fairly small-scale reports on the visitors to a specific site such as *The Wordsworth Museum Visitor Survey 1991*, a report prepared for Dove Cottage, the museum of the Words-worth Trust, by the Tourism Research Group of the Department of Geography at the University of Exeter, UK (University of Exeter 1992). Many museums are using surveys such as these as management tools to aid in monitoring change or in forward planning. The Dove Cottage survey, for example, showed that the pattern of visitors had remained relatively constant comparing 1990 to 1991, although visitors from the London area had fallen slightly. The report also pointed out that 80.2 per cent of the museum's visitors came by car and used the Dove Cottage car park. There are implications in both of these bits of information for forward planning. It is not always easy to use museum visitor surveys for research purposes as they are generally regarded as internal management tools and are not therefore published, but many museums will release details if asked.

Recently, museum visitor research has followed a new direction. With an increasing professional concern for democracy and access, it has become clear that talking to *visitors* does not help in discovering what it is about museums that keeps some people away. The only way to discover this is to go and ask them. Some research has therefore focused on the attitudes and perceptions of people who fall into one of the many groups that are unlikely to visit museums. This generates qualitative as opposed to quantitative data.

Bringing History and the Arts to a New Audience: qualitative research for the London Borough of Croydon (Susie Fisher Group, 1990), is an example of this new approach. Carried out by a market research company, the report discusses how focus group interviews were held with people who agreed that they 'wouldn't be seen dead in a museum'. The research objectives are concerned with discovering attitudes and perceptions, digging down to people's personal meanings and interpretations of experience. The findings of the research are reported using (some of) the words of participants rather than tables full of figures. This research is being used to inform the development of a new museum in Croydon. A second example is *'Dingy Places with Different Kinds of Bits': an attitudes survey of London museums amongst non-visitors* (Trevelyan 1991). The London Museums Consultative Committee, a London-wide body representing the interests of all museums in London, having seen the work done by Mass Observation for Greater London Arts, and the market research methods used by the Susie Fisher Group in Croydon, commissioned Mass Observation to carry out rather similar research with a London-wide museum application.

The range of material for research into the use of museums is wide and is seldom gathered in one place. It is often difficult to use as different parameters for the research are used, which makes comparison problematic. For many people it is very trying to make sense out of figures as relatively raw data. However, for all the reasons discussed above, it is important to try to develop some kind of a picture of museum and gallery visits.

WHAT DO WE KNOW?

In Britain, museums and galleries attract a mass audience. Estimations of numbers of visits include 72.8 million in 1984–5, between 75–8 million in 1989 (Middleton 1991: 153; Myerscough 1991: 16) and 74 million in 1990 (Eckstein and Feist 1992: 70). It is likely that the museum and gallery market is Britain's largest sightseeing draw: of the visits in 1989 it is probable that visits from overseas tourists accounted for some 20 per cent, approximately 15 million visits. School party visits are estimated at 5 million, with visits made by British adults accounting for the remaining 55–7 million visits (Middleton 1991: 153). The number of visits to museums and galleries made by overseas tourists appears relatively constant for 1990 (Eckstein and Feist 1992: 70).

Seven museums (British Museum, National Gallery, Tate Gallery London, Natural History Museum, Royal Academy, Science Museum, Glasgow Museum and Art Gallery) were among the thirty-nine tourist attractions with more than one million visits in 1990 (Eckstein and Feist 1992: 70). The British Museum attracted 5,410,000 visits in 1991, the National Gallery 4,300,000 and the Science Museum 2,525,000. Very large attendances are the exception for museums, with *Sightseeing in the UK* pointing out that 83 per cent of museums attracted annual attendances of 50,000 or less in 1990, 15 per cent recorded between 50,000 and 500,000 and only 2 per cent achieved more than 500,000 (British Tourist Authority 1991). Birmingham Museum and Art Gallery attracted 559,000 visits in 1990, and the Castle Museum Nottingham 632,000. The average attendance at the 1,547 museums surveyed by the British Tourist Authority was 48,000, the same as in 1988 (Eckstein and Feist 1992: 70).

Middleton (1990: 23) estimates that around 29 per cent of British adults (13 million people out of a population of 45 million) visited a museum at least once in 1989. If this is the case, they visited a museum on an average of four visits each. However, opinions differ as to what proportion of the British public visits museums. Merriman (1991: 48) suggests that between 47 per cent and 58 per cent of British adults visit museums at least once a year, and he reminds us that this figure is close to the figures of some other researchers. Time Use Surveys from the Henley Centre Leisure Futures suggests a figure of 47 per cent for Britain, and this figure remains more or less constant over their regular quarterly surveys.

The Canadian museum survey (Dixon, Courtney and Bailey 1974) suggests that more than half the Canadian public (55–60 per cent) visited Canadian museums; and an American survey carried out by the National Research Centre for the Arts estimates 56 per cent of the public visit a history museum at least once a year, with slightly fewer people visiting art galleries and science museums.

The English Tourist Board survey of 1982 proposed that 24 per cent of the adult public visited a museum at least once during the preceding year; while the Touche Ross report (1989) suggests that 44 per cent of the adult population have visited a museum in the last two years, considerably more than the 25 per cent which have visited an art gallery. The *RSGB Omnibus Arts Survey* (Arts Council 1991b) suggests that 32 per cent of British adults were museum visitors and 18 per cent were gallery visitors (see Table 5.3), with 10 per cent visiting photography galleries or exhibitions. This survey also points out that once all types of exhibitions and museums are considered together, 48 per cent of the population visit 'nowadays'. 'Nowadays' is a market research term which is taken to mean 'at the present time'. It is likely that had people been asked if they had visited a museum, gallery or exhibition within the last two years, this percentage would have been considerably higher.

Many researchers do not include visitors under 16 in their surveys, but where they have been included, they very often make up the largest group of visitors, for example making up half of the museum audience in Ipswich and a quarter in Glasgow (Myerscough 1988).

The figures overall are very confusing, and it is difficult to form a complete picture of what proportion of the population visits museums on a regular basis. The discrepancies may be due to a number of factors, such as whether the definition of a museum includes art galleries, how the public perceive this distinction, how the surveys are carried out, what system of weighting is used to adjust the figures and what period of time is covered by the questions asked. However, in terms of numbers, the RSGB findings are interesting and encouraging (Arts Council 1991b).

✳Reviews of a range of surveys enable the identification of the general characteristics of museum visitors (Merriman 1991: 42–56). Students and higher-status socio-economic groups tend to be over-represented in proportion to their numbers in the population in general, while lower-status groups, the retired, the unemployed and the disabled tend to be under-represented. Museum visitors tend to be educated beyond the minimum school-leaving age, or are still in full-time education. Museum and gallery visiting is less likely among older people. Middleton's research (1990) shows the pattern of visiting to museums, compared with demographic patterns in general (see Table 5.1), while the 1991 *Target Group Index* research (Arts Council 1991a) shows how art galleries attract an even more exclusive audience than museums (see Table 5.2). The Research Surveys of Great Britain survey makes a direct comparison between museums and art galleries (see Table 5.3).

All the tables confirm that museum visiting decreases with age. As people grow older, their interests tend to be more home-centred, but this tends not to happen until some years after retirement, whereas the tables show this process beginning in museums at a much earlier stage. More thought for the needs of this group, and more directly targeted provision would increase visits. This is particularly important as the elderly as a percentage of the population is expanding and it is likely that British society is moving away from a culture dominated by youth to a culture dominated by the over-fifties. The growth will be in the group aged 45–59. An extra 1.5 million people will be entering this age-group during the next decade, while there will be no change in the group aged 60–79 (Middleton 1991: 140–1). People aged 45–59 are active, energetic, have generally completed or nearly completed their child-focused years, and have more time and often more money to spend on themselves. Those reaching this age-group during the next few years are those who were born after the Second World War, and who were young during the 1960s. Their expectations are far higher than those who were born and grew up during harsher and more austere times. They are a prime target for museums and galleries during the next few years.

Table 5.1 Museum visiting by British adults in 1989

	GB population (millions)	% visiting museums
All adults	45.1	29
Male	21.7	30
Female	23.4	27
Age		
15–24	8.7	29
25–34	8.1	31
35–44	7.7	36
45–54	6.1	30
55–64	5.8	28
65+	8.7	20
Class		
A/B	8.3	43
C1	10.3	34
C2	12.7	24
D	7.8	21
E	6.0	18

Source: Middleton (1991), and published in Eckstein and Feist (1992)

Table 5.2 Attendances at art galleries or art exhibitions in Britain

	% currently attending art galleries	% going more than once per year
All adults	21.4	9.2
Men	21.0	9.1
Women	21.8	9.4
Age		
15–19	25.2	9.5
20–24	22.4	9.8
25–34	23.3	10.1
35–44	25.9	9.9
45–54	22.5	9.2
55–64	20.7	10.7
65+	13.3	6.7
Social grade		
AB	41.4	20.4
C1	26.9	11.8
C2	15.0	5.3
DE	11.3	4.3
Terminal education age		
14 or under	8.4	4.1
15	12.7	4.6
16	16.6	5.7
17/18	27.7	11.8
19 or over	49.4	25.4
Still studying	38.1	16.5

Source: *Target Group Index, 1990/1*, and published in Eckstein and Feist (1992)

The largest group visiting museums is in the 25–44 age-range (with a bulge in the 35–44 age-group) and by implication this is likely to consist of people with children. This is not the case with art galleries and art exhibitions, where visits are more evenly spread throughout adulthood, with a possible increase after the family has grown up. This is interesting as it suggests that where museums are seen as suitable for young children, art galleries are not. Art galleries are not generally targeting the family audience in the design of their displays, and as long as this continues it is unlikely that art galleries will attract a much larger proportion of leisure or tourist visits. The *RSGB Omnibus Arts Survey* (Arts Council 1991b) suggests that while 32 per cent of all adults visit museums, only 18 per cent visit art galleries. The Touche Ross survey indicated that 44 per cent of the population had visited a museum during the last two years, while 25 per cent had visited an art gallery (and 35 per cent had visited a National Trust property or stately home) (Touche Ross 1989: 14). However, the growth of the over-fifties age-group presents opportunities for art galleries.

Table 5.3 Attendances at museums and art exhibitions and galleries

	% visiting museums	% visiting exhibitions/galleries
All adults	32	18
Men	34	17
Women	30	19
Age		
16–19	31	18
20–24	33	18
25–34	35	15
35–44	30	20
45–54	36	21
55–64	29	20
65+	22	14
Social grade		
AB	51	35
C1	39	23
C2	29	11
D	24	9
E	17	11

Source: *RSGB Omnibus Arts Survey*, and published in Eckstein and Feist (1992)

The group of adults of young family age is also expanding as a percentage of the population, with an extra 1.1 million entering the age-group 30–44 during the next decade. The family visitor has already become one of the more important targets for museums and this will become increasingly important during the next decade.

Although most museum visitor surveys do not include young people under the age of 16 (presumably because they are not expected to know what they think or do!), this group represents a further point of growth. While the group currently aged 15–29 years is expected to decrease by about two million in the next decade, those currently in the age-group 5–14 will expand by about one million (Middleton 1991: 140). Targeting children in families directly, and targeting schools will become important marketing strategies. The combination of the growth in numbers of family-formers and the growth in numbers of young children means that the small group consisting of adults and children visiting together will become perhaps the most important group to plan for in considering displays, events, comfort facilities and literature.

The level of education is a very important variable in indicating whether an individual is likely to become a museum visitor. The more highly educated someone is, the more a museum or gallery visit becomes likely. This has been confirmed by research in many other countries (Dixon, Courtney and Bailey 1974: 30; Arnell, Hammer and Nylof 1980). It is clear from the tables that museums appeal more to the higher social classes (social classes ABC1). It is also the case that visiting museums is less popular among Asian and Afro-Caribbean ethnic groups. As *Cultural Trends*, 1991 states baldly: 'museum visiting in the UK remains primarily a white upper/middle class pastime' (Eckstein and Feist 1992: 77).

It is easy to under-emphasize the appeal of museums to a wide public. Even if the rather pessimistic figure of 29 per cent of the adult population is taken as a guide to the proportion of the public visiting museums in Britain, and this is agreed by both Middleton (1991) and Myerscough (1991), museums and galleries would appear to reach a broader cross-section of the population than many other cultural institutions. In Glasgow, for example, 30 per cent of the museum audience is made up of people from social classes C2, D and E, and in Merseyside the proportion of lower status groups is 47 per cent. These figures are considerably higher than those for theatre and concert audiences (see Tables 5.4 and 5.5) (Myerscough 1991: 20). Middleton (1990: 23) suggests that one in five of museum visitors are on average from social classes D and E. The market for museums and galleries is also younger than for theatres and concerts.

The market for museums and galleries varies with different types of museums. Art galleries tend to attract more female than male visitors, and more highly educated visitors; science and transport museums attract more men than women, and visitors tend to be less highly educated.

In Canada, there is evidence that open-air museums attract a broader cross-section of the public than other types of museums, and that art galleries attract the least democratic audience (Dixon, Courtney and Bailey 1974).

It is likely that, of visitors to museums in general, approximately one-third are very infrequent, while of the others, possibly a further third are regular users, going perhaps

Table 5.4 Social class of visitors to museums in the three regions of study

	Glasgow	Merseyside	Ipswich
ABC1	70%	53%	67%
C2DE	30%	47%	33%

Source: Myerscough (1988)

Table 5.5 Social class of visitors to theatres and concerts in the three regions of study

	Glasgow	Merseyside	Ipswich
ABC1	80%	73%	67%
C2DE	20%	26%	33%

Source: Myerscough (1988)

three or four times per year or more (Middleton 1990: 23). The Touche Ross survey stated that of the museum visitors interviewed, just under half had been to a museum three or more times in the past year, and one-third had made their previous museum visit in the past month (Touche Ross 1989: 15).

In relation to repeat visits, surveys of the patterns of visiting for individual museums reveal very individual patterns. At the National Portrait Gallery in Trafalgar Square, for example, an area popular with overseas and home tourists, but also with a large and consistent day-time population, the following pattern was found in 1985: of the UK visitors, 43 per cent were first-time visitors, and 57 per cent were returning visitors; of the overseas visitors, 71 per cent were first-time visitors and 29 per cent were returning visitors (Harvey 1987: 8). In contrast, frequent visitors (those who had been three times or more) to Dove Cottage and the Wordsworth Museum in the Lake District during 1991, for example, consisted of only 0.5 per cent of the visitors. People who were visiting the museum for the first time during the same year formed 86 per cent of visitors (University of Exeter 1992).

The Leicestershire survey found that there was a core of relatively frequent visitors, with rather different characteristics from those who visited less frequently (Prince and Higgins 1992: 98). Those who described themselves as frequent visitors tended to belong to a group described by the researchers as IPT-A (Index of Population Type – A). This group in general consists of professionals, managers and white-collar workers who occupy secure and high-salaried jobs, and have been educated to a high level. Frequent museum visitors from this group were aged between 35 and 54, and were likely to have also joined a group concerned with conservation or heritage. Self-defining infrequent visitors came from IPT-C, a group that as a whole consisted of manual workers in industrial jobs, where take-home pay might well be high, but where job security was low. The education level of this group was typically low and, interestingly, those visiting the museums were in the age-group 16–34. They tended not to have joined any related society.

Why do people visit museums? From the tables above it is clear that social class and educational background are important determinants. Socialization, family habits and attitudes, interests related to collections and exhibitions, all play their part in disposing people to make visits. When asked why, many people give rather general answers, but themes do emerge. The Touche Ross survey found that an overwhelming majority of their interviewees in a national poll considered that museums should be both educational and entertaining. The main reason for visiting was interest in the displays or the collections, cited by one-third of the respondents. The second most popular reason for making a visit was as an entertainment or as part of a holiday (Touche Ross 1989: 16). Very few of those interviewed as part of the national poll visited museums in connection with their studies. Average visit length seems to be about one hour, although it tends to be longer when paid for through entry charges. Interactive exhibits were regarded as being the most popular type of exhibit, especially among younger respondents, while older people tended to prefer what they knew, static exhibits (Touche Ross 1989: 2). More than three-quarters of museum visitors thought that more should be done to promote exhibitions and events. Facilities such as seating, toilets, cloakrooms, signage and floor-plans received some criticism (Touche Ross 1989).

Those people who did not visit museums were cited by Touche Ross (1989: 15) as giving not enough time as one of the main reasons, and this reason also appears in more qualitative accounts (Trevelyan 1991: 24; Susie Fisher Group 1990: 44). However, the qualitative accounts also reveal other attitudes, including a feeling that museums are for people with education and specific interests, and people who want to learn. One of the major reasons why some people don't visit museums and galleries is because of bad experiences in the past. Many people still see museums as they were at that time, and think that museums are austere, forbidding, dusty, empty, church-like and remote (Trevelyan 1991: 34–6). The research for Croydon revealed deep-seated psychological barriers relating to participation in the arts: 'Arty people are hypocrites, do-gooders'; 'Black artists? Our country's culture shouldn't be changed for them'; 'They should fund hospitals, not the Arts'. Many people revealed fears of being shown to be ignorant, of feeling self-indulgent, neglecting more important basic chores, of looking ridiculous, of being treated as in need of charity (Susie Fisher Group 1990: 44–6). These barriers are very real, and not always easy to break down, although many of the recommendations in the report are very sensible. The suggestions made for the museum and arts complex at Croydon recommended a complex of small related experiences, rather like a small shopping centre. Opportunities for eating, drinking, sitting and watching offer a non-threatening and welcoming first-level experience of the centre, with arts and crafts workshops, video and object-based displays, exhibitions on the past and the future easily accessible for a more in-depth exploration.

It is very clear that museums are competing for customers in a relatively static market. The average number of visitors per museum reporting has steadily declined during the last decade from 72,000 in 1978, falling to 61,000 in 1982, 51,000 in 1986 and 48,000 in 1988. The average number of visitors per museum remained at 48,000 in 1990. During the period from 1978, museums reporting data to the English Tourist Board rose from 716 to 1,222. Museums surveyed by *Sightseeing in the UK* in 1990 numbered 1,547 (British Tourist Authority, 1991). In part, the fall in the average number of visitors per museum is accounted for by the growth in number of museums. In part too, the average figure is distorted by the accommodation of huge visitor losses at those national museums that have introduced charges – for example, admissions at the Natural History Museum were 47 per cent lower in 1991 than in 1981, and at the Science Museum were 53 per cent lower (Eckstein and Feist 1992: 73). However, it would appear that it is not going to be easy to sustain visitor numbers, particularly in a period of recession.

Visitor research is an essential management information tool. It should include both qualitative and quantitive research, and be carried out as part of a systematic and planned programme. In the past, museums and galleries have seen this as expensive and time-consuming, but as museums strive to get closer to their audiences, the need to know first who they are, and second, what they think, will become more and more imperative.

This paper first appeared in E. Hooper-Greenhill (1993) Museums and their Visitors, *London: Routledge.*

REFERENCES

Arnell, U., Hammer, I. and Nylof, G. (1980) *Going to Exhibitions*, Stockholm, Sweden: Riksutställningar.
Arts Council (1991a) *Target Group Index*, London: British Market Research Bureau/Arts Council.
Arts Council (1991b) *RSGB Omnibus Arts Survey: report on a survey of arts and cultural activities in GB*, London: Research Surveys of Great Britain Arts Council.
British Tourist Authority (1991) *Sightseeing in the UK: a survey of the usage and capacity of the United Kingdom's attractions for visitors*, London: BTA/ETB Research Services.
Dixon, B., Courtney, A. and Bailey, R. (1974) *The Museum and the Canadian Public*, Toronto: Arts and Culture Branch, Department of the Secretary of State, Government of Canada.
Eckstein, J. and Feist, A. (1992) *Cultural Trends* 1991: 12, London: Policy Studies Institute.
English Tourist Board (1982) *Visitors to Museums Survey 1982*, Report by the English Tourist Board Market Research Department and NOP Market Research Limited, English Tourist Board.

Falk, J.H. and Dierking, L.D. (1992) *The Museum Experience,* Washington D.C.: Whalesback Books.

Greater London Arts (1990a) *Arts in London: a survey of attitudes of users and non-users,* Greater London Arts.

Greater London Arts (1990b) *Arts in London: a qualitative research study,* Greater London Arts.

Harvey, B., (1987) *Visiting the National Portrait Gallery,* London: OPCS/HMSO.

Heady, P. (1984) *Visiting Museums: a report of a survey of visitors to the Victoria and Albert, Science, and Natural Railway Museums for the Office of Arts and Libraries,* London: Office of Population and Census Surveys/HMSO.

Loomis, R. J. (1987) *Museum Visitor Evaluation: new tool for management,* Nashville, Tennessee: American Association for State and Local History.

Lucas, A. M., McManus, P. and Thomas, G. (1986) 'Investigating learning from informal sources: listening to conversations and observing play in science museums', *European Journal of Science Education* 8(4): 34–52.

McManus, P. M. (1987) 'It's the company you keep . . . the social determinants of learning-related behaviour in a science museum', *International Journal of Museum Management and Curatorship* 6: 263–70.

McManus, P. M. (1988) 'Good companions . . . more on the social determination of learning related behavior in a science museum', *International Journal of Museum Management and Curatorship* 7: 37–44.

McManus, P. M. (1989) 'Oh, yes, they do: how museum visitors read labels and interact with exhibit texts', *Curator* 32(3): 174–89.

McManus, P. M. (1990) 'Watch your language! People do read labels', in *What Research Says about Learning in Science Museums,* Washington: Association of Science-Technology Centres: 4–6.

McManus, P. M. (1991) 'Making sense of exhibits', in G. Kavanagh (ed.) *Languages: objects and texts,* Leicester, London and New York: Leicester University Press: 33–45.

Merriman, N. (1989) 'The social basis of museum and heritage visiting', in S. Pearce (ed.) *Museum Studies in Material Culture,* Leicester, London and New York: Leicester University Press.

Merriman, N. (1991) *Beyond the Glass Case: the Past, the Heritage and the Public in Britain,* Leicester, London and New York: Leicester University Press.

Middleton, V. (1990) *New Visions for Independent Museums in the UK,* West Sussex: Association of Independent Museums.

Middleton, V. (1991) 'The future demand for museums 1990–2001', in G. Kavanagh (ed.) *The Museums Profession: Internal and External Relations,* Leicester, London and New York: Leicester University Press.

Miles, R. S. and Tout, A. F. (1991) 'Impact of research on the approach to the visiting public at the Natural History Museum, London', *International Journal of Science Education* 13(5): 534–49.

Millward Brown/Arts Council (1991) *Galleries and Museums Research Digest,* London: British Market Research Bureau.

Museums and Galleries Commission (1993) *Quality of Service in Museums and Galleries: customer care in museums – guidelines on implementation,* London: Museums and Galleries Commission.

Museum Education Roundtable (1984) *Museum Education Anthology, Perspectives on Informal Learning: a decade of Roundtable reports, 1973–1983,* Washington, D.C.: Museum Education Roundtable.

Museum Education Roundtable (1992) *Patterns in Practice: selections from the Journal of Museum Education,* Washington, D.C.: Museum Education Roundtable.

Myerscough, J. (1988) *The Economic Importance of the Arts in Britain,* London: Policy Studies Institute.

Myerscough, J. (1991) 'Your museum in context: knowing the museum industry; the background statistics', in T. Ambrose and S. Runyard (eds) *Forward Planning: a handbook of business, corporate and development planning for museums and galleries,* London and New York: Routledge.

Newsom, B. Y. and Silver, A. Z. (1978) *The Art Museum as Educator,* Berkeley, Los Angeles and London: University of California Press.

Prince, D. and Higgins-McLoughlin, B. (1987) *Museums UK: the findings of the museums data-base project,* London: Museums Association.

Prince, D. and Higgins, B. (1992) *The Public View: the findings of the 1991/92 study of the perception and use of Leicestershire museums, arts and records service,* Prince Research Consultants Limited.

Royal Ontario Museum (1976) *Communicating with the Museum Visitor: guidelines for planning,* Toronto, Canada: Royal Ontario Museum.

Susie Fisher Group (1990) *Bringing History and the Arts to a New Audience: qualitative research for the London Borough of Croydon,* London: The Susie Fisher Group.

Touche Ross (1989) *Museum Funding and Services – the visitor's perspective,* report of a survey carried out by Touche Ross Management Consultants.

Trevelyan, V. (ed.) (1991) *'Dingy Places with Different Kinds of Bits': an attitudes survey of London museums amongst non-visitors,* London Museums Service.

University of Exeter (1992) *The Wordsworth Museum Visitor Survey 1991. A report prepared for the Wordsworth Trust,* University of Exeter: Tourism Research Group, Department of Geography.

6

Why don't people go to museums?

Tanya Du Bery

Mass-Observation was commissioned to carry out a study in London to research the attitudes to museums of people who don't normally use them. Museums were seen as worthy and as having an educational purpose, but at the same time this was seen as very boring. Although many people had visited the large national museums and found them difficult to decode, many small local museums were unknown. Afro-Caribbean and Asian interviewees wanted more of direct relevance to their contribution to the nation's art and history.

Lack of knowledge of the existence of museums and of the ways in which museums have become more interesting on the part of non-users points up the need for better, more focused marketing and outreach work.

Mass-Observation was commissioned by the London Museums Consultative Committee to conduct research into attitudes to museums among those who do not generally visit them. The aim of the research was to identify the barriers – both physical and psychological – which discourage Londoners from visiting both national and local museums.

As far as the methodology of the study was concerned, altogether six group discussions were conducted. Five among current non-users of museums and one among occasional visitors to museums. Each group consisted of six to eight respondents. All discussions were conducted within Greater London and the composition of the groups ensured different sectors within London were represented. In this study, not only were age and sex taken into account, but also particular minority groups (such as ethnic and disabled) in order to determine whether they had particular and distinctive needs.

The research revealed that while most non-users had a strong interest in the past, museums were not felt to put the past over in an interesting and involving way. Museums have a negative image. They are seen as boring, musty, gloomy and stuffy. The atmosphere was likened to being in a church or library. Many non-users had formulated their negative image long ago but as they had not been back to museums, this image had not changed. Non-users with recent experience of the big London museums often reported back favourably on certain aspects of the exhibitions and realized that museums could be exciting and interesting places. But they still tended to have an unfavourable overall image of museums.

It was recognized, however, that museums have a worthy purpose – that of preserving, and educating people about cultures and artefacts – and this was perceived as an important role. Local museums were believed to have a distinctive purpose of preserving and communicating the history of their local area.

Most non-users had some experience of visiting the big national museums. Those who had visited most recently tended to be parents or grandparents accompanying children.

There was, however, little enthusiasm for the idea of visiting museums. Non-users tended to see them as places that would appeal mainly to children, the elderly and various other types such as 'boffins' or those with nothing better to do with their time.

Non-users were much more likely to have visited the big national London museums than their local museum. There was a very low awareness of local museums among non-users and sometimes they disputed whether individual local facilities even qualified as museums, given their small size and very limited range of exhibits.

The main factors discouraging visits to museums were the belief that they had an unwelcoming, unattractive atmosphere; lack of interesting exhibits; lack of change in exhibitions; cost; and transport problems. Women with children and disabled respondents also anticipated access difficulties inside the buildings. Inadequate provision of refreshments also made museums unattractive places to visit.

Additional factors discouraging visits to local museums in particular were a lack of awareness of them and the expectation of few – and unexciting – exhibits.

When asked what would encourage people to visit museums, the main suggestions were to make museums into brighter, more lively and more exciting places with a more relaxed, casual atmosphere. In addition, there was a requirement for more exciting, involving exhibitions and for exhibitions to change on occasion.

Famous exhibitions were seen as an attraction, but non-users also wanted exhibitions showing aspects of everyday life in the recent past, as well as in earlier times. People also felt that museums should show the present and future to demonstrate how progress takes place. Afro-Caribbean and Asian non-users wanted coverage of black and Asian culture to show the contribution made by these cultures and to recognize the part ethnic minority groups had played in this country's history. This was also generally encouraged by white respondents.

Museums should make a special effort to appeal to children, it was argued, as they were the main reason for going to museums in the first place. Mothers wanted creches for their children.

As far as local museums were concerned, people felt they have an important role to play in preserving and communicating local history, that they could be developed and promoted, and that they would encourage visitors to the area.

Non-users wanted local museums to focus on the local area. It was suggested that exhibitions in these facilities should demonstrate the part the local area had played in national events, tell the visitor about famous residents in the area, show aspects of everyday life as it had been – and perhaps include an element of sensationalism by covering local crimes and disasters.

In the research, non-users were prompted by images of different types of displays and asked which types most appealed to them. Of the alternative types shown, there was most demand for interactive and multi-media displays as these involved the visitor and helped to bring the past to life.

It was felt appropriate for local museums to have displays encouraging community involvement. There was quite widespread interest in the ideas of family or local history discovery centres, mobile museums, and displays in non-museum venues which would encourage interest and could stimulate a follow-up visit to the main museum.

Local museums, it was felt, needed to advertise themselves better and could use leaflets, local papers, libraries and posters to do so. Advertisements should project a bright, cheerful image and make it clear that children were welcome. Advertising should be aimed at different groups of the community such as children and young people.

Overall, there was a feeling that museums should try to sell themselves harder and convince individuals that a visit was a worthwhile and an enjoyable, exciting experience.

(The report of the findings of the study is available from the London Museums Service, AMSSEE, Ferroners House, Barbican, London EC2Y 8AA. Price £20.)

This paper first appeared in Museum Development *(March 1991), pp. 25–7.*

7

Problems in visitor orientation and circulation

Stephen Bitgood

On arrival at an unfamiliar museum, what information is available to enable visitors to decide what to do? Often this vital aspect of a museum visit is neglected by museum staff and the visitor is left either to struggle or leave.

This paper identifies conceptual orientation, wayfinding or locational orientation, and circulation as the three major elements of orientation within the museum. Each of these aspects is discussed in detail and many helpful and practical suggestions made. The literature on this topic is referenced. Although much of the content of the paper may seem like simple common sense, a test at the nearest museum or gallery will demonstrate how small a part common sense plays in designing the visitor experience, and how irritating the results are for visitors.

INTRODUCTION

The topic of orientation and circulation was not my first choice for this paper. I would much rather have chosen subject areas that I know more about. For example, exhibit labels or exhibit design. I chose orientation and circulation because it is, in my opinion, the most neglected area of visitor studies. It is also one of the most important areas since it influences whether or not people actually visit a museum/park/zoo/aquarium, whether or not visitors see particular exhibits, what they learn from their experience, what they tell friends and relatives, and whether they will return.

Considered broadly, visitor orientation and circulation is related to all aspects of the museum experience. Orientation problems do not start at the front door. They begin long before people enter the facility and continue long after they are home again, since visitors pass on their experiences to their friends and relatives who in turn develop their own expectations (see Adams 1988; Hayward & Brydon-Miller 1984). Thus, orientation and circulation play a key role in marketing/public relations, education, audience research, exhibit design, and visitor services. In a sense, systems of orientation and circulation tie these various areas together.

We have all experienced the slings and arrows of outrageous orientation systems – when we can't find our way to our destination; when we can't find our way inside a building; when we can't find the rest rooms; when we can't find our way out of a building; or when we can't find where we parked our car. Most of these slings and arrows can be avoided if our orientation and circulation systems are carefully designed. In this paper we will identify some of the major problems in orientation and circulation and make some suggestions for minimizing these problems. While systems of orientation and circulation are most critical for first-time visitors, it would be a mistake to ignore the effects of these systems on repeat visitors. Recently, we evaluated user orientation in a medium-sized shopping mall and found that a high percentage of users did not know what was located in the back corridors of the mall, despite the fact that the vast majority of these shoppers used the mall at least once or twice a month (Bitgood and Hulac 1987). Repeat visitors may also need orientation if the facility has changed since their last visit. We recently found at the Alabama Space and Rocket Center (Bitgood 1988) that many of the repeat visitors had not visited in the last three or four years. Since substantial additions have been made in the Center during that time, visitors were surprised to find that there were many new areas.

There are three major elements to visitor orientation and circulation: conceptual orientation, wayfinding, and circulation. Conceptual orientation (also called 'thematic' orientation) includes an awareness and understanding of the themes and subject matter organization of the facility. Although visitor expectations and prior experiences play a key role in conceptual orientation, the most important factor appears to be on-site orientation systems. The role of both 'off-site' and 'on-site' orientation will be discussed below.

Wayfinding, or 'topographical' or 'locational' orientation, involves being able to find or locate places in a facility. Orientation devices such as maps and direction signs are critical for wayfinding. Other factors such as the complexity of the facility can also have a profound impact on wayfinding.

Circulation describes how visitors make their way through the facility. What pathways do they take? Do visitors circulate the way the designers intended? Do visitors miss key exhibits because of the architectural design of the facility? Which direction do visitors turn when they reach choice points? Do visitors have a circulation strategy (e.g., 'Turn right and follow the perimeter') or do they simply wander more or less aimlessly?

It is obvious that orientation and circulation are intimately tied to one another. Factors that affect one are likely to affect the other. Because of this close relationship, we believe that it is extremely important to consider these two factors together. Orientation will influence the circulation patterns of visitors and circulation designs influence the users' orientation.

For purposes of this paper, problems of orientation and circulation will be divided into seven problem areas. Each will be discussed individually. These problem areas are:

- pre-visit or off-site
- arrival at the facility
- finding support facilities (restrooms, food, gift shop, etc.)
- orientation and circulation during exhibit viewing
- exiting or leaving the facility
- measurement of visitors' orientation and circulation behavior.

LITERATURE ON ORIENTATION AND CIRCULATION

Readers unfamiliar with the literature on orientation and circulation are referred to several sources. The classic studies of Melton (e.g., Melton 1935; 1936) are a must for all professionals dealing with visitors. In a series of observational studies, Melton demonstrated that visitors have a strong tendency to turn right when they enter an exhibit gallery and that exits compete with exhibit objects such that visitors often walk out an exit, whether or not they have viewed all or even most of the exhibit objects in the gallery. Melton showed that these results occurred in both art museums and science museums, and replication was obtained in several galleries. It should be noted, however, that the right-turn bias depends on several factors such as placement of attractive exhibits, signs that prompt turning in a particular direction, etc.

Literature on environmental cognition and cognitive mapping are relevant to orientation and wayfinding (e.g., Fisher, Bell and Baum 1984). Lynch (1960) suggested that one can describe such cognitive pictures in terms of five components: landmarks, paths, boundaries (edges), districts, and nodes (intersections). Designers of orientation and circulation systems would be wise to consider explicitly these components in the development of their systems.

Levine's (1982) work on You-are-Here maps also provides useful information for the designer of orientation and circulation systems. He suggests that a viewer must have two items of information in order to relate the map to the environment. A 'You-are-here' symbol telling the visitor where he/she is provides one useful piece of information. Signs and labels on the map can also provide important information. Distinctive landmarks (asymmetrical structures) can aid the viewer in identifying location, and providing redundant cues is helpful. The map should be arranged so that it parallels or is aligned with the environment ('forward-up equivalence'). He suggests the 'two-item theorem' for producing effective orientation: either two pairs of points or one pair of points and a direction need to match in order to produce an overall figure match. Some of these principles were demonstrated in a later study (Levine, Marchon and Hanley 1984).

After studying a display at the British Museum (Natural History), Griggs (1983) formulated 13 recommendations for developing systems of conceptual and topographic orientation (wayfinding). While these suggestions are not exhaustive, they do identify some important areas of consideration. For example, Griggs advises that orientation be integrated into the development phase of exhibit areas instead of after-the-fact. Although it should not have to be said, Griggs insisted that orientation devices should be 'user-defined' instead of being 'defined' by the museum professionals. Many museums/zoos still appear to have a 'visitor-be-damned' attitude about their orientation systems.

Hayward and Brydon-Miller (1984) published an article that is unique in that it studied 'off-site' as well as 'on-site' orientation at Old Sturbridge Village, an outdoor history museum in Sturbridge, Massachusetts. They surveyed visitors in four areas of 'off-site' (pre-visit) orientation: personal recommendation (discussion with friends and relatives); school field trip (information from a child's visit or museum education programme); read about facility (travel guides, books, advertising, brochures, newspaper articles); and visited a similar place (experiences at other museums). Over 70 per cent of the sample of visitors stated that they visited a similar place; 58 per cent stated that they had discussed Old Sturbridge Village with friends or relatives; 41 per cent had read about the facility; and 10 per cent received information from school trips.

Loomis (1987) reviewed most of the writing on visitor orientation in a separate chapter of his book, *Museum Visitor Evaluation*. This chapter has some very practical suggestions on how to evaluate museum orientation. Sample checklists and outlines are included and these materials should be useful to the novice evaluator. In addition, Loomis reviewed some of the literature on orientation in non-museum settings.

Cohen, Winkel, Olsen, and Wheeler (1977) evaluated board maps and direction signs in the National Museum of History and Technology. Both board maps and direction signs were found to improve visitor orientation, but each was used in a different way. Board maps were used primarily for conceptual orientation, while direction signs were used more for wayfinding.

Shettel-Neuber and O'Reilly (1981) studied orientation and circulation of visitors at the Arizona-Sonora Desert Museum in Tucson, Arizona. They used both direct observation and survey methods. Among other findings, they demonstrated that the circulation route of the visitor determined, to some extent, how confused visitors became during their passage through the Museum. One of the many points of interest in this report was a rationale for obtaining visitor circulation patterns. First, people prefer a suggested path. Knowledge of visitors' preferred path can aid in selecting a suggested route since people may be more likely to follow a route that is freely chosen. Second, circulation knowledge can aid the facility in planning for exhibits and programmes. Interpretive talks, special presentations, etc. can be timed and physically arranged to coincide with visitors' circulation patterns. Third, this circulation knowledge provides a basis for museum staff to alter visitor behaviour.

Falk (1988) discussed several issues related to orientation and circulation in his book, *The Museum Experience*. For example, Falk cites a study of public school student groups visiting the National Zoo. This study showed that students who were given pre-visit orientation (what they would see, when they would eat lunch, when they would visit the gift shop, etc.) learned more than other groups of students even when they were given a more learning-oriented pre-visit preparation.

The above review only scratches the surface of writings available. The interested reader is encouraged to examine a special issue of *Visitor Behavior* (1987, 1(4)) for further information and references. Other references that readers may wish to look at include:

- Yoshioka (1942)
- Parsons and Loomis (1973)
- Carpman (1986)

PRE-VISIT ORIENTATION

The first type of problem occurs before visitors get to the facility. As Loomis (1987) states: 'Orientation begins with the images and messages that inform the public of the existence and location of a particular museum' (p. 165). Such pre-visit or off-site experiences are often not thought of as part of orientation by professionals in visitor studies. However, it is obvious, after a little reflection, that this aspect of visitor orientation is extremely important. We see three areas of possible difficulty during this stage of orientation:

- Prior visitor experiences and expectations
- Obtaining directions to the facility
- Following directions

Prior experiences and expectations

Visitors hold diverse expectations of what they will experience before they visit an exhibition type facility (Hayward and Brydon-Miller 1984). How do prior visitor experiences and expectations influence orientation? Hayward and Brydon-Miller found that about one-half of the visitors to Old Sturbridge Village received information from friends and relatives. In addition, one-half to three-fourths had visited similar facilities. These experiences clearly had some impact on whether or not these people visited. At the present time, we don't know how much these prior experiences and expectations influence visitors. This is an important question – one that should be studied more thoroughly. The public has some stereotyped beliefs of what museums, parks and zoos are like. We need to know these beliefs; we need to change some misconceptions and foster the development of more positive attitudes.

We also need to study the non-visitor (e.g., Hood 1983;1986). Why do people choose not to visit a facility? Hood (1983) suggests that visitors do not perceive the facility as providing their desires.

Don Adams (1988) points out the importance of word-of-mouth in public relations. Such word-of-mouth obviously provides pre-visit orientation experiences to the visitor. Often the information from this experience is inaccurate. Hayward and Brydon-Miller (1984) found that visitors had misconceptions about what they would experience at a historical village. On the other hand, Bitgood (1988) found that first-time visitors were often knowledgeable in describing what they would see and do at the Alabama Space and Rocket Center. Much of their information came from friends and relatives who had previously visited.

Suggestion: Evaluate word-of-mouth experiences and earmark orientation experiences to your public relations efforts. This evaluation can be accomplished through self-report measures (i.e., interview, survey); but, remember that people have a tendency to tell you what they think you want to know.

Obtaining directions

I believe that visitors usually get their directions from brochures, from road signs, from tourist information centres, or from family and friends. To evaluate thoroughly an orientation system, I think you need to know where visitors received their directions. It is common for museums to ask where visitors heard about the facility; but, it is rare for museums to ask where they obtained directions. In our study at the Space and Rocket Center in Huntsville, Alabama, we did ask such questions. We found that 78.5 per cent of visitors attempted to use the special Space Museum/Space Center road signs directing people to the Center. Unfortunately, 18.9 per cent found these road signs confusing because of conflicts in the signage, a lack of signs at critical points, and because the size of these signs was relatively small.

Suggestion: Ask visitors where they obtained their directions and find out what problems they may have had in following these directions.

Following directions

You also need to know whether or not these directions were effective. Were visitors able to easily follow these directions? If visitors have difficulty following directions, the difficulty should not be attributed to the stupidity of the visitors, but rather to the inadequacy of the directions. When street signs are confusing, street numbers not easily read, and buildings not clearly marked, wayfinding can be difficult and frustrating. I recently gave up looking for a science museum in a Southern city because it wasn't where I thought it should have been and there was too much traffic to stop and ask.

Suggestion: Ask visitors if they had trouble finding the museum/zoo. You might also role-play a naive visitor and see if road signs and other types of directions are easy to follow. Type of transportation may also be important to investigate, since brochures that give directions should include public transportation and/or parking directions.

ARRIVAL ORIENTATION

Three common problems associated with arrival are: parking, finding the entrance, and entrance orientation.

Parking

Parking is often a problem in an urban facility. If finding parking spaces is a problem, it may be worth attempting to solve this problem. I have been discouraged several times from visiting a facility because of parking difficulties. Although I know of no empirical reports concerning visitors, I would not be surprised if this is an important reason for *not* visiting.

Suggestion: Determine (by survey) if visitors have difficulty parking. If so, provide directions for parking and information on public transport to reach your facility.

Finding the entrance

This can be difficult in large facilities. Many large museums have multiple doors, only one of which is the correct entrance. The entrance is not always clearly marked.

Entrance orientation

A more obvious problem and one that is discussed frequently in literature (e.g., Loomis 1987) is orientation (or lack of orientation) at the entrance to the facility. Screven (1986) suggested that there are three types of advance organizers that play a role in orientation: conceptual pre-organizers (brief information about exhibits); topographic organizers (e.g., simplified maps); and overviews (what can be seen and done; what can be learned). These advance organizers can be presented in several ways. Some facilities (such as Colonial Williamsburg) have an orientation centre separate from the main exhibition area. Others have a small area as one enters the facility; others have orientation displays in each theme area of the facility; and others have little, if any, orientation. Sceptics might argue that each of these approaches is equally ineffective. However, I think there is evidence to suggest that orientation systems do work, if they are designed carefully. Both the placement and the content of these orientation areas is critical.

Suggestion: Entrance orientation should be designed to meet the following criteria: (1) attracting power (displays should elicit a high percentage of use); (2) holding power (visitors should use the displays for a sufficient amount of time to process necessary orientation information); (3) comprehension (visitors should easily understand information presented). To meet these criteria orientation devices should: be easily accessible to visitors (preferably in the visitors' normal pathway); information should be concisely displayed (since visitors won't spend much time in an orientation area); involve multimedia (visitors seem to prefer a variety of devices including film, slides, posters); and not compete with exhibits (if exhibits are visible from the orientation area, visitors tend to bypass the orientation displays).

ORIENTATION TO SUPPORT FACILITIES

In times of need, locating lavatories may reach crisis importance. Why do some facilities appear to hide their lavatories. After travelling in their cars to reach your museum/zoo/aquarium, families are likely to head for the lavatories immediately upon their arrival. In addition to lavatories, one must consider the location of gift shops, food concessions, and resting places for weary visitors. We have observed that in some facilities, people visit the museum specifically to purchase items or browse in the gift shop. If possible, it is a good idea to allow visitors to shop without paying entrance fees.

Suggestion: Visitors should be given information about the location of lavatories and other support facilities as they enter the building.

ORIENTATION AND CIRCULATION WHILE VIEWING EXHIBITS

Exhibit viewing problems can be divided into three areas: (1) conceptual orientation; (2) wayfinding; and (3) circulation. Conceptual orientation and wayfinding will be considered together.

Conceptual orientation and wayfinding

Orientation devices come in many forms. Floor directories, wall maps, hand-held maps, direction signs, information kiosks, and information desks are some of the most popular. Many questions can be asked regarding orientation.

- What information do visitors want before they circulate through a facility?
- How can you design orientation devices that will be attended to?
- How would they like this information presented?
- Which orientation devices are actually used by visitors and how often?
- Where should these devices be placed in order to be most effective?

What kind of information do visitors want?

Shettel-Neuber and O'Reilly (1981) studied orientation and circulation at the Arizona-Sonora Desert Museum. They asked visitors what information would have been most helpful before starting their visit. Most people (55.6 per cent) wanted information on conceptual orientation (i.e., information about the exhibits and what to see). Only 18.5 per cent wanted wayfinding information. It remains to be seen whether this data is typical of other facilities or not. If so, facilities need to do a better job giving information on conceptual orientation. Shettel-Neuber and O'Reilly also asked how visitors would like this information presented. Visitors were more likely to state that they prefer a short film (45 per cent) or signs and posters (33 per cent) than any other device. However, based on this data, we don't know which device they actually choose when confronted with a real situation. Self-report information can be misleading.

Designing orientation devices that will be attended to

Introductory orientation devices are often ignored, perhaps because visitors want to get right to the exhibits. Griggs (1983) found that visitors did not use orientation devices as they were planned by the museum staff. Only 49 per cent of visitors were observed using the orientation exhibit and no visitor spent long enough to experience the entire content. Griggs suggested that the orientation material was in competition with the exhibits. If orientation material is to be attended to, it must be designed in such a way that it is not competing with exhibits.

What devices are actually used and how are they used?

Several studies have asked visitors which orientation devices they actually used. These studies suggest that hand-held maps are the most-used device for wayfinding. For example, Shettel-Neuber and O'Reilly (1981) found that 64.7 per cent reported using the hand-held map, 44.1 per cent used exploring; 32.4 per cent used knowledge from a previous visit; and 35.3 per cent used direction signs. In a study at the Birmingham Zoo (Bitgood and Richardson 1986) we found that 77 per cent of visitors who received hand-held maps were observed using them. We also found that visitors who were given hand-held maps viewed a greater percentage of the exhibit areas (86 per cent) compared with a group who were not given a map (78 per cent). Hayward and Brydon-Miller (1983) found that 99 per cent of visitors used the hand-held maps at Old Sturbridge Village, a facility with much greater circulation complexity than the Arizona-Sonora Desert Museum from the Shettel-Neuber and O'Reilly study.

The evidence is strong that hand-held maps are used extensively for wayfinding. However, we don't know how often hand-held maps are used for conceptual orientation. Casual observations suggest that hand-held maps are important contributors to conceptual orientation if enough information is provided.

Wall (board maps *vs* direction signs)

Cohen and her colleagues (Cohen *et al.* 1977) found that wall maps and direction signs seem to serve a different function. Wall or board maps were used primarily to determine which exhibits to visit. Direction signs, on the other hand, were used primarily for wayfinding.

Visitors' understanding of exhibit themes is another area of conceptual orientation that must be carefully considered. We asked visitors at the Anniston Museum to match specific exhibits with theme areas of the Museum. Only four out of 15 exhibits could be accurately placed in their correct theme area. By 'accurate' I mean that visitors were able to match the exhibit with the theme area above the 60 per cent level. The average level of accuracy for all 15 exhibits was less than 40 per cent.

Suggestion: Use formative evaluation in the development of a complete orientation system. Include visitor input at all stages of this evaluation.

Another common wayfinding problem occurs when visitors look for the location of scheduled events such as demonstrations, bus tours, etc. Wayfinding cues must consider such problems. Since staff are bombarded with wayfinding questions if the cues are not adequately provided, this is not a difficult problem to diagnose.

Circulation

It is generally assumed that visitors will circulate through most or all of the exhibit areas. Studies have shown that this is not the case. Whether or not visitors actually do circulate through particular exhibit areas depends upon three factors: (1) visitor characteristics (e.g., tendency to turn right; fatigue; boredom); (2) architectural characteristics (e.g., placement of exits); and (3) exhibit characteristics (e.g., size, movement).

71

Visitor habits appear to play a role in circulation. The classic studies on visitor charac-teristics were conducted by Robinson (1928) and Melton (1935). Melton (1935) described a series of studies showing that, in the absence of more powerful factors, visitors have a strong tendency to turn right. Many people when faced with a complex environment such as a museum or large shopping mall develop a strategy that follows the rule: 'Take a right when entering the facility and follow the perimeter until you reach your starting point.' However, at other times visitors appear to 'browse' (Loomis 1987). Loomis states: 'Most visitors' movement through exhibits is closer to what might be called a "random walk process" where visitors move about without a clear pattern of progress toward any specific destination' (p. 162).

The architectural characteristics of facilities also play an important role in determining circulation patterns. As noted above, Melton convincingly showed the effects of exits in a series of studies. Obviously, physical barriers and direction arrows are useful devices for directing the circulation flow of visitors. In one study (Bitgood, Benefield, Patterson, Lewis, and Landers 1985) we found that less than one per cent of visitors violated direc-tional signs in the Birmingham Zoo's Reptile House when the traffic flow was changed from two-way to one-way.

The role of lighting should also be noted (Loomis 1987). Visitors are reluctant to enter dark areas. They are more likely to follow lighted pathways.

Finally, exhibit characteristics must be considered. Visually salient exhibits will draw the attention of visitors and influence their circulation. Melton (1936) showed that introducing movement (from a gear-shaper machine) in a museum gallery changed the circulation pattern. Originally, most visitors turned right when entering the gallery. Movement from the gear-shaper, however, drew their attention and resulted in visitors travelling straight ahead toward the source of movement instead of turning right.

Suggestion: Take all factors (visitor characteristics, architectural characteristics, and exhibit characteristics) into consideration when designing circulation pathways. It is often important to provide visitors with a suggested circulation pathway.

EXIT ORIENTATION

Two problems can exist in exiting a facility. First, it may be difficult to find the exit. Occasionally, a facility is well-marked for finding a specific location, but not for return-ing. Recently, I have had two disorientation experiences trying to find my way out of hospitals. I was called to consult with some hospital administrators to study their orientation system (or lack of it). Finding the administrator's office was bad enough. Trying to find my way out of the hospital was even worse since there were no direction signs. A second experience occurred when I took my daughter to a hospital for X-rays. The direction signs to the X-ray department were easy to follow. Unfortunately, there were no return signs. We had to wander until we found someone who could tell us how to get out of the hospital.

Suggestion: Make sure orientation cues are provided both in to and out of the facility.

A second problem is finding your car or other source of transportation. Parking lots are usually carefully marked with number and colour codes. In addition to these cues, facilities like Epcot remind visitors as they board a tram from the parking lot where they have parked their car. If visitors do not have their own transportation, problems can arise finding public transportation or a taxi.

Suggestion: In a large facility, it may be necessary to provide locational cues and reminders to visitors while they are still in the parking lot so they can find their way back.

MEASUREMENT OF ORIENTATION AND CIRCULATION BEHAVIOUR

Measurement of visitors' behaviour requires knowledge of assessment methodology that may not always be obvious. One of the first problems encountered is what measures should be included. It is my feeling that both self-report (surveys, questionnaires, interviews) and direct observation (tracking, etc.) should be used. The specific form of the questions and the particular instruments depend on the situation. Multiple measures of orientation/circulation are generally necessary because of the complexity of the problems. One instrument or device is unlikely to produce all of the information necessary to understand orientation/circulation problems. In general, such measures should probably include: pre-visit knowledge, an understanding of theme areas, wayfinding knowledge, ability to use orientation information to plan a visit (especially with respect to time), knowledge of visitor services (food, gift shops, etc.), and circulation pathways taken by visitors.

In addition to the questions of what measures to include, important questions of reliability and validity must be considered. If visitor evaluators are not aware of possible measurement problems, faulty conclusions can easily be made.

Reliability

Reliability refers to the consistency or stability of the measurements. For example, if two observers are recording the same visitor, will they count the same behaviours? While this question may sound trivial and the answer 'yes' in most cases, studies of reliability among independent observers are often quite surprising. It is more difficult to obtain such agreement between observers than is often thought. This is particularly true if behaviour must be coded into different categories. For example, while studying the relationship between visitor behaviour and animal activity in zoos, we found it difficult to code different categories of animal activity (Bitgood, Patterson and Benefield 1988). Yet we have not found one visitor study that suggests reliability among independent observers may be a problem. We must take care to ensure that our measurement systems are standardized and used in the same way by all observers in research and evaluation projects.

Self-reports

In the hands of a skilled practitioner such as Marilyn Hood, self-reports in the form of surveys and interviews can be very useful. But, there are pitfalls to this method as there are with any other. People do not always report events accurately. For example, it has been observed that visitors tend to overestimate time at an exhibit or at the facility (Bitgood and Richardson 1986: Shettel-Neuber and O'Reilly 1981). In addition, Bitgood and Richardson found that visitors were only 60 per cent accurate in retracing their steps through the zoo.

Direct observation

Direct observation has at least two major problems. First, it is labour intensive and thus costly in terms of observer time. Second, if visitors know they are being observed, reactivity may result.

Interpretation of data

Not only must the validity of the measures be questioned, but the interpretation of data must be carefully considered. In one study (Bitgood and Patterson 1986b) we found that visitors responded differently to the question: 'Which method would best help you find your way around the museum?' If visitors were asked this question before they entered the exhibition hall, they were less likely to indicate 'self exploring' and more likely to indicate 'direction signs'. However, if visitors were exiting the museum, they were more likely to check 'self exploring'. How should this be interpreted?

Another problem of interpretation is overgeneralizing a result. At this stage of visitor research, we must be cautious in assuming that a result found in one setting will generalize to another.

CONCLUSIONS

In conclusion, although we know much about visitor orientation and circulation, we need to know considerably more if we are going to design our facilities in the most effective manner. I believe that research and evaluation need to focus on several aspects of orientation and circulation.

- We need a systematic study of visitor orientation and circulation. Thus far, we have had a few hit-and-run projects, but these projects have lacked a long-term systematic thrust.
- We need to integrate all of the literature into a consistent conceptual scheme – a scheme that will give us working guidelines or rules for designing effective orientation and circulation systems.
- We need to pressure museums, zoos, parks, etc. to apply what is already known about orientation and circulation.
- We need to look critically at our measurement procedures to ensure that they are reliable, valid, and inclusive of all the important orientation/circulation elements.

This paper first appeared in S. Bitgood, J. T. Roper and A. Benefield (eds) (1988) Visitor Studies 1988 – Theory, Practice and Research, *Proceedings of the First Annual Visitor Studies Conference, Jacksonville, Alabama: Center for Social Design, pp. 155–70.*

REFERENCES

Adams, G. Donald (1988) 'Understanding and influencing word-of-mouth', in S. Bitgood, J. T. Roper Jr, and A. Benefield (eds) *Visitor Studies – 1988: theory, research and practice,* Jacksonville, AL: Psychology Institute, Jacksonville State University: 51–60.

Bitgood, S., Benefield, A., Patterson, D., Lewis, D., and Landers, A. (1985) 'Zoo visitors: Can we make them behave?' *Annual Proceedings of the 1985 American Association of Zoological Parks and Aquariums,* Columbus, OH.

Bitgood, S. and Hulac, M. (1987) *People in Public Places: a study of Quintard Mall users,* Technical Report No. 87–20, Jacksonville, AL: Psychology Institute, Jacksonville State University.

Bitgood, S. and Patterson, D. (1986a) 'Principles of orientation and circulation', *Visitor Behavior,* 1(4): 4.

Bitgood, S. and Patterson, D. (1986b) 'Orientation and wayfinding in a small museum', *Visitor Behavior,* 1(4): 6.

Bitgood, S. Patterson, D., and Benefield, A. (1988) 'Exhibit design and visitor behavior: Empirical relationships', *Environment and Behavior.*

Bitgood, S. and Richardson K. (1986) 'Wayfinding at the Birmingham Zoo', *Visitor Behavior,* 1(4): 9.

Bitgood, S. (1988) *Summary Report: visitor orientation at the Space and Rocket Center,* Huntsville, AL: unpublished report.

Carpman, J. (1986) 'Wayfinding in hospitals: solving the maze', *Annual Proceedings of Society of Environmental Graphics Designers.*

Cohen, M., Winkel, G., Olsen, R. and Wheeler (1977) 'Orientation in a museum – an experimental visitor study', *Curator*, 20(2): 85–97.

Falk, J. (1988) *The Museum Experience*, unpublished manuscript.

Fisher, J. D., Bell, P. A. and Baum, A. (1984) *Environmental Psychology,* 2nd edition, New York: Holt, Rinehart, & Winston.

Griggs, S. (1983) 'Orienting visitors within a thematic display', *International Journal of Museum Management and Curatorship*, 2: 119–34.

Hayward, G. and Brydon-Miller, M. (1984) 'Spatial and conceptual aspects of orientation: visitor experiences at an outdoor museum', *Journal of Environmental Systems*, 13(4): 317–32.

Hood, M. (1983) 'Staying away', *Museum News*, 61(4): 50–7.

Hood, M. (1986) 'Beware of catch-22', *Visitor Behavior*, 1(2): 10.

Levine, M. (1982) 'You-are-here maps: psychological considerations', *Environment and Behavior*, 14(2): 221–37.

Levine, M., Marchon, I., Hanley, G. (1984) 'The placement of you-are-here maps', *Environment and Behavior*, 16(2): 139–57.

Loomis, R. (1987) *Museum Visitor Evaluation: new tool for management*, Nashville, TN: American Association for State and Local History.

Lynch, K. (1960) *The Image of the City*, Cambridge, MA: M.I.T. Press.

Melton, A. W. (1935) *Problems of Installation in Museums of Art*, New Series No. 14, Washington, DC: American Association of Museums.

Melton, A. W. (1936) 'Distribution of attention in galleries in a museum of science and industry', *Museum News*, 14(3): 6–8.

Parsons, M. and Loomis, R. (1973) *Visitor Traffic Patterns: then and now*, Washington, DC: Smithsonian Institution, Office of Museum Programs.

Robinson, E. S. (1928) *The Behavior of the Museum Visitor*, New Series No. 5, Washington, DC: American Association of Museums.

Screven, C. G. (1986) 'Exhibitions and information centers: principles and approaches', *Curator*, 29(2): 109–37.

Shettel-Neuber, J. and O'Reilly, J. (1981) *Now where? A study of visitor orientation and circulation at the Arizona-Sonora Desert Museum*, Technical Report No. 87–25, Jacksonville, AL: Psychology Institute, Jacksonville State University.

Yoshioka, J. G. (1942) 'A direction-orientation study with visitors at the New York World's Fair', *The Journal of General Psychology*, 27: 6–9.

8

Sending them home alive

Anita Rui Olds

What ideas from environmental psychology can museums use to increase the enjoyment of a museum visit? 'Aliveness', and the resultant feelings of well-being and enjoyment can be achieved by designing an ambience with sufficient environmental stimulation to keep the brain at optimal levels of stimulation by meeting four basic needs: movement, comfort, competence and control.

Through the discussion of the ways in which people react in a range of different types of environment, we are made aware of the social, physiological, and psychological factors that come into play during a museum visit. Ideally a balance between movement, comfort, competence and control is necessary for physiological and psychological harmony. In museums, where it is often necessary to restrict one or more aspects, special care should be taken to increase provision for the others.

Ideally, a museum visit is a memorable experience that affects a person's life beyond the museum's walls. To be changed in this way, however, people must be fully *alive* where they are; free to drop their self-consciousness, their roles and facades, their fears of knowing too little, or of needing to judge and analyse; free to allow the objects and events to become part of themselves. Over and above the design requirements and neutral architectural backdrop of an exhibit, there is the opportunity and challenge to make each space a more successful place of learning and creativity, where people get more in touch with who they really are and what they might be. The following summary of ideas gathered from research in the field of environmental psychology suggests that achieving such 'aliveness' depends on designing an ambience with sufficient environmental stimulation to keep the brain at optimal levels of alertness by meeting at least four basic needs: movement, comfort, competence, and control.

MOVEMENT

The freedom to move about in space, assume different body postures, create one's own boundaries, and enter diverse territories is a prime way in which people manifest health and power and fulfill their potential. Indoors, however, the presence of many bodies moving in unpredictable ways is often experienced as discomforting. And because motion is more apparent in small spaces and can make space feel more congested, it is not encouraged where square footage is limited or focused attention is required. In most museums and galleries, visitors are expected to be quiet, move carefully, and behave in a formal and subdued way. These restrictions tire the body and dull the mind.

People feel most alive, however, when they can move freely within a setting to explore its limits and facets, have access to needs (lavatories, telephones, lockers, food), and can vary the pace of their activities over time. Thus museum visitors, especially children, may prefer to give an exhibit a 'once over' at the outset to determine its physical and informational scope and then proceed to absorb its contents step by step. Some visitors are content to follow a given sequence, while for others the visit is enriched by a more random approach.

It is particularly helpful, therefore, for aspects of an exhibit to allow for fine and gross motor interaction with the materials (pushing buttons, ringing bells, using body weight to unbalance or relocate objects) and encourage different types of movements and body postures: sitting (on chairs, floor, loft with feet dangling); standing; climbing (on stairs, ladders, inclines); lying (under or inside something); encircling something; bending or stooping (through lowered doorways); reaching; looking up, over, or under; moving (through wide and tight spaces, forward and backward, on level or inclined ground, with clear or minimal visibility, and with some or no light at the end of the tunnel). Where participants cannot be permitted to interact with the materials, demonstration by a craftsperson or operator can still have the powerful effect of introducing movement and change into the setting.

Just as a brisk walk may clear the mind, a period of standing or sitting to look at something, if followed by an active experience of walking a distance, changing levels, or using the body vigorously, helps wake up the brain. If this motion takes one to a space with an entirely different configuration and mood, so much the better. In homes, living rooms, kitchens, and bedrooms are distinct places involving different levels of activity, body postures, and degrees of privacy. Moving through such different rooms is often (as in the Pepsi ad) 'the pause that refreshes'. Similarly, moving through an exhibit in varied ways, through spaces with distinctly different moods and qualities, and using one's body (or someone else's) to make things happen in a display are all ways of creating movement, the *sine qua non* of life.

COMFORT

In addition to bodily movement, the senses also must 'move' and receive changing stimulation from the external environment. Our eyes see by scanning a visual field but are reduced to 'nonsight' when forced to stare at a stationary image. Our ears hear when sound waves strike and vibrate the ear drum.

Dramatic fluctuations in stimulation level can be frightening and disorienting. But an environment that provides rhythmic patterns of predictable sameness combined with moderate diversity enables the senses to maintain optimal levels of responsivity and makes us feel 'comfortable'. Natural elements, such as blazing fires, babbling brooks, and gentle breezes exemplify this principle well. They are always moving in ways that are fairly predictable. Yet moderate variations – a flicker or flare, a new pitch, a cooler or warmer draft – prevent boredom or withdrawal by introducing a change that catches the attention and reawakens the nervous system.

The difference-within-sameness so exquisitely present in nature is difficult to create within the static built world. Clearly, in a museum one does not want the background to have such arousal levels that it detracts from the exhibit itself. Paradoxically, it is often the sensorial blandness of a museum's setting that makes it difficult for visitors to absorb the details of even a particularly wondrous exhibit. The old adage, 'Variety is the spice of life', is the best guideline for generating an ambience that supports aliveness and learning.

This guideline means, first of all, that all the senses should be moderately stimulated. If an exhibit is largely visual, a quiet background of pleasantly varied sounds, odours, textures, and opportunities for movement will actually enhance the visual experience. Variety in physical parameters – scale, areas of light and shadow, floor levels and ceiling and partition heights, room size and number of occupants, degrees of intimacy, activities that are messy and clean – can also powerfully contribute to comfort and heightened awareness.

Attention to detail, especially to the finish materials used on floors, walls, ceilings, windows, and furniture, can have a more powerful impact on users and on the overall 'feel' of a place than any other single factor. The textures, colours, and forms applied (or not applied) to interior surfaces are the environmental qualities with which occupants come most closely in contact. These are 'read' continually as people experience any setting. Finishes and design details affect what is seen, heard, smelled, and touched, and therefore how people feel in a space.

To the extent that a comfortable environment is aesthetically integrated and whole, it is also beautiful. Its physical wholeness and harmony transmit psychic wholeness and tranquillity, elevating the spirit and encouraging the senses to play with surrounding events and forms.

A powerful way to design for aesthetic richness is to conceive of all elements of a room (floors, ceilings, walls, horizontal and vertical supports, objects, forms, and architectural details) as interactive surfaces that can be sculpted, painted, draped, and moulded, much the way artists, sculpt, paint, and mould wood, clay, canvas, fibres, colours, and forms. An environment is most comfortable when there are varied moods throughout the facility, created by interesting things to look at, unexpected surprises of light and shadow, sound, warmth, and colour, nooks and crannies, and things that respond, smell, or feel inviting. Then the senses can play everywhere, not solely with the exhibits.

All environments affect people in at least two ways: they suggest a range of activities that can or cannot occur in a setting, and they evoke feelings. Thus environments are always both emotionally felt and mentally interpreted by each occupant. Exhibits tell people what they can do, whereas the beauty and aesthetic qualities of a facility affect people's emotions and convey messages about their self-worth. A context of wholeness that unites body, mind, and spirit, thought and feeling, head and heart, invariably uplifts and transforms, helping people to learn and experience things they do not know and making them feel good about themselves and life. When the inner loveliness of the visitor meets the outer loveliness of an exhibit, then there is magic!

COMPETENCE

Aliveness also comes from being able to care for one's basic needs autonomously and from being successful at meaningful activities. Museum-goers often experience a sense of inferiority and submissiveness since they come to encounter the unfamiliar. They are unable to stake out territories over which they have jurisdiction or to control their activities and levels of social interaction in customary ways. To compensate for this loss of control and status, visitors should be helped to feel that they belong by being able to make their way easily through the facility and to participate in activities that grant them some control over territory, materials, and social encounters. An interpretable physical layout, reinforced by good signage and graphics in lobbies, corridors, elevators, exhibit areas, and at critical junctures, can help people get to where they want to go. Facilities that enable them to fulfil basic personal needs without assistance – coat racks, coffee machines, water fountains, clocks, telephones, baby-changing tables, conveniently located lavatories – honour independence and personal power.

Where people of a variety of ages and physical conditions are present, adaptive facilities, as well as those scaled to meet a range of developmental and educational levels and interests, further affirm the inherent learning capacities of each participant. Dioramas and full-scale mock-ups of a setting, which create an environment or contextual framework for an exhibit, help all visitors make inferences that bridge the gaps between the familiar and the unknown.

A sense of competence is also boosted by an ordered space whose parts are distinguishable from one another. Areas or zones within a room can be set apart by the amount of physical space between them, distinctive lighting and pools of light, boundaries and dividers, and the use of colour – our most powerful visual organizer. With different colours on work surfaces and sitting surfaces at the visitor's eye level, even a visually chaotic environment becomes interpretable. Seeing a red, blue, or green space within a room communicates more powerfully than signage that where the colours begin and end, so do the activities.

There is another sense in which competence can be addressed. Studies of cognitive and personality styles suggest that people process information in different ways (left brain/right brain, screener/non-screener, reflective/impulsive) and primarily along one of three dimensions: visual, auditory, or kinesthetic. A kinesthetic learner, for example, will have a hard time absorbing information from a purely visual display where there is nothing to touch or manipulate. To ensure that no one is 'disabled', a successful exhibit presents the same information in at least these three modalities so everyone can approach and interpret the material in the way that suits him or her best.

CONTROL

Because we do not have eyes in the backs of our heads and cannot protect ourselves from attack from the rear, control and physical security depend upon having something solid at our backs, with the ability to see and hear what approaches head-on. Thus people move across beaches, fields, and parks and stand still only when their backs are against a wall, a tree, or a bench. If protection at the rear is impossible, security may also be achieved by sitting or standing close to a wall, sitting or lying close to the ground, or attaining a position of height from which to survey the surrounding terrain. Most spaces have a zone (usually a corner) that is recognizably more protected than all other points in the room. It is there you will find the teacher's or doctor's desk, dad's favourite chair, and storage for precious items. People instinctively gravitate to a protected zone and like to stay there. Activities requiring a willingness to sit still and concentrate work best when placed in this location.

Physical security also depends upon being able to make predictions about territories and events beyond one's immediate spatial sphere. Broad vistas, rendered by an architecturally open plan, achieve this sense of security best. Interior windows or walls of glass, however, bold graphics, lighting that does not create mysterious shadows, and balanced acoustics can be intentionally employed in more enclosed settings to provide the 'extension of the senses' that is required.

A CONCLUDING THOUGHT

Psychological and physiological harmony depend upon the balance maintained among movement, comfort, competence, and control. Whenever one factor is limited (when movement is restricted, for example, because an exhibit requires the visitor to sit), the value of the other factors must be increased (a more stimulating background ambience, more back protection, varied sensorial modes for approaching the information). Because museum environments often produce many limitations at once, including restricted movement, interaction with unfamiliar materials, and restricted territorial control, the comfort dimension is exceedingly important and requires far more attention than is often characteristic of exhibit design practice. But, when all four needs are met and balanced to complement the extremes of visitor and exhibit limitations and excesses, then the setting truly lives and people leave the museum renewed and more alive.

This paper first appeared in Journal of Museum Education *15(1) (1990), pp. 10–12.*

FURTHER READING

Alexander, Christopher (1979) *The Timeless Way of Building*, New York: Oxford University Press.
Alexander, Christopher *et al.* (1977) *A Pattern Language*, New York: Oxford University Press.
Bachelard, Gaston (1969) *The Poetics of Space*, Boston: Beacon Press.
Fiske, D. W., and Maddi, S. R. (1961) *Functions of Varied Experience*, Homewood, Ill.: Dorsey.
Mehrabian, Albert (1976) *Public Places and Private Spaces: the psychology of work, play, and living environments*, New York: Basic Books.
Walter, Eugene Victor (1988) *Placeways: a theory of human environments*, Chapel Hill, N.C.: University of North Carolina Press.

9

Image and self image

Marista Leishman

The most effective mode of communication is often face-to-face. Warders and attendant staff are often the only members of the museum staff that visitors meet. Their role has been changing in recent years, and new duties tend to emphasize their function in interpretation and visitor service. New training programmes are developing to enable these new functions to be carried out, as two case studies demonstrate.

> In England, where ignorance, vulgarity, or something worse are the characteristics of the lower orders, and where frivolity, affectation, and insolence are the leading traits of a class of lounging persons who haunt most public places, it would be the excess of folly for gentlemen who possess valuable museums to give unlimited access to the public.

In 1806, when this was written for the catalogue of the gallery at Cleveland House it was also requested that in wet or dirty weather visitors would arrive in carriages. Some fifty years earlier the British Museum opened in Montagu House and one of the trustees noted: 'If public days should be allowed, then it will be necessary for the trustees to have the presence of a committee of themselves attending, with at least two justices of the peace and the constables of the division of Bloomsbury.' The need to guard valuable collections has as long a history as the admittance of visitors, so spare a thought for today's warders and attendants working within a tradition which once allowed ticketed entrance only to 'studious and curious persons'.

All dressed up with nowhere to go, most attendants have about as much to look forward to as an underemployed sub-policeperson. After all, rarely do thieves remove paintings in broad daylight, or vandals spoil precious objects. And it is not that often either that curious hands fondle exhibits, umbrellas jab enthusiastically at canvases or children stick chewing gum onto the noses of statues. But these are the few moments in which the traditional attendant comes into his or her negative own, fulfilling the message of the stern uniform, and mingling assumed authority with the sheer relief of having something to do. Intervention becomes the high point of the day.

Most of the time the job is unspeakably boring and even staying awake becomes a problem. One attendant described his patch as 'a beautiful prison, into which not many people come, not even troublemakers'. Not surprisingly, visitors are put off by this band of melancholy minders who communicate their dejection, subtly suggesting that museums perhaps aren't very interesting after all.

TRAINING FOR ALL

Staff at Ironbridge Gorge Museum subscribe to the philosophy that taking care of the visitor is as important as taking care of the collection. High standards of service are expected of each and every member of staff.

At the end of 1991, to ensure that museum staff did not become too isolated in their separate departments, the museum instigated a completely different kind of training for all staff, from cleaner to curator, from typist to tourist information officer, sales receptionist to steam-winding operator.

The following March, all 230 members of staff took part in customer care training, which was organised by Insite and part-funded by West Midlands Area Museum Service. Staff responded enthusiastically to the training sessions which took them back to basics, forcing everybody to rethink their roles. Through this process many staff realized that they too were valued because of the role they played, even if they were invisible to the public.

In a typical day, Ironbridge staff will be asked a wide variety of questions often unrelated to their official functions. It is vital that they are able to respond, and want to respond, positively to all demands. The coffee shop manager at the Museum of Iron must be able to tell the enquiring visitor about the Jackfield Tile Museum and vice versa, and recruitment and training must take all this into consideration. At the beginning of the main season all staff attend tours to all the museum sites to familiarize themselves with visitor facilities and with the history of Ironbridge.

The attendant at Ironbridge has never conformed to the stereotype – the barely civil, uninterested philistine clothed in grey uniform and wearing a peaked cap. Ironbridge attendants could be better described as facilitators, particularly those in costume at Blists Hill Open Air Museum. Visitors expect these members of staff to be accessible, to talk to them and to answer their questions. This kind of service can be very demanding and there is intensive training for these staff, mainly at the beginning of the season.

Katie Foster, head of public relations,
Ironbridge Gorge Museum

KNOCK-ON EFFECTS

Most larger museums grew up in the nineteenth century often as assertions of civic triumphalism: the demeanour of the warding staff was consistent with the grand manner of such institutions But, since the 1960s many new places have opened. As well as the steady acquisition of properties by the National Trust and the National Trust for Scotland, historic houses in private ownership, heritage centres, visitor centres attached to open-air sites and theme parks began to compete for the public attention. Independently run specialist museums appeared: for the first time there were specific collections for cycles, pencils, lace and lawnmowers. In 1984 English Heritage began work to present some 400 historic properties with push and profile and their Scottish counterpart followed. The royal palaces continued to absorb millions of visitors, the cathedrals even more.

These new 'visitor attractions' (the phrase itself is significant) use new kinds of staff. Historic houses may be staffed by volunteers who take pride in knowing about the history of the house and its inhabitants. At mining or maritime museums staff may be ex-miners or seamen – proud of their pits and their ships, and more concerned with the safety of the visitors than the exhibits. The farmstead at Aden Country Park in Grampian is staffed by farmworkers who explain what they are doing. At Blists Hill Open Air Museum, part of Ironbridge Gorge Museum, demonstrators dressed in character work as locksmiths, ironworkers, candlemakers and so on while at the same time chatting with the visitors. At hands-on science centres like those at Catalyst, Snibston Discovery Park and the Museum of Science and Industry in Manchester, staff are there to explain how things work, to see they don't go wrong and, occasionally, as at Eureka!, to engage the interest of younger visitors. At Amberley Chalk Pits Open Air Museum volunteer staff drive the traction engine and work in the sandwich bar.

In most of these places the staff that visitors meet have responsibilities and objectives different to those of traditional museum attendants. They are there to welcome and to answer questions rather than to exercise a watching brief. This puts pressure on museums with displays of valuable and vulnerable objects to provide the same service to their visitors, and to encourage them to feel at home, but without putting collections at risk. There was no place for traditional warders ('les gardiens-robots') at the Pompidou Centre in Paris when it opened in 1977. Instead, 'hotesses d'accueil' combine the tasks of welcoming and interpreting with responsibility for security. At the 1991 Japan exhibition at the Victoria and Albert Museum separate staff responded to visitors' enquiries in addition to normal warding staff – a solution out of the reach of smaller museums.

Other museums and galleries are reassessing the role and image of the traditional warder. At the Royal Naval Museum in Portsmouth, Melanie McKeown, customer services manager, seeks to relate customer care to security. One of the warders, Ken Shergold, tells how he 'thinks customer' by asking himself how would he like to be treated if he were a visitor. Susan Bourne, curator of Burnley's Towneley Hall Art Gallery and Museum believes that appearance and personal pride are important and that police-style uniforms are now redundant. At the National Museum of Scotland, Alan Young, head of administrative services, looks forward to a service which is rewarding for staff and more welcoming for the public. This calls not for a reduced security role, but for a more discreet one which replaces an aloof presence (with matching uniform and persona) with a more out-going image (without a peaked cap) but with authority still intact. Windsor Castle, despite, or perhaps because of the blaze, will continue to be near the top of the league table of visitor numbers. In the view of the management the formal dress of the warders makes ever more important their need to relate well to the thousands of visitors.

BUILDING CONFIDENCE

In spite of these changes traces of the old culture persist in some museums. There is still the unmistakable feeling that makes the visitor ill at ease, that forces him or her to experience the museum as solemn and the staff as grim. Too often, visitors keenly seeking information are met with attendants who neither know nor care. For a visitor fresh from an historic house where questions are likely to be encouraged such treatment is unlikely to prompt a return visit.

Recently, in reply to a visitor's very ordinary question, an attendant in a national museum quickly said he had no idea. 'I'm only a menial here,' he explained. Museums may be working on the external image of their attendants but are they looking to improve the self-image of the individual? Christopher Amey, head of security at the National Portrait Gallery, feels that warders must be conversant with the subject of the gallery's exhibitions. To work well and to project a positive image, attendants need support and training. Attendant staff need to be fully integrated. This means keeping them informed of what is happening in the museum, why and when. If attendants are not told about a new development, given an explanation of a new exhibition or the chance to ask questions, they receive the unequivocal message that they are unimportant and that the important matters are going on elsewhere. It also means more than team briefing, feeding information from the top down. Managers must listen to the experience and advice of attendants who regularly witness the reactions of the public. As Sir John Harvey-Jones says: 'We make pathetically inadequate use of the capabilities of our people.'

At Stoke-on-Trent Museum there is a regular exchange of information between front-of-house staff and curators. At Tullie House Museum in Carlisle, director Nick Winterbotham, like management at Marks and Spencer, regularly arranges temporary closures for in-house training. Duties are rotated hourly because boredom is inimical to a happily operating institution and curators as well as front-line staff meet the public. Staff at the National Museum of Wales are considered the public face of the museum, and their training programme involves everybody, at all levels. Training programmes at Ironbridge Gorge Museum include site maintenance workers, curators and telephonists. At the National Maritime Museum the view is that 'we are here for the customers'. Regular team briefing and training are embodied in the museum's corporate plan, according to Stephen Deuchar, development manager.

But training is not so simple. Disappointingly, the Hale Report on museum professional training and career structure (Museums and Galleries Commission, 1987) does not recommend career structures for attendants. Failing to notice the ways in which the role of the attendant has changed, the report offers little in anticipation of continuing development. Instead it proposes a core syllabus – an inadequate response to an important need.

In addition, training alone is not enough. In the Industrial Society Magazine (March 1989), David Turner regrets that training is becoming 'hung up on standards, qualifications, status and accreditation. The real issue is how to move away from standardization in favour of individuality and from conformity to creativity.' He goes on to note that the concept of accumulated competences for training at all levels is sound, 'blending the skills, knowledge, aptitudes, temperament and personal qualities' that are needed by all members of the workforce. But when these competences 'are required to conform to a set of standards defining a performance requirement' and leading to an award, something is missing. A single national set of standardized competences, however diligently prepared, should be understood as a menu and not as a diet. Museums, people and circumstances all vary; museum managers and attendants need to be able to choose from a broad spectrum of training material and approaches.

When training becomes a prescription for action, it shows. The telephonist, lifelessly delivering a formula response ('Good morning, Jones and Baker here, Brian speaking, how can I help you?') voices a contradiction between style and content. At one gallery the double doors are importantly flung open by an attendant on either side at the approach of every visitor. Flattered, a visitor enters, only to catch part of an uninterrupted dialogue on pay and conditions from the other side of the gallery. The mechanics of training are there but the central matter is lost. Managers should encourage human rather than mechanical responses, and give attendant staff the confidence to relate easily to visitors. This will help them to remain interested, alert and welcoming and to convey through their attitude the message that all questions will be dealt with politely, that information or assistance is there if needed and that complaints will be taken seriously.

QUIET REVOLUTION

Since 1990 Glasgow Museums staff have seen their duties, career opportunities and the service they provide for the public completely redefined. The first group to have their duties reviewed were those in the front-line, the people on the museum floor, the visitors' first point of contact. Security attendants, cleaners, shop assistants, porters and enquiries staff were amalgamated into a new hybrid museum assistant whose role encompassed all these former duties.

The new scheme has three grades designed to give a clear career path. The basic grade A for new recruits involves training in security, cleaning, portering and customer care/information duties. In the next grade, B, training covers: handling enquiries, museum shops and added security measures in control room duties. The top grade C deals with collection information and involves curatorial staff in training.

Staff progress from one grade to the next through on-the-job training and assessment and through specific courses developed with Glasgow City Council's central personnel department and the Museum Training Institute. Training beyond grade A is voluntary but applications from staff have exceeded expectation. Attaining the necessary skills not only means a higher salary, it also offers job enrichment and personal satisfaction.

The first line managers in the scheme are known as museum officers (MOs) who are on higher graded posts linked to curatorial scales. MOs are themselves trained in administrative and supervisory skills.

The scheme aims to create a highly motivated team dedicated to improving visitor and staff access to collections. The scheme is designed to:

- help staff develop a knowledge and interest in the collections
- teach principles of communication
- develop interpersonal skills in order to relate to visitors' expectations
- enable staff to evaluate public response to all museum services and to play a part in forward planning
- empower staff to take ownership of their role in Glasgow Museums.

Now in its third year of operation, the scheme has not all been plain sailing. Although we are still learning, we are well on the way to creating a team of ambassadors for the museum.

Stewart Coulter, deputy director,
Glasgow Museums

Museums have come a long way from those early days when they worked to keep the public at bay. Those museums who through their staff are 'engaged in a dialogue with the public', as Val Bott, curator of the Passmore Edwards Museum, put it *(Museums Journal* February 1990, p. 28) are now getting the results they deserve by investing in front-of-house staff, museum managers can move attendant staff out of the category of 'the menial' to their proper place at the forefront of the museum experience.

This paper first appeared in Museums Journal *93(6) (1993), pp. 30–2.*

REFERENCE

Museums and Galleries Commission (1987) *Museum Professional Training and Career Structure: the Hale report*, London: HMSO.

10

Outline of a technology for effective science exhibits

Roger S. Miles and Alan F. Tout

Exhibitions are a major mode of communication in museums and galleries. Since the 1970s, research on exhibition communication has been systematically carried out at the Natural History Museum in London.

This is an early paper that describes the theoretical position taken by Roger Miles and his team at the beginning of the attempt to develop a museum technology – a set of critical standards and a body of objective knowledge in the design of exhibitions. Based in educational technology, a number of elements are identified that will produce effective science (and other) exhibits.

These elements focus on the structure of the exhibition in terms of the use of space and the division of ideas and concepts. The ideas proposed were and remain of vital importance. However, a focus only on the structure of the exhibition will not result in effective exhibitions, as the 'effectiveness' of exhibitions is located within the subjectivity of the visitor.

A useful companion paper which deals with the response of people within communicative situations is to be found in chapter 12 by Sam H. Ham.

Most curators of palaeontological collections tend to be involved to some extent in exhibition work, and therefore the philosophy behind it is an important part of curation. The views set out in this paper have been acquired during the first stages of work on a large new exhibition scheme in the British Museum (Natural History) (Miles and Tout 1978). This scheme will eventually deal with all aspects of natural history and we believe that our conclusions apply therefore to palaeobiological as well as to other scientific displays.

Museum displays have often been the subject of criticism in specialized publications and the popular press, but whether the opinions expressed have any meaning or value has seldom been considered. Are they purely subjective, or are they at least potentially objective like judgements in scientific research? Can the quality of the criticism be explained, defended, and above all improved? These are the questions considered in this paper, which stems from a conviction that if we can improve the quality of our criticism then we can improve the quality of our exhibits. Displays have often been modernized by changing their style (Swiecimski 1977a, b, c), but there have been few attempts to analyse their purpose, assess their effectiveness, or systematically improve their performance (see also Loomis 1973). At the moment exhibition design is a somewhat haphazard process, but if we can agree on a set of critical standards, and build up an organized body of objective knowledge, then we can begin to make real progress in this field.

Criticism is an intellectual skill which plays a recognizably important role in the human-ities and the fine arts, but it has an even more fundamental role in science (Macdonald-Ross and Waller 1975). The argument that criticism is essential to the growth of scientific knowledge has frequently been expressed, particularly by Popper (e.g. 1976: 22, 23):

> . . . the only intellectually important ends are: the formulation of problems, the tenta-tive proposing of theories to solve them; and the critical discussion of the competing theories. The critical discussion assesses the submitted theories in terms of their rational or intellectual value as solutions to the problem under consideration; and as regards their truth, or nearness to truth. Truth is the main regulative principle in the criticism of theories . . .

A statement about exhibition design such as 'exhibits should be well lighted', regardless of its intrinsic merit, has a logical status which depends very much on the context in which it is made. In the context of criticism, it defines a criterion against which to judge existing exhibits; in that of planning, it has a prescriptive or normative role telling us how to reach accepted goals. Both contexts occur in this paper. In the first part we shall discuss a scientific approach to the problem of improving the effectiveness of museum exhibits, with particular emphasis on the role of criticism. In the last section we shall gather together an initial set of precepts resulting from this approach and thus provide the prescriptive context.

SCIENCE MUSEUMS AND MUSEUM SCIENCE

Museums differ in their purposes. Many, especially those concerned with the arts, tradi-tionally have the aim of collecting and preserving objects of intrinsic merit and of putting at least some of these on public display. Others are concerned with science, and consequently tend to place less emphasis in their exhibits on objects and more on ideas. For this last category there is no logical reason why the scientific method (which has led to a vast increase of knowledge and understanding in many different fields) should play an important part in the advancement of knowledge and then be ignored when it comes to diffusing this knowledge more widely.

This outlook provides a framework within which it is possible to take a fresh look at the process of exhibition design. This framework is characterized by the criticism-based schema of Popper (1972: 287), a three-stage iterative process of trial and error:

$$P_1 \longrightarrow TT \longrightarrow EE \longrightarrow P_2$$

where P = problem, TT = tentative theory, EE = '(attempted) error elimination, especially by critical discussion'. Once it is accepted that exhibits may be regarded as trial solutions to suitably defined problems, the four entities linked in these three stages can be identified in the context of exhibition design:

1 *Initial problem.* Problems take many forms in exhibition design. For example, they concern the effectiveness of exhibits in communicating facts and ideas, the visitors' difficulties in finding their way around the exhibits, and the attraction and holding of visitors' attention. Such problems may be difficult to identify and describe, but each must be clearly formulated if a solution is to be proposed and tested.
2 *Tentative theory.* This is the trial solution to a problem. In the practical context of exhibition work the solution normally takes the form of specifications for an exhibit or larger part of an exhibition.

3 *Error elimination.* This involves the criticism of the trial solution by the realization of an exhibit or larger part of an exhibition, and the evaluation of its performance against previously fixed standards. In other words, the theory is put to the test to reveal its limitations.

4 *New problem.* The elimination of errors in a theory leads ideally to a more refined solution. The new solution can then be be pitted against a deeper interpretation of the original problem. We must assume that it is always possible to make further progress (i.e. learn how to do the job better) because we have no means of knowing when we have arrived at a perfect solution. This assumption gives purpose and direction to work, though in practice it may never be feasible to test and improve exhibits beyond the point where they function adequately according to the criteria applied to the exhibition as a whole.

The same framework underlies the approach in the broader field of operational research (e.g. Churchman *et al.* 1957; Waddington 1973: 25–30), and the more specific one of educational technology (e.g. Rowntree 1974) in which there are many ideas relevant to the design of museum exhibits.

THE SCIENCE MUSEUM AS AN ENVIRONMENT FOR LEARNING

It seems reasonable to assume that most science exhibits are set up with the aim of communicating ideas, e.g. to tell a story, explain a concept, suggest a new attitude, or reveal the interest of a particular object or phenomenon that might otherwise escape attention. We may also assume that most visitors enter a science museum with the expectation of learning something, though frequently such expectations may be ill-defined. From these two assumptions it follows that science museums are potentially places where people learn (Shettel 1968, 1973; Screven 1969, 1976; Lakota and Kantner 1976). That is, science museums can provide learning environments for the general public. Further, the sort of learning environment provided by a public science museum is unique in its informality and in the freedom afforded to the learner. Thus, visitors can extend their knowledge and understanding in whatever direction they choose; they do not have to conform to any set of values other than their own; and they can come and go as they please, moving about at their own pace and on their own terms. The only thing asked is that visitors behave in a socially acceptable manner.

These points have, *inter alia*, been summarized by Thier and Linn (1976: 234):

1. People come to science centres and museums generally by choice.
2. People choose activities suited to their own needs.
3. Individuals can interact with materials that might not otherwise be available.

THE RELEVANCE OF EDUCATIONAL TECHNOLOGY

Discussion above refers to science in connection with museums and the link of technology with education. Since our principal concern in what follows is with museum technology (Oppenheimer 1968: 169; Miles and Tout 1978), it is appropriate to distinguish between the ways in which we use the terms 'science' and 'technology'. Both are associated with the idea of research as a purposeful activity by which knowledge is advanced. However, not all research is scientific and not all scientific research follows the same pattern.

The present discussion relates only to that which is conducted according to Popper's schema (see above), and we recognize the following categories:

1. *Applied research*. The main purpose is to find a way of doing some particular thing.
2. *Pure research*. The main purpose is to advance knowledge. Two kinds may be distinguished.
   2.1. *Basic research*. The purpose is to advance knowledge in a particular field to make it easier to solve problems in that field.
   2.2. *Fundamental research*. There is no apparent prospect of putting the new knowledge to practical use.

Different names are sometimes used for these three types of research, but this is less important than distinguishing the underlying differences in purpose.

Science (in a restricted sense) is the underlying body of objective knowledge built up by applied, basic, or fundamental research. A technology, for our purposes, is a body of scientific knowledge relevant to a particular field of activity. Technology (as an activity) is the application of science to the solution of practical problems. It may use the results of fundamental research, but technological research must be either applied or basic because its purpose is never just the increase of knowledge. There are thus three important aspects of technology:

1. The organized body or objective knowledge which results from scientific research.
2. The extension of this knowledge by scientific research.
3. Practical purposes which underlie this further research.

Purpose is so central to technology that it must be defined unambiguously by clearly stated objectives.

The technological approach to design in education began with programmed learning, which led to the ideas underlying educational technology, i.e. the learner not the teacher as the focus of attention; giving the learner control over his or her own rate of working; and providing for mixed ability and attainment, e.g. by introducing branching points into the sequence of instructional material. Science museums are different from schools and adult institutes in formal education (Thier and Linn 1976: 234) but the learning process is much the same everywhere. Therefore, museum technology and educational technology are distinct but the two have considerable overlap. The biggest differences arise from the extreme heterogeneity of museum visitors and their freedom of action.

The museum, no less than the teacher (e.g. Tammadge and Starr 1977), has to (1) motivate (2) set the scene in which learning can take place, and (3) present information in such a way that learning becomes enjoyable and rewarding. The affective aspects of the learning process (Krathwohl *et al.* 1964) present more difficulty than the cognitive ones, and perhaps carry slightly more weight in the museum than in formal education, but apart from this the features of educational technology most relevant to the museum exhibition are listed below. Most of these are characteristic of programmed learning, but for continuing changes in emphasis (Shettel 1968, 1973; Screven 1969, 1976; Macdonald-Ross 1969; Davies 1971; Rowntree 1974; Lakota and Kantner 1976).

1. The statement of aims is in the form of specific objectives, i.e. in potentially measurable terms.
2. The content of the course of study (exhibition) is carefully arranged so as to present the underlying ideas in a logical sequence. Not all writers accept that this feature is appropriate to museums (Cameron 1968: 37; Shaw 1972: 43), but axiomatically this

precept must be followed if the museum wishes to provide a proper setting for indi-vidualized learning and at the same time present science as an organized body of knowledge.

3. The interaction between the learner and the subject material (exhibits) is carefully controlled by:

   (a) arranging the material in digestible steps;

   (b) making provision for various levels of ability, knowledge, and interest, *inter alia* through 'enrichment' material;

   (c) making provision for participation or active responding, though not necessarily through overt responses;

   (d) making arrangements for immediate confirmation of responses (i.e. 'feedback' after a correct response).

4. The medium is matched to the subject material and learners at all stages. This subject is largely beyond the scope of this paper and therefore receives only passing mention.

5. The materials are subjected to validation and evaluation.

THE EMERGENCE OF A MUSEUM TECHNOLOGY

Until recently, the role of trial and error and the importance of objective criticism were not widely recognized as relevant to the design of exhibitions. Thus, Parr (1962: 36–7) was able to write:

> beyond the esthetic satisfaction it provides, we have no evidence of what effects good design may have upon our ability to communicate knowledge and create understanding by visual means. In fact, we do not even seem to have rigorous proof that design makes any difference at all to the educational value of an exhibit, how-ever great our personal faith in the designer's art. And we are making no serious attempt to arrive at objective appraisals in performance in the tasks to which we are dedicated.

The turning point came more or less at the same time as the publication of a small-scale study on the criteria habitually employed by specialists developing, producing, and teaching from exhibits (Shettel 1968). Shettel argued that if these criteria (e.g. 'exhibits should be well lighted') were necessary and sufficient for the design of effective exhibits, then experts in the field, upon examining a given exhibit, should agree whether it did or did not meet these criteria. In other words, he was interested in discovering whether existing precepts for effective design provided adequate critical standards for judging exhibits.

A draft list for measuring exhibit effectiveness was produced with fifty-five criteria drawn from the literature. These criteria were sorted into fifteen basic sets (Shettel 1968, table 1) 'including: ability to attract attention; accuracy of information presented; rela-tion of exhibit to surrounding area and other exhibits; design of exhibit including use of colour, light and contrast, etc.; the items contained within the exhibits; and the use of various communication techniques such as sound, motion, demonstration, films, etc.'. Initially these were rated on a six-point scale, but after trial this was replaced by a four-point scale.

We may ignore some of the subtleties in the design of the draft list, e.g. to check the internal reliability of the ratings, and it will be sufficient to consider only the results of its first trial. As Shettel (1973: 35) notes, these were not very encouraging. For example, 'One of the items queried: "How would you rate the overall design of the exhibit?" The following results were obtained from six specialists who were rating the same exhibit: One said it was "excellent"; one said it was "very good"; one "high average'; one "low average"; and two "fair". Whatever *overall design* means to the authors of the exhibit literature, it certainly meant different things to the six raters.'

Shettel's results came from a small experiment using draft criteria, and involved a heterogeneous group of experts (designers, production staff, interpreters, etc.). Therefore, we must be cautious in interpreting these results. Also, it would be wrong to dismiss the tacit knowledge of designers just because it is the result of experience rather than book learning, and has not been developed by orthodox experimental methods (Macdonald-Ross and Waller 1975: 77). However, applying this knowledge to the criticism of existing designs is one of the ways it becomes public knowledge, and Shettel's work showed that in one trial at least, tacit knowledge did not provide criteria for the consistent judgement of science exhibits. This does not mean that common sense has no part to play (e.g. see Hjorth 1971). But it does strongly suggest that more exacting, more objective criteria are needed before better exhibits can be developed in a systematic way. Shettel's (1968: 150) own major conclusion has considerable interest for the last section of this paper:

> One observation stands out very clearly as a result of this small-scale study, and that is the need for more clearly stated objectives for exhibits.
> ... The question which should be asked is, 'Specifically *what* do you want *whom* to do, know, or feel after seeing the exhibit that they could not do, know or feel before seeing the exhibit?' Answering such a question in adequate detail would cut through much of the ambiguity, and even mystique, that surrounds the exhibit field.

Shettel's work was followed by two events of major importance. These were the realization that some aspects of educational technology might usefully be applied to exhibit design (Screven 1969; Shettel 1973; Lakota and Kantner 1976; Thier and Linn 1976), and the rediscovery of observational work on museum visitors (Melton 1935; Lakota 1975; Lakota and Kantner 1976). The linkage of educational technology and observational work led in turn to the emergence and development of museum technology.

Technology facilitates the making of predictions (e.g. about the interaction between visitors and exhibits), with the practical aim of making better decisions in particular circumstances. In this context, Lakota, Shettel, Screven, and other American workers apparently believe that man's actions, though they stem from a small set of basic drives, are fundamentally responses to external stimuli. This leads to the questionable conclusion that the visitor's behaviour can be determined completely by controlling the conditions. However, this question need not concern us because the matter is surely of theoretical rather than practical interest. The body of objective knowledge making up museum technology can *not* be regarded as a set of laws which permits the prediction of the future state of a fully deterministic system. People visit museums for many different reasons (Morris 1962; Alt 1977: 254–5) and there is no means of telling what knowledge or interest any given visitor will bring to bear on the exhibits, how he will interact with other people in the museum, or how he will be influenced by his expectations of the visit. In short, the number of stimuli to which visitors might respond and the degree to which the response can vary from one individual to another are so great, that it would be a hopeless task to predict the behaviour of a particular visitor. The only practicable possibility is of making predictions concerning populations, not individuals. This has been recognized in the training field, where the original criterion of 100 per cent of the learners attaining 100 per cent of the learning objectives has largely been replaced by the more realistic 90/90 criterion or something similar.

In museums, where the visitors form an extremely heterogeneous population, sights must be set much lower, but this does not mean that museums should abandon educational exhibits. Treating a museum exhibition as a medium for education gives purpose to the process of design in a way that, as far as we are aware, no alternative view of museums does. Persons producing exhibits should, in this view, take it for granted that they are working in an educational medium, in the same way that most teachers know that their job is educating 'regardless of the number of failures among their pupils' (Alt 1977: 248). Of course, it is a legitimate part of the designer's art to capture the imagination of the casual visitor and turn him or her into a serious learner. This is the same as the teacher motivating the pupils, but it is not the same as assuming that people are infinitely mouldable, and whatever the intention of the authors we cite when discussing the evaluation and improvement of exhibits, we reject this assumption.

APPLYING THE TECHNOLOGY

The extent to which the precepts of educational technology are applicable in the informal learning environment of a science museum, and that to which the results of limited observational studies in disparate institutions can be applied to science museums in general, can only be established by a process of trial and error. At the very least, applying precepts from these two sources provides a starting-point for the development of more effective exhibits, as in de Morgan's paradox – 'wrong hypotheses, rightly worked from, have produced more useful results than unguided observation' (Løvtrup 1974: 491). The outcome from applying these precepts is a set of specifications for an exhibit or larger part of an exhibition, which we have identified with the 'tentative theory' of Popper's schema (p. 88), and which is then put to the test by realization, followed by measurement of performance and comparison with previously fixed standards or criteria. Here we can again draw on educational technology and observational studies, this time to provide objective criteria of greater use than those examined by Shettel (1968).

The process of testing is complicated by the very large number of variables involved in the design of even a single exhibit. But more importantly, testing is not possible until another problem has been solved, that of defining effectiveness and specifying the effectiveness criterion in precise terms. Exhibit effectiveness may be defined as 'the measurable transmission of information about scientific principles from the exhibits to the visitors' (Eason and Linn 1976: 46); but what information, and what kind of visitors?

In making predictions about interactions between visitors and exhibits it is not possible to consider individuals even if we limit ourselves to the serious learner. Our predictions must concern populations of visitors. And the confidence with which we can make these predictions depends on two things; (1) the risk which we are prepared to accept of being wrong, which we can control; and (2) the variation within a particular population, which we cannot control, though we can subdivide the total population into less heterogeneous parts. Such a subdivision was tacitly made above, when the casual visitor was distinguished from the motivated learner.

Criticism and the consequent attempt to eliminate errors together constitute the process which has come to be known since the early days of programmed learning as evaluation. In terms of when, rather than how it is carried out, a distinction may be drawn between formative and summative evaluation (Scriven 1976; Screven 1976). Formative evaluation is carried out during the development of an exhibition and the results are used to improve the effectiveness of the final product. This evaluation can be carried out on all aspects of an exhibition, including the materials used in its construction, its ability to attract visitors and hold their attention and its communications effectiveness. It is usual to use cheap, easily modified mock-up versions of the exhibits for this work. Eason and Linn (1976: 49) give a list of the questions answered by one specific programme of formative evaluation:

1. Do the exhibits work as planned?
2. Are the directions at an appropriate reading level?
3. Can visitors follow the directions provided?
4. Are diagrams clear to visitors?
5. How long do visitors generally spend at each exhibit?
6. What part of the visitor population is interested in optics?

Summative evaluation is carried out after an exhibition has been developed and installed, and aims to discover how well the original planning goals have been achieved. It forms the basis of further action if the exhibition is to be revised, partly replaced, left to stand as it is, or scrapped completely. Formative and summative evaluation are not, of course, mutually exclusive, and there is no reason why formative evaluation should not take place during modification of a completed exhibition, in the light of the summative results.

In both formative and summative evaluation it is necessary for the test criteria to be appropriate, effective, and practical (Davies 1971: 212). Failure in one or more of these respects may explain some of the disappointing results obtained so far in measuring the effectiveness of science exhibits (Alt 1977). Test criteria based on detailed factual knowledge may be inappropriate if Thier and Linn (1976: 234) are correct in their assumption that visitors are not attracted to science museums to learn facts but rather to discover new and interesting phenomena. And the devising and administration of pre-tests and post-tests to measure changes in knowledge, beliefs, and attitudes, while appropriate in formal education, are not necessarily so in the convivial setting of a public museum (Linn 1976). Factors such as these are probably more important than the problem identified by Shettel (1968: 138), of 'designing appropriate measuring instruments that are sensitive to changes'.

Observational work offers a more direct approach to the evaluation of exhibit effectiveness than pre- and post-test questions. The basic premiss is that unless certain readily observed 'conditions of learning' are fulfilled, an exhibit or exhibition cannot possibly be effective. Attraction and holding do not measure the power of an exhibit to increase the visitor's knowledge or change his attitude and beliefs. It is possible for an exhibit to perform well in both respects and still communicate nothing. However, we can be more certain that an exhibit which fails to attract and hold attention will not communicate, regardless of its potential effectiveness in transmitting information. This is knowledge worth having because it forms a firm basis for practical action.

THE DESIGN OF EFFECTIVE EXHIBITS

In this last section we present a set of precepts for the design of effective exhibits, based on the work of Lakota (1975; Lakota and Kantner 1976). As already explained, these define conditions for learning for the visitor whose goal is museum learning. However, we believe that they permit a positive, directional approach to the work of mounting science exhibits, to the benefit of all visitors. The precepts form two overlapping sets. The first is derived from observational studies and concerns exhibit architecture – which Lakota and Kantner believe to have an overwhelming influence on visitor behaviour. The second set is based on the aspects of educational technology already mentioned.

Architectural and organizational factors

1. The exhibition space should be partitioned into smaller areas with chambers or alcoves large enough for groups of about ten to observe some aspect of the exhibition

Melton (1935) found that visitors spent most of their time near the entrance of an exhibition and less and less as they approached the exit. The exhibits receiving most attention were those in a direct line between the point where the exit becomes visible and the exit. Even so, speed of movement increased rapidly as the exit was approached. This exit gradient effect can be lessened by constructing exhibitions in a cul-de-sac form with a single entrance and exit (Fig. 10.1A). In the case of large rectangular galleries, this means that the entire area must be partitioned into a series of culs-de-sac with a comb-like arrangement (Fig. 10.1B). The 'comb' may be regular, or topologically distorted to reduce the exit gradient effect still further (Fig. 10.1C). Both types allow for a separate entrance and exit. The culs-de-sac may then be further subdivided into chambers or alcoves off the main traffic paths. This is believed to increase holding power by dividing the content into well-defined steps, isolating the visitor from the distractions of crowd noise and adjacent exhibits, and allowing small groups to interact socially. Large open galleries present such a daunting prospect and seem to require such a large commitment, that many visitors do not progress further than the entrance.

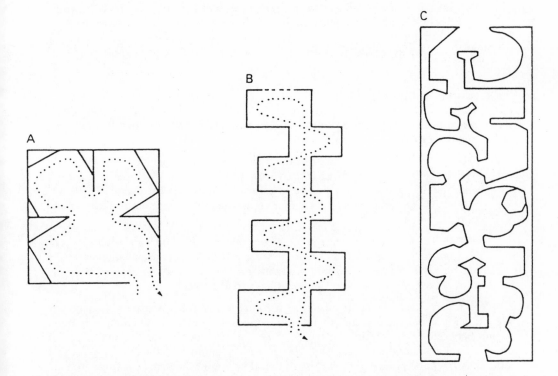

Fig. 10.1 Subdivision of exhibit space, after Lakota and Kantner 1976. Possible exit shown by broken line in B; main routes shown by dotted line in A and B

95

2. The organizational structure of the exhibition should be clear to the visitors

Exhibitions with a clear organizational structure appear to have greater holding power than those which have not. This idea presents few problems in the design of small cul-de-sac exhibitions, where visitors can see the over-all arrangement of the exhibits at a glance. The main problem with large galleries is that the over-all organization may not be obvious to visitors. Therefore, in order to guide them an orientation area should be provided at the entrance. This should communicate the organizational plan of the exhibition, and be linked to headings in the individual display areas which clearly state the concepts that are covered. The term 'organizational plan' is intended to cover more than the provision of a map of the gallery, where this is necessary. The aim should be to tell visitors what the exhibition is about, what it has to do with them, how it is organized conceptually, and what they can expect to learn from it. Ideally, all four should then be related to a map of the arrangement of the displays. With a large or complex exhibition, it seems clear that this information should be repeated at given points in the gallery, particularly where visitors might be faced with a choice of routes and therefore a decision about where to go next.

3. Island display units should be avoided or sited off the main routes through the gallery

The ability of a gallery to handle large numbers of visitors seems to depend primarily on the width of its major path. Exhibitions with free-standing island displays apparently possess significantly less holding power than those without such displays. It would appear that islands tend to be situated in the middle of the major path through the exhibition and thus reduce path width and increase crowd pressure. Anyone standing around such a display would be essentially blocking crowd flow at its most congested point.

Educational technology factors

1. Exhibits should have explicitly stated objectives which specify exactly what visitor effects are intended

Objectives here refer to the behaviour of the learner. Thus an objective for an evolution exhibit might be that after studying it the visitor will be able *to cite* three of Darwin's arguments against Special Creation. The case for objectives has been stated by Rowntree (1974: 35) in an epigrammatic form that applies equally well to both education and exhibition planning:

> If you don't know where you're going, you're liable to land up some place else! Or, of course, no place at all. But even if the some place else were useful and interesting (and usually it is not) you would probably find yourself with no time or resources left to get to the place you really should have tried to reach.

The practical value of objectives to those working in museums is that they encourage clear thought about the content, organization, and style of exhibits; facilitate communication between those working on the exhibits; and provide an honest foundation for evaluation. Lakota and Kantner (1976: 98), however, go much further, and suggest that objectives might be presented to visitors so that they know what can be learned from an exhibit. It is hypothesized that this will give direction to learning and aid visitors in organizing exhibit content. Highly specific objectives will concentrate attention on particular details of an exhibition and decrease incidental learning, while high-level objectives will increase, motivate, and promote incidental learning. An example (after Lakota and Kantner) of a caption with highly specific objectives for a palaeontological exhibit might be:

Look closely at the fossils in this exhibit. By finding their scientific names, and reading their labels, you will be able to:

- Name each fossil when shown its picture;
- Recognize the picture of each fossil when shown the name;
- Identify the order in which the fossils appeared from the oldest to the most recent.

Try it. Test yourself at the end of the exhibit, and see how well you did.

2. Careful thought should be given to the order in which information is to be learned and this order should be carried through to the design of the exhibits

Many exhibitions set out to tell a story, and most stories are not disorganized collections of facts (Shettel 1973: 40). Wittlin (1971: 149) makes the general point that 'Our understanding and appreciation of information grows when details are presented in a clear sequence and in a general context. A message with a beginning and an end has appeal to us.' However, this begs the question of how the information should be sequenced for any given exhibition, although we might assume that the traditional rules of sequence remain useful. These are: proceed from the known to the unknown; from the simple to the complex; from the concrete to the abstract; from observation to reasoning; and from a whole view to a more detailed view of the whole (Davies 1971: 41). Other strategies include beginning to end (e.g. in a historical or developmental context), deductive (from reasoning to observation), and geographical. Clearly the published rules sometimes contradict one another, and therefore have to be applied with discretion according to the nature of the exhibition. To this end we have adopted the notion of a concept or learning hierarchy (Gagné 1970) in organizing new exhibitions in the Natural History Museum (Miles and Tout 1978). This hierarchy is based on the theory that in order to understand C, the learner must first understand B. C is usually a concept, and B, its basis, two or more lower-order concepts. It is possible to draw on most of the familiar rules of sequence in constructing a hierarchy, but without having to follow them uncritically.

3. The material should be arranged in steps of appropriate size

This point has already been discussed in the context of dividing up the exhibition space into alcoves or chambers. But there is more to be said on the subject from other points of view, and these imply a further subdivision of the material within the alcoves. Firstly there is the fact noted by many authors (Melton 1935; Shettel 1973; Thier and Linn 1976; Linn 1976) that the typical visitor spends less than one minute on any one item in an exhibition. Wittlin (1971: 149) suggests that we 'like to use the human capacity to exercise our judgement in keeping with the brief measure of time we spend standing in front of a display'. Secondly, for physiological and perceptual reasons (reviewed by Wittlin 1971), the visitor needs to focus his eyes on single objects that interest him; he needs vacant spaces between these objects; and both his eyes and brain need to rest. Thirdly, from a psychological point of view there is a limit to the amount of information that can be communicated at any one time. Exhibits should provide the visitor with an opportunity to rest his mind; this 'is particularly true of the amount of text on a particular label, which can be easily controlled by dividing up the material into smaller pieces' (Shettel 1973: 40). A further method of reducing the length of text is mentioned below.

4. Provision should be made for various levels of ability, knowledge, and interest

Defining the target audience, for the practical purposes of design, is an exceptionally difficult task in a public museum. One advantage of the learning hierarchy is that it includes all the steps in the story of the exhibition, beginning with the most basic. These basic concepts are those which are assumed to be familiar to visitors when they arrive. The learning hierarchy thus allows for an exhibition which leads even the most uninformed visitors from the familiar through the less familiar to some totally unfamiliar concepts. Nevertheless, it is also important to provide sufficient information for the quicker, better-informed visitors, and the exhibition must be organized so that they do not have to work laboriously from one end to the other, with no freedom to 'skip' familiar material.

Wittlin (1971) has stressed the dangers of trying to combine displays which deliver an interesting and stimulating message to the general visitor (an 'interpretive' exhibit) with a 'scholar's library of specimens' (an 'underinterpretive' exhibit). She contends that such compromise exhibits remain underinterpretive and may even become misinterpretive, with the visitor's attention focused on the design rather than on the subject-matter. One answer to this problem is to provide an interpretive exhibit leading to another of limited interpretation. The general visitor, primed by guidance received in the first, can move on to the second if he or she so wishes. Such exhibits of limited interpretation are equivalent to the enrichment booklets of some modern school courses, and can be regarded as serving the same function i.e. satisfying the needs of the quicker, more highly motivated learner.

5. Provision should be made for visitors to engage in active response

The hypothesis behind this precept is that 'active participation heightens the acquisition and retention of information' (Shettel 1973: 40). Several lines of evidence support the case for active rather than purely passive learning (Thier and Linn 1976). However, there is a reason why active participation is particularly appropriate in a science museum. Science is a creative, exploratory activity, and therefore science museums should be places where visitors can ask questions and answer them by their own observations and experiments (Oppenheimer 1968: 174).

We must not forget that visitors do in any event, respond to exhibits, and that the aim in developing interactive exhibits is to improve the *quality* of that response, and thus the learning that results from it (Lakota and Kantner 1976: 122). However, responses do not need to be overt, and in many instances covert responses may be equally effective in stimulating learning, providing they are consistent with the objectives of the exhibition. Overt responses are perhaps most closely identified with mechanical, electronic, or electromechanical devices, but it is with these that the greatest danger of irrelevant activity arises. 'Flipping a switch, pushing a button and turning a crank are, in many instances, examples of participation for participation's sake, and have no useful function in achieving the objectives of the exhibit' (Shettel 1973: 40). Further, such devices tend to present severe maintenance problems. Nevertheless, participatory exhibits have been described that are not overtly complex in design. Wittlin (1971), for example, has described a very simple participatory exhibit on human teeth, in which the visitor provides all the elements of movement and response.

Labels which ask questions elicit a special class of covert responses. To be effective, questions should relate to the important features of the exhibition, particularly to specific objectives, and should focus and maintain attention on the objects on display. Question-asking labels have the additional advantage of brevity, and it is claimed that a single question can often communicate more to a visitor than an extensive text panel. With questions as with objectives, the highly specific ones will concentrate attention and reduce incidental learning, while the general ones will stimulate a wider view and increase incidental learning. Lakota and Kantner (1976: 108–10) recommend that highly specific questions be used liberally to maintain visitor attention, and contend that they are best placed before that part of the exhibition containing the related material. On the other hand, general questions, which promote incidental learning and are better for the casual visitor, should be placed after the material. At all events, the best results are obtained when the questions are placed in the closest possible proximity to the exhibit area they refer to.

6. Feedback should be provided after a correct response

In designing for a response, the question that designers have asked themselves is: how will visitors know when they have got it right? The notion of feedback in relation to museum learning was originally developed (Screven 1969: 9; Shettel 1973: 40) on the basis of laboratory experiments on reinforcement. However, being told that your answer is correct is now thought to be less important in learning than was previously believed. Lakota and Kantner (1976: 108–10) have summarized the present state of knowledge as follows: (1) unless feedback conveys new information it has no positive effect on retention; (2) right/wrong feedback is preferable to feedback which corrects a mistake by identifying the correct answer; and (3) it is better to give no feedback at all than to risk giving it before the response has been made.

This paper first appeared in Curation of Palaeontological Collections: Special Papers in Palaeontology 22 (1979), pp. 209–24.

ACKNOWLEDGEMENTS

We thank Kim Dennis for reading and commenting on the manuscript, and M. Alt for his comments on an earlier draft.

REFERENCES

Alt, M. (1977) 'Evaluating didactic exhibits; a critical look at Shettel's work', *Curator* 20: 241–58.

Cameron, D. F. (1968) 'A viewpoint: the museum as a communications system and implications for museum education', *Curator* 11: 33–40.

Churchman, C. W., Ackoff, R. L. and Arnoff, E. L. (1957) *An Introduction to Operations Research*, London.

Davies, I. K. (1971) *The Management of Learning*, London.

Eason, L. P. and Linn, M. C. (1976) 'Evaluation of the effectiveness of participatory exhibits', *Curator* 19: 45–62.

Gagné, R. M. (1970) *The Conditions of Learning*, 2nd edn, New York.

Hjorth, J. (1971) *How to Make a Rotten Exhibition*, 2nd edn, Stockholm (reprinted in *Curator*, 1977, 20: 185–204).

Krathwohl, D. R., Bloom, B. S. and Masia, B. B. (1964) *Taxonomy of Educational Objectives. Book 2. Affective Domain*, New York.

Lakota, R. A. (1975) 'The National Museum of Natural History as a behavioural environment. Part I. An environmental analysis of behavioural performance', Office of Museum Programs. Smithsonian Institution, Washington: 1–96.

Lakota, R. A. and Kantner, J. A. (1976) 'The National Museum of Natural History as a behavioural environment. Part II. Summary and recommendations', Office of Museum Programs. Smithsonian Institution, Washington: 1–123.

Linn, M. C. (1976) 'Exhibition evaluation – informed decision making', *Curator* 19: 291–302.

Loomis, R. J. (1973) 'Please not another visitor survey', *Museum News Washington* 52(2): 21–6.

Løvtrup, S. (1974) *Epigenetics*, London.

MacDonald-Ross, M. (1969) 'Programmed learning – a decade of development', *International Journal of Man-Machine Studies* 1: 73–100.

MacDonald-Ross, M. and Waller, R. (1975) 'Criticism, alternatives and tests: a conceptual framework for improving typography', *Programmed Learning*: 75–83.

Melton, A. W. (1935) 'Problems of installation in museums of art', *Publications of the American Association of Museums*, N.S. 14: 1–269.

Miles, R. S. and Tout, A. F. (1978) 'Human biology and the new exhibition scheme in the British Museum (Natural History)', *Curator* 20.

Morris, R. E. (1962) 'Leisure time and the museum', *Museum News Washington* 41(4): 17–21.

Oppenheimer, F. (1968) 'The role of science museums', in E. Larrabee (ed.) *Museum and Education*, Washington.

Parr, A. E. (1962) 'Some basic problems of visual education by means of exhibits', *Curator* 5: 36–44.

Popper, K. R. (1972) *Objective Knowledge. An Evolutionary Approach*, Oxford.

Popper, K R. (1976) *Unended Quest*, revised edn, London.

Rowntree, D. (1974) *Educational Technology in Curriculum Development*, London.

Screven, C. G. (1969) 'The museum as a responsive learning environment', *Museum News Washington* 47(10): 7–10.

Screven, C. G. (1976) 'Exhibit evaluation – a goal referenced approach', *Curator* 19: 271–90.

Scriven, M. (1976) 'The methodology of evaluation', in R. E. Stake (ed.) 'Perspectives of curriculum evaluation', *American Educational Research Association Monograph Series on Curriculum Evaluation* 1, Chicago: 39–82.

Shaw, E. (1972) 'The Exploratorium', *Curator* 15: 39–52.

Shettel, H. H. (1968) 'An evaluation of existing criteria for judging the quality of science exhibits', *Curator* 11: 137–53.

Shettel, H. H. (1973) 'Exhibits: art form or educational medium?' *Museum News Washington* 52(1): 32–41.

Swiecimski, J. (1977a) 'The problem of modernizations in museum exhibition design', *Museologia* 7(1): 3–25.

Swiecimski, J. (1977b) 'The problem of direction of exhibition modernizations and their causal basis', *Museologia* 8(7): 3–21.

Swiecimski, J. (1977c) 'Marginal forms of modernization of museum displays', *Museologia* 9(12): 3–25.

Tammadge, A. and Starr, P. (1977) *A Parent's Guide to School Mathematics*, Cambridge.

Thier, H. D. and Linn, M. C. (1976) 'The value of interactive learning experiences', *Curator* 19: 233–45.

Waddington, C. H. (1973) *O. R. in World War 2*, London.

Wittlin, A. S. (1971) 'Hazards of communication by exhibits', *Curator* 14: 138–50.

11

Impact of research on the approach to the visiting public at the Natural History Museum, London

Roger S. Miles and Alan F. Tout

Following nearly two decades of research into the effectiveness of exhibitions at the Natural History Museum, the approach used, which was originally based on programmed learning and educational technology, has been changed. While still using sound basic principles of communication and upholding the original educative purpose, recent exhibitions are more visitor oriented. They are designed on the basis of detailed knowledge of the audience, pay more attention to the entire gallery as an experience rather than concentrating on the individual exhibits, and take affective, or motivational, as well as cognitive objectives into account.

INTRODUCTION

In the early 1970s the Natural History Museum in London drew up long-term plans to renew its public galleries because the existing exhibitions were believed to be dull, old-fashioned, irrelevant and too technical. The aim was to produce educational exhibitions which would help the general public to understand current science. The first new exhibition, the *Hall of Human Biology*, opened in 1977. This paper sets out to show how subsequent research has shaped our design philosophy. A great deal of exhibition research has been carried out in Europe and North America since the pioneering work of Robinson (1928) and Melton (1935). Research in this field has certain inherent difficulties to which we refer later, but nevertheless far more has been carried out than we have space to deal with here, so we have concentrated on two studies which have significantly affected our approach to the task of developing educational exhibitions. A list of published work based on studies in the Natural History Museum is appended to illustrate the range of investigations undertaken by staff and others.

THE STARTING POINT

Our new-style exhibitions were from the outset aimed at improving the public understanding of science. In the beginning the only technology relevant to this aim was that of programmed learning (Miles and Tout 1978, 1979, Miles 1986). In order to communicate an understanding of the concepts and processes of modern science the exhibitions were therefore designed:

(a) from the bottom up, i.e. from the concepts to be communicated rather than from the gallery space to be filled, so that the emphasis was placed on the intellectual content of the exhibits rather than on objects *per se*;

(b) with well-defined aims and objectives;

(c) with the subject matter divided up into easily managed chunks, organized in a clear logical sequence, with this sequence made manifest in the physical form of the exhibition;

(d) using a variety of media of communication and embracing hands-on ('interactive') and dynamic exhibits;

(e) with a range of supplementary books and other materials for use either within or outside the museum.

The museum was seen as providing an informal environment for learning, with individuals (except those in school parties) providing their own agendas. We believed that in comparison with what had gone before, our approach was learner- (i.e. visitor-) oriented, with attention paid to affective as well as to cognitive objectives. The exhibitions certainly attracted visitors, but as the list above suggests, the initial emphasis was entirely on the subject-matter and the efficient transmission of information, and it was only later that we began to understand and respond to the meaning of a museum visit to the visitor.

EARLY RESEARCH

Human Biology was seen as an experiment, a prototype that allowed us to test a range of ideas and approaches under real conditions. Our plan was to build the exhibitions, study how well they worked (summative evaluation), then use the results to revise weak exhibits and inform work on subsequent projects. We discovered that this approach did not work (Miles 1988a). Consequently, summative evaluation was largely replaced by the testing of mock-up exhibits during development (formative evaluation) and audience analysis during planning (front-end evaluation). Research of this type is mostly concerned with short-term problem solving, so the results are often not written up in a formal way and consequently not published (but see Griggs 1981, Griggs and Manning 1983, Jarrett 1986).

Summative evaluation has two practical (as distinct from financial or political) disadvantages that lessen its value to the exhibition developer. First, any attempt to measure factual learning from exhibitions by comparing separate random samples of visitors before and after their visit is inappropriate because it makes no allowance for the way people use museums (see below), and also makes impossible demands on the visitor's memory. Second, it does not show how to correct any fault it has uncovered. Recommendations appended to a summative evaluation of the orientation system (maps, signposts, etc.) in the museum's 1981 *Origin of Species* exhibition (Griggs 1983) come not from the study but from the literature of psychology.

THE IDEAL EXHIBIT

A central factor in the study of how visitors behave towards museums is what the visitor conceives to be the ideal exhibit. In a pioneering attempt to evaluate this, Alt and Shaw (1984) asked each of twenty visitors to the Natural History Museum to comment on three exhibits out of forty-five in the *Hall of Human Biology* and used the results to draw up a list of exhibit attributes. In the second part of the study 990 visitors were each asked to say whether or not the listed attributes applied (a) to each of two of the forty-five exhibits and (b) to what they considered to be the ideal exhibit. Efforts were made to balance and randomize as appropriate when selecting the exhibits for a particular visitor, which is why the number of visitors involved in the second part of the study was so much larger than in the first.

Normally, evaluation is seen as an investigation of a simple, two-sided relationship: an exhibit and how a visitor reacts to it. But this is an artificially isolated relationship which ignores visitors' more general expectations of museum exhibits. Alt and Shaw's study added another dimension by asking visitors not only how well the exhibit worked for them, but also how they rated it against their conception of an ideal.

By using this technique, Alt and Shaw were able to identify characteristics which visitors felt an ideal exhibition should have. These formed a spectrum from positive attributes which ideal exhibits should have, through neutral to negative attributes which would be absent in an ideal.

Positive:

- makes the subject come to life
- makes its point quickly
- has something for all ages
- is memorable

Neutral:

- participatory
- deals with the subject better than textbooks
- is artistic
- makes a difficult subject easier

Negative:

- badly placed; not easily noticed
- does not give enough information
- one's attention is distracted by other displays
- is confusing

When applying the authors' conclusions in the context of museums as a whole it should be remembered that the attribute list, which has a vital role, is based on a single small sample drawn over a short period.

Griggs (1990) extended Alt and Shaw's technique to compare seven exhibitions in the Natural History Museum, three modern, three traditional and one recently completed but of traditional rather than modern style, *British Natural History*. As a first step, in 120 interviews, he asked visitors to describe the exhibits in these exhibitions in their own words. From this he collected over 350 descriptions which he categorized and summarized into fifteen statements. These represented the visitors' point of view. To these he added a further six which fell into one or other of two categories and represented the museum's concerns. Some reflected criteria which the design team felt to be important because of previous experience, the others reflected criteria which pinpointed differences between the old and new style of exhibitions but which were not adequately covered by the initial list. In the second part of the study another group of 650 visitors were interviewed as they left one of the seven exhibitions. They were shown each of the twenty-one statements and asked to say how well the statement described the particular exhibition. They were also asked to say how much it mattered if an exhibition did or did not have the characteristic in question. The aim was to discover which characteristics visitors used to discriminate between the various exhibitions.

Griggs found some characteristics to be generally desirable, e.g. visitors expected the subject-matter to be well explained and easy to understand irrespective of the style of the exhibition. However, a few characteristics, some desirable and some not, discriminated between old and new style exhibitions (with *British Natural History* in an intermediate position). The lists below are in descending order of importance.

Desirable characteristics:

- It is obvious where one should begin and how one should continue.
- Uses a lot of modern display techniques which help one to learn.
- Uses familiar things and experiences to make its points.
- Includes a comprehensive display of objects and/or specimens.

Undesirable characteristics:

- Subject-matter not sufficiently explained.
- Exhibits not realistic enough: difficult to relate to the real world.
- Appealing to children but less so to adults.
- Traditional in style; old-fashioned.

Discussion

Alt and Shaw (1984) acknowledge the difficulties of museum research, to which we referred in our opening paragraph. A balance has to be struck between scientific rigour and practical considerations. The major difficulty is that interviews which are numerous enough to be statistically adequate and long enough to provide substantial information interfere too much with the subject's visit. Furthermore, museums invariably have insufficient funds available to do all the things they would like to do, so the resources available for what amounts to market research are pitifully small in comparison with those available in industry. What manufacturer would base his marketing plans on a mere twenty interviews?

The result of these difficulties is that one invariably ends up trying to draw useful conclusions from a paucity of data and has to make do with tentative rather than well-tested hypotheses. However, the studies we have referred to are particularly significant because, when coupled with the knowledge acquired through experience in mounting exhibitions and informally observing visitors to the Natural History Museum over the past fifteen years, they provide strong empirical data consistent with the emerging picture of a typical museum visit.

Many studies have shown that the time a visitor spends at an exhibit is both on average short (around thirty seconds) and variable – from nil to three-quarters of an hour. The upper limit is much longer than the designers of most exhibits expect. As Alt and Shaw point out, truly interactive, or participatory, exhibits generally make much bigger demands on the visitor's time than non-participatory ones. Where little explanation is required adequate time is fairly readily given, but lengthy instructions tend to put the visitor off. Participative and non-participative exhibits therefore need to be sharply distinguished and treated accordingly.

People (except in school parties) visit museums in their leisure time, and for many the visit is a social occasion – a chance to be with family and friends. They expect to learn something, but entertainment and social interaction are as important, if not more important, reasons for the visit (Miles 1988b). The average visit lasts less than two-and-a-half hours, and only half or less of the time is devoted to the exhibits. Most of the time the visitor is moving around, actively exploring, more concerned with the gallery as a whole than with individual exhibits. Most exhibits are inspected somewhat casually, with time and effort devoted only to those that, for one reason or another, engage the attention. Fatigue, in the form of object satiation rather than physical tiredness, becomes apparent after about thirty minutes. After this visitors stop at exhibits less often, and the number at which they stop for a long time diminishes progressively (Miles and Tout 1991, with refs).

This composite picture of the typical museum visit provides the context within which we have to work, so the better we understand what happens during the typical visit, the better we are able to plan exhibitions which will meet the aim of providing an environment in which informal learning can take place. It is clearly no longer good enough to offer visitors what we think is good for them and hope that they will spend as much time on it as is necessary for them to fulfil our educational goals. Instead we must attempt to convince visitors that what is on offer is something beneficial and worth the time they must spend on it.

The researches of Alt and Shaw and Griggs give us a further insight into the overall perceptions and expectations of our visitors and provide a practical basis for designing successful educational exhibitions. However, we should also note that Griggs's results in particular are consistent with secular principles of communication, tacitly known to generations of human beings, of purpose, structure, variety and pacing, and which are, *inter alia*, formalized in educational technology. In the case of the Natural History Museum the new paradigm has led to a shift in emphasis (but no more than that) from cognitive to affective objectives, from individual exhibits to the entire gallery as an experience, and from evaluating exhibits to learning about the audience. In the wider context the view of museums as storehouses of factual information to be memorized has been discredited and replaced by one in which they are seen as places where people find new vistas opening up and their interests awakened, so that they may be launched on paths of learning and find guidance on how to move onwards.

There is sometimes a sense of disappointment when one cannot say what people learn in museums, but we can now see that this stems from a wrong conception of what museums are. They are not 'machines à apprendre', though there certainly exist techniques for measuring the potential of exhibitions to deliver clear messages to suitably motivated audiences. In reality they are places people visit for a variety of social reasons, places which offer, amongst other things, opportunities for learning if, and only if, visitors decide that this is what they want.

This paper first appeared in International Journal of Science Education 13(5) (1991), pp. 534–49.

ACKNOWLEDGEMENT

We are grateful to Dr Giles Clarke for his critical comments on our first draft.

REFERENCES

Alt, M. B. and Shaw, K. M. (1984) 'Characteristics of ideal museum exhibits', *British Journal of Psychology* 75: 25–36.

Griggs, S. A. (1981) 'Formative evaluation of exhibits at the British Museum (Natural History)', *Curator* 24(3): 189–202.

Griggs, S. A. (1983) 'Orientating visitors within a thematic display', *International Journal of Museum Management and Curators* 2: 119–34.

Griggs, S. A. (1990) 'Perceptions of traditional versus new style exhibitions at The Natural History Museum', *ILVS Review* 1(2): 78–90.

Griggs, S. A. and Manning, J. (1983) 'The predictive validity of formative evaluations of exhibits', *Museum Studies Journal* 1(2): 31–41.

Jarrett, J. E. (1986) 'Learning from developmental testing of exhibits', *Curator* 29(4): 295–306.

Melton, A. (1935) 'Problems of installation in museums of art', *Publications of the American Association of Museums*, N.S. 14: 1–269.

Miles, R. S. (1986) 'Lessons in "Human Biology": testing a theory of exhibition design', *International Journal of Museum Management and Curatorship* 5: 227–40.

Miles, R. S. (1988a) 'Exhibit evaluation in the British Museum (Natural History)', *ILVS Review* 1(1): 24–33.

Miles, R. S. (1988b) 'Museums and public culture, a context for communicating science', in P. G. Heltne and L. A. Marquardt (eds) *Science Learning in the Informal Setting*, Chicago, IL: Chicago Academy of Sciences: 157–69

Miles, R. S. and Tout, A. F. (1978) 'Human biology and the new exhibition scheme in the British Museum (Natural History)', *Curator* 21(1): 36–50.

Miles, R. S. and Tout, A. F. (1979) 'Outline of a technology for effective science exhibits', *Special Papers in Palaeontology*, London: The Palaeontological Association 22: 209–24.

Miles, R. S. and Tout, A. F. (1991) 'Holding power: to choose time is to save time', *ASTC Newsletter* 19(3): 7–9.

Robinson, E. S. (1928) 'The behavior of the museum visitor', *Publications of the American Association of Museums*, N.S. 5: 1–72.

APPENDIX: ADDITIONAL PUBLISHED PAPERS BASED ON STUDIES IN THE NATURAL HISTORY MUSEUM

Alt, M. B. (1979) 'Improving audio-visual presentations', *Curator* 22(2): 85–95.

Alt, M. B. (1980) 'Four years of visitor surveys at the British Museum (Natural History) 1976–79', *Museums Journal* 80: 10–19.

Alt, M. B. (1983) 'Visitors' attitudes to two old and two new exhibitions at the British Museum (Natural History)', *Museums Journal* 83: 145–8.

Falk, J. H. (1983) 'Time and behavior as predictors of learning', *Science Education* 67(2): 267–76.

Griggs, S. A. and Alt, M. B. (1982) 'Visitors to the British Museum (Natural History) in 1980 and 1981', *Museums Journal* 82: 149–55.

Lucas, A. M., McManus, P. and Thomas, G. (1986) 'Investigating learning from informal sources: listening to conversations and observing play in a science museum', *European Journal of Science Education* 4: 341–52.

McManus, P. M. (1985) 'Worksheet induced behaviour in the British Museum (Natural History)', *Journal of Biological Education* 19: 237–42.

McManus, P. M. (1987) 'It's the company you keep . . . The social determination of learning-related behaviour in a science museum', *International Journal of Museum Management and Curatorship* 6: 263–70.

McManus, P. M. (1988) 'Good companions: more on the social determination of learning-related behaviour in a science museum', *International Journal of Museum Management and Curatorship* 7: 37–44.

McManus, P. M. (1988) 'Do you get my meaning? Perception, ambiguity and the museum visitor', *ILVS Review* 1(1): 62–75.

McManus P. M. (1989) 'What research says about learning in science museums: Watch your language! People do read labels', *ASTC Newsletter* 17(3): 5–6.

McManus, P. M. (1989) 'Oh, yes, they do: how museum visitors read labels and interact with exhibit texts', *Curator* 32(3): 174–88.

Miles, R. S. (1985) 'Formative evaluation (Prozessevaluation) und der Entwicklungsprozess von Ausstellungselementen im British Museum (Natural History)', in B. Graf and G. Knerr (eds), *Museumsausstellungen: Planung, Design, Evaluation* München: Deutsches Museum: 35–44.

Miles, R. S. (1987) 'Museums and the communication of science', in D. Evered and M. O'Connor (eds), *Communicating Science to the Public*, Ciba Foundation Conference, London: Wiley: 114–30.

Miles, R. S. (1989) 'Audiovisuals, a suitable case for treatment', *Visitor Studies: Theory, Research and Practice* 2: 245–51.

Miles, R. S. and Alt, M . B. (1979) 'The British Museum (Natural History): a new approach to the visiting public', *Museums Journal* 79: 1158–62.

Morris, R. G. M. and Alt, M. B. (1978) 'An experiment to help design a map for a large museum', *Museums Journal* 77: 179–80.

12

Cognitive psychology and interpretation: synthesis and application

Sam H. Ham

Research into how we learn (cognitive psychology) offers some useful hints on how to structure and present communicative acts, whether they are exhibitions, talks, or texts.

Meaningfulness, relevance and conceptual organization are identified as key elements for information processing. The focus of the article is on the way in which people respond within a communicative situation. Ways to shape interpretation so as to enable people to respond are suggested. Although focusing on face-to-face communication the ideas discussed are of great relevance to exhibitions.

This paper makes a useful companion piece to chapter 10 by Roger Miles and Alan Tout.

Although interpretive research has traditionally borrowed from other behavioural sciences (e.g., educational psychology, social psychology, and sociology), little attention has been given to the existing vast body of research on human cognition. Dick *et al.* (1974) based an earlier paper on the contention that interpreters were often unaware of communication principles that could be derived from social psychology and persuasion research. Although otherwise impressive in its breadth, the Dick *et al.* paper was notably void of references to cognitive psychology.

The purpose of this paper is to show the application of cognitive psychology in interpretive research and practice. As such, the focus is both theoretical and applied. The first part of the paper examines past experiments on human cognition and suggests five propositions for future interpretive research and theory. The second part of the paper discusses potential applications of cognitive psychology in designing interpretive presentations.

COGNITIVE PSYCHOLOGY AND INTERPRETATION

Cognitive psychology examines how humans gain and store external information in memory, and how they utilize it to direct their attention and behaviour (Solso 1979). It includes such topics as sensory perception, pattern recognition, attention, memory, mental imagery, semantic organization, thinking and problem solving. Although a discussion of each of these topics is beyond the scope of this paper, interpreters should intuitively find many of them relevant. Consequently, it has probably *not* been a lack of relevance that has prevented interpretive researchers from considering cognition research, but rather that cognitive psychology has not traditionally focused on human communication *per se*.

Nevertheless, knowledge of how humans gain, organize and store information can be useful in better understanding interpretation. Hammitt (1981), for example, borrowed heavily from cognition research to reformulate Tilden's seminal principles of interpretation, and Tai (1981) and Hammitt (1978) both adopted a cognitive psychology framework to evaluate the effectiveness of self-guided interpretive services. In this paper I attempt to apply cognitive psychology to the problem of designing personal interpretive presentations, with emphasis on the variables of audience attention, comprehension and recall.

For present purposes, 'interpretation' is viewed as an agency's communication with non-captive audiences in leisure settings. The distinction between captive and noncaptive audiences is necessary since it is well accepted that people in leisure settings place special demands on interpreters and interpretation (Field and Wagar 1973). Perhaps the most important of these demands state: 1) interpretation must be entertaining and interesting since external incentives for audiences to pay attention (e.g., exams, grades, etc.) do not exist in leisure settings; and 2) interpretation must be understandable and therefore relatively easy for audiences to process mentally. Central to the interest and understandability of interpretation are factors of *meaningfulness, relevance* and *conceptual organization*. I will discuss these factors as they relate to the development of personal presentations for noncaptive audiences. (See Witt (1983) for a discussion of psychology pertaining to audio-visual presentations.)

The meaningfulness of information presented to audiences (particularly noncaptive audiences) is important to achieving the purposes of presentations – recall, conceptual understanding, and so forth. Considerable research in cognitive psychology focuses directly on this topic, and a number of studies have indirect bearing. Most of this research empirically substantiates what Freeman Tilden (1977: 9) said in his first principle of interpretation:

> Any interpretation that does not somehow relate what is being displayed or described to something within the personality or experience of the visitor will be sterile.

For instance, Glucksberg *et al.* (1966) found that when a child located on one side of an opaque screen was given verbal instructions for a recognition task by another child on the opposite side of the screen, performance was fair to poor. However, when the same child was later read *his/her own* instructions (the same ones he/she had earlier given to another child), performance improved dramatically. The authors suggested that people can more readily understand information if it is presented exactly as they themselves would say it.

Commenting on the Glucksberg *et al.* study, Dale (1972) attributed the results to ego-centrism (the child's inability to see reality through another's eyes). A *meaningfulness* hypothesis, which holds that improved understanding is due to the similarity between the information presented and the recipient's own verbal style, would be even more pertinent.

Meaningfulness can be viewed as the number of semantic associations a person has for a particular word. The greater the number of associations, the more meaningful the word (Ellis, 1978). This conceptualization is consistent with results of the Glucksberg *et al.* (1966) study, given that people describe their world in the most meaningful descriptors possible. Therefore, it might follow that the more similar the semantic structure of a message and the verbal style of an audience, the more meaningful the audience will find the message. Thus we see today's trend toward plain-language contracts and insurance policies, as well as Bibles written in twentieth-century style.

Meaningfulness, of course, is only one factor determining our interest in a message. Perhaps even more important is the relevance of the message (i.e., the degree to which we have prior ego-involvement with the topic). An interesting phenomenon illustrating the importance of ego-involvement has been repeatedly observed in laboratory experiments on selective attention. These studies have utilized an experimental method called 'shadowing' in which a subject is presented simultaneous tape recordings of two messages, and is instructed to focus attention on one and ignore the other. In addition, the subject is asked to repeat (shadow) the attended spoken message as it is presented. To control for the discriminating effect of voice tonal qualities the same speaker records both messages. The subject usually wears stereo headphones to prevent overlap of messages in the same ear.

Cherry (1966) conducted such an experiment and found that his subjects were reasonably able to shadow under certain conditions, but that the content of the shadowed message was poorly remembered. The unattended message, of course, was even more vague. In fact, it was so poorly understood that a switch from English to German on the unattended channel went undetected. In an earlier study Moray (1959) obtained similar results and discovered that subjects could say little about the unattended message despite the fact that selected words were repeated up to thirty-five times. However, when he prefaced the unshadowed message with *the subject's name* the subject paid more attention to it and remembered more about it.

An experiment by Neisser (1969) demonstrated that the same striking phenomenon occurs when we read. Neisser had his subjects read the lines of one colour from a text consisting of sentences in alternating colours. As in the Cherry and Moray experiments, little was retained from the unattended message except when the subject's name appeared. Thus, people appear to listen to and look at the world selectively. Although individuals pay attention to only a small number of stimuli at one time, there is considerably more monitoring going on than is realized. And, it is evident people will readily switch their attention to those stimuli most important to them. Solso (1979: 122) summed up the universality of this phenomenon:

> And isn't this also true at the cocktail party? Someone on the other side of the room says: 'And I understand Bob and Lee . . . ' And, until then completely engrossed in other conversations, all the Bob's and Lee's turn a live ear to the speaker.

E. F. Hutton stock consultant advertisements on television present a similar example of selective attention. Also consider how well parents can distinguish between the shouting of countless children in a nursery or playground and that of their own.

Based on results of these studies, it can be hypothesized that audiences will be more interested in presentations that occasionally mention their names. This not being very likely (or practical) under most circumstances, one might speculate that presentations which (as Tilden suggested) rely on information important to the *common experiences* of the audience will command greater attention. Numerous investigations have shown the influence of self reference on audience retention of information. In fact, there is evidence to indicate that simply *telling* audience members to use themselves and their experiences to judge the relevance of presented information can significantly improve learning and recall (Rogers 1977, Cartwright 1956). In other studies, Craik and Tulving (1975) and Rogers *et al.* (1977) reported that subjects' recall of words that remind them of themselves was superior to their recall of other words. Consistent with Craik and Lockhart's (1972) 'Levels of Processing Theory', these findings demonstrate that personally relevant information is more deeply encoded than other kinds of information, and hence more easily remembered.

Put another way, human perception capabilities are limited. There is a constant trade-off between what we attend to and what is ignored. People will consciously choose to focus on information which is most important to them for the moment. That is, temporarily at least, some information is more relevant than the other stimuli vying for attention. High relevance seems to make perception and processing of information easier. (Consider the sometimes extreme effort required to pay attention to boring presentations one is later expected to know something about.) Thus, people are more sensitive to relevant information than to stimuli of questionable relevance. Such information is sometimes termed *low threshold* since it easily enters the conscious experience despite the existence of considerable competing stimuli (Morton 1969, Tulving and Gold 1963).

In summary, the relevance of a message appears to be strongly influenced by the recipient's background. A person's name, members of his/her family, occupation, religion, values, semantic style and other factors which exist permanently in memory can significantly affect the perceived importance and meaningfulness of information to that individual. To be most relevant and most meaningful, presentations must be geared to audience characteristics that enhance ego-involvement and understanding of the topic.

A presentation that is relevant and meaningful at one point, however, may not necessarily be so at the next. If the topic becomes confusing or dull, or for any reason requires the audience to expend undue effort to maintain attention, the audience will likely tune it out by switching attention to a more gratifying stimulus.

Clearly, the presentation must remain relevant throughout, and it must be organized in a way that allows the audience to process incoming information as rapidly and as efficiently as possible. When the organization of the presentation becomes fuzzy to the audience, the audience must work harder to maintain the train of thought. This effort is then spent at the expense of processing subsequent information; it also (especially for noncaptive audiences) increases the likelihood of attention switching. Therefore, not only should presentations be geared toward common experiences of the audience, but they must also be couched in an organizational framework which helps audiences organize and understand the connections between separate bits of information.

THE EFFECT OF CONCEPTUAL FRAMEWORKS

Without a clear conceptual framework an audience will usually attempt to provide its own. This may be accomplished by asking questions of a speaker. Although few non-classroom settings are conducive to two-way interaction, at least one study (Ham and Shew 1979) suggested that opportunities to participate verbally significantly increased audience enjoyment of interpretive activities. If circumstances or inhibition prevent the individual from asking questions in order to clarify the conceptual framework, he/she may resort to an implicit (or assumed) organization. Thus, when people enter a movie or conversation late, the information they attempt to process is out of context. Normally, they wait until they think they have got the gist of the conversation before jumping into it. Undoubtedly, some are less patient and are willing to guess about conceptual frameworks earlier than others. Often such guesses result in 'off-the-wall' (out of context) statements and provide humour and embarrassment for the conversationalists and newcomer, respectively.

It seems individuals are continually checking what they *think* is the conceptual organization of a message against each new piece of information processed. As long as the pieces fit into the context perceived up to that point, the processing of information occurs efficiently (almost effortlessly). When a piece does not readily fit the conceptual framework, however, it is held out of context until the organizational 'error' has been discovered. If the error is discovered relatively soon, little interest or understanding is lost. If, on the other hand, a workable framework is not soon constructed, considerable extraneous information may build up out of context and the individual becomes hopelessly confused. At this point attention switching is likely to occur, especially for non-captive audiences not willing to spend the extra effort to sort things out.

Studies on how humans recognize and utilize patterns help to demonstrate the effect of conceptual frameworks on learning and understanding. Many studies (e.g., Allen *et al.* 1978; Biederman *et al.* 1973; Lockhart 1968; Palmer 1975; and Tulving and Osler 1968) have collectively demonstrated that: (1) one pays more attention to information rich in association, while tending to ignore unassociative (out-of-context) information; (2) a conceptual framework will add meaning and relevance to new information only to the extent that the new information is consistent with the conceptual framework; (3) once established, the conceptual framework is used by the audience to judge the relevance of subsequent information; (4) information not readily processed into the conceptual framework is lost in a relatively short period of time; and (5) people can consciously control attention and often appear to do so on the basis of contextual clues and ease of processing. Thus, there is strong evidence that recall and learning are made easier by contextual information, and this is precisely what conceptual frameworks do for verbal presentations.

Of particular importance to interpreters are experiments by Thorndyke (1977) which illustrated the influence conceptual frameworks can have on audience comprehension and recall of information presented in story format. Thorndyke presented his subjects four different versions of the same story. The versions were nearly identical in information content but varied in how the information was organized within the story. His findings revealed that story comprehensibility and audience recall were indeed determined by how much 'plot structure' a story contained.

A major finding was that presenting the theme (plot structure) at the outset of a story served as a major organizer which allowed subjects to see the context of subsequent information. In fact, in presentations containing no theme statement at all, even presenting sentences in *random order* made no difference in subjects' recall or comprehensibility ratings of the story (i.e., both were low). Thus, an athematic presentation can make as little sense to us as a random presentation of unrelated sentences. In addition, when subjects were later asked to summarize the story in their own words, they tended to remember information reflecting the conceptual organization of the story, and to forget details and other subordinate information. This indicates that not only do conceptual frameworks facilitate the processing of information, they also constitute most of what is retained in memory after a message is communicated.

Contextual clues also permit a phenomenon called *chunking* (or clustering). Chunking is the term given to our ability to consolidate diverse pieces of information into a lesser number of manageable conceptual *chunks* (i.e., putting similar pieces of information into categories or patterns).

The human mind is limited in the number of unrelated stimuli it can simultaneously process. Miller (1956) demonstrated a principle that still stands: human perceptual capacity is limited to about seven (actually seven ± two) discrete stimuli. Thus, processing four pieces of unrelated information would be relatively easy for most people, whereas processing eight or more pieces would provide insurmountable difficulty. Cognitive chunking considerably (perhaps indefinitely) increases the raw amount of information that can be simultaneously processed by humans. In short, if contextual clues are available, meaningful associations among diverse stimuli can be recognized and *categories* rather than individual pieces of information are held in memory. Thus seven ± two) categories, each containing several associated elements can be processed.

There is much support for the idea that chunking makes pattern recognition possible for humans. Biederman and his associates (Biederman 1972; Biederman *et al.* 1973) found that subjects could more accurately and more rapidly recognize test objects when the objects were located in real world rather than jumbled scenes. Palmer (1975) obtained similar results and concluded that contextual clues provided by situational characteristics normally associated with an object (e.g., a college campus, or a line drawing of a face) provide a meaningful conceptual framework which makes possible recognition of the object (a particular dormitory or an isolated part of the drawing). In recognizing a face or a campus scene, of course, countless stimuli are simultaneously perceived and recognized as a pattern. Similarly, Chase and Simon (1973) found that although master chess players and beginners could think ahead the same number of moves, engaged in similar searches for strategies, and spent about the same amount of time scanning the board, the masters could reconstruct a chess pattern from memory much more rapidly and accurately than beginners. As Solso (1979: 67) pointed out:

> ... these data indicate that the ability to see 'chunks' or meaningful clusters of chess pieces made it possible for the better players to gather more information in the given time.

A series of experiments by Tulving (Tulving and Gold 1963; Tulving and Pearlstone 1966; Tulving and Osler 1968; Tulving and Psotka 1971; Tulving 1974) dramatically demonstrated the influence of chunking on learning and recall of information. In all cases, subjects who memorized contextually-related words were better able to recall them at a later time than subjects who had memorized unrelated words. Furthermore, when the words to be remembered were explicity asked for in terms of category names that helped organize the word list, recall was as efficient as the original learning itself, even after ten minutes. In no case, however, had subjects been given the category names ahead of time; nor had they been permitted to rehearse the lists of words (ranging from 24 to 120 total words) during the waiting period. Bower *et al.* (1969: 340) who conducted similar experiments, summarized the significance of such findings.

> If (a subject) can discover or learn a simple rule or principle which characterizes the items on a list and which relates them to one another, then he uses that rule as a retrieval plan in reconstructing the items from memory, with a consequent improvement in his performance.

In the Bower *et al.* study, recall was two to three times better for organized presentations than for randomized lists of words.

The implication of these studies for applied communication is that presentations must be carefully designed to direct audience members' natural tendency to chunk discrete information into meaningful generalizations. Since much information in interpretive activities may be new to audiences, it is important that contextual clues be readily discernible. If these clues already exist (or have associates) in a person's memory, they will be even more useful organizers of information. For instance, consider the difficulty one might have recalling the letter serial:

FB ... IPH ... DTW ... AIB ... M

If, however, the serial was changed so that the sequence of the letters elicited associations from long-term memory, the task might be remarkably easy. That is essentially what Bower and Springston (1970) found when they presented the same serial to subjects as:

FBI . . . PHD . . . TWA . . . IBM

The results for this serial (and others) were that recall was more accurate when the discrete letters were presented in meaningful context (i.e., only four pieces of information had to be stored in order to recall the twelve-letter serial).

Clearly, the processing of incoming information is made easier when the information is presented in a way that encourages chunking. For instance, the complex natural history of a mammal might seem amazingly simple if presented in the context of just three or four key organizers (e.g., food, cover, space or niche, habitat and competition). Therefore, although perceptual capacity is only about seven units, the amount of raw information contained (chunked) in each unit can vary enormously, and according to one psychologist (Solso 1979), perhaps up to the limits of the central nervous system itself. Consequently, the *amount* of information presented in an interpretive activity may not be as important as the conceptual framework used to present it. As previously emphasized, the easier it is for audiences to receive a message, the more likely they will pay attention and be able to recall it later.

RECOMMENDATIONS FOR DESIGNING PRESENTATIONS

An old cliché in speech communication goes: Tell them what you are going to say; then say it; and then tell them what you said. From the standpoint of providing a conceptual framework, this is undeniably good advice. But it may oversimplify a complex task by ignoring the issues of meaningfulness and relevance outlined earlier. The following discussion attempts to integrate the research described by suggesting a more theoretically-grounded approach to planning and organizing interpretive presentations. Central to this discussion is the concept of *theme* which is presented in some detail.

Selecting the theme of a presentation is an important organizational step for interpreters. *Theme* and *topic*, although frequently used synonymously, are not equivalent. Whereas the topic delineates the *subject matter* of a presentation (thereby restricting the range of possible themes), the *theme* is viewed as the underlying thought or major point the interpreter wants to make (Lewis 1980). Thorndyke (1977) describes it as 'the general focus to which the plot adheres'. In essence, the theme is the answer to the question, 'So what?' The theme of a presentation whose topic is desert animals might be: 'Desert animals have developed unique ways of adapting to hot environments.' An alternative theme might be. 'Many desert animals are nocturnal.' Although related in content, development of these alternative themes might be substantially different.

Clearly, *how* a theme is developed is important to whether audiences will find it easy or difficult to follow (Thorndyke 1977). It is therefore recommended that the body of the presentation be produced first in a flow chart format showing the theme and cognitive pathways through which it is to be developed (Fig. 12.1). People do this covertly in a variety of situations. Consider the mental processing one uses to recall and retell a joke he/she has not told for some time. Normally one first thinks of the punchline, the 'so what' of the joke (theme). Then the attention turns to the pieces of information required and the sequence in which they must be mentioned to ensure that the intended humour will be realized (and hopefully appreciated) by the listener. After one has considered these things, he or she has implicitly developed a conceptual framework around a theme, and has designed the framework to accomplish predetermined ends.

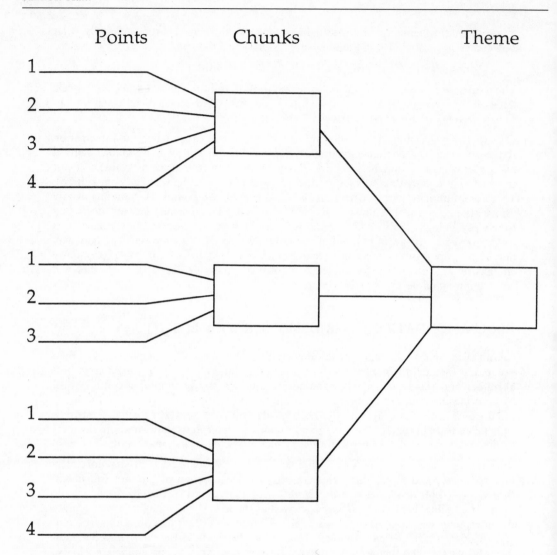

Fig. 12.1 Conceptual relationship between individual pieces of information, cognitive 'chunks' and the theme of a hypothetical presentation

Usually, the development of other types of presentations will require three distinct parts – an introduction, body and conclusion. In addition, careful thought should be given to the *vehicle* with which the theme is to be developed. Each of these considerations will now be discussed.

The way the theme is introduced and concluded depends entirely on the specific points to be mentioned in the body. For this reason, the body of the presentation should be developed first. This should be approached as in the 'joke' example above. Based on the theme, one should select the discrete points that need to be presented (Fig. 12.1). Consider the sequence of these points required to provide contextual clues and to enhance the listener's processing of information. Changes in thought or direction will require transitions. Transitional phrases are often overlooked in interpretive presentations, yet if these crucial threads are lacking, an otherwise well-organized presentation may fall apart. Transitional phrases demonstrate the relationship of what *has* been said to what *will* be said. Thus they facilitate chunking and reduce required audience effort.

The discrete points selected, their sequence of presentation, and the nature of transitional phrases depend on the *vehicle*. Even the most carefully designed conceptual frameworks can be dull. The vehicle is essentially a strategy adopted to enhance the audience interest in the topic.

If, as Craik and Tulving (1975) and Rogers *et al.* (1977) suggest, the *appeal* of information is a function of its personal relevance, one can readily see why the vehicle of a presentation can be so important. One could develop the theme, 'forests are important renewable resources and must be managed wisely' by presenting awesome quantities of statistics about wood production and use. Another vehicle might be used to relate a vivid fictional (but believable) account of a twenty-first-century community which differs strikingly from its twentieth-century counterpart because wood products are scarce. Further analogies might be drawn between the twenty-first-century 'wood shortage' and the all-too-familiar twentieth-century 'oil shortage'. The analogous vehicle might be more effective because it is more personal. Other story vehicles could include irony, humour, suspense, mystery, sadness, melodrama, or surprise.

The conclusion of the presentation follows logically from the body. Its tone and organization also depend in part on the introduction. It is necessary, therefore, that concurrent thought be given to the introduction at this point, but it is suggested that the introduction be developed last. The main purpose of the conclusion should be to wrap up the theme. It should offer an answer or answers to the 'so what' question. It should present the big picture or the moral to the story. In other words, the conclusion demonstrates the wisdom of the conceptual framework and vehicle adopted for the presentation.

Such wisdom is verified if the audience readily sees the logic between what was presented and what was concluded. The most profound conclusions often suggest (explicitly or otherwise) some new action or perspective on the part of the audience. If, as Tilden recommended, the answer to the 'so what' question is couched in experiences the audience is likely to have in the future, the likelihood of inspiring (or at least provoking) the audience is increased.

Developing the introduction after the body and conclusion often improves the presentation. This makes sense if one considers the two main purposes of the introduction: (1) to entice the audience to select the presentation instead of the countless other stimuli that vie for its attention, i.e., make the audience *want* to hear more; and (2) to establish the vehicle and conceptual framework upon which the rest of the presentation will hinge. Only *after* the rest of the presentation is designed can the interpreter really know *what* is to be introduced and *how* it should be done. Thus, the introductory remarks that later conjure up irony, humour, sorrow, etc., are developed with full knowledge of the direction of the theme and its conclusion.

It is during the introduction that audiences learn what the theme is and how it is going to be organized. Concurrently, they decide whether the conceptual framework is relevant enough to pay attention. They also receive important clues that suggest chunking strategies and help audiences to process the rest of the presentation. Because of the influence the introduction can have on listeners' attention and information processing, it may well be the most important and most difficult part of the presentation.

Obviously, this '2–3–1 Rule' (body-conclusion-introduction) is flexible. While it makes intuitive sense to proceed in the order described above, it would be impractical to ignore other parts of the presentation while focusing on the design of one. In fact, it seems essential not only to plan each phase in light of the others previously designed, but also to rethink everything at each step of the process.

SUMMARY AND CONCLUSION

I have suggested possible applications of cognitive psychology to interpretation, focusing on verbal presentations for noncaptive audiences such as those attending interpretive activities in parks and other leisure places. Although research in cognition is infrequently used to illuminate findings of interpretive research, at least five principles can be seen that have their grounding in cognitive psychology. These can be stated as general propositions:

1 matching the verbal style of a presentation with that of the audience increases the meaningfulness (and interest) of the presentation;
2 audiences will attend more faithfully to presentations which elicit associations from long-term memory as new information is presented. This is because such associations make the new information more meaningful and more relevant to the audience;
3 keeping the number of perceptual units to be processed by the audience at or below seven increases the likelihood that the audience will pay attention for the duration of the presentation;
4 providing a conceptual framework that enhances audience opportunities for chunking information will facilitate information processing, and thereby increase the likelihood that the audience will attend for the duration of the presentation;
5 information rich in associative character and couched in meaningful context will be more accurately recognized, recalled, and understood by audiences.

On the basis of the research reported, a strategy for planning interpretive presentations was discussed. It appears that cognition research may prove insightful in improving interpretive efforts. Thus, cognitive psychology should be examined for its potential contribution to theory and practice in interpretation and related fields.

This paper first appeared in Journal of Interpretation *8(1) (1983), pp. 11–27.*

REFERENCES

Allen, G. L., Siegel, A. W. and Rosinski, R. R. (1978) 'The role of perceptual context in structuring spatial knowledge', *Journal of Experimental Psychology; Human Learning and Memory* 4(6): 617–30.
Biederman, I. (1972) 'Perceiving real world scenes', *Science* 177(1043): 77–80.
Biederman, I., Glass, A. L. and Stacy, E. W. (1973) 'Searching for objects in real world scenes', *Journal of Experimental Psychology* 97(1): 22–7.
Bower, G. H., Clark, M. C., Lesgold, A. M. and Winzenz, D. (1969) 'Hierarchical retrieval schemes in recall of categorized word lists', *Journal of Verbal Learning and Verbal Behavior* 8(3): 323–43.
Bower, G. H. and Springston, F. (1970) 'Pauses as recoding points in letter series', *Journal of Experimental Psychology* 83(3): 421–30.
Cartwright, D. (1956) 'Self-consistency as a factor affecting immediate recall', *Journal of Abnormal and Social Psychology* 52(3): 212–19.
Chase, W. G. and Simon, H. A. (1973) 'Perception in chess', *Cognitive Psychology* 4(1): 55–81.
Cherry, C. (1966) *On Human Communication*, 2nd edn, Cambridge: Massachusetts Institute of Technology.
Craik, F. I. M. and Lockhart, R. S. (1972) 'Levels of processing: a framework for memory research', *Journal of Verbal Learning and Verbal Behavior* 11(6): 671–84.
Craik, F. I. M. and Tulving, E. (1975) 'Depth of processing and the retention of words in episodic memory', *Journal of Experimental Psychology: General* 104(3): 268–94.

Dale, P. S. (1972) *Language Development: structure and function*, Hinsdale, Illinois: The Dryden Press, Inc.

Dick, R. E., McKee, D. T. and Wagar, J. A. (1974) 'A summary and annotated bibliography of communication principles', *Journal of Environmental Education* 5(4): 8–13.

Ellis, H. C. (1978) *Fundamentals of Human Learning, Memory and Cognition*, 2nd edn, Dubuque: William C. Brown Publishers.

Field, D. R. and Wagar, J. A. (1973) 'Visitor groups and interpretation in parks and other outdoor leisure settings', *Journal of Environmental Education* 5(1): 12–17.

Glucksberg, S., Krauss, R. M. and Weisberg, R. (1966) 'Referential communication in nursery school children: method and some preliminary findings', *Journal of Experimental Child Psychology* 3(3): 333–42.

Ham, S. H. and Shew, D. L. (1979) 'A comparison of visitors' and interpreters' assessments of conducted interpretive activities', *Journal of Interpretation* 4(2): 39–44.

Hammitt, W. E. (1981) 'A theoretical foundation for Tilden's interpretive principles', *Journal of Interpretation* 4(1): 9–12.

Hammitt, W. E. (1978) 'A visual preference approach to measuring interpretive effectiveness', *Journal of Interpretation* 3(2): 33–7.

Lewis, W. J. (1980) *Interpreting for Park Visitors*, Philadelphia: Eastern National Park and Monument Association (Acorn Press).

Lockhart, R. S. (1968) 'Stimulus selection and meaningfulness in paired-associate learning with stimulus items of high formal similarity', *Journal of Experimental Psychology* 78(2): 242–6.

Miller, G. A. (1956) 'The magical number seven, plus or minus two: some limits on our capacity for processing information', *Psychological Review* 63(2): 81–97.

Moray, N. (1959) 'Attention in dichotic listening: affective cues and the influence of instructions', *Quarterly Journal of Experimental Psychology* 11(1): 56–60.

Morton, J. (1969) 'Interaction of information in word recognition', *Psychological Review* 76(2): 165–78.

Neisser, V. (1969) 'Selective reading: a method for the study of visual attention', paper presented to the 19th International Congress of Psychology, London.

Palmer, S. E. (1975) 'The effects of contextual scenes on the identification of objects', *Memory and Cognition* 3(5): 519–26.

Rogers, T. B. (1977) 'Self-reference in memory: recognition of personality items', *Journal of Research in Personality* 11(3): 295–305.

Rogers, T. B., Kuiper, N. A. and Kirker, W. S. (1977) 'Self-reference and the encoding of personal information', *Journal of Personality and Social Psychology* 35(9): 677–88.

Solso, R. L. (1979) *Cognitive Psychology*, New York: Harcourt Brace Jovanovich, Inc.

Tai, D. B. (1981) 'An evaluation of the use and effectiveness of two types of interpretive trail media in Yellowstone National Park', unpublished M.S. thesis, University of Idaho, Moscow, Idaho.

Thorndyke, P. W. (1977) 'Cognitive structures in comprehension and memory of narrative discourse', *Cognitive Psychology* 9(1): 77–110.

Tilden, F. (1977) *Interpreting Our Heritage*, 2nd edn, Chapel Hill: University of North Carolina Press.

Tulving, E. (1974) 'Cue-dependent forgetting', *American Scientist* 62(1): 74–82.

Tulving, E. and Gold, C. (1963) 'Stimulus information and contextual information as determinants and tachistoscopic recognition of words', *Journal of Experimental Psychology* 66(4): 319–27.

Tulving, E. and Osler, S. (1968) 'Effectiveness of retrieval cues in memory for words', *Journal of Experimental Psychology* 77(4): 593–601.

Tulving, E. and Pearlstone, Z. (1966) 'Availability versus accessibility of information in memory for words', *Journal of Verbal Learning and Verbal Behavior* 5(1): 381–91.

Tulving, E. and Psotka, J. (1971) 'Retroactive inhibition in free recall: inaccessibility of information available in the memory store', *Journal of Experimental Psychology* 87(1): 1–8.

Witt, G. A. (1983) 'Media psychology', *Technical Photography* 15(1): 38–40.

13

Collaboration: towards a more holistic design process

Hank Grasso and Howard Morrison

The production and design of exhibitions is most effectively achieved as a team effort. The team should include curatorial, design, and education specialists. Scriptwriters and subject researchers are also of great value. This paper describes a holistic collaboration between members of an exhibition team, and discusses the processes that were followed in the various stages of the exhibition.

Visitors to *American Encounters* a Columbian Quincentenary exhibition opening 24 June 1992, at the Smithsonian Institution's National Museum of American History, will see some of the ways American Indians and Hispanics have interacted with each other and with Anglo-Americans in New Mexico for nearly 500 years. Visitors to the exhibition will *also* see the result of a unique, collaborative exhibit development and design process.

Nearly three years ago, the museum assembled a team of four curators, a scriptwriter, an education specialist, a designer, a New Mexico-based researcher, and a project manager; one of the curators served as project director. Such teams usually function as autonomous collectives in which individuals responsible for a particular domain meet merely to coordinate the execution of their separate tasks; but the *American Encounters* team functioned as a collaborative body.

Collaboration does not preclude individual responsibility and accountability; team members were assigned specific duties and areas of concern. But, at each crucial decision-making point, they *shared* roles and responsibilities. Everyone participated in the decision making that determined the content and design of each part of the exhibition. Collaboration is more difficult when some team members are contractors rather than staff employees; contracts link payments to specific tasks and must be written to accommodate some blurring of the lines of responsibility.

Many exhibits might benefit from this kind of holistic approach. When the entire team participates in all aspects of the development and design process, individual differences in perspective and interpretation as well as in personality and agenda become assets rather than liabilities. There are fewer surprises, fewer last-minute (a.k.a. costly) demands for changes by competing interests. There are also more opportunities for sharing potential solutions with colleagues outside the team, test audiences, and a wide variety of consultants – in this case, tribal and community representatives, artisans, photographers, collectors, and scholars.

The challenge, as anyone who has ever tried to do anything by committee knows, was to establish a collaborative rhythm within a group of diverse individuals. What follows are brief descriptions of the series of group problem-solving exercises that allowed the *American Encounters* team to arrive at collaboration in the development and design of the exhibit.

EXERCISE I: IDENTIFYING INTERPRETIVE GOALS

What is the most important message the exhibit should convey to the audience? What is the essential aspect of that message that the audience must understand for the exhibit to have meaning? The first step in answering these fundamental questions was to allow each member of the team to express what he or she believed to be the purpose of the exhibit. The free exchange of ideas was crucial; for there to be collaboration, everyone on the team must have a say, must have a stake in the exhibit.

The *American Encounters* team retreated to West Virginia for three days of brainstorming with a professional meeting facilitator. The result was not consensus but a collection of wide-ranging, commonly acknowledged interpretive goals to show cultural continuity, cultural change, cultural diversity, and cultural unity.

These and other goal statements provided the basis for in-depth audience studies using visitor surveys and interviews as well as focus groups. In addition, a broad-brush statement of purpose was presented in an illustrated brochure produced on a colour photocopier. The brochure was distributed to community and scholarly consultants as well as to potential financial backers.

EXERCISE II: ORIENTING CONCEPTS AND EXPERIENCES

What core ideas should the exhibit present? What kinds of visitor experiences should it provide? Even though members of the *American Encounters* team had differing ideas on the exhibit's abstract goals, they were able to work collaboratively when answering these and other concrete questions.

For this exercise, everyone on the team literally had to put their suggestions on the table by means of a paper swatch floor plan. Each specific content idea or exhibit experience was written on a small, medium, or large square of paper and taped to a single over-sized sheet of paper. Suggestions were assembled in relation to each other. Some needed more space; others less. Some needed to come before others; some after. Some were transitional; others were unrelated.

This exercise produced a seemingly helter-skelter wish list, but, in the process, core ideas and experiences began to emerge.

EXERCISE III: EXAMINING POSSIBLE SEQUENCES OF VISITOR EXPERIENCES

By translating the swatches of paper into large and small circles, it was possible to lay out the interrelationships of concepts and experiences in a bubble diagram. The result was a schematic representation of the sequence and relative importance of ideas and experiences.

EXERCISE IV: DEVELOPING A PRELIMINARY FLOOR PLAN

Spaces in the exhibit were allocated by superimposing the bubble diagram on a plan that showed the size and configuration of the actual space available. How must the space be entered? How may it be exited? How many different ways can visitors move through the space? Team members, with pencils in hand, joined in marking up floor plans to develop various possible layouts for the preliminary floor plan.

The transfer of elements from bubble diagram to floor plan provided a reality check on the sequence and scale of proposed concepts and experiences. Ideas that were vastly too large for the space available were dropped or shifted to video or other media that can compress many images into a compact experience.

Ideas over which the group disagreed often found a place in the exhibit simply by configuring a wall in a certain way or by changing the amount of space allotted to a certain element. Persistent disagreements were dealt with outside the group forum. A mediator shuttled between differing parties carrying proposals back and forth to work out agreements.

This exercise was the most difficult one in the series because the team had to define real visitor experiences in terms of actual sections of the exhibition.

EXERCISE V: CHOOSING OBJECTS AND IMAGES

What objects and images are available to tell the stories identified on the preliminary floor plan? The team began to assemble snapshots of objects and graphics (paintings, illustrations, and archival photographs, in a series of plastic sleeves housed according to exhibit section in loose-leaf binders. Objects and images were shuffled, added, deleted, or returned to various exhibit sections with ease. In this way, team members defined sets of two- and three-dimensional items for each section of the exhibit. These interpretive sets in turn helped the team refine specific stories that would be told in each part of the exhibit. For example, pottery suggested itself as a metaphor for continuity and change among Pueblo Indians; weaving did the same for Hispanics.

EXERCISE VI: VISUALIZING EXHIBIT CONTENT

How will the objects, images, and stories selected for the exhibit actually work when they are brought together? The next step in the development and design process was to render the exhibit in a series of storyboards. Colour copies of graphic images and of photographs or drawings of objects were mounted to section-specific illustration boards along with a brief statement of teaching goals.

These storyboards provided an affordable way for team members to visualize the exhibit. The boards helped them to fine tune preliminary organizational decisions. Storyboards also provided colleagues, museum management, outside consultants, and ordinary visitors an opportunity to respond to plans for the exhibit. The boards produced for *American Encounters* were used for presentations and meetings. They were then installed in the museum's exhibit preview area where visitors were invited to write their comments on forms provided. A more formal audience survey was not conducted but would have been useful.

EXERCISE VII: VISUALIZING THE EXHIBIT SPACE

The next step was to build a three dimensional foam core model of the exhibit. The model enabled team members to see in scale how spaces and elements within the exhibit related to each other when viewed during a walk-through. The model was a working tool not a presentation piece. Foam core walls went up and came down, exhibit cases were moved, and vantage points were shifted. To reinforce larger interpretive messages, spatial patterns within the exhibit were derived from cultural forms: the Pueblo Indian section of the floor plan is circular, suggesting the cyclic patterns common in their culture, while the Hispanic community section is rectangular, like a village plaza.

After repeated trials and discussions, the model became the basis for detailed construction drawings. These drawings, which were prepared in consultation with an architect, included exhibit-specific information on wall placement and case openings as well as public space-specific information on acoustic attenuation and electrical, lighting, audio-visual, and emergency systems.

EXERCISE VIII: SELECTING FORMS, COLOURS, AND TEXTURES

Team members regrouped to decide on specific personalities for each section of the exhibit, using the model to test various solutions. They looked to objects in each section that suggested certain patterns and hues. They drew upon cultural or environmental elements related to exhibit content that could be abstracted in forms and textures. The team also decided to incorporate actual contextual elements from each community in New Mexico (being careful to avoid those elements that were clichéd or stereotypical): adobe and carved wooden architectural components, stone label substrates, coyote fencing, and signs.

Material palettes with samples of fabrics, paints, floor and wall coverings, and label panel were developed for each section of the exhibit. Only materials that met durability requirements for public spaces, fire codes, and conservation mandates were considered.

EXERCISE IX: DEVELOPING A GRAPHIC IMAGE VOCABULARY

The goal was to devise a palette of type styles and symbol sets that could be employed to convey ideas. Because the abstract qualities of typefaces and symbols are hard to articulate, the designer prepared several sample solutions for the group to consider. He selected a wide range of typefaces; he created symbol sets using various combinations of elements derived from cultural icons to identify things such as exhibit sections and labelling hierarchy.

The group discussed these and chose those that seemed better or more appropriate. The group selected a single typeface for the entire exhibit but used distinctive symbol sets for each section. For example, the section of the exhibit that looks at twentieth-century tourism in New Mexico uses a chili pepper symbol and graphic organizational bars that fuse dollar signs with patterns derived from weavings. A graphics designer could be engaged to assist with this exercise.

121

EXERCISE X: ESTABLISHING HUMAN FACTOR OR ERGONOMIC PARAMETERS

A full-scale mock-up of a typical exhibit component made using foam core, colour photocopies of objects and photographs, and photocopies of sample labels and graphics was used to address various design solutions as well as federally mandated accessibility requirements. The team experimented with the arrangement of objects and the size and placement of labels. They tested vertical heights, viewing distances, and angles of reading surfaces – exercises typical of industrial design services. They tried various ways to code maps, timelines, and other information-dense graphics.

Once the team settled on a range of standards, the mock-up was moved to a public area. A visitor study was conducted using a mock-up of entrance panels and two exhibit cases, one from the Pueblo Indian section and one from the Hispanic section. Visitor observations and interviews conducted by an audience research firm suggested changes that were incorporated into the design control drawings.

EXERCISE XI: FINDING AN EXHIBIT VOICE

The preparation of the label script for *American Encounters* began with three curators writing labels for specific content areas (the group as a whole had already established a four-level labelling hierarchy: main labels were written first, then section, group, and object labels). To make three different voices one, the team's writer reworked each label, preparing a draft script for the entire exhibit.

The team regrouped at this point to review the draft. Reading aloud, they went through the script line by line, day after day, considering everything from conceptual intent to word choice. *Every* team member participated; everyone made contributions to all sections of the exhibit, resulting in the final script. The document was reviewed by colleagues, the museum's director, its management committee, consulting scholars, and community members in New Mexico. Once revisions based on their comments were incorporated into the script, it was sent to copy editors.

EXERCISE XII: CONSIDERING CASE-SPECIFIC SOLUTIONS

Having begun this series of exercises with the broadest possible focus, the team made a series of decisions about increasingly specific design questions. As team members resolved each question, they moved on to the next one; they wasted no time retracing their steps. Now it was time for the last step.

The team used white models – renderings of each exhibit case with scale likenesses of objects, supports, pedestals, and graphic and label panels – to consider final designs for each exhibit case. The models enabled the team to decide not only on the placement of elements within the exhibit case but on other design questions as well. For example, should object supports in a given exhibit case be abstract or realistic?

In the course of their discussions, the team (joined in 1991 by a collections manager) worked closely with conservators to ensure that the overall design of each exhibit case as well as specific object supports and brackets met conservation guidelines.

The final designs for each case were rendered as case elevations or production drawings and turned over to exhibit fabricators.

These problem-solving exercises allowed the *American Encounters* team to arrive at collaboration. Why? The exercises provided the structure that made it possible for team members to set aside job-title divisions; at crucial decision-making points they were able to share roles and responsibilities in a noncompetitive environment. The exercises gave team members a common language and made it necessary for them to use it; when they spoke to each other of alternative solutions, they were spared the confusion that results from speaking in curatorese or designerese or educatorese. Finally, the exercises were solution specific; team members had to focus on the narrowly defined problem at hand, ensuring that their discussions were creatively motivated. The cumulative result was a kind of gestalt that influenced the development and design of the exhibit at every step.

The *American Encounters* team included Richard E. Ahlborn, co-curator; Harold Closter, project manager; G. Benito Cordova, researcher; Richard Doty, co-curator; Lisa Falk, education specialist; Hank Grasso, designer; Rayna Green, co-curator; Howard Morrison, writer; Susan Ostroff, collections manager; and Lonn Taylor, co-curator and project director.

This paper first appeared in History News 47(3) (1992), pp. 12–15.

14

Learning to make an exhibition of ourselves

Pat Rabbitt (introduced by Andy Millward)

'I've come all the way from bloody Blackburn on the bloody bus because I read this was a MAJOR bloody exhibition! This is a tatty collection of bits and pieces!' – salutary lessons in exhibition production.

Being a University Museum, we at the Manchester Museum are always interested in being approached by other departments to help present their work to a wider public. Some time ago we were asked if we would like to present an exhibition on *Memory* by Professor Pat Rabbitt of the Age and Cognitive Research Unit. The first meetings were not a great success as people forgot to turn up!!! The full tale, or one person's view of the full tale appeared in the February 1989 issue of *The Psychologist* and we are very grateful to them and the author, Pat Rabbitt, for permission to reproduce it. It includes many gems of common sense along with the odd character assassination which makes it more fun to read. What did I think of the result? Well my vote goes to the man from Blackburn, so read on.

Andy Millward

If you consider mounting an exhibition, our first and most vital piece of advice is that you should wait and hope that the feeling will pass.

You should intensely distrust your initial enthusiasms – which may betray you, as they did us, into a situation from which you will be very lucky to escape without shame and actual financial loss. If you must go ahead, try to be businesslike and keep to a tight agenda from the very beginning.

Our initial *planning* meetings were carried out in a spirit of casual, not to say fatuous, enthusiasm. Meetings were continually deferred on short notice and slight pretext and when, by chance, any two of us actually remembered to turn up at the time arranged, rapidly became gossip sessions. Only the steadily rising pressure of our moral commitments to our credulous sponsors brought us to the most important discovery we have to pass on:

> *Planning a museum exhibition is an extremely demanding task, and the essence of it is not a grand sweep of ideas but a remorseless and nagging attention to detail.*

Until all concerned realize this nothing useful happens. Nothing would ever have happened if we had not eventually hired Tansy Arthur to keep our discussions to the point, to reject our procrastinations, to force decisions upon us and to be very, very rude to us as often as was necessary. Someone must take on this demanding and unpopular role. She will never do it again – even for money.

We had other instructors. The most proficient, and sage, was Alan Warhurst, Director of the Manchester Museum. He gently made us see that, since exhibitions require a great deal of time to prepare, and since schedules may lag for good reasons, large and active museums have to programme at least a year in advance. To maintain a constant turnover, directors must keep a shrewd eye on the progress of each individual project and override the optimism of lagging exhibitors, swiftly judging replacements at the first sign that any one of them is falling behind deadline.

Alan also taught us that the planning of cycles of exhibitions requires ruthless opportunism. Successful projects must be over-run into slots previously reserved for less attractive, or less prepared ventures. We found ourselves gazumped by Lindow Man, and once again shifted onto a new slot when his time in Manchester was extended. The only way to counter such steely Directorial flexibility is to be able to stake firm claims based on demonstrably complete preparations. Raising the voice a few octaves and by 80 decibels sometimes also helps to establish sincerity and clearness of purpose.

Our next tutor was Andy Millward of the museum's display department. To describe Andy as *blunt* is to describe Margaret Thatcher as *positive*. Perhaps his occupational characteristics have been acquired while teaching people like us two important things.

First, an exhibition is not a poster session in which the style of all displays can be unrelated. If displays are not planned as a whole, by talented people like the admirable Alez Hamilton and Kathy Webb of the MUTV team who created the entire finished exhibition, the result is visually emetic. The moral: design something about which one must consult professionals, and for which one should be prepared to find cash support if necessary.

Andy's second and most important lesson was even more painful: an exhibition has to be written as well as assembled. All exhibits, large or insignificant, need captions which, collectively, tell an interesting story very concisely, and in very simple words, aimed at a very general audience. This needs extraordinarily tight writing. Like all things which are unexpectedly hard to do, this takes an unexpectedly long time. Once devised, captions have to be impeccably edited and elegantly produced. Thank you again, Jackie Andrade. The moral: if you plan an exhibition, make sure to clear your diary first.

Andy's tutelage brought to life earlier advice from Richard Morris whose enthusiasm, interest and practical help, based on his own experience in designing the Natural History Museum's permanent *Exhibition of Ourselves* were a great prop to our queasy morale. We were neurotically concerned that we might not have enough different displays. It took us time to realize that the real problem is to have a few, but very good, displays tightly coordinated to tell interesting stories in a simple way. An important fact is that visitors to an exhibition very seldom spend more than five minutes in the same room. If pictures, objects and captions cannot make a point within that period they have little impact.

These successive discoveries gradually made us realize that people planning an exhibition are entirely on their own. In our first euphoria, a continual excuse for postponing decisions on details was that, if things came to a crunch, all we had to do was ring up friends, well known for their brilliance and flair, who would overwhelm us with remarkable ideas and material.

Every one of the many colleagues we approached was, indeed, extraordinarily kind, encouraged us, and assured us that an exhibition on human memory was far too original and exciting an idea to possibly fail. All knew of an undergraduate project in their department, already nearly begun, which might easily be worked up to make a fascinating demonstration. Some were sure that they still had, somewhere, parts of poster displays which had gone down well at BPS London meetings between 1974 and 1983, and which they would be glad to search out and pass on. One had a (only slightly torn and foxed) poster advertising the Ebbinhaus Centenary Symposium, and a framed portrait photograph of William James which we could have if we promised to take very great care of them and to return them immediately when the exhibition was over. There was wild talk of a giant phrenological head . . .

The very best replied promptly to our letters and said that they would be delighted to help in any way they could, as fast as possible, if we could tell them exactly what we wanted. These excellent realists were, of course, never troubled. In the frame of mind in which we asked, if we had known exactly what we wanted we would not have enquired. The moral: do not expect your colleagues to generate ideas you do not have yourself.

Other illusions languished one by one. A particularly bitter loss was the fantasy of cornucopias of eager commercial sponsorship – banks, building societies, manufacturers of computer memories, Filofax Ltd (geddit?), pharmaceutical companies and publishers jostling to be associated with *The Great Event*. Replies, when written, were world-weary and negative. The splendid exception was Penguin Books – who offered us £20 on the condition that we devoted much of our display space to a selection of their output. We did not accept, but take this opportunity of publicly expressing our warm thanks for the thought. The moral: be sure that you have all the sponsorship you need before you bid for your time-slot. To work out what you need, think in the most ample terms, of all you might possibly spend, treble it. Only a very generous last-minute grant from The Royal Society saved us from financial ruin.

Nothing so unpleasantly constipates the mind as the threat of an unpayable overdraft.

One discovery, at least, was delightful: University librarians are charming and helpful people who have experience at organizing very large exhibitions. They are also enormously knowledgeable and imaginative. Any organizers will be fortunate if they can find individuals as promptly sympathetic, at ludicrously short notice, as Mrs Ferguson and her colleagues at Manchester University Library. They will also be lucky if they gain access to as rich a source as the John Rylands collection.

This raises an important point of budgeting: rare books, and other valuable, desirable, or simply fragile objects must be protected and insured. Electronic security and insurance do not come cheap, and have to be negotiated well in advance.

The other costs are mainly psychological. A bad paper is not read by most of your colleagues, and even a dreadfully inept public lecture is soon forgotten, but an exhibition which lasts for weeks in the street outside your office is a thing of duty which can destroy forever.

Apparatus breaks down and has to be repaired. Posters go missing. Replacement handouts must be xeroxed at short notice.

Memorable experiences are accidentally gained by overhearing sharp 11-year old hackers (*'Gawd, all they've got are rotten old beebs and Apples'*), deride inelegancies of graphics and learnedly discuss how most amusingly (i.e. obscenely) and efficiently to *fix* the demonstration programmes. Or hearing an apoplectic geriatric tear a strip off a guiltless security attendant (*'I've come all the way from bloody Blackburn on the bloody bus because I read that this was a MAJOR bloody exhibition! This is a tatty collection of bits and pieces!'*). Or noting how many punters glance about for fifteen seconds and hastily leave. To the

Manchester Department of Psychology research students who put up with all this and more, while guarding and demonstrating for four hours a day, our sympathy and inadequate thanks.

There are also pleasures. An important thing to realize is that an exhibition can be a lively backdrop, and a source of publicity, for other concurrent related activities. With witty and learned help (Mike Gruneberg, Charles Hulme, Alan Parkin and Jim Reason), Andrew, Graham and I ran a series of six public lectures on memory. We had expected to break even with audiences of about forty. The gate was never less than 120 and peaked at 164. It is still a great pleasure that members of our ACPRC research panel go out of their way to say how much they enjoyed the series, and to press us to run another.

If you are running an exhibition you should seriously consider what other events you might mount at the same time. Once again it is a good idea to find and consult your local professionals first. Bill Jones and his colleagues of the Manchester University Extra-Mural Board secured the lecture theatres, printed the tickets, collected the money, kept the books, bribed the University porters, located absconding projectionists, stacked the chairs, organized the publicity – and underwrote the considerable financial risk. (We had learned a bit by then.) Had we given them more time their enthusiasm might have taken them to dangerous lengths. Out of our timid success has come the much more complicated and daunting fantasy of *The Manchester Science Faculty Annual Christmas Lectures*. But that rich collection of unrelated nouns and minefield of potential embarrassments will make quite another story.

The exhibits were designed to be easily transportable, and have now been to Aberdeen, where Bob Logie displayed them in the Department of Psychology, and during his International Conference on Thinking, and then passed them on to Aberdeen City Museum, who wish to copy some of them for long-term display. The displays will then travel to Swansea where Graham Beaumont will use them as he thinks fit. There is some demand for the residue, on later dates, from local museums and institutions in the North West.

We feel great relief at having accomplished most of what we promised our very generous sponsors: the Scientific Affairs Board of the BPS, who provided a pump-priming grant; the Experimental Psychology Society, the Cognitive Section of the BPS, and The Royal Society (through their Committee for the Public Understanding of Science, *COPUS*). To all these our very warm gratitude.

This paper first appeared in Museum Design 1 *(1990), pp. 5–7.*

15

Cheap and cheerful: techniques for temporary displays

Mark O'Neill

A practical description of simple techniques used in a very small museum that produces its own exhibitions. Suggestions are made of what kind of materials to use, which give an indication of the kinds of thinking to be done in planning from scratch. Area Museum Councils (in the UK) and other museums are useful places to go for help and ideas. Techniques for writing the text and displaying the objects are discussed.

Our museum, Springburn, is fortunate enough to have a staff designer, but we still felt a need for a kit of graphic products which would enable anybody to put together a display that is at least presentable. This is mainly because we do not have permanent exhibitions. With six or seven temporary exhibitions a year, we wanted a system that made them look permanent, but would nonetheless be as cheap and quick to produce as possible. This is the kit we have devised.

SCREENS

The nylon-covered screens available commercially were the first things we discounted, as they look very temporary, and are very expensive. We therefore had screens made from three-quarter inch blockboard (Summerlee uses Medium Density Fibre Board and finds it it satisfactory), cut into sheets 1 metre wide and 2 metres long and edged with a hardwood lipping. The standard sheets measuring 8 by 4 feet are very tall and can be oppressive in a small space, and the edges look rough without the lipping. In 1986 these boards cost £35 each from a local joinery. They are joined by Klem Klamps, which come in silver or white. Their brightness can be obtrusive, but the company can match any colour for minimum orders of 100. Alternatively you can have the clamps dipped in the same colour as the screens. (The other most widely used clamp are made by Nexo, which are more expensive, but give greater flexibility.) This gives a very versatile system. The screens are heavy, and it requires two people to set them up or re-arrange them. However the solid wood means that framed paintings or photographs can be attached with screws. A great variety of layouts can be created through combining screens, and, best of all in a small museum with a gallery which cannot be sectioned off from the public, panels can be installed and removed very quickly. Even with the clamps our system cost less than half that of commercially available nylon fabric type systems, retains its appearance longer and is more easily renewed.

The cases were designed before the screens, which are the same height and painted as near an identical colour as we could find. The screens have a thin rail to support the graphic panels at the same level as the bottom of the glass in the cases. Thus if you have inherited old cases you can have screens made which match them in size, and have both painted or stained the same colour.

Our cases are simple boxes supplied by Harley Shopfitters Ltd. The anodized aluminium is a dark metallic brown so that it looks discreet but modern, and at the same time does not clash with the wood panelling of the museum; we wanted the display system to be as nearly invisible as possible. The cases have solid 'cupboard' bases for two reasons: being able to see people's legs through cases distracts attention from the exhibition; and they provide very valuable storage space.

THE EXHIBITION SCRIPT

When we are planning an exhibition we begin by estimating its size in terms of the number of panels and cases required. Even if this changes later, it is a useful way of thinking about the script, as a supplement to the display and not a book which is being written. Everyone thinks that their labels are masterpieces of clarity and conciseness. One must be ruthlessly humble and pass one's script on to an objective third party, ideally a teacher or journalist, but any handy lay person will do. At the very least you should do the Fry test for readability (see chapter 18); you should aim for a reading age of about 13, which is what the average adult finds easy while standing up. And if your exhibition contains more than 2–3,000 words, it's too long.

EDITING THE TEXT

We then divide the text into sections and give the panel dealing with each section a title heading. Along with the main photograph, the title conveys the point without the need to read any further. The introductory panel should have 100 to 150 words following the heading, and the remainder of the panels 50 to 75 words. Individual photographs, diagrams etc. should have captions of no more than 20 words. Both types of label can be split into two tiers, with the main statement in larger or bolder letters. Sometimes the demands of the narrative will be such that the material will not divide this way, but in this case the key statements should be typeset in bold letters. Thus even if it is embedded in a longer text, someone skimming through will pick up the essentials. It may be useful to think in the way journalists are trained to write – in the expectation that their copy will be cut back from the end, so that important statements should appear first, and not be spread throughout the panel. It is much more difficult to write short accurate captions than long ones, but it is always worth the effort.

DESIGNING THE LAYOUT

As the exhibition is about to go into production, our designer has a file for each panel, containing all the relevant text and photocopies of all the photographs and maps etc. She then does a layout for each panel in the form of a simple scale drawing, indicating the size and position of photographs, captions, headings, etc. If you don't have access to a designer, this is the key stage at which to get help, whether from an art teacher or someone who has a 'good eye'. It is important that someone other than the person who wrote the text at least looks at it objectively – the writer will be too close to the material. One person should design the whole thing, otherwise it will not have a coherent overall feel.

PUTTING IT TOGETHER

The first design decision is choosing the mounting board – i.e. the background colour of the exhibition. 'Swatches' or samples of the full range of colours and sizes of board can be obtained from art materials suppliers. The colour you choose can be symbolic or just a nice colour. Test it against the kind of material which will be used on it – colour or black and white photographs. Too strong or garish a colour may be overpowering in large quantities or in a small space.

HEADINGS

All our main headings are in Eurotext, a vinyl self-adhesive lettering system which offers a wide range of colours and typefaces. Again, a catalogue of these is available. Eurotext is ordered by post, usually through a graphic art supplier such as Millers or Sime Malloch, or direct from the manufacturer. The words arrive by post, usually within 48 hours, on a paper strip, which is very easy to apply straight. It is very expensive (about 30 pence per letter), but one buys only the letters one needs, so that even one or two headings in a carefully chosen colour will brighten up an exhibition considerably. It can also be used to put headings on the glass in cases, and to make signs. The main heading can also be made from Letraset or Mecanorma, which comes in sheets of (mainly black) dry transfer lettering. Again, catalogues of the wide range of typefaces are available from graphic art suppliers.

PRODUCING LABELS

Typesetting improves labels from typewriting beyond all recognition, and it is worth spending a significant part of your budget on it. If you can't find a typesetter in the yellow pages, your printer will be able to advise you on who can do it for you. A local college, library service or businesses may have desktop publishing facilities which they may let you use. The quality will not he as good as typesetting but is still much better than typewritten labels. Your local newspaper may also be willing to help as they will have full typesetting facilities.

Finished typesetting comes on a white glossy paper, and usually needs to be transferred into another form. Using the invaluable photocopier, the labels can be copied onto coloured paper to match the mounting board and the heading letters. This can either be a lighter hue of the same colour or a lighter different but complimentary colour – beware of having too high a contrast, or the labels will form a jumpy pattern of their own across the panels. The important contrast is between the paper and the lettering, to make for easy reading. Some photocopiers will also reduce or enlarge the lettering to the required size. All labels of the same category (main, secondary, photographs, object) should have the same size lettering. The labels themselves should also however extend the full length of any photograph they accompany. It is therefore necessary to measure the longest photograph, and the size of the lettering for that will determine the size for other labels. Remember that many elderly people with failing eyesight find larger writing easier to read – never go below 12 point (typefaces sizes are measured in 'points') for even the smallest label.

TRANSPARENT LABELS

Transparent labels work very well on light coloured mounting board. The best quality is achieved with Agfa Copyproof 'CP Frisket' (used in conjunction with 'CP Negative'), which is a light-sensitive adhesive backed plastic. An A3 sheet of transparent labels costs about £3 and requires a process camera – again your local newspaper may have one of these and may be willing to help. A cheaper but more opaque product is made by Rank Xerox, called Self Adhesive Drafting Film, which costs about 25 pence per sheet and can be photocopied on to. Transparent labels tend to peel if placed in cases. You can also photocopy onto to transparencies designed for overhead projectors. These are not self adhesive, but are very clear, and can only be used for small captions on laminated panels. In cases they can be placed in those little acrylic frames which prop up photographs on your desk.

DRY MOUNTING AND LAMINATING

Dry mounting involves placing a tissue of glue between the photographs and the mounting board and melting them together in a special press. This is by far the most secure way of fixing photographs to boards. All our display panels are laminated, at the same time and using the same press. This involves heat-sealing a transparent sheet of plastic onto the boards, prolonging their life indefinitely. Laminating presses cost over £1,000, and small museums could consider clubbing together to buy one, or jointly applying for grant aid for one. You should note that original documents and photographs should never be laminated! We only use the press in the few days before each exhibition but it has paid for itself many times over. The laminating film and the dry mounting tissue only cost about £5 per panel, while the commercial cost would be as much as ten times that amount.

CASES

One of the main problems in local history displays is relating objects in cases to the general narrative in an exhibition. Our basic strategy for this is to line the cases with the same mounting board that we use for the graphic panels. Photographs, documents, graphics and text are also included in the cases so that artefacts are not physically separated from their supporting material. However it is also important to have a variety of interpretive styles – we vary the amount of interpretation both within and between exhibitions.

It is important to note that the display system described is suitable for temporary exhibitions of prints, copies and robust local history material. Fragile and valuable objects from museum collections will require special security and environmental control arrangements, and should not be put on display without expert advice.

This paper first appeared in Scottish Museum News *(Spring 1990), pp. 17–19.*

REFERENCE

Sorsby, B. D., and Horne, S. D. (1980) 'The readability of museum labels', in *Museums Journal* 80(3): 157–9.

16

Museum text as mediated message
Helen Coxall

How does language work to construct meaning? Museums and their texts are active agents in shaping opinion and identity. Language is socially determined and therefore articulates ideologies, generally through the assumptions which underlie texts. Museum writers need to be aware that this is happening in order to identify the assumptions that our texts will be built upon.

The writer demonstrates with examples from museum labels how linguistic variables such as the agentless passive, naming devices, and evalutive adjectives construct meanings which contain assumptions (which may be racist, sexist or biased in other ways) that the writers are unaware of and would probably not want to support.

My Ph.D. research into museum language is an exploration into how language means, that is, the process by which language conveys meanings. A large part of the research consists of linguistic analyses of texts from selected galleries and museums, with regard to social and ideological implications.

The following passage from the introduction to Gerda Lerner's book *The Creation of Patriarchy*, highlights both directly and indirectly, two very important issues that are relevant to my investigations. First, the significance of gaps in textual information and second the issue of discrimination:

> Until the most recent past historians have been men, and what they have recorded is what men have done and experienced and found significant. They have called this History and have claimed universality for it. What women have done and experienced has been left unrecorded, neglected and ignored in interpretation. Historical scholarship, up to the most recent past, has seen women as marginal to the making of civilisation and as unessential to those pursuits defined as having historical significance.

> Thus the recorded and interpreted record of the past of the human race is only a partial record, in that it omits the past of half of humankind, and it is distorted in that it tells the story from the viewpoint of the male half of humanity only.

If history is only a partial record of the past it follows that one way of looking at history is in accordance with the omissions in the text. In other words the world view of the historian can be understood in relation to what the account does not say, because a way of saying is also a way of seeing. In this case the gap in the information suggests a particular stereotypical attitude to the role of women in society. However an omission in this quote itself foregrounds the fact that different ways of seeing the world are not limited to female or male perspectives alone. Here is an example to explain what I mean.

Dr Jeanne Cannizzo wrote an article 'How sweet it is; cultural politics in Barbados', about the Museum of Barbados whose collection was (until recently) not a record of the history of the black Barbadian people, who form the majority on the island, but a record of the predominantly white Barbadian merchants and planters and their adoption of European culture. She makes the point in her article that:

> Museums and their displays are often active agents in shaping all kinds of identity. By not displaying the cultural heritage of the majority of the population, the museum has taken from them, by implication, their role as history makers, as active participants in their own past.

Thus, not only do the gaps in this museum's collection reveal the writers', and in this case the museum directors', ideological stance, they imply a meaning that is communicated to whoever reads the text. In other words, the writer is perpetuating and reinforcing their own ideological bias: the mediated message in this case being that the black Barbadians are not worthy of historical record. The responsibility that this implication places on any writer involved with educational institutions, such as museums, is obvious.

Mark Leone puts this point very forcefully in his article 'Methods as message: interpreting the past with the public'. 'Reading, writing, telling and performing history are *active* and *form* modern opinion, modern nationality, modern identity, class interests and social position' (my italics). Thus, assumptions that are embedded in language are all pervasive and cannot be ignored. My interest is in the way the avoided subjects in the text and the language itself transmit both the personal world view of a writer of museum texts and the official policy of the museum itself.

In their book *Language as Ideology* Kress and Hodge make the following observation: 'The world is grasped through language. But in its use by a speaker, language is more than that. It is a version of the world offered to, imposed on, enacted by someone else.' They go on to make the claim that the grammar of a language itself is a theory of reality. Which perhaps sounds a little far-fetched to start with. Nevertheless, social structures not only determine discourse but are themselves produced by discourse. Subsequently, if you think about it, our system of communication (our language) is already in existence before our children learn it and in learning this language they learn words that appear to stand for value-free, common-sense concepts but are actually socially-determined ones. For example they learn the name of the person who delivers their letters every morning as 'postman' which seems straightforward enough until you stop to think that implicit in this name is the fact that all such people are men.

This does not mean that because our language is socially determined we are unable to escape the unconscious articulation of underlying ideologies. But it does mean that we must become clear about what these underlying assumptions are if it is not our wish to perpetuate them. Therefore, if the grammar of a language is indeed its theory of reality it should be possible to uncover its hidden agenda, for if writers are saying things they are unaware of, critical linguistic analysis can serve as a valuable means of exposure and therefore of consciousness raising. Furthermore, it should be possible for an aware writer to draw on other discourses in order to create a new perspective. And this applies as much to historians as to writers of museum texts.

I will return to this issue later when the implications contained in selected museum texts will be examined. To return for now to Gerda Lerner's book; she does obliquely acknowledge that gender discrimination is not the only kind of discrimination found in historical records. She says:

> As formerly subordinate groups such as peasants, slaves, proletarians, have risen into positions of power, their experiences have become part of the historical record. That is the experiences of the male group; the females were, as usual, excluded. The point is that men and women have suffered exclusion and discrimination because of their class. No man has ever been excluded from the historical record because of his sex, yet all women were.

However, although Lerner only explicitly acknowledges gender and class discrimination, it seems to me that racial discrimination is also implied in her reference to slaves. By concentrating upon awareness of gender discrimination it is possible to overlook the fact that the same insidious discriminatory process is being perpetuated by methods of recording histories of many groups of marginalized peoples on the grounds of race, class, religion, politics and age.

In his essay 'Belief and the problem of women', Edwin Ardener refers to women as a *muted* group as opposed to the male dominant group. This is a particularly appropriate term as it not only refers to the process by which women have been written out of history but the process by which they are rendered inarticulate, as they are forced to communicate in male-orientated language. Thus the term muted indicates a problem both with language and with power.

However, women are not the only group that are effectively muted by the constructed language of the dominant group. Let us look at some texts that illustrate the problem for writers of text in social history museums who seek to redress the balance contained in previous historical accounts. Not everyone, of course, does seek to redress the balance, and it would not be surprising to find that there are some museums staff (as indeed there are historians) who, according to historian John Tosh 'reject theory and remain blissfully unaware of the assumptions and values which inform their own selection and interpretation of evidence'. But this position is difficult for staff to defend in the light of the fact that museums are regarded by the public as centres of excellence and knowledge that are automatically endowed with authenticity. However, is it possible to give an authentic historical account? John Tosh goes on to say: 'The record of recent centuries is so voluminous and varied that contradictory results can be obtained simply by asking different questions.'

Surely therefore, it is the questions that are being asked that provide the key to differing interpretations of history? After all, it is possible to provide a completely one-sided version of any event, past or present, by simply avoiding certain facts, as we have already acknowledged, or to put it another way, by avoiding certain questions. By examining the lexical and syntactical choices (that is the choice of words and grammar) in a text it is possible to find first, evidence of the position of the writer; second, what they were saying; third, what they were choosing not to say and why; and last who they appeared to be addressing. It is also appropriate to enquire whether or not the information was both relevant and accessible to the potential audience. The purpose as I mentioned at the outset, is to raise awareness about the ways that language choice can reflect a pre-determined way of seeing and to suggest alternative ways of saying that avoid unintentional bias.

The writers of museum texts have a responsibility to the public and therefore have to be very careful that they do not convey implicit, unintentional meanings. Thus museum writers are not justified in being familiar only with their own subject but must also concern themselves with their mode of communication.

Linguistic variables can create meanings that are at first glance not apparent. For example, the use of the passive as opposed to the active form can create problems for writers if they are unaware of the effect of using this particular language construction. If a writer uses the passive form they are able to avoid naming the perpetrators of an event and simply make a statement about the end result. For example, the newspaper headline that says simply 'Three passers-by were shot during riots'. Now, if the journalist had used the active instead of the passive form s/he would have had to identify who did the shooting and the heading would therefore have implicated somebody, for example: 'The police shot three passers-by during riots' or 'Rioters shot three passers-by'. Of course from a journalist's point of view, if there were some confusion about who did the shooting this method of reporting is convenient, however, the same practice is used deliberately by politicians to avoid uncomfortable facts.[1] It can also be used quite innocently by writers with unfortunate results. Here is an example taken from the Georgian section of a social history museum.

> Under the influence of the Adam brothers furniture was simple, refined and strongly classical in form and ornament. . . . Hepplewhite designed oval and shield shaped backs to many of his chairs and both he and Sheraton, the other great furniture designer of this time, emphasised lightness of construction and elegance of treatment.

Note the specific naming of the individual designers and the use of the active formation. Compare this with the updated version of the same exhibit label:

> Neo-classical shapes and motifs were popular, like the lyre shape on the back of the music stand. This style of furniture is now often called Hepplewhite and Sheraton.

Here the furniture is named by the abstract noun *style*, the agentless passive is used, and when the designers are named it is only in reference to the name of their style of work which has miraculously detached itself from themselves as creators. It is like referring to a Shakespearian style of writing and denying the existence of Shakespeare himself. It does not take much imagination to guess that the writer did not intend the latter interpretation to be communicated, however, it does demonstrate the problems that can arise when adopting this 'impersonal' academic style of language.

The effect of the agentless passive here is two fold. First, it avoids telling the reader who exactly performed the work referred to. Second, the writer avoids identifying her/himself at all and therefore apparently remains objective. The facts being recorded acquire that aura of authenticity as they cannot be seen to be subjective. Thus the writer's choice and combination of lexicon and syntax control the meanings that can be read into the text by the museum's visitor. Let us look at a few more examples.

The various uses of nouns can mediate the meanings. We have already seen how the use of proper nouns (the specific naming of the designers in the last text) conferred status upon them. We have also already come across the use an abstract noun (style) which contributed to the text's vagueness. Abstract nouns used frequently can create complexity. There is another type of noun that is used frequently by politicians which is called a noun construction. This is a noun that has been constructed from a verb which, like the use of the passive, usually has the effect of avoiding identifying the agent of the sentence.

George Orwell wrote a fascinating essay entitled 'Politics and the English Language' in which he attacked political language or 'the institutional voice' as it is called nowadays. Although written in 1945 it still applies today: this is how he defined it.

> In our time political speech and writing are largely the defence of the indefensible . . . political language consists largely of euphemisms, question begging and sheer

cloudy vagueness. [And he gives the following example] Defenceless villages are bombarded from the air, the inhabitants driven out into the countryside, the cattle machine-gunned, the huts set on fire with incendiary bullets: this is called *pacification*. [Pacification is a noun construction – he continues –] Such phraseology is needed if one wants to name things without calling up mental pictures of them.

To demonstrate how this can be applicable to museum texts here is another example taken from the late eighteenth century section of a social history museum.

The family here would have had three or four servants whose life would have been a lot less comfortable. They would have done all the shopping, cooking, cleaning and household chores, including looking after the children, in return for their keep.

The use of the generic noun *servant* under-values the status of this group of workers. Presumably this generalization is intended to cover parlour maid, chamber maid, kitchen maid and perhaps nanny and governess too. We can only guess as we are not told. Such a generalization suggest an attitude to this kind of worker but does this originate in the mind of the writer or was it intended to reflect the class-conscious attitudes of the period?

As we have already observed, naming workers as *designers* identifies them as individuals by virtue of their trade. In this passage, however, it is only the work that the servants performed that is given significance. The activities are described by noun constructions: *cooking, cleaning, shopping, looking after children*. In other words a noun has been created out of a verb which deflects importance from the doer to the work itself. Thus the verb *to cook* is transformed into the noun *the cooking* and the necessity to refer to the doer, in this case the cook and her occupation, is avoided in favour of a description of the activity itself. Thus the cooks are demoted by the writer. Such terminology suggests that the people themselves who were probably mostly women were not important and that anyone could have done the job. It is also interesting that the children are parallelled linguistically with household chores which is a strange attitude for a social historian to take unless this was indeed the attitude to children at the time, in which case this surely warrants an explanation.

In the following text slaves are parallelled with mahogany, cotton, tea and spices.

London was a huge port and trade centre and London's merchants were wealthy. Of all the trades, the slave trade was perhaps the most profitable for London merchants and bankers, and many of them kept black slaves in their London homes. Trade with the British colonies provided the raw materials for the many luxury goods now found in British homes. Mahogany was imported from Jamaica and Cuba, tea, cotton and spices from India, sugar from the West Indies, as well as porcelain from China. London was a cosmopolitan city attracting skilled workers from many parts of the world. Many of these like the French Huguenot silk weavers who had settled in Spitalfields, influenced the look of furniture and furnishings in Britain.

The writer makes no linguistic differentiation between the trade in people and inanimate objects: both are referred to as commodities of contemporary trade. It is quite clear from the claim that 'rich merchants and bankers kept black slaves in their London homes', that this was a status symbol. The text reinforces this by the barely differentiated possession of slaves and luxury goods in the home.

It is well known that slave traders did not treat their 'commodities' as human beings, however, it seems rather strange that a text written in the 1980s should attempt to perpetuate, even condone, that view, for, by not mentioning the attitude to slaves at that time, this is the impression given. By using the verb , *kept* in 'kept black slaves in their London homes', the parallel with a domestic animal is conjured up. After all, one *keeps* a dog but *employs* a cook. The *Oxford English Dictionary*'s definition of *kept* is 'financially supported and privately controlled by interested persons'. This may have a bearing on the fact that servants were given such little status in the previous passage quoted if they were also black slaves. If the museum considers history to be part of an on-going process of social development which embraces past, present and future, this issue should surely be addressed or at least acknowledged, as failure to do so actually influences social attitudes.

The passage itself reads more like a promotion for London in a holiday brochure than an historical account. It commences with the name London and ends with the name Britain. In only six sentences London is repeated five times and Britain three times. Repetition is a linguistic technique used frequently in advertising. Although a certain amount of repetition is unavoidable and even desirable, for purposes of clarity, the repeated use of the name London in this text is a good example of linguistic redundancy: 'the slave trade was perhaps the most profitable for *London* merchants and bankers, and many of them kept black slaves in their *London* homes . As the reader is aware right from the start that London is the subject of the paragraph, neither of these repetitions is necessary.

Also the choice of evaluative adjectives adds significantly to the impression that London is being promoted, thus: *huge* port, *profitable* (trade), *wealthy* (merchants), *luxury* goods, *British* homes, *cosmopolitan* city, *skilled* workers. *Huge, profitable, wealthy* and *luxury* are being used as maximizers to emphasize one very specific aspect of London life in the 18th century. *British* homes, without the qualification of 'some' or 'certain' before it, is very misleading as it implies that all homes in Britain possessed luxury goods, which is very far from the truth.

> London was a cosmopolitan city attracting skilled workers from many parts of the world. Many of these like the French Huguenot silk weavers who had settled in Spitalfields, influenced the look of furniture and furnishings in Britain.

Although the *OED*'s definition of cosmopolitan is 'belonging to all parts of the world', the word has assumed other, more exotic, connotations through its frequent use in travel brochures. Also the choice of the verb *attracting* is interesting. Historians will know that the French Huguenots were driven from their own country by the religious persecution that followed the revocation of the 1685 Edict of Nantes. Therefore, as the Huguenots were refugees, the suggestion that they were part of a body of skilled workers that London attracted from all over the world is not only misleading but historically questionable.

The choice and combination of words contributes significantly to the mediation of versions of events. An alternative to *attracting* for example, could be 'employing', and to *French Huguenot silk weavers*, 'immigrant refugee workers'. The text would have given a very different impression if these words had been altered. It is also interesting that the black slaves are parallelled linguistically with inanimate trade commodities whereas the white Huguenots are named specifically and thus given status on three counts, one by virtue of their nationality, 'French', two, their religion, 'Huguenot', and three, their trade, 'silk weavers'. Thus, the choice and combination of language represents not just a way of talking about the world but also a way of seeing it.

To return to Jeanne Cannizzo whom I quoted earlier, it would be difficult to contest her assertion that 'museums are carefully created, artificially constructed repositories; they are negotiated realities'. It is fair to add however that those involved in writing museum texts are often unaware of the implications of the language they use. Indeed, some would be very surprised to discover prejudices that they were unaware of appearing in the words they have written. It is clear that all discourses are socially constructed and museum staff are not exempt from the articulation of this process. Until authors of museum texts become more aware of the underlying ideological construction of their own world view, their personal angling of historical events will continue to mislead visitors because: 'the world is grasped through language. But in its use by a speaker, language is more than that. It is a version of the world offered to, imposed on, enacted by someone else' (Kress and Hodge 1974).

Thus we have looked at texts that discriminate against women and race. The last example relates history from a classist perspective:

> Whole suburbs sprang up in a matter of years; most of Holloway appeared in the 1860s and 1870s. The commuter had arrived. He made his money in the City, but could escape city life.

> Others were not so lucky. Commuter railways cut through vast slum areas; pools of cheap labour, used and yet avoided by the suburban resident. . . . At a time when everyone was supposed to 'know their place', where you lived was very important. Really wealthy and fashionable people lived either in the West End, in the country (or both).

Those people living in the suburbs are named by this text as *commuters*. Those living in the West End are named *really wealthy and fashionable people*, but those living in the slum areas are given no human status at all. instead they are indicated with the metaphor *pools of cheap labour*. The noun *pool* is the name of something from which water can be drawn, the anonymous people being the water which could be drawn from the pool. In other words the working classes are named linguistically as a resource for the better-off and have no title, sex or trade.

The two verbs in the following clause, qualifying pools of cheap labour, are very significant: '*used* and yet *avoided* by the suburban resident'. This is clearly written from the point of view of the suburban resident, not the slum resident. The fact that these people are being *used* as *cheap labour* indicated quite clearly that they were being exploited. If the writer had used the verb *employed* instead of *used* s/he would not have appeared to be condoning this practice. Also, the fact that these people were to be avoided indicates that the text is written from the point-of-view of the suburban resident. To elect to describe people and their homes from the point of view of those who exploited and avoided them, can hardly be claimed as an unbiased perspective.

I am not trying to suggest that it is possible for museum staff to produce exhibitions that are completely impartial and value-free. This would not be realistic and there is even a case to argue that it would not be desirable. However, it would be possible to raise the consciousness of writers in order that they are more aware of the process by which meanings are constructed and communicated. If this could be achieved they would have more control over the unconsciously mediated messages in their texts.

This paper first appeared in Women, Heritage and Museums (WHAM) *14 (1990), pp. 15–21.*

NOTE

Helen Coxall works as a freelance Museum Language Consultant and teaches at the University of Westminster.

1 For more on this see C. L. Learman, 'Dominant discourse: the institutional voice and control of topic', in Howard Davies and Paul Walton (eds) (1983) *Language Image Media*, Blackwell.

REFERENCES

Ardener, Edwin (1978) 'Belief and the problems of women', in S. Ardener (ed.) *Perceiving Women*, New York: Hammond.

Cannizzo, Jeanne (1987) 'How sweet it is cultural politics in Barbados', *Muse*, Winter.

Kress, Gunther and Hodge, Robert (1974) *Language as Ideology*, London: Routledge & Kegan Paul.

Lerner, Gerda (1886) *The Creation of Patriarchy*, Oxford: Oxford University Press: 4–5.

Leone, Mark (1983) 'Methods as message: interpreting the past with the public', *Museums News* 62(1): 35–41.

Orwell, George (1946) 'Politics and the English Language', in David Lodge (ed.) (1972) *20th Century Literary Criticism* (first published in *The Collected Essays, Journalism and Letters*), Harlow: Longman: 361–9.

17

Combating redundancy: writing texts for exhibitions

Margareta Ekarv

Margareta Ekarv writes easy-to-read books for adults and here describes how she applied lessons from this style of writing to exhibition texts. Most people find reading in museums difficult after a few minutes, often because of simple physical factors. The easy-to-read style often does not mean that language or subject matter must be simplified.

Sentences are short, normal word order is preferred and lines are about forty-five characters long. The end of a line of text coincides with the end of a natural phrase. Subordinate clauses, and unnecessary adverbial modifiers are avoided.

This style of text writing, based on this article, has been tried out in some museums in England very successfully.

Is there really any need for words in a museum? Aren't pictures, exhibits, labels and sets enough? Aren't our modern museums so loaded with messages of various kinds that visitors can learn all they need from the exhibits without the written word?

Far from it. By using written material for other purposes than mere labels and summaries we can put words on a par with the other exhibition material. We can use words to give a new, deeper dimension to our visual experience. Words make us think, and our thoughts conjure up pictures in our minds. Is it not through mental pictures like these that we discover the world around us?

When I was asked to write the texts for the Postal Museum's permanent exhibition *A Letter Makes All the Difference* I was confronted, together with producer Elisabet Olofsson and designer Björn Ed, with a number of questions. Elisabet and Björn knew about these problems and they were agreed that in this exhibition the texts were to have the same status as the documents and other exhibits, that it was worth devoting time and energy to this written material rather than turn out something slapdash at the last minute.

An exhibition text has to put up with more competition than most other written material. It has to compete for people's attention with all the other material and tends to be the last thing to catch their eye when they stand in front of the exhibits. They have to read the text *standing*, probably after a tiring walk on hard stone floors. The light is poor compared to their reading lamps at home, and it is impossible to vary the reading angle as with a book or newspaper. We are up against great odds, and the only way to overcome these obstacles is to make the text *easy to read*.

'EASY READING FOR ADULTS'

When the Postal Museum approached me I had just finished writing an easy-to-read book for adults. It was therefore natural for me to use the easy-to-read method for this project. I believe this method can be a great help, and also an inspiration, to those who write exhibition texts for museums.

Ever since the 1960s the National Board of Education has given grants for the publication of easy-to-read books for adults. A condition for financial support for the publication of these books is that the writers must write simply and straightforwardly. However, this does not mean simplification either of the language or the subject matter. The sentences are short, normal word order is preferred and the lines are about forty-five characters long. In dividing the text into lines the principle is to let the end of a line coincide with the end of a natural phrase. Subordinate clauses, complicated attributive constructions and unnecessary adverbial modifiers are avoided. To take an example of the sort of text you might see in a museum: 'Most of the manure was spread during late winter when there was still snow on the ground, but some of it was also spread in the summer'. A corresponding easy-to-read text would be phrased as follows:

The farmers spread manure
in late winter and in summer.

Does the reader miss anything essential in the latter version? Not as far as I can see. The information given in both cases refers to the time when the manure is spread. The easy-to-read version favours the active form of the verb, the subject confronting the reader with the natural order of things. Moreover, there is no division into syllables when an easy-to-read text is printed. Museum material, on the other hand, often contains syllable division, which is neither easy to read nor very attractive to the eye. In the following example it seems the length of the line was the decisive factor:

The trade from the coastal districts of Northern Sweden and Finland went through the country's capital, Stockholm, which consequently became an important transshipment centre.

A STEP-BY-STEP PROCESS

I was asked to write the texts about five months before the exhibition was to be opened. The exhibition concept had already been decided on, and also the arrangement by rooms, but not the final appearance of the rooms. Work had just started on the building of the exhibits. Documentation for each room was in the pipeline. My first task was to read up on the subject so as to be able to make judgements of my own. The factual information was to be provided by others.

The work of writing the texts took a little over two months. My texts were based on the data compiled by various museum officials and on the conversations I had at regular intervals with the producer and the designer *in the room where a particular text was to be shown*. It was important to relate to the exhibition room in each case.

Thus I began writing the texts long before the rooms themselves were finished. My first efforts were rough drafts. Elisabet and Björn read them and gave their views, which was not so easy since we did not yet have a definite idea of how the rooms would look. To start with I just wrote to get acquainted with my subject, and the reactions I got gave me inspiration and a sense of direction. I went home and rewrote the texts. My collaborators read through the new texts and we again had discussions together. Each new version and discussion resulted in significant changes. The spirit of these dialogues was open and critical, and the texts also provided ideas for the design of the exhibition rooms. This method of writing the material may sound time-consuming, but it worked. Choosing the subject matter, putting it into words, rejecting some parts and altering others is a process that takes time. It was important to try the texts out, and my job was made easier by the fact that Elisabet and Björn had very definite ideas about what the exhibition was to convey.

The factual information in the texts was checked by those who had written the documentation. After altering and making clean copies of the texts we had them enlarged and taped them in place in the exhibition itself. Although I tried to keep in touch with each exhibition room while work was in progress, I was aware of the risk of producing armchair material. The texts must be an integral part of the exhibition environment, and we had to delete and change parts that we had already approved when we saw that reading the texts in the exhibition room gave a different impression from that intended. We typeset the texts with the typography we had decided on, we tested different sizes for readability and mounted the texts in frames to get as clear an idea as possible of what the finished results would look like. We were, however, aware that the finished result always has one or two surprises in store, since the overall impression depends on a combination of so many elements.

In the exhibition *A Letter Makes All the Difference* the historical process is illustrated in fragments, by the lives and work of certain people. Some of these people are represented by full-scale wax figures. These figures were made at the same time as the texts were being written, and when their faces were being completed the texts were already in the typesetting state. If I had seen these faces first I would have been able to make some of the texts more authentic. This is just one example of the fact that the writer should always keep in touch with what is going on in the exhibition room, and of course the problem becomes increasingly acute in the final stages when everyone is pressed for time.

CONCENTRATING THE TEXT

When writing texts for exhibitions we constantly have to condense the material and delete everything superfluous until there remains a bare minimum necessary to convey the essential content. This situation makes great demands on style. The words must be well chosen and precise and each phrase must be concrete and clear to enable the reader to absorb it rapidly. This does not mean that a factual text must be dry as dust; the language can be full of associations and provide food for thought. I believe that you can concentrate such texts to an almost poetic level, though the object is not to write poetry. But you should be attentive to the sounds and rhythm. Even in a factual text you should bear in mind that the language depends on interaction between the different sounds of the language, especially the vowels. The melody produced by this interaction can be turned to account for rhythmical purposes, and a suitable rhythm makes a text easier to read.

We know from studies that have been carried out that few visitors, if any, read all the texts accompanying an exhibition. My goal in writing the exhibition texts was that if a visitor starts reading one of the texts, it should be so easy to read and interesting that he or she reads to the end of the paragraph. This is one of the reasons why the texts are divided into independent paragraphs, the other being that this division is made necessary by the content. I also hope of course that a visitor who reads one such paragraph with appreciation will go on to the next one.

In my view the language of these texts should match the subject, according to the time-honoured principle of harmony between form and content. So if I am writing for a historical exhibition I might use some words with an archaic ring. We should not forget our linguistic heritage: words like betide, regal and chattels help to create an atmosphere, and if the meaning of a word is not immediately apparent the context may offer a solution. At the same time, the text should also be addressed to the reader. There may seem to be a contradiction here, but in fact this is quite natural. Visitors reading a text in a museum should have the feeling that a knowledgeable guide is standing right beside them and talking to them. The tone and conversational expressions will help them to understand. I also think that these texts should be stimulating, conjure up pictures and make the reader feel 'this is really terribly interesting', as the Swedish writer Bengt Anderberg has said about just about everything in life and literature. It is true that the museum repertoire is 'classical' but as in the theatre it is the performance and the production that still bring the old truths home to us. The selection of historical facts, real life in fact, can be produced in a museum in such a way as to make us sit up and think. An important part is played in the production by the written material.

CAPTIONS, CATALOGUE?

This exhibition had no captions in the rooms. This was not because we had forgotten them, we simply could not find a satisfactory solution to the problem. It is difficult to produce captions which do not limit your scope or oversimplify. Perhaps we will find a solution when we evaluate the exhibition and make additions. No exhibition should be so permanent that it remains completely unchanged year after year.

What about a catalogue? How should it be written and what should be the relationship between catalogue and exhibition texts? The texts for the exhibition *A Letter Makes All the Difference* are intended as a brief introduction, an inspiration to the visitor to find out more about the subject somewhere else, in a comprehensive catalogue for example. Such a catalogue would give us a chance to fill in the details, such as the material we had to exclude from the documentation provided by the museum officials. There is no reason why we should not write the catalogue in an easy-to-read style too. We have not yet started on this task, however.

Words certainly have an important function in a museum. Let us give them the chance to fulfil this function by broadening the visitors' experience while stimulating their interest. Don't we owe this to the museum visitor?

This paper first appeared in Exhibitions in Sweden 27/8 (1986/7), pp. 1–7.

How old is this text?

James Carter

Readability tests can help ensure that texts can be understood. The Fry and the Cloze tests are described. Although these measures can be useful, some caution is suggested in their use. Neither of them have been specifically designed for museum use.

Do your readers really understand you? Readability – the measure of how easy a text is to read and comprehend – depends on many factors. The reader's motivation is a major one. For example, an 8-year old will work hard to understand a complex or poorly trans-lated computer game instruction book, but wouldn't attempt a financial report of the same complexity. Typeface and layout also affect how fluently you can read text. But the complexity of the language is a factor too, and reading age tests can be a useful check on whether your writing is likely to be understandable or not.

They have been developed in the education sector, where it's obviously important to match the abilities of children who are learning to read with the style and complexity of the books their teacher gives them.

There are many different methods, some of which rely on involved mathematical formulae. The Fry test is easy to do and relatively quick.

1 Select at random three passages of 100 words. If your text isn't this long (and often it shouldn't be!) use just one passage.
2 Count the total number of sentences in each passage and take the average of these numbers.
3 Count the total number of syllables in each passage and again take the average. It's easiest to do this if you go through the text writing the number of syllables in pencil above each word.
4 Plot these two averages on the graph (Fig. 18.1).

If you want a benchmark to aim for, try writing for a reading age of 12 for panels in an exhibition for the general public. If that seems low, just think about your readers. You can't rely on them being highly motivated: most interpretation is about provoking interest, not satisfying a desire for detailed knowledge. They're likely to be standing up, perhaps outdoors, with distractions including wandering children, low-flying jets and ice-cream stalls. It's not that you're writing for people who have a reading age of 12, just that you need to make your text as easy to read as possible.

It's important to recognize that reading age is not related to physical age or mental age. The method above is simply a measure of how complex the word and sentence structure is, and therefore of how easy it is to read. A recent test on a copy of the *Sun* and on a

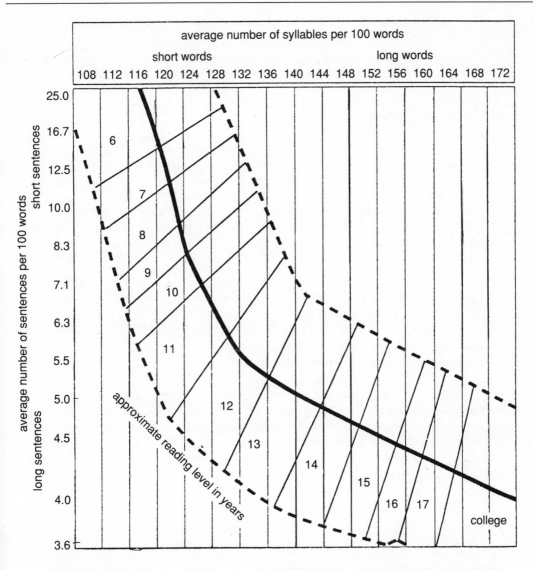

Fig. 18.1 The Fry Test for reading age. This graph has been redrawn from the *Journal of Reading*, April 1968; the dotted lines indicate the boundary of the region of maximum reliability of the test.

feature in *The Independent on Sunday* magazine gave reading ages of 11/12 and 15/16 respectively. The *Sun* isn't written for people who are stupid, just for those who prefer something easy to read (whatever else you may think about it!).

MIND THE GAP

The Fry test only measures complexity of language. It's quick and easy, but it can't tell you whether your intended audience actually understands what you've written. Cloze

Procedure gives an indication of how your readers interact with your text, and how much they really understand it.

The name cames from *closure*, a concept in Gestalt theory which suggests that we will mentally complete any incomplete pattern. For example, a diagram of a circle with gaps in it will still be perceived as a circle. As applied to readability and comprehension tests, the procedure has many possibilities and variants, but the version which follows is appropriate for interpretation intended for adults.

1   Select a passage from your text and prepare a version of it in which every fifth word is replaced by an equal-sized blank. The passage should start at the beginning of a paragraph. A length of about 250 words is recommended, but not essential. Leave the first and last sentences intact, and ensure that you don't remove proper nouns unless they have already occurred.
2   Show this prepared text to a representative sample of your audience, and ask them to guess the missing words. Allow as much time as necessary. The equal-size blanks prevent guesses on the basis of word length.
3   Calculate the score as a percentage. Count an answer as correct only if it is exactly the same word as in the original, though you can allow minor mis-spellings. Numbering the gaps interferes with the readers' flow, and makes it more difficult for them, so find some other method of checking the completed passages.
4   Scores below 40 show that your readers may have real difficulty with your text. The table in Figure 18.2 shows the relationship between cloze scores and comprehension.

These comprehension levels indicate how well readers might do in a multiple-choice questionnaire based on a full version of the text.

'Independent' is equivalent to a score of 90% or better – complete understanding. 'Instructional' means a score of between 75% and 89% – in a classroom setting, enough for full understanding with some assistance. This should be acceptable for most interpretation: you're not aiming to equip visitors for an exam. Visitors are often in groups, and their companions will fill in gaps in any individual's understanding. They can also pick up clues from other text, or from objects on display.

Comprehension level	Frustration	Instructional	Independent
Cloze score	0 40	 60	 100

Fig. 18.2   Correlation between comprehension and cloze scores. Good interpretation should give a cloze score above 40. From Rye (1982)

'Frustration' level, however, means that the text is too difficult even with some help. It's time to go back to the drafting stage!

PASS THE SALT

There are many other tests for readability, some of them available as computer programs. But perhaps they all need to be taken with a healthy pinch of salt. They can mask real difficulties – a poorly written short sentence can be less comprehensible than a well written long one. They can draw attention to apparent faults which would cause no difficulty, especially if they involve comparing text with lists of 'familiar' words. One computer package, for example, rejects 'Brighton', 'Royal' and 'dragons' in a children's guide to the Royal Pavilion in Brighton. It's worth remembering that some 'familiar words' lists were compiled in the United States in the 1930s!

Above all, tests like these are no substitute for writing with feeling and power. Writing solely to match a particular reading age could easily be dull: the trick is to write simply, but with an enthusiasm that makes your writing worth reading.

This paper first appeared in Environmental Interpretation *(Feb. 1993), pp. 10-11.*

REFERENCES

If you want to know more about readability, try these books:

Gilliland, John (1972) *Readability*, London: Hodder and Stoughton.
Rye, James (1982) *Cloze Procedure and the Teaching of Reading*, Oxford: Heinemann Educational.

19

A writing checklist

J. Carter and D. Hillier

Although extremely short, this list gives some very useful basic guidelines for writing museum texts of all sorts, and is of particular relevance to interpretive panels and labels.

Good writing develops with practice. The more you do, and the more you think about it, the more you develop an 'ear' for what makes good text. This checklist gives some guidelines to start you off.

- Use **short sentences**. Put just one or two ideas in each sentence. Vary the pace by using some longer sentences, but avoid using many sub-clauses, separated by commas, which build sentences that go on and on, rather like this one: notice the contrast between it and the two before.
- Use **active** verbs rather than passive 'Henry VIII broke the monasteries' power in 1564' rather than: 'The monasteries' power was broken in 1564'. The passive form sounds guarded and dull; it also removes people from the story and suggests that events happen by themselves.
- Make your writing **personal**. Involve your reader by using 'you'; if you need to refer to your organization, use 'we'.
- Use the expressions and language you'd use if you were **talking** to someone. 'We bought the Reserve in 1979' rather than 'The Council purchased the Reserve'. Do you go down to the shops to purchase some bananas? Try reading your draft to a friend (better than a colleague) and get them to tell you when it sounds like 'officialese'.
- Describe things you know **people can see**, or are likely to see, rather than rarities.
- If you have a lot of information, use a **text hierarchy**. This is particularly useful in exhibitions: a headline to summarize the panel, a short block of text (100–150 words) to give essential points, then more information in other blocks or picture captions. Make the different levels of importance clear by different type sizes or styles, and by the position of the text on the page/panel.
- Be **selective** about how much you write! Choose the most important or interesting things, and be concise. You may be able to write more if the panel is describing something particularly interesting, or is in a place which people will have made a special effort to get to.

This checklist first appeared in Environmental Interpretation *(Feb. 1993), p. 21.*

20

Worth a Hull lot more

Elizabeth Frostick

A history exhibition case study. History exhibitions used to focus on national history, divided chronologically into 'ages' or centuries. This exhibition focuses on local and individual histories, and the exhibition is divided according to life-stage. The emphasis is on the 'how was it for you' approach to understanding the past. Consultation with local people, and research into the past of a very specific locality and the people who do and did live there has resulted in a very successful exhibition.

In the five months since the official opening on 11 September 1990 by Hull's very own superstar, Roland Gift (lead singer of the Fine Young Cannibals), *The Story of Hull and its People* attracted 35,000 visitors. This is not bad going for a predominantly working-class city of almost 300,000. The tremendous level of support for this venture is a reflection both of the approach taken by the Old Grammar School Museum and the pride with which local people hold their own history and their museums.

The Story of Hull and its People is a new permanent exhibition about the history of ordinary people who have lived and worked in Hull over the past 700 years. Although a self-contained exhibition, it is the culmination of some four years' work in social history in Hull and a number of specific temporary exhibitions. The new exhibition, which occupies a modest space of about 180 square metres is situated on the first floor of the Old Grammar School Museum in the heart of Hull's medieval 'Old Town'.

The Old Grammar School is a new museum – first opened in May 1988 – with the function of telling the social history of Hull. The Old Grammar School itself, as its name suggests, was originally Hull's Grammar School, built in 1585. The Old Grammar School complex, however, also includes two adjacent buildings which provide an education room and research room on one side, and a lecture room on the other.

The new displays, *The Story of Hull and its People* (also the subtitle of The Old Grammar School museum) mark the completion of the major phase in a two-phase, permanent exhibition about the social history of Hull. Much time was spent deliberating the logistics of an exhibition to be mounted in 180 square metres of space.

Self-censorship not only causes the curator psychological hang-ups, it also prevents many important subjects from ever reaching the public domain. There are enough constraints upon a curator already, acting as 'hold-all' for the wishes of politicians, chief officers, directors, local societies, ordinary people, and professional colleagues, to name but a few. The point is that exhibitions should provoke a response, and people do not have to like the content of history for it to be important. Taking the plunge into areas where approval is not guaranteed takes a certain amount of courage: the guiding principle adopted in Hull, however, was to represent the history of the majority of ordinary people and not bow to pressure from an articulate minority.

The significance of *The Story of Hull and its People*, in this respect, is that it does depart fundamentally from the approaches taken in traditional social history and local history galleries. A chronological approach was felt to be too restrictive; this frequently leads to 'books on the wall' (until the nineteenth century), and unsuccessful models taking up vital space, but most importantly produces exhibitions which say very little about people. The traditional local history gallery relies on an historical or geographical understanding of history which puts topography before an explanation of the development of an essentially human experience. Alternatively, there are object-centred approaches where human experience may be frozen at a particular point in time; here, all aspects of life are recreated in a room, town or village setting which can still fail to explain the relevance of it all to people's lives. Such static displays also inherently fail to address the dynamics of history. The problem with such approaches is that they have failed to develop the 'people dimension' to any satisfactory level.

The Story of Hull and its People aims to retrieve people from the history of place-names, buildings, famous men (and occasionally women), governments, officialdom, exceptional events and inanimate objects. It takes more of a 'how was it for you?' approach. In other words it celebrates people's actual lives. What did people do, think, fear, celebrate, experience and actually feel in the past. Why shy away from the most fascinating and important history of all? It is only through the investigation of personal experiences that we can balance the years of 'official' history, preserved in documents and the written word, representing such an imperfect picture of the past.

The introduction to the exhibition focuses upon two local people, Ray and Elsie, who are still very much alive and whose families have lived in Hull for at least five generations. Their personal stories are illustrated by the photographs, documents, objects and recollections drawn together for the museum, and they provide an insight into at least two of the individuals that together make up the history of Hull. This way every visitor is invited to think about themselves and their own personal histories. We all have a history to tell.

The exhibition then relates Hull's history through the various stages of life common to the people who have lived in Hull, rather than by a year by year account. This exhibition is not the definitive account of Hull's history, but it is an attempt to put people first in trying to understand the past. The story begins, at the beginning of a person's life with 'Childhood' and ends with 'Death'. In-between the story traces the following themes: 'Adolescence', 'Skills for Life', 'Courtship and Marriage', 'No Place Like Home', 'Running a Home', 'Childcare and Health' and 'Earning a Living'. Part Two of the development will complete the life-cycle by looking at history through more communal activities, like 'Politics', 'War', 'Leisure', 'Custom and Beliefs', 'Old Age', and finally 'Death'.

An explanation of the 'Childhood' section reveals more of the approach taken here. This first main section looks at many different aspects of childhood in Hull's history, and does not shy away from the fact that some of these were extremely unpleasant. 'The Fight for Life', 'Death takes its Toll' and child mortality statistics are a grim reminder of a past struggle for survival. A height chart allows children today to measure themselves against the smaller heights of children earlier this century. The issue of child abuse is not evaded. The exhibition then celebrates the various aspects of play, with among other things, giant snakes and ladders, fantastical characters and toys for children to play with. The design throughout the exhibition is lively and colourful and provides a friendly and warm environment for visitors. 'Childhood' in Hull would not be complete without a look at orphans.

Throughout, the exhibition tries hard not to avoid 'difficult' subjects: the courtship section includes local people talking about the 'mating game' – there are even a few 'Mates' on display. A section on 'Childcare and Health' includes information about the many thousands of women who died in childbirth, and the central role that women have played for centuries in nurturing the next generation. A video about the history of housing in Hull, made by the museum, is candid about the Yorkshire Development Group (YDG) 'misery maisonettes' of the 1960s and 1970s and the problems of homelessness. The TV-Video is situated within a young couple's 'typical' living room of 1989/90, where visitors can rest their weary museum feet.

Another feature of the exhibition is 'The Game of Life', a simple interactive device which allows visitors to take part in the exhibition itself. Assisted by Hull's celebrated attendants, (see *Museums Journal*, March 1989: 12) visitors are invited to take a card which reveals one of six different characters. Based on probable local lives over the five centuries, the fate of a particular character is revealed in the different parts of the exhibition. This device helps to create an active response from visitors, but has also allowed the museum to stress that experiences in the past were different for different individuals and dependent on many factors.

The exhibition has been built with extensive involvement by local people; much of the oral history research has been incorporated directly as audio tapes, but also as people's own words on the panels. Much of the collection has been successfully built up through staging a series of temporary exhibitions in Hull and through direct appeals for *The Story of Hull and its People*. It is important to stress the high level of involvement by large numbers of local people in shaping the exhibition. Ray and Elsie, for example, were able to build their own family histories, and their role within the displays evolved over a period of time. A local photographer was asked to produce many contemporary images of Hull, partly to fill gaps where material was difficult to acquire, like pawnbroking, but also to bring the story up to date and to have a record for the future. Large numbers of people shared memories and discussed and donated material. Not surprisingly, a number of museum staff helped in the realization of the exhibition, the total cost of which was £170,000. An 80-page book expanding the ideas in the exhibition has been published jointly by the museum and Hutton Press, a local publisher, which will sell at £3.95.

Meanwhile, the curator's potentially fiercest critics – local people – who form a majority of the 35,000 visitors so far, think it is great.

This paper first appeared in Museums Journal *91(2) (1991), pp. 33–5.*

21

Art history for all the family
John Millard

An art exhibition case study. Art displays are often designed with little thought for the visitor, and the result is that only those with a prior knowledge of art and art history visit the gallery. Generally fine art and decorative art are categories around which displays are built, and they are generally kept apart.

'Art on Tyneside' set out to appeal to the non-specialist with two specific target audiences: children 8 to 12 years, and people with disabilities. Categories of material were mixed, the learning and access needs of the target visitors were paramount, market research and consultation were undertaken seriously as part of the exhibition planning and production process.

David Phillips reviews the exhibition.

Art on Tyneside, recently opened at the Laing Art Gallery in Newcastle upon Tyne, brings together the Laing's collections of silver, glass, ceramics, paintings and costume to tell the story of art on Tyneside over some 300 years. The novelty of this art display is the use of ideas from other museum disciplines and even from Jorvik or Wigan Pier: it is the first art display to use scenic recreations, interactives, sounds, smells and models, not to mention a talking tug-boat.

To some, such techniques are inappropriate for high culture. One arts pundit was thrown into a fury when he visited with his family. He felt that the display debased the art. However his children approved, and, if the gallery's comments book is any guide, visitors welcome the friendly approach of the display. 'Transformation! Glorious transformation!' wrote one.

The Laing has an imposing portico and marble halls, which were meant to create a hallowed atmosphere for art when it opened in 1904. This sort of intimidating architecture is familiar enough, but it now suggests to many that art and art galleries are 'not for the likes of us'. The Laing, as Newcastle's city art gallery, cannot afford to project such an exclusive image. Newcastle suffers from problems of inner city deprivation and unemployment, and saw riots in the summer of 1991. The gallery runs the risk of being seen as marginal, or even unsustainable in a city with scant resources to deal with serious social and economic problems.

The area of the Laing now occupied by *Art on Tyneside* used to contain a shanty town of new and old cases which had been gradually installed over a 15-year period, giving rise to displays that were disjointed and lacked focus. There were separate sections for costume, glass, watercolours and so on. Art galleries often separate categories of objects in this way and, as any contemporary craftsperson can tell you, there is hierarchy of materials, with painting at its apex. Such displays may be useful to students or collectors, but they are not for a general audience. The new display shows that the range of media in the Laing's collection can be brought together in a coherent display in which they have equal status.

Research on a series of exhibitions at the Laing suggested that regional art was a good candidate for this multi-media approach. Newcastle was a flourishing centre for silver and glass production before the fine arts had even a foothold in the area. The wood-engraver Thomas Bewick, a major figure on Tyneside, emerged from an eighteenth-century craft workshop specializing in a variety of media; and Victorian woodcarving, glass and pottery was at least as exciting as the painting of the time.

A chronological narrative was constructed with a series of settings, which show works of art in a historical context and give an impression of changes that took place in the cultural climate. A significant proportion of the display is devoted to the present, with video and exhibition areas showing art and architecture in the local environment, and encouraging visitors to take part in art in the region.

The key target audiences selected for the display were 8- to 12-year-olds and people with disabilities. Exhibitions at the Laing targeted at children had been successful, and a series of 'Freedom To Touch' exhibitions had been pioneered by education officer Gwen Carr for people with special needs.

Contact with Equal Arts (formerly Northern Shape – the arts and disability agency for the Northern region) and teachers' advisers in Newcastle was essential for reaching these target audiences.

Equal Arts put together a team of consultants with experience of a range of disabilities, and they were shown the initial design. This included a model of the display, which proved to be an invaluable aid to the consultants, one of whom had difficulty reading plans and none of whom were museum specialists. They produced a report with a list of recommendations. Many could be carried out at no cost, but more costly aspects included, for example: non-reflective glass to help visitors with impaired vision; an induction loop in the video area for hearing-impaired visitors; and raised floor-track for blind and partially-sighted visitors. Eventually grants and sponsorship were found to finance all of the disability consultants' recommendations.

As the display team worked on catering for the target audience of 8- to 12-year-olds, outside designers Redman Design Associates contributed crucial experience of using interactives and other non-verbal forms of interpretation from museum disciplines other than art. The education officer was asked to take a lead on producing copy for the panels, and a small team worked on their wording and on cartoons to complement the story-line for younger visitors. Tensions arose among staff, particularly over the graphic panels for each area. Some curators worried about over-simplification, but encouragement came from an unexpected quarter. The text of the graphic panels was translated for leaflets in Gujarati, Urdu and Cantonese, the main languages apart from English used in Newcastle, and the translators were enthusiastic about the clarity of the story it told. The story of *Art on Tyneside* is told in about 1,500 words on around a dozen panels and the text was checked by local school advisers.

The key target audiences have responded well to the display and are visiting in increasing numbers. The focus of the display on younger children and people with disabilities has also signalled to a general audience that the Laing is serious about access. As a visitor wrote in the Laing's comment book: '*Art on Tyneside* was brilliant and it was a very good idea to make it easier for blind and disabled people. It's good for children too.'

The attendants' uniforms were changed for the opening of the display, from the traditional navy blazer and tie with a blue shirt, to polo shirts and sweatshirts with a logo. Many visitors noticed and commented on the changes:

- A breath of fresh air compared to the usual image of art galleries
- About 300% better than it used to be
- What a transformation from a year ago
- About time! I feel as though you've just reopened the Laing's doors – very enjoyable

During its first few months *Art on Tyneside* attracted about 70% more visits than the same period in the previous year. It cost just over £300,000 including £75,000 from the Wolfson Fund. Only time will tell whether this will be followed with the further investment needed to develop the gallery. Early indications are that visitors, politicians, business-people and even many art enthusiasts recognize and welcome *Art on Tyneside*'s attempt to appeal to people who would not normally think of going to an art gallery.

ART ON TYNESIDE: REVIEW
David Phillips

Don't tell anyone, but most of the works of art ever made look the way they do because that is how someone paid for them to look. Art galleries, for some reason, like to keep that secret. But now the Laing Art Gallery has blown the gaff with *Art on Tyneside*, which seeks to bring the arts on Tyneside to life as part of social process.

First, a description. We enter a room dominated by a large mural of art on Tyneside. Sounds of pillage tempt us through a doorway in the mural into the first of a sequence of small spaces, each devoted to a theme in a chronological survey, such as border warfare, picturesque landscape, classical Newcastle or the swinging sixties, and containing works of art in a theatrically suggestive multi-media *mise-en-scène*.

Although the display is aimed at a particular age-group (8- to 12-year-olds) the interpretative methods accommodate a wide range of visitors. For instance, as well as the cartoon-style sub-commentary, in which two children travel through history in a sequence of Asterix-like encounters, individual cases of objects bear more conventional museum-style labels about their contents. There are various opportunities for hands-on activities. We can sit at a table in an eighteenth-century coffee-house and read the *Newcastle Courant* for 3 January 1757; or have a go on a magnetic board on which we may try out our own combinations of the elements of a classical architectural façade. There are also touch samples, and a map on which push-button selections tell where distinguished buildings may still be seen in the city. There are videos, a slide show and an audio-visual presentation, video-disk-style selections and an audio point which seeks to present the experience of artists and craftspeople of the past in their own words, related to a quiz.

A first question must be whether, given the brief to bring in a new audience, and the decision to target children, an essentially didactic historical show was the right vehicle. I feel that for such an audience the visit needs to be centred on activities. For all the activities which the designers have been able to build into *Art on Tyneside*, the theme is a resistant one for this kind of treatment. Perhaps there are other aspects of art collections which would have been more accessible to activity-based exploration, as science is experienced in a science centre.

A second question is whether, from an aesthetic and academic point of view, this use of collections can be justified at all, or whether it simply interferes with our chance to see the works of art. One must respect (whether agreeing with it or not) the strong case which can be made for the most conventional presentation of collections considered pre-eminent, where the displays look marvellous and manifestly attract and engage a substantial audience, as in the new galleries of the National Gallery. But nobody can seriously claim that the majority of regional British galleries work like this. Their collections are the result of an attempt, which failed, to ape the canonical collections of the national institutions. Haunting as these municipal accumulations are for those of us who have spent much of our lives working with them, every passing year makes the segment of cultural history and human achievement which they celebrate with such pomposity seem more parochial. How refreshing to abandon the pomp, and show them as revealing vehicles of very human aspirations and pretensions, social as well as aesthetic. When the aesthetics work, the display does not get in the way. *Art on Tyneside* only uses part of the collections in part of the Laing so there is plenty of conventional display left for the visitors who do prefer it.

So how well has it been done? It is fun, informative, good-looking and very imaginative, with evidence of a great deal of thought both about the subject and about the audience coming to see it. Inevitably there are problems, but it is a compliment to such an ambitious and novel project to discuss the interesting problems which it raises. Some of the problems are practical. The spaces are confined, and can get very hot. The shrieks of the initial scene of pillage linger obtrusively through the successive centuries, interfering with the new sounds. One or two works of art were not as easy to see as one would have wished, for instance the Turner and Girtin watercolours, (though many other things were easier to see than they might be in a more conventional display). On the day I visited, the gallery did not seem quite on top of the burden of maintenance such a display involves: while much was working, and it would have been easy to go around without happening on anything amiss, I did find the first audio-phone out of order, one video and the Victorian photographer's slide projector not working, a problem with the lighting around the John Martin painting and no quiz sheets available.

More generally, I was not sure that the balance between illusionism and suggestion hit the right note. At one or two points one felt that an attempt had been made to present the past illusionistically, as if by a costumed figure in a heritage centre, as when a voice on an audio-phone says: 'I'm Mary Beilby from the Beilby family workshop, and Newcastle folk seem to like the glass and silverware that I design and make.' But the visitor whose suspension of disbelief survives that has also to come to terms with other display conventions which seem to undermine any illusion, as if with a Brechtian device. An example is the tableau, (commemorating a heroic event in which the women in a fishing community dragged a life-boat along the coast to launch it for a rescue), in which a ragged figure and seagull look for pickings on the sea shore with a massive oil painting by John Charlton hanging on a wall behind them. Such a mixture of conventions might be intended to carry a message in itself, for instance that what the visitor sees is not 'The Truth', but only a representation. However, the mixture here, though lively and imaginative, did not seem to say anything so coherent.

More significantly, the youth of the target audience means that, perhaps inevitably, the history presented is bland and conventional. I felt that the concept team may have started from the art and then tried to find suitable glimpses of historical context for it, rather than starting from a more coherent historical theme. When the art concerns Newcastle's strong tradition of maritime painting, the approach is unobtrusive and works fine; but with, for instance, the Turner and Girtin, it seemed less successful, demanding an excursion into 'the picturesque landscape' which did not seem to fit into the spirit of the place in the same way. Generally, the display succeeds in getting across the message that art arises as part of a social process, and in suggesting parts of the process. Perhaps it is unfair to expect such a display to attempt a more up-to-date exposition of sub-texts, whether structuralist, feminist, Marxist or psychological. Hopefully another gallery will take the Laing's cue, but aim at an older audience so as to include more acknowledgement that, to many contemporary commentators, the pictures almost burst out of their frames with the burden of such sub-texts.

But these are mostly discussion points rather than criticisms. The most important question about the display is what kind of experience it provides for most of its visitors. Attendance at the gallery is reportedly very substantially up, but only time will tell whether this is a temporary fillip, or a sustained reward for so much effort and investment. On a Sunday afternoon when I visited, the displays appeared to be successfully holding the attention of a modest number of visitors of all ages and, most valuably, to be provoking discussion.

But a display which includes so many experimental features requires very careful study for anyone anxious to know, for example, whether the interactive aspects are effective aids to comprehension, or whether they are more of a distraction. One hopes there will be opportunities for such studies to be done.

This paper first appeared in Museums Journal *92(2) (1992), pp. 32–3.*

22

Multiculturalism incarnate

Jane Peirson-Jones

An 'ethnographic' exhibition case study. Re-displays of often long-held ethnographic collections involve museums entering one of the most difficult and exciting arenas of contemporary cultural politics. Indigenous peoples the world over are reclaiming their cultural heritage and demanding an involvement in representations of their world. In many examples, 'ethnography', the view from the other, has become 'social history', the view from within.

This exhibition was mounted within this context of re-negotiation and reclamation. With many cultural and ethnic groups represented, and with a collection that was made within a colonial and imperialist ideology, the exhibition is themed according to cross-cultural issues and activities.

Anandi Ramamurthy reviews the exhibition.

'I notice some other visitors don't quite know what to make of it. You don't 'look at' Gallery 33 in the same way as you 'look at' other galleries. Nothing else in the museum prepares them for it.' . . . 'I began to see that the exhibition was about beliefs, customs, values and art from around the world and the relationship between them. It's about our culture, society and out place in it.' . . . 'I enjoyed my visit to Gallery 33 because you could join in and put on face masks, write things down on a piece of paper and put it on a totem pole.' . . . 'The first thing I remember are the masks . . . We all enjoyed trying them on and seeing how they changed our personalities.' . . . 'I thought it was very colourful and made you feel happy compared with the rest of the museum.'

The Gallery 33 project had twin goals: to put on public display the city of Birmingham's ethnographic collection, which had been in store for nearly thirty years, and to create a new kind of gallery which offered the visitor an interesting, challenging and enjoyable experience. In his brief the director, Michael Diamond, proposed that the display should be multicultural, multidisciplinary and multimedia: multicultural in the way it made reference to Birmingham's multicultural population, multidisciplinary in its use of the different disciplines within the museum service, and multimedia in its use of a range of interpretative media. To his list I contributed additional objectives: that the display should be concept-led not object-led, that it should be as interactive as possible and that the design should have a contemporary feel. Two major issues needed to be addressed in the interpretation: first, the representation of 'other' and secondly the colonial context of the ethnographical collection itself.

As there are over one hundred distinct cultures represented plus gender and social differentiations, there are many 'others' to take into consideration. Several steps were taken to address the ethnocentrism inherent in the display development process and to mention the politics of representation in the display itself. The first was to broaden the 'authoring base' by working with an advisory group on multicultural issues. Second, features about the way in which indigenous peoples in Canada, USA and New Zealand are taking charge of their representation in museums, were incorporated into the 'information stands'. Third, the cross-cultural juxtapositions of artefacts within topics such as religion, ethnic identity, gender are meant to challenge visitors' perceptions of themselves and encourage an examination of what is meant by 'other'. The visitor survey indicates success in this, as two thirds of the respondents reported that the display had caused them to ponder on the similarities and differences between their own and other cultures. Fourthly, we worked hard on the selection of positive images and the use of language to minimize an implicit use of 'us' and 'them'. This has been partially successful and for a number of reasons the use of language will continue to be contested. An attempt was made to treat western and non-western artefacts equally but this can be difficult because of traditional museum practice.

It was necessary to explore the history of the collection in a direct way in order to raise issues about ownership of cultural property, the implicit racism in the museum process and the multiple meanings which ethnographic artefacts hold. This has been tackled in two ways. There is a diorama in which three important benefactors to the collections, a missionary, a colonial administrator and a private collector are exhibited and their motives discussed. Alongside this an interactive video explores different attitudes to collecting and cultural traditions in the Solomon Islands with four characters; two from the present day and two from the 1920s. These exhibits can take the visitor into a deeper level of understanding of the gallery as a whole and provide a focus for anti-racist education as distinct from the cross-cultural multicultural resource in the rest of the display.

The implicit challenge of the project was to make a museum collection, formed in the first thirty years of this century as an outcome of Birmingham's colonial endeavour, say something of relevance to present day Birmingham with its very different demographic, social and economic components. To this end, contemporary artefacts have been included and all the photographs were taken in the 1980s. The hi-tech design and graphic presentation by Bremner and Orr Design Consultants Ltd attempts to link Gallery 33 with the outside world. The lively colour scheme inspired by Ndebele women's mural art from South Africa and the bold use of metal finishes are controversial features, but Bremner and Orr have succeeded in creating an exciting, informal space where visitors are expected to, and do, behave differently. As the Saturday activities bear witness, performers feel comfortable and visitors are relaxed and can enjoy themselves.

How have the visiting public responded to the exhibition? An extensive visitor evaluation programme, directed by communications consultant Paulette McManus, was designed to study the volume and pattern of visitor use and the emotional and intellectual impact of the displays. This consisted of an exit questionnaire, a tracking study, a visitor memories survey, an observation and questionnaire study of the interactive videos and analysis of visitors' written comments. Analysis of visitors' comments and questionnaire replies reveals an overwhelmingly positive response although there is a wide range of opinion on all aspects of the design and content of the gallery. The extremes of this range are represented by some who see the gallery as far too radical and some who think it is much too conservative. The most popular and memorable exhibits are the hand-held replica masks with the interactive video (IV) and musical instruments joint second. The survey shows that visitors find the IV easy to use, it has good holding power and visitors are stimulated to think about the issues raised (Peirson Jones 1992).

The response from within the multicultural arts community in Birmingham has been mixed. Gallery 33 cannot fulfil the many and various expectations which have been placed upon it. It is an anthropology display, not an exhibition about Black- and ethnic-minority visual arts or history which many would like to see. One gallery cannot carry the responsibility for covering the multicultural agenda for the museum as a whole. Multicultural interpretation needs to be fully integrated across the museum service. However, Gallery 33 has acted as a catalyst for discussion and dialogue between people within the Black- and ethnic-minority arts community and museum staff. The agenda has shifted from the role of Gallery 33 to broader issues about policy and practice in the museum as a whole.

With hindsight there are aspects of Gallery 33 which I would change. Instead of addressing seven related topics I would take one concept and explore it in a cluster of exhibits which would complement and reinforce each other. I would make greater use of the information stands and develop more effective graphic communication in them. In the interactive video it would be more effective to start with the contemporary issues and work back into the archival material. I would be much more direct and confrontational about controversial issues such as the return of cultural property now that I have better understanding of visitors' thinking. In terms of project management I would carry out far more consultation with a wider range of people on a broader agenda. I would give more authority to key advisers and I would include formative evaluation in the planning stage. Consultation stimulates the creative process, informs decision-making, increases confidence and reduces the risk. It should be an integral part of all exhibition development, not just those on 'sensitive' topics. Because Gallery 33 was new, in terms of concept and design, it called for an innovative approach from everyone who worked on its realization. It was an exercise in the management of change and much was learnt about sponsoring change, risk management and team-building.

How should Gallery 33 develop in the future? A degree of flexibility to accommodate change has been designed into Gallery 33. In 1992 display changes focused on world music as part of the *Sounds Like Birmingham* festival. Teachers' packs on cross-curricular multicultural approaches have been introduced and the first of a series of discovery boxes have been trialed and evaluated (Peirson Jones 1993). The Saturday activity programme, *Family Festivals*, which has attracted first-time visitors as both performers and audience, will be expanded. A promotional strategy needs to be drawn up. The visitor survey shows that 80 per cent of the audience finds the exhibition by chance. To date there has been no targeted promotion aimed at new audiences and appropriate marketing remains a key issue.

An important question still to be resolved concerns future acquisition policy. Should we collect contemporary material from cultures already represented in the collection or should resources be shifted to collecting related to Birmingham's ethnic minority communities? The answer to this question will lie in the development of a broader multicultural policy. The interpretative approach taken in Gallery 33 throws out a continuing challenge to both visitors and the people who work within it. Whether it inspires, confuses, informs, entertains or annoys, the bold design and mix of objects and images elicits a response. The text does not invite passive absorption of information but actively encourages visitors to form personal opinions. Over half the visitors surveyed said that they enjoyed having questions raised which made them think. Of the visitors, 40 per cent were immediately made more conscious of their own cultural heritage by their experience of visiting the exhibition. Daily we see visitors physically interacting with the hands-on exhibits. Survey evidence suggests that they also engage intellectually with the concepts about cultural identity presented in Gallery 33.

GALLERY 33: REVIEW
Anandi Ramamurthy

Gallery 33 represents a new approach to exhibition design, far from the dreary rows of identical cases in which some museums seem permanently entrenched. The gallery itself is the exhibit, in which historical and contemporary material culture can be found. Bright colours, a 'fun' approach, the interactive videos, all this provides plenty to stimulate the interest of the young audience for whom the gallery was presumably intended. Gallery 33 also brings a breath of fresh air in its ability to question ideas and history and to acknowledge ideas as interpretations. The organic gallery, growing and changing, is here to stay. Yet Gallery 33 fails because of its central notion: 'a meeting ground of cultures'. It refuses to recognize that cultures will not interact on equal terms until societies operate on the basis of equality. The imperial aggression of Europe and America, over the past two centuries, has ensured that the concept of a global village has been hurled a long way into the future.

While hanging on to the concept of a global village by, for example, juxtaposing birthday cards with Indian wedding jewellery (both expressions of celebration), curator and designers are obviously aware that the issue of conflict within society needs to be discussed. Questions of race and class are presented as: 'how did you gain your position within society?' Next to these words is a picture of the Queen writ large. Below this is a photograph of a slave advertisement with the text: 'Black people have lived in Britain for 400 years. Between 1600 and 1800 most were bought as slaves to work as domestic servants. Eventually the slave trade was banned throughout the British Empire in 1807 and slavery itself was abolished in 1834.' These words, although factual, are dishonest. Millions of people were kidnapped by force from Africa, hauled on to slave ships in such appalling conditions that, by the time they reached their destination, over a third of them were dead. All this was carried out because of white people's desire for wealth at the expense of all else.

The selection of information changes the experience. Gallery 33, like the multicultural policies which engendered it, sanitizes the areas of conflict to give the impression of a new direction without any substantial change in attitude. In this, the mask-making, body-painting, music-making themes are predominant. And in the never-ending obsession with cross-cultural comparisons, it is non-European people that are left misrepresented. It is non-European objects and images which have no context, and the image of Arab women in burkas is again dragged out in the wrong context. The veil is not a mask.

Many issues are raised in Gallery 33 without being fully discussed. The collectors of the gallery's ethnographic collection are presented, speaking for themselves. Ida Wench, for example, describes why she went to Melanesia: 'It was waiting for me and I could not disappoint them.' With virtually no context, this sort of speech only acts to endorse her imperialist ideas. To answer questions about why and how these objects were collected, we not only have to ask the collectors, but also those from whom they were collected. In many ways, collectors have been speaking for decades, through their collections. Since we probably do not know the people from whom the collections were bought, this may seem an impossible task. Yet simply asking the question serves a purpose. Information itself is suffused with the issue of power: power to articulate; to preserve; to know and to interpret. It is this central issue which Gallery 33 does not raise.

Such side-stepping allows the multicultural totem pole to exist as though permissive and all encompassing. It does not anticipate that, as on the day I visited, a nationalist Brit would have erected the British flag in it, as though staking their territory.

This paper first appeared in Museums Journal *92(1) (1992), pp. 32–3.*

REFERENCES

Peirson Jones, J. E. (1990) 'Interactive video and the Gallery 33 project', *Museum Development*, June.
Peirson Jones, J. E. (1992) 'The colonial legacy and the community' in Ivan Karp, Christine Muller Kreamer and Steven D. Lavine (eds) *Museums and Communities*, Washington and London: Smithsonian Institution Press.
Peirson Jones, J. E. (ed.) (1993) *Gallery 33 – a visitor study*, Birmingham Museums and Art Gallery.

23

Alternative perspectives
Gaby Porter

Although science centres have been enormously popular across the world for some years now, some science museums remain unreconstructed – difficult to understand without specialist knowledge, and of limited interest to many.

On the other hand, we all experience science in our daily lives at both a micro and a macro level. How can science museums make more links between the ideas and objects of science, and people. Broader definitions of science, approaches using social history, and greater efforts to integrate the context for science and technology are suggested.

> I have expectations of science museums. I expect not to understand them. I expect a visit to leave me feeling alienated, confused and exhausted. Should the museum concerned also be a museum of technology, my heart hits my boots.
>
> (Kavanagh 1992)

Many museums of science and technology tell (hi)stories of scientific achievement with technological objects. Museum displays narrow down the open-ended activities of science into objects and knowledge which may be only one alternative or outcome of the scientific endeavour. Science as a process of enquiry, experimentation, uncertainty and testing gives way to science as it is 'materialized' in objects: the end product. Interactive science exhibits, intended to encourage open-ended experimentation and exploration, are often constructed in a closed form of press-the-lever-and-see-what-happens. History is written by the winners and the stories told in museums are generally success stories: in physics; civil and mechanical engineering; transport and aeronautics – the areas which define science and technology in museums. They follow a linear pattern of development, from earliest to latest and from inventor to market (less often onward to actual use). Many museums of science and technology focus on the front end of research and innovation: the workplace is the laboratory, not the factory, warehouse or household. They downplay production and distribution; they neglect consumption, use and reproduction, which are for social history museums.

When collecting and interpreting science as it is applied in industry, museums of science and technology focus on the core technologies: the 'hardware' of machinery and motive power; they pay less attention to the 'software' of chemicals, finishing processes and products. For example, the textile collections in museums in the north west represent and duplicate spinning and weaving machinery; they under represent and omit bleaching, dyeing and the many and varied finishing and making-up processes. When these museums collect and interpret domestic technologies, they tend to be the hard technologies of buildings and appliances, rather than the soft technologies of soap and cleaning materials, food and drink, textiles and furnishings.

SCIENCE IN SOCIETY

Science as innovation and progress is all around us: for example; scientific developments are quoted in advertising copy to sway purchasing decisions for washing machines, cosmetics and cars. At the same time, 93 per cent of the population are scientifically illiterate, according to research such as that carried out by John Durant (1989). To reach this figure, certain facts were identified as fundamental to measuring how much science people know and how far their beliefs differed from formal and official science. These facts were used as a yardstick to measure scientific literacy: 7.1 per cent of British citizens met the criteria. In this way, science defines 'us' in its own terms, and perpetuates a 'top-down' approach to science learning. Such studies ignore the informal, amateur and lay methods of acquiring scientific knowledge and practising scientific techniques – amateur astronomers, environmental groups and many others.

Public interest in and concern for science issues is high; but the concerned public, or publics, may wrest these issues out of the scientific sphere and place them in the wider social and political context. People understand and evaluate new techniques such as new reproductive technologies through the social relationships they are seen to create and affect. In a recent collection of studies of the public understanding of science, edited by Alan Irving and Brian Wynne, people were asked about strongly scientific and technological issues – Chernobyl, the hazards of living near chemical plants, genetic diseases. In response, they spoke of the importance, and difficulty, of establishing hard facts and obtaining reliable and independent information. Again, in the 1992 evaluation of the *Flight!* gallery at the Museum of Science and Industry in Manchester, respondents gave high ratings to the ideas which incorporated 'social' and 'technical' issues – such as the changes in air travel and comfort over time, and airline disasters. But when the dominant scientific practice screens out social and cultural issues and downplays uncertainty, legitimate public debate can quickly become polarized into 'public fears' in the face of 'scientific progress'.

In response to the exclusion and exclusivity of science, a small number of forceful and articulate people have acted and spoken from 'outside' science to place it firmly in the societies which produce it. In the peace camps at Greenham Common, and in movements for peace against nuclear power and weapons and for the environment, women and men have challenged the scientific establishment, demanding that science be responsible and accountable, and proposing alternatives.

The 'classical' view of science as intellectual activity endorses the pursuit of goals in a vacuum, internally driven and not concerned with or responsible for social consequences. New gender studies of science address the social – and 'gendered' – relations of science and technology. They are committed to changing both the organizations in which knowledge is produced, and the knowledge that is produced. These studies challenge the Enlightenment view of science: that nature is 'given' and that science 'discovers' it. In her influential work *The Death of Nature*, Carolyn Merchant re-read the texts of the 'founding fathers' – above all of Francis Bacon. For her, they provided the rationale for a violent and misogynist science which sought power and control over both women and nature. In peace and environmental campaigns, and in gender studies, women continue to stress the links between the scientific and military establishments: they view science in its organized, institutional forms as contaminated and dangerous. Particularly in military and weapons research, and in the nuclear field, they see the drive for rationality, abstraction and ever more sophisticated technologies as 'masculine', mad and ultimately totally destructive.

163

Museums in Britain are reticent about the military character of science and technology – although most of these museums have been established in the post-war period, when science and technology have been largely military. David Edgerton refers to 'the deeply warlike orientation of English science and technology' in this period, describing it as the 'warfare state', not the 'welfare state'. He argues that the aviation industry's development has been misrepresented as benign, with transforming powers to bring people together around the world in the global village; the nationalistic and military character of that development has been concealed in histories and in museums.

Last year I attended an international conference on gender, technology and ethics at Luleå, in northern Sweden. My visit to Luleå served as an allegory for this paradox of the presence and invisibility of the military in science, in society and in museums. The city is in the centre of a large military base. As the aeroplane descended, passengers were instructed to take no further photographs until we entered the city. When we left the airport, we were confronted by a huge black sculpture of a soaring military jet, which overshadows the exit road. In the region, hunting is a popular weekend pastime, particularly with men; many Luleå households have guns. These aspects of the regional economy are both everywhere and concealed. They are not mentioned in Teknikens Hus, the popular interactive science centre at Luleå University, although the centre is supposedly committed to showing technologies in the context of the economy and technology of the region.

At the conference, speakers and delegates again and again urged that science and technology studies should encompass the full cycle and effects, not just the 'front end': impact as well as innovation. They advocated an approach which acknowledges the two-way process that shapes scientific developments – the interaction between people and technology – and explores alternatives, offering technology development as a process of social choice. Such an approach also emphasizes the full product cycle, including use and disposal; and with a global perspective and concern notes, for example, that processes and products declared unsafe in the 'First World' may be exported and dumped to contaminate and injure workers and consumers in other parts of the world.

One area of major concern for women who do not wish to lose control of their bodies and futures is that of reproductive technologies and genetic engineering. These have profound implications for the social relations of reproduction. Here, women are urging that the technologies should be assessed in actual social contexts, rather than in clinical trials, investigating observable particulars and relying on repetition of events. They also address the division of labour by sex and value in the fields of medical research and treatment where these new technologies are developed and practised.

For museums, these approaches imply that much stronger links and crossovers should be built between science and technology and social history. The scope and techniques of fieldwork and collecting should be extended to include oral histories, photographs, records and documents to give a wider context for scientific objects. Methods of display should be developed that fully integrate technical and social stories, and place them as linked and in dialogue, rather than a linear chain in which the 'social' is placed apart from, and usually at the end of, the technological story. The museum in Russelsheim, the home of the Opel car works, has shown how effective these approaches can be through exhibitions such as *Mensch und Natur*, held in 1990. In a very different way, the exhibition *Sixth Sense* at the Museum of Work in Norrköping, Sweden, deals with the interactions between people and technologies that are used in the workplace, and how people's senses can be used creatively or exhausted and destroyed in the course of their work. Museums might also explore the symbolic aspects of science and technology through representing fiction, film and fantasy as forms which also shape our understanding and experience. Rather than choosing the 'natural' evolution from one technology to another, museum displays might focus on critical moments or phases when an object, or group of objects, takes on new and different meanings: for example, the moment when, after concerns about safety and food poisoning, the microwave oven was reshaped socially as well as technically, to appeal more strongly to women and to emphasize traditional cooking methods.

Museums of science and technology deal with a narrow range of sciences and technologies. They might usefully broaden their scope, and therefore their definitions of sciences and their publics. For example, the Eksperimentarium in Copenhagen, Denmark, ran a public programme in the spring of 1993 on perfumes and smells with exhibitions, workshops, and lectures; they included industrial applications, such as additives to materials such as rubber and plastics, and the cosmetics industry, as well as body and animal smells; they drew in new audiences to science and to the centre. New developments in science suggest that museums must converge or rearrange their identities. At present, life ('biological') sciences and physical ('technical') sciences are usually separated in different museums; museums are oriented towards science and technology as it used to be defined. While an orientation towards the past may be appropriate for museums, they must be ready to record, collect and represent the full range of present and future technologies, including biotechnologies and genetics. This is the new 'Big Science', replacing physics and chemistry.

Perceptions of science are immense and varied. For example, people view the 'science' in weapons research very differently from the 'science' in seeking a treatment to counteract the HIV virus. Science in its social and cultural context – in different social groups, in commerce, in research, in governments, in different countries – means many different things. The major challenge for museums throughout the world charged with conveying information about, and communicating, science and technology is to represent and engage with the dialectic process, to acknowledge the diverse views of science and to take them on board in exhibitions and other programmes.

This paper first appeared in Museums Journal *91(11) (1993), pp. 25–7.*

REFERENCES

Durant, John (1989) 'Understanding of science in Britain and the USA' in R. Jowell *et al. British Social Attitudes*, special international report, Aldershot: Gower.

Easlea, Brian (1983) *Fathering the Unthinkable: Masculinity, science and the nuclear arms race*, London: Pluto. See also 'Men's madness: science and technology from a feminist perspective' (1990) Lusia Films for Channel 4.

Edgerton, David (1991) *England and the Aeroplane*, Manchester: Manchester University Press.

Irving, Alan and Wynne, Brian (eds) (1993) *Science in Everyday Life, Flight! Evaluation Report*, 1992, Museum of Science and Industry in Manchester.

Kavanagh, Gaynor (1992) 'Dreams and nightmares: science museum provision in Britain' in John Durant (ed.) *Museums and the Public Understanding of Science*, Science Museum/COPUS.

Merchant, Carolyn (1980) *The Death of Nature: women, ecology and the scientific revolution*, New York: Harper & Row.

24

Science by stealth
Patrick Sudbury

All museum collections can be used in interdisciplinary ways, and often, these are the most interesting ways for them to be used. This paper gives examples of the use of a range of collections and exhibitions in the development of an awareness of science.

The vital role of science and technology in human existence is perhaps the strongest reason for trying to increase the representation of science within non-science museums and galleries. (It is also considerably cheaper and more effective to supplement existing interpretation than to build new science centres.) But museums tend to group, collect and interpret objects according to subject area: art objects are appreciated for their artistic content and science objects are interpreted for their scientific connections. This approach often reflects the knowledge, skills and attitudes of those in charge of the collection rather than the objects themselves. The total separation that often exists between the arts and the sciences is both artificial and unnecessary. Collections are an amazing resource to be interpreted in endless ways. Exploiting the inherent science in objects enables institutions to use their collections fully. Objects can be used mutely for their sculptural and aesthetic qualities (form). They can be examined for their intrinsic significance (function). Or they can be used to illustrate a theme or concept (association).

Colleagues in museum education departments have been using interdisciplinary approaches for years and the national curriculum actively encourages them. However, the significance of this work has not yet been fully exploited by those concerned to increase the public understanding of science. The fault is partly with museum education staff, who see nothing significant in their approach and fail to publicize their own work, and partly with the scientific community, which tends to disregard the con-tribution museums can make. Curatorial staff who are often uneasy about the cross-curricular use of their collections should also take some of the blame. What is needed is to take the interdisciplinary elements out of the museum's education department and make them available to the individual and family visitor as well as to school-children.

The beauty of using virtually any collection to convey scientific concepts is that it does not require any initial scientific interest or knowledge on the part of the teacher or visitor. A primary school teacher with limited training in science (an all-too-common situation) can usually deal effectively with small chunks of science if liberally coated with a subject they know better. The same goes for many members of the public who feel that science is not for them. Some dislike the idea of science. Others feel inadequate when faced with a scientific subject because they are not trained scientists. It is often better not to bill displays as 'scientific' and to allow the scientific content of the objects to emerge gradually. Enthusiasm for the information will dispel worries that might be felt about something that is overtly scientific.

UNUSUAL ANGLES

Impossible to imagine a world without it; yet somehow only when there is too much of it do we really become aware of sound. *Sounds Great* was a Livesey Museum children's exhibition that encouraged its visitors to explore the world of sound and think about its production, transmission and how it is electrically manipulated. Individual exhibits allowed visitors to create and look at sound waves, to store messages and play them back at different speeds and to experiment with a delay phone.

Like many Livesey exhibitions, the theme was deliberately chosen from the common experiences of the museum's young visitors. Without setting out explicitly to be 'scientific', the museum tackles simple subjects from unusual angles. This approach uncovers scientific ideas that are still attractively wrapped in familiar cultural contexts; rubbish and water are other themes of recent Livesey exhibitions. The Livesey is located in a depressed inner city area, which means that children who might not ordinarily come across this type of innovative educational service find it on their doorstep.

Sounds Great was based on interactive exhibits produced by Science Projects. Many of the ideas, say Stephen Pizzey, of Science Projects, come simply from pursuing phenomena he is personally interested in. This approach carries over into the exhibits, for though they provide ideal material for teachers to draw on, they are meant more to generate curiosity and enthusiasm than to be formally didactic. The visitor, says Pizzey, is much more used to a magazine than, say, an academic lecture; and in *Sounds Great* people wandered from exhibit to exhibit like casual readers.

The exhibits were grouped into two broadly thematic sections and the show's visual coherence was enhanced by setting the exhibits against a backdrop of lively mural displays that drew on record covers and the like in a reference to the material culture associated with (musical) sounds. Teachers' packs and work sheets were also available for those who wanted to structure their visits further.

Popular with both organized groups and other more casual visitors, *Sounds Great* raised smiles and made people think. But where this style of exhibition comes into its own is in the encouragement it gives people to learn from each other. Children, commonly the first to touch an interactive exhibit, would often go on to show adults how to 'do it'; adults tended to read aloud the accompanying interpretive labels. Enjoyable and instructive, *Sounds Great* created an arena for both subtle scientific exploration and social learning.

Ken Arnold is exhibitions officer at the Wellcome Institute for the History of Medicine and was formerly assistant keeper at the Livesey Museum

It is possible to persuade visitors to do scientific experiments without them realizing that they are treading in the domain of science. Thus, in time, visitors may become accustomed to some of the strengths of science in posing questions and testing outcomes. They also come to recognize some of the fictions of science in terms of 'weightless objects', 'frictionless pulleys' and 'perfect gases'. The limitations of simple theories when faced with the complex reality should be readily admitted. The idea of the 'right' answer needs to be replaced by the concept of the 'best' answer in light of the available evidence.

Museums face a difficulty in communicating the uncertainties of science without giving the impression that the results are too unsure or trivial to be worth considering. While a message displayed mutely in the gallery may create a confused and unconvincing impression, a public lecture, a demonstration or a drama performance can convey the process of approximation, of getting a 'wrong answer' and of explaining why it was wrong.

It often helps to provide visitors with something to do so that they can find out for themselves. The techniques are well tried at Launch Pad, the Exploratory, Techniques and the former Technology Testbed in Liverpool. Children take to hands-on activities spontaneously, while adults normally require more encouragement. Here again, the method has some weaknesses because many experiments allow for some ambiguity, which is reflected in the visitor's response. This ambiguity can lead to visitor frustration and disappointment if there are no trained demonstrators on hand to assist. The solution to this problem is better scientific input, better design, good training and a grouping of related experiments that give a consistent and sustainable result.

ADDING COLOUR

The *Art/Science Alliance* at the Dulwich Picture Gallery is a good example of how a non-science collection can be scientifically interpreted. At Dulwich the head of education, Gillian Wolfe, and artist and painting conservator Philippa Abrahams have operated regular cross-curricular sessions for primary and secondary school children, and adults, over the past four years.

A brief introductory tour uses the gallery's collection to explain how some pictures were made. This leads on to a discussion about different natural and synthetic pigments, the media that are used to bind them, and the supports and grounds that are used to provide the stable surface for the paint. The session describes how the organic and mineral substances are treated to make different colours and the students are allowed to grind and mix them. Staff emphasize that many of these processes are not new; they used to be, and sometimes still are, part of the everyday knowledge of the artist.

The beauty of the session is that it is held in the gallery surrounded by the paintings. The children are able to see and to handle the materials from which the paintings are made in a way that relates to their experience of the world around them. After such a session the experience of seeing a picture or even the painted wall of a room could hardly be the same again. In the space of an hour the children become aware of a technological and scientific tradition that stretches back for thousands of years. It is all done without a formula or an equation in sight.

Patrick Sudbury is assistant director (central services) at the National Museums and Galleries on Merseyside

Most museum educators glean the basic science that they think they need and then impart it in a way that they think others can understand. They teach in an interdisciplinary way using museum objects. The potential for learning is enormous but a class is of finite length. Because of their (mainly) arts backgrounds many museum educators hand much of the scientific learning potential to the teacher for post-visit classroom work. This can be less than satisfactory if the teacher, too, has limited scientific knowledge.

THE WIDER PICTURE

In 1988 the National Gallery began its series of *Art in the Making* exhibitions, which examined the structure and technique of works in the collection – by Rembrandt, from fourteenth-century Italy, or by Impressionist painters. Considering paintings as physical objects, the exhibitions drew attention to the way in which people's understanding and appreciation of a work can be enhanced by a greater knowledge of how it was made.

In each exhibition a group of related works that had been extensively examined by the gallery's conservation and scientific departments were displayed with information about the way the paintings were made and the materials and pigments used. Often the technical examinations cast light on how a picture had been painted. For example, tiny grains of sand embedded on the surface of a Monet beach scene indicated that it was indeed painted out-of-doors. Sometimes, as in the case of certain paintings in the Rembrandt exhibition, discrepancies in the technique and materials cast doubt on the authorship of the painting.

The National Gallery now has a series, *Making and Meaning*, in which technical examination is only one approach among several used to elucidate the meaning of a great work of art. With the help of loans of related works, the exhibitions investigate the meaning of a picture, relating what can be discovered about the physical nature of the work and its technique, to what is known about its origin, purpose, content and history. Like *Art in the Making*, these exhibitions are the result of the collaboration between art historians, conservators and scientists.

The first picture to undergo this treatment is the Wilton Diptych, a rare and enigmatic work from the end of the fourteenth-century, probably painted for the English king, Richard II. In spite of its great beauty, little is known about the origins and purpose of the diptych. The exhibition investigates its complex subject matter and treatment, relating it to contemporary illuminated manuscripts, stained glass, sculpture and painting in an attempt to find answers to the many questions that surround it.

Michael Wilson is head of exhibitions and display at the National Gallery

---

SCIENTISTS AND EDUCATORS

Education staff are trained to filter, absorb and communicate knowledge. They undoubtedly do a good job. By contrast, many scientists are poor communicators who would confuse, upset and alienate their audiences and destroy the very enthusiasm and interest the museum is seeking to create. The strengths of both disciplines need to be combined. Evidence from Technology Testbed shows that opportunities can be missed and messages become garbled through lack of scientific knowledge allied to careful communication.

SCIENCE COACHING

'I liked the bus so much I didn't want to leave.' This was the enthusiastic response of one of Belfast's inner city schoolchildren to the Ulster Museum's innovatory, award-winning Science Discovery Bus. This project was made possible by the imaginative support of the Department of Education (Northern Ireland) under a special initiative *Making Belfast Work*. The bus takes the riches and resources of the museum to the economically and socially deprived areas of the city.

Children engage in a wide variety of activities structured to fit in with the science curriculum for Northern Ireland. Under the direction of museum education staff they carry out experiments and explore the variety of natural history specimens, rocks and impressive fossils. They use computers to study the weather and microscopes to explore the fascinating landscape of their finger prints. Using objects with a variety of different colours, textures, shapes and smells, children are encouraged to use all their senses. The bus can be full of excited five-year-olds all holding something and excitedly shouting: 'Miss, Miss, look!'

For older children, schools choose one of five themes directly related to the primary science programmes of study. Each theme is explored through eight activities that use science equipment and museum specimens. The children take part in an exciting circus of experiments and practical activities. Becoming scientists, they forget the artificial barriers of physics, chemistry, geology and biology in their enthusiasm to finish one task so that they can move on to the next. They are unaware of time and the two hours disappear too quickly for most – even in the final week of term when concentration is at a low ebb.

The themes – *Light, Materials, Rainforest, Earth in Space, Ourselves* – use the resources of the museum to relate aspects of science to everyday life. Butterflies camouflaged to hide in their environment are as much a part of the exploration of light as investigating reflection and refraction using light boxes.

Materials explores the properties of metals through electricity, magnetism and ductility. Coke cans are used alongside bauxite to emphasize the importance of recycling. Children are amazed when they see bauxite. It never occurs to them that aluminium might come from anything other than large lumps of metal in the ground.

Beautiful tropical butterflies and extraordinary-looking beetles are used to illustrate the wealth of the rainforest. Its riches also include a variety of fruits and spices. Many of the exotics that are taken for granted are new to children who eagerly look forward to the tasting session with their teacher. Occasionally the session is interrupted by the crashing of weights as the balsa wood breaks in the flexibility experiments.

Earth in Space and *Ourselves* are also popular topics. All are carried out with enthusiasm that often leaves teachers refreshed and delighted by their pupils approach. 'A busy, worthwhile and enjoyable session and a great stimulus, not a single child was less then enthusiastic,' said one teacher.

'The bus was very big. I liked the seats because we could swing around in them.' This may have been a design fault – but one no child would like corrected. The inside of the bus is a surprise as the one-way glass gives no hint of the conversion inside. The smart cupboards, work-tops and seats, although functional, give a feeling of space and sophistication that the children react to with surprise. 'It's like going into a Tardis, Miss.' In a two-hour session small groups of children will move round eight activities.

Since the bus lacks the space of a real Tardis, half of the activities are set up in the classroom. With the new emphasis in the Northern Ireland curriculum on primary evidence, hands-on experience is essential, but individual schools do not have the necessary resources. The bus has been visiting schools since its launch in May 1990. Three years on there is still a long waiting list and, although constantly requested, no school has yet had a repeat visit.

The idea of an outreach facility devoted to science occurred when the Northern Ireland curriculum was being implemented in primary schools. The emphasis on group activities, follow-up ideas and background materials in the form of six primary science topic booklets has been greatly valued. The outreach programme also includes Stuffee, a loveable six-foot-high soft sculpture from the Children's Museum in Pittsburg. Stuffee, who receives most of the fan mail, is used in a unique health education lesson. Not only do children marvel at his 20-foot intestine but they also giggle at his enormous sandwich as it emerges from his oversized lunch box.

The Science Discovery Bus illustrates the museum's commitment to the local community. When the bus is not visiting schools in areas like Andersonstown, Shankill and Falls it teams up with community groups or other institutions. Perhaps the most successful was the *Multi-coloured Road Show* with Belfast Zoo.

Children from inner-city schools are now coming to the museum in increasing numbers both for exhibitions and handling lessons. A series of museum-based science lessons for 5- to 11-year-olds has been developed to support the Northern Ireland curriculum and extend the work of the Science Discovery Bus. The next venture will find the bus providing support for pupils with special needs. They too will enjoy the facilities. As one teacher wrote: 'The visit was like a little bit of the museum brought specially for us and we were allowed to touch!'

Sally Montgomery is science education officer at Ulster Museum

Scientists are sparsely represented on the staff of museums and galleries and a competent scientist is needed to advise not just education staff but, also curatorial, interpretation and design staff. A scientist will recognize and define scientific links between seemingly non-scientific objects and check that the greatly simplified interpretation built upon the curators' and educators' experience of their public is not misleading or wrong.

A (fictitious) example may help to illustrate the relationship. A museum that has a collection that includes a fire engine may be in the care of a social history curator. An education officer may be keen to exploit this attractive item as a focus for school and public interest. The key requirement for a fire engine is the ability to pump water to the top of a high building. This presents a fascinating opportunity for dealing with head pressure. Neither the curator nor the educator may have the time or the expertise to represent simply and accurately the fundamental relationships that exist between head pressure, hose diameter and flow rate. A scientist can make sure that any description is technically correct and can also ensure that the display refers to wider issues, such as the conversion of kinetic and potential energy.

The scientist should have an important continuing relationship with the demonstrators or role players who are helping interpret a display with scientific and technical elements. As time goes by and staff forget, become stale or leave, the original message can become garbled. Continuing quality control and training is best provided on the technical side by someone with a good grasp of the science and technology that is being presented.

STEALTH ON MERSEYSIDE

Today the 'science by stealth' approach occurs to a large extent in the primary school programme of the National Museums and Galleries on Merseyside. Almost every primary school session in the museum covers science in a cross-curricular sense. In essence, every object is approached from three directions. First, there are the aesthetics of its appearance and decoration; second, is the human aspect of its role in society and the use that people made of it; third, the scientific element looks at the science and technology that underpin the object, sustain the society and make possible the human and aesthetic outcomes.

This approach has evolved in Merseyside over a long period of time. For example, there has been an interdisciplinary interpretation of Liverpool Museum's decorative art collection of European docks and watches since the 1970s. At that time the objects in the gallery were interpreted mainly in terms of their decorative features. In a number of instances the works of the clocks and watches were shown and named, but that was a far cry from trying to interpret the history and scientific development of time measurement. In 1975, Peter Reed, as newly appointed education officer for science, developed a school programme comprising a gallery visit and a museum classroom session based on this display.

Reed noted how time had always been important to people, that it had been measured in various ways, by sundials and nocturnals, the flow of water or sand, or the regular burning of an oil lamp or candle. The gallery session gave the class a chance to appreciate the aesthetics and complexity of the objects while the classroom session introduced combustion, water flow and the pendulum to lead on to the quartz crystal and caesium atomic clocks of the twentieth century. Fluid properties, thermal expansion and crystal lattices were all visited on the way. Due to space constraints in the gallery, the programme involved a split session, part of it in the galleries, part of it in a classroom behind the scenes. As such, it was difficult and expensive to operate, illustrating the need to consider this kind of interpretation during gallery design.

A PARROT'S PERSPECTIVE

When Oldham Museum received a substantial grant from the Museums and Galleries Commission to tour an exhibition about parrots, it was on the understanding that it would integrate natural history, art, literature and humour (Museums Journal, November 1992: 30).

Showcases explaining the natural history and conservation problems of parrots are mixed in with Ralph Steadman sketches, Michael Rothenstein prints, Punch cartoons, Edward Lear prints and nonsense verse, Tiffany glass, Indian costume,

---

Spode pottery, Maori bags and a bizarre knitted sculpture. This integrated approach has proved popular with the Oldham public: the exhibition appealed to a wide range of people, particularly primary schoolchildren for whom it offers good cross-curricular activities.

Not that the exhibition was without problems. It was organized by Oldham's natural history exhibitions officer Sian Owen, who, while fully conversant with the wildlife and conservation aspects of parrots, was less experienced when it came to art. The etiquette and regulations governing the loan of works of art had to be learnt from scratch although, fortunately, colleagues at Oldham Art Gallery provided much-needed advice. Formal training sessions on handling and packing were arranged via the art gallery while a reliable and secure transportation company was recommended to collect loaned material. The benefits of in-house training and advice were enormous, not only did it save time and money but it also helped to demystify a previously unknown set of rules. Research into art, literature and humour although also new territory for natural history staff, was enjoyable.

Less entertaining was obtaining copyright permission, which although freely given required time and patience. Take-overs in the book publishing world require the copyright chaser to turn detective.

By far the most perplexing and ultimately unsatisfying aspect of mounting an integrated exhibition is its marketing. A journalist was hired to produce separate press releases, specifically targeted at specialized and general interest publications and radio. Despite excellent regional coverage, which focused largely on the Monty Python/talking-budgie angle, the response from the national media was disappointing.

Attracting the attention of a capital-centred press is always difficult for a provincial museum but the wide-ranging nature of the exhibition made it hard to 'sell' to editors. Exhibition sections in the broadsheets are headed Visual Arts and Arts; *Parrots* has a lot more in it than just art, but that seemed to work against us.

Women's magazines, apart from *Women's Weekly*, were lukewarm and, in retrospect, should have been targeted specifically for the 'cute and funny' angle. The weightier science publications blew hot and cold, presumably confused by the broad range of subjects covered in the exhibition.

A possible lesson here is to be even more specific with press releases; editors concerned solely with science should only be made aware of the natural history angle, while the lighter, novelty aspects should be left to general interest editors.

So is it worth putting on an integrated exhibition? Definitely. As long as the central theme of the exhibition is strong, an exploration of different genres can provide stimulating mental, aural and visual variety.

Bruce Langridge is museum officer (natural history) at Oldham Museum

One of Liverpool Museum's most popular galleries is the transport gallery with its road vehicles, bicycles and railway items displayed statically as nineteenth-century sculpture. The interpretation is historic, basic and factual. To bring the objects alive to children, education staff have, over the years, emphasized in worksheets and teachers' notes the potential for scientific learning. Lion, the world's oldest working locomotive, provided the opportunity to explain the social revolution in personal mobility that railways initiated. These school sessions also explained that the locomotive burns coal (which very few primary school children have ever seen); that the burning coal generates hot gas; that the hot gas turns water to steam; that the steam is contained at high pressure like the steam in a pressure cooker; and that the steam forces the pistons to and fro. These transformations of energy and the accompanying losses are part of the wider study of thermodynamics.

In another area an educational session on the Ancient Greeks looks at the designs and the pictures on their pottery. The pictures reveal much about the appearance, dress and activities of the people, while the colouring of the red pottery ground and the black decorative designs are explained in terms of the different degrees of oxidation of different clays in the furnace. The opportunities are endless. Women of fashion in ancient Egypt used galena, malachite and hematite for face make-up; pumice and talc for the skin; and alabaster, serpentine and slate for containers and palettes. The geology and chemistry of these few items have recently provided the substance of a small display in the archaeology discovery centre in Liverpool Museum.

Further examples are to be found in the shipping collections where the use of flags is obvious in early paintings. The story of the commercial need for rapid communications and precise time keeping leads from signal flags and heliographs, through chronometers, the 'one o'clock gun' and the telegraph to telephones and radios. The session on Victorian toys shows ceramic-faced dolls with cotton bodies, pressed metal figures coloured with lead paint, a wooden dancing bear, and a board game with coloured painted card. All reveal a notable absence of the plastics, synthetic fabrics and acrylic paint that make some modern toys light, colourful and less toxic. Opportunity for such cross-linking is not limited. As we have seen, a fire engine can lead quickly to a session on hydraulics; a crane to forces; a brake block to friction; musical instruments to sound, waves and vibrations; paintings to light and colour.

The Piermaster's House in the Merseyside Maritime Museum illustrates different forms of energy – muscle power, clockwork, coal and gas, but not electricity – which can be used to inform a discussion about the arduous work load of the Edwardian piermaster's wife and link between physical and social science. Ship models and paintings from the maritime history galleries show the hundreds of designs used to exploit and resist the forces of nature in a practical way. Thanks to a grant from the Gatsby Charitable Foundation, staff have built hands-on units for stability experiments (with a tow-tank) and made a short video to introduce the underlying science. The right scientific input at the right time, well supported by education and curatorial expertise, will transform interpretation of the huge and diverse collections of art and human history. That input needs to be at the stage when new displays and interpretative programmes are being developed; when they are first implemented; and on a continuing basis to provide quality control and retraining. There is scope the other way round as well. All too few people appreciate the rugged power of a beam engine, the exquisite perfection of a large telescope mirror or understand the lives and motivations of the people who make and use them. Still less do many people understand the classic simplicity of a mathematical equation. Perhaps the time has come to emphasize the aesthetics and humanity of science as a further stage in the quest for public understanding and awareness.

This paper first appeared in Museums Journal 93(11) (1993), pp. 27–31.

25

Happy hands-on
Nick Winterbotham

Interaction need not mean high-tech computers or expensive new galleries. This short paper sets out the good and the bad of lower-technology approaches.

There is no doubt that interactive exhibits enhance the visitor experience. Even the flip-up lid and the push-button can do more to elicit favourable response than passive exhibits, by involving visitors and giving them added value.

Whether interpreting science, art, history or anything else, an interactive exhibit will be memorable. Though sometimes for the wrong reasons, the visitor will be shaken out of the glazed and passive role of the ambulant couch-potato into that of the agile mental gymnast.

THE GOOD

The most enjoyable interactives are probably those which have variable outcomes. Randomness, infinite choice and multiple controls can make for a more absorbing experience. Exhibits which allow (or require) more than two hands on are frequently very popular. Interactivity should dispense with the need to interpret in other media, allowing relevant exhibits to have little or no labelling at all but still to impart a sophisticated but non-verbal message. Furthermore, the act of making something work can impart understanding at different levels. For example corn-grinding is hard work for slow progress, rotary action is easier than reciprocating, you've got to keep your fingers from being pinched, sometimes you get the angle wrong and it doesn't grind properly . . .

On the other hand, the message from interactives can sometimes be confused and people may take away erroneous ideas from an exhibit. In identifying what people learn, we can draw a distinction between 'cognitive' gains – the facts you get to know, and the 'affective' gains – the degree to which you enjoyed the process and how you feel about it afterwards. The role of all museum exhibits may always be more successful in the affective domain than in the cognitive and while visitors may in due course forget the detail of what was served up, they are unlikely to forget the enthusiasm that such exhibits can generate. For some, the exhibit which poses unanswered questions can be rewarding in itself. For many others, exhibits which pose problems requiring dexterity and coordinative skills are highly attractive. Some interactives can pay for their own maintenance. Interactive donations boxes are one example; activities such as electronic leaflet generation or brass-rubbing can be financed simply by an honesty-box system. Interactives encourage conversational and didactic interaction between visitors. Often a child will have a go first, followed by the accompanying adult. Each enables the other to overcome reticence and take a risk at learning.

THE BAD

An interactive exhibit may blight involvement in other exhibits within a radius of several metres. Careless combinations of passive and active exhibits – while aiming to vary the pace of a gallery – may result in some items not being noticed.

Interactives can be extremely expensive and often fail to illustrate satisfactorily the original objective. Also, and especially in the realm of science. there is a limited range of gallery experiments which work well. These can be found in many museums and exhibits round the globe, but adopting such 'off-the-shelf' successes can lead to a departure from the display objectives. 'If in doubt, get a plasma ball' seemed to be the spirit of the 1980s, and much of the message of individual galleries may have been lost in public wonderment at the medium.

Interactives don't have to be high-technology. If they are, you will need a high-technician and one for whom repair and maintenance is a joy and not a chore for a rainy day. Complex interactives frequently break down and should thus be removable or disguisable. A 'temporarily out of action' notice has a very negative public-relations value. A sign-writer with a sense of humour will come in handy when exhibits are recalcitrant.

THE WHEREWITHAL

It is important to have individuals or teams responsible for maintaining exhibits with a guarantee of limited 'down-times'. A philosophy of 'if it breaks, it's our fault' is the most appropriate to adopt. Controls, switches and hands-on objects ought to all have military-grade design specification.

Low-tech interactives tend to be a lot cheaper to purchase and maintain than their high-tech counterparts, may not require power supplies and tend to appeal across a wider spectrum of the visiting public. As the success of a visit is often rated according to what was accessible to all the members of a family group, these exhibits contribute greatly to visitor satisfaction by providing a cohesive and social experience. But low-tech exhibits break down too and need care and maintenance in the same way as high-tech ones.

Galleries where interactivity is promoted may argue with galleries where it isn't. A traditional art show next to a science exploratory exhibit may suffer paint picking or animated poking, but it may also benefit from the switching on of enquiring minds.

Interactive exhibits often cost more per square metre than noninteractive ones and they certainly require more ongoing care and maintenance. But visitor surveys and gallery staff will tell you that they are worth their weight in gold.

This paper first appeared in Museums Journal 93(2) (1993), pp. 30–1.

26

History: in hand, low-tech and cheap

Harriet Purkis

How to stimulate visitors through problem-solving, handling and interaction.

Hands-on History, a special exhibition put together by St Albans Museum, was all about getting to grips with history for yourself by touching museum objects, questioning historical evidence at first hand and trying your hand at being an historian.

It aimed to show that studying history is about active questioning and problem solving rather than reading a prepared narrative. It aimed to encourage visitors to solve problems through active and tactile interaction with real objects from Roman times to the present. It was self-service to allow people to choose the things they wanted to do, to allow interaction between children and parents or teachers, and to let people explore at their own pace.

The main target audience was school groups at history key stages 2 and 3. Teachers' notes and a feature in the museum's regular schools newsletter outlined the exhibition and listed the attainment targets that it met and the primary source material used. Other target groups were families with children, and the over-sixties who were invited to a series of Memory Afternoons with tea.

The exhibition looked broadly at objects, photographs and documents as evidence; and ways of recording and preserving history in museums. Objects were on open display – on the floor, on tables, in drawers and in trays. The interaction involved physical activities combined with thinking, guessing and questioning. Activities included picking up objects; trying on shoes; posing or being the photographer in a recreated Victorian photographic studio; measuring, sorting and drawing objects; opening drawers; sticking broken plates together; reading the news to camera; and changing captions to photographs on a magnetic board.

The interaction was guided by brightly coloured text panels which addressed people as 'you', began with direct, familiar phrases, and used questions. The text gave instructions about what to do in each section and also explained why historians themselves carry out the activity. For example, one section consisted of a pile of shoes on the floor, from the 1930s to the present and from clogs to cycling shoes. The text panel asked 'Can you be a history detective and use guess work and imagination to try and find out what the people who wore these shoes were like? The checklist of clues and questions may help you.' Another section, *The Same but Different*, featured food packaging from Roman amphorae to milk cartons, and invited visitors to sort the packages into groups (how they were sealed, what they were made of, what was in them).

Visitor response was gauged by a comments sheet and observation – which found people talking a great deal, parents reading out the panels and children doing the activities.

This exhibition proved that a visitor's experience of history in museums can go beyond passively reading or listening to the story of a town or history of an industry. By using everyday objects, historical concepts and questions can be addressed.

Why not introduce hands-on elements in your permanent history displays? Its proven to be cheap, effective and fun. Don't leave it to the science centres and high-tech computer specialists. Get your visitors hands-on history. Every museum can do it!

This paper first appeared in Museums Journal *93(2) (1993), p. 31.*

27

Increased exhibit accessibility through multisensory interaction

Betty Davidson, Candace Lee Heald and
George E. Hein

An evaluation study of a natural history gallery at the Boston Museum of Science resulted in the installation of multisensory consoles which developed the gallery audience and enabled much greater retention of information. Different learning styles were observed. Although people with disabilities were a major target audience, the changes made improved the experience for everyone, except those wanting a very quiet, solitary visit.

In 1985, the Boston Museum of Science conducted an accessibility audit, a self-evaluation of the physical and intellectual accessibility of its programmes and exhibits. It proved useful to the Museum for exhibit design, long-range planning, and staff development. As one result of this self-evaluation, the Museum sought and obtained funding from the National Science Foundation to modify one exhibit hall. The intent of the modifications was to make both the environment and the content more available to all visitors, including those with disabilities. This article describes the evaluation of those changes and suggests how these findings can be applied in a variety of museum settings.

Before modifications, the New England Lifezones Hall consisted of a large U-shaped gallery, approximately 30 by 60 feet, containing six dioramas of wild animals native to New England. Each animal species was depicted in its natural habitat: presentations of deer, bear, moose and beaver, and two dioramas of birds (those that frequent a sandy shore and others native to a rocky coast). The dioramas consisted entirely of visual material. Text panels were backlit, in small print, at adult shoulder height. The exhibit was similar to ones found in many natural history museums.

Our evaluation consisted of studies before, during, and after modifications (baseline, interim, and final). The gallery continued to function with a steady stream of visitors throughout the redesign activities. Since the major goal of the project was to make the hall more physically and intellectually accessible, one of the primary audiences for our evaluation was the disabled visitor. However, the total inaccessibility of the original dioramas to visually disadvantaged visitors and the lack of accommodation of the exhibit to other disabled populations precluded any studies on this population of visitors before modifications: we would not be able to collect any baseline data on responses to the gallery for visually impaired visitors, and we felt that it would be inappropriate to ask other disabled visitors to tour a gallery that could provide them with little or no satisfaction. We did carry out case studies of special-needs audiences during the changes for formative feedback to exhibit developers. We also looked at the behaviour of 'ordinary' visitors before, during, and after modifications. The term *ordinary* is placed in quotation marks for three reasons.

1 One in six people in the United States population is classified as having some form of special need (*Disabilities Studies Quarterly* 1990), either physical or mental. Thus it is safe to assume that the general museum public includes a significant number of members with a range of special needs or disabilities.

2 The differences between those characterized as belonging to one group or the other cannot be sharply drawn but represent a continuum, a finding that became evident as we studied visits by both the general audience and special-needs groups.

3 The need for and benefits of accessibility extend to the entire museum public; the consequence of limited accessibility are the same, regardless of the cause. If a museum visitor cannot read a label because he or she has (a) vision impairment, (b) limited reading capability, or (c) limited understanding of English, the net result will be the same: the visitor will not understand the exhibit message. Similarly, benefits of accessibility are shared by multiple groups; for example, tactile elements placed low are accessible to visitors in wheelchairs and children.

EXHIBIT CHANGES

The modifications represent a new approach to accessibility: the intention was to make the exhibit more accessible to all visitors, not just to provide some form of substitute accessibility to those with handicaps. For example, visually impaired visitors have utilized guides or tapes to provide auditory access to dioramas in the past, but these have not been coordinated with other exhibit modifications. Audible descriptions alone do not provide access for visually impaired people, nor do multisensory experiences provide access without audible explanations and interpretations of them. As a visually impaired consultant for the New England Lifezones project commented (Bloomer 1987) on the use of auditory descriptions alone, 'Just send me the tapes, I'll stay home'. The modifications in the gallery consisted of three major components, plus additional materials.

Labels

All the dioramas received new and expanded sign panels. The old labels were all mounted at the side of each diorama at approximately shoulder height. The new 'signs' included information that could be accessed in several modes. The original labels were modified, rewritten, and the manner of their display altered, so they were easier to read and easier to understand. In addition, each diorama had constructed before it, approximately 2 feet off the ground, a console that contained an audiotape with descriptive material about the diorama and a 'smell box' that, when turned on, fanned an aroma associated with the animal or its habitat to the visitor. Two of these consoles also included something to touch; one had a pair of deer antlers, the other had a moose hoof.

The two bird dioramas originally had buttons on a panel mounted on the wall to the left of the diorama. When the buttons were pushed, a light shone on the species identified. The buttons were small and positioned so that it was not possible to hold the button and see the light in all instances. The buttons for each diorama were replaced with larger ones, easier to manipulate, and moved to a console in front of the exhibit.

Animal mounts

Three-dimensional representations of some of the species in the diorama were added in the gallery. These included a mounted specimen of a beaver and one of a black bear positioned near their respective dioramas. Two bird models, made of bronze, were also displayed. Each of the animal models could be touched.

Interactive exhibits

Three free-standing hands-on displays related to animal adaptations, the theme of the exhibit, were installed. They were animal coverings to touch and to view through a microscope, a comparison of animal features with human tools (e.g., claws and a hand cultivator), each of which had model animal parts and human tools that could be touched and wooden pieces from which various mock animals could be constructed. All three new components illustrate a feature of animal adaptation. Also, all of them are deliberately relatively 'low-tech', easily constructed and installed in any museum setting.

Exhibit introduction

A triangular kiosk explaining the exhibit was provided in the open entrance of the gallery, and some materials on the floor unrelated to the exhibit's theme were removed.[1]

During the interim period, some but not all of the new components were installed. The additional components were also tried out in several versions. For example, some labels were altered after visitors were observed to have difficulty seeing them; the structure of the free-standing components was modified after it was noted that visitors in wheel-chairs had difficulty using them, and the placement of components was modified.

An important feature of the final renovations was that all descriptive components were installed consistently in parallel locations; for example, earphones were always placed at the right-hand edge of the panels and free-standing exhibits. In addition, label and recorded message information contained considerable redundancy; repeated material was one of the various forms used to provide the visitor with access.

EVALUATION PLAN

We carried out three separate but related activities.

1 Formative feedback to the exhibit designers as components were added to the gallery. This work was carried out throughout the period of the modifications; it consisted of discussions with exhibit designers based both on the structured observations and interviews used in the summative evaluation and informal observation of general visitors and visitors with special needs.
2 Case studies of groups of special-needs visitors who were invited to use the exhibit purposes after some or all of the modifications were complete.
3 Observation of general visitor behaviour and interviews (a) before modifications, (b) approximately halfway through the modifications, and (c) after all the changes had been made. This paper reports primarily the results of the third evaluation component.

For the structured observations, visitors and visitor groups were chosen at random and observed from one position in the gallery. Since the entire exhibit was contained in a single large room with no major obstructions, there was no need to track visitors as they proceeded through the gallery. The first person (or group) who entered the exhibit area was selected for observation. When one observation was finished, the next person (or group) to enter was observed, and so on. One visitor group was defined as one unit of observation. The dates of observations, number of visitors observed, and composition of groups are recorded in Table 27.1.[2]

Table 27.1 Numbers and percentages of visitor groups observed and interviewed

Composition of groups	Observations					
	Baseline 7–27 Aug. 1987		Interim 20 Apr.–14 May 1988		Final 7 Feb.–5 May 1989	
	No.	%	No.	%	No.	%
Adult-only groups	36	53	25	25	13	16
Mixed groups	25	37	69	68	57	70
Children	7	10	8	8	12	15
Total number of groups observed	68	100	102	101	82	101

	Interviews		
	18 Aug.–3 Sept. 1987	8–13 June 1988	5–20 Apr. 1989
Total, all groups	37	29	31

For the interviews, the first available person (or group) exiting the exhibit when the interviewer was ready after completing the previous interview was selected and questions were directed to the group. Multiple responses were encouraged and tabulated as separate opinions. Therefore, the total number of answers to any one question can exceed the sample size. Interviews were conducted at approximately the same time as observations and included primarily open-ended questions. The interview form used for the first 10 baseline interviews was modified for all subsequent interviews. Quantitative comparisons reported in this paper are for questions that were consistent for the two forms. Not every respondent answered each question.

The interview sample included all three categories of visitors – adults, mixed age groups, and children – as did the observations. Since the interview sample was gathered by the same method as was the observation sample, at comparable times, the two samples are likely to have the same composition.

RESULTS

The observation study provided information on visitor composition and behaviour, primarily on length of time in the gallery and flow patterns. The interview study provided information on visitor attitudes and learning. All data in the following tables and figures refer to the sample sizes indicated in Table 27.1.

1. Audience composition

The data in Table 27.1 illustrates that as the exhibit changed to include more interactive materials, so did the composition of the audience who viewed it. The proportion of children and family groups increased. In the same period, there were no significant variations in the composition of the Museum of Science audience that could account for this change.

2. Time in gallery

Visitor time in the gallery has gone up dramatically following the modifications. This is true both for average time and the fraction of visitors who spend more than three minutes there. Conversely, and illustrating the same trend, the number of in-and-out visitors has decreased dramatically (Tables 27.2 and 27.3, Fig. 27.1).

Table 27.2 Time in gallery

Average time in gallery:	Baseline Minutes	Interim Minutes	Final Minutes
Children	1.0	3.0	2.6
Mixed groups	3.0	3.9	5.3
Adults	3.3	2.9	6.1
All visitors	3.1	3.6	5.3

Table 27.3 Percentage of all visitors in gallery

	Baseline %	Interim %	Final %
3 minutes or more	50	52	73
1–2 minutes	31	38	23
Less than one minute	19	10	4

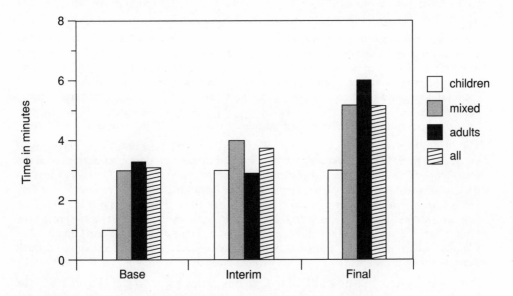

Fig. 27.1 Average length of time spent in the hall by groups of visitors

183

3. Visitor flow patterns

In the baseline data, the predominant patterns observed among all visitors were groups who stopped and looked at several displays, those who browsed through the gallery in constant motion, and a high proportion of visitors (approximately one-third) who walked into the gallery and straight out again or walked in, looked at the moose exhibit and perhaps the beaver lodge, and then turned and went out.

In the interim data, and more clearly in the final evaluation, when all the components were on the floor, a number of other patterns emerged. As the quantitative data demonstrate, the number of in-and-out visitors had decreased. In addition, the new components filling the centre of the gallery encouraged movement between them, particularly for the groups with children. There was also a physical dialogue, movement back and forth between activity stations and diorama windows. This was particularly evident around the bear and beaver mounts and their related exhibits.

Finally, many children and some special-needs groups showed a preference for a particular sensory modality. They made a circuit of the smell boxes, the touch models, the auditory labels (earphones), and even the bird lights.

The net result of these varied visitor flow patterns was that the visitors, when viewed as a whole, appeared to engage in random motion through the exhibits; but this randomness resolved itself into purposeful paths when individual visitors were observed.

4. Attracting power

The attracting power of each exhibit component – that is, the fraction of the total visitors who stopped before that component – could be determined from the observation data. For this study, attracting power is defined as any instance in which there is an indicator in the field note that the visitor has had some observable interaction with the exhibit component. The results for the original dioramas and after modification are provided (Table 27.4, Fig. 27.2).

Before the modification, there was clearly a major difference in attracting power for the various dioramas; the moose, with almost 66 per cent of visitors stopping before it, was more than four times as popular as the deer, which had only 16 per cent attracting power. After the changes, the difference between the various dioramas decreased; all of them fall in a band of attracting power at 60 per cent ± 10 per cent, with the difference between the most popular and the least only 19 per cent. In addition, most of the new free-standing components also attract up to approximately 60 per cent of the visitors.

The qualitative observations and the interviews support these results. A teacher who entered the room asking his students if they wanted to see the moose got sidetracked at the microscope. The class never did get to the moose. In another group, Cub Scout leaders tried to get their group away from the microscope by talking about the moose. When they failed to move the group into the gallery, the leaders asked if the scouts wanted to see the lightning show. The group moved on. Parents often surveyed the gallery and spotted the build-a-beast as something for their children to do. 'Here's something for Jamie to do'. Groups of kids were most animated by the activity stations and called back and forth between them, 'Come, see this.'

When visitors were asked 'Which of the exhibits in this room do you like the best?' the moose was most frequently mentioned in the baseline data. In the summative data the bear was the most popular exhibit, and the deer, the beaver, and the 'touching' things all were mentioned more frequently than the moose.

Table 27.4 Attracting power of exhibit components (per cent of visitors who stop and interact with exhibit)

Component	Baseline %	Interim* %	Final† %
Coastal birds	37	19	61
Beaver	41	56	68
Moose	66	48	70
Shore birds	43	32	59
Deer	16	22	59
Bear	32	21	59
Smell box†		25	-
Build-a-beast		27	37
Microscope		41	54
Tools			34
Beaver mount			59
Bear mount			63

* As the exhibits were modified, the number of components increased. Some components were present during both interim and final evaluation phases, others were added after the interim observations.

† During the interim period, a smell box was installed as a separate component. In the final phase, smell boxes were incorporated into the panels in front of each diorama.

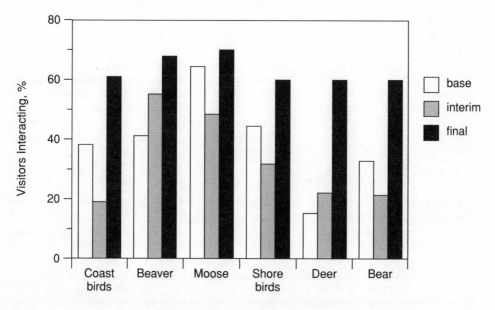

Fig. 27.2 The attracting power of dioramas at three stages

5. Label use

Both observations and interviews indicated that after changes visitors interacted more with the labels, both written and recorded. (See samples of labels on pages 187–9.) The recorded labels were particularly popular; after modifications, more than twice as many visitor groups (72 per cent compared to 34 per cent) were observed using the recorded labels as compared to the written labels.

In the interviews, visitors were specifically asked about their use of labels. The responses to the question 'Did the labels provide you with any information?' are summarized in Fig. 27.3. They indicate that the exhibit modifications increased the use of labels both in the amount and in the diversity of information obtained.

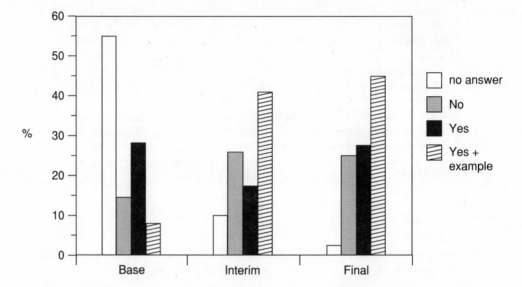

Fig 27.3 Responses to 'Did the labels provide you with any information?'

In the baseline data, half the sample did not answer this question, and an additional 15 per cent said that they didn't read the labels. Only 7 per cent of the visitors could give specific new information. In the final data, 45 per cent of the respondents gave some piece of information, including references to reading about the mounted animal specimens, and bird and place identification. Those who reported new information included some who cited examples from both the recorded tapes and the activity stations, as well as from the printed labels. Identification of birds was the most frequent animal-related information, followed by reference to the bear label on hibernation.

In general, the level of information and knowledge in the final data interviews and observations (from conversations overheard) showed an increase from baseline to the interim data, and from interim to final data, although the acknowledged reading of labels decreased for the interim data, compared to the baseline data. This combination of results suggests that information increasingly came from sources other than the written diorama labels; visitors knew more, and they gained that knowledge in a variety of ways. For example, when asked if he read the labels, one visitor said, 'No', but when asked to give an example of some new information, he repeated the recorded beaver label almost verbatim. Another 'no' response to the question about reading labels was coupled with the response to the question about gaining new information 'reading about the tool things'. Visitors also cited 'the smells' and 'that beaver fur feels soft' as new information they had learned from the exhibits – information obviously gained through means other than reading.

Whitetail Deer Diorama: Labels for the original, interim, and final whitetail deer diorama and audio script for the final exhibit.

Original Label: Left of diorama

WHITETAIL DEER
Odocoilius virginianus

SQUAM LAKE, NEW HAMPSHIRE

WHITETAIL DEER, OFTEN CALLED "VIRGINIA DEER," ARE THE MOST PLENTIFUL AND BEST KNOWN OF AMERICAN BIG GAME MAMMALS. THEY LIVE IN OPEN WOODLANDS, USUALLY NEAR WATER, EATING GRASS, TWIGS AND LEAVES. WHEN STARTLED, THESE DEER BOUND AWAY, THEIR WHITE TAILS RAISED AS A SIGNAL OF ALARM.

THE DOE (FEMALE DEER) AND FAWNS SHOWN IN THIS EXHIBIT SPEND THE SUMMER TOGETHER; THE BUCK STAYS ALONE. WHITETAILS LIVE ABOUT TWELVE YEARS.

FAVORITE FOODS Many of the plants shown are favorites on the deer menu; blueberry, wild cherry, sensitive ferns, wild rose, lichens, and swamp grass. Can you recognize them? In the fall they gorge on acorns.

THE DEER'S YEAR The deer's mating season is in November. The fawns, usually twins, are born in June, and are concealed from enemies by their spotted coats which resemble the sunflecked forest floor. In winter, a small band of bucks, does and half grown fawns yard up in a sheltered place, trampling the snow to make feeding easier.

ANTLERS Only the buck has antlers, which are shed in January. New antlers begin to grow in April or May and are first covered with sensitive skin, or "velvet." In August, the antlers are fully formed and the velvet is rubbed off, leaving hard, sharp spikes for battling other males during the mating season.

HISTORY Whitetail deer were valuable game animals to the Indians and early settlers. The slaughter was so great that whitetails almost became extinct but under protection of the law they have now increased to an estimated four million in the United States. In some areas the food supply is not sufficient to last through the winter, and many deer would starve if hunters did not reduce the numbers.

RACES There are several races of whitetail deer, varying in weight from 35 to 400 pounds, ranging over most of North America. Related forms are found in South America.

SEE THE LABEL TO THE RIGHT FOR INFORMATION ABOUT THE LOCATION OF THIS GROUP.

Original Label: Right of diorama

ENVIRONMENT OF THE WHITETAIL DEER GROUP

THIS EXHIBIT SHOWS ONE OF NEW HAMPSHIRE'S MOST TYPICAL SIGHTS — WOODED LAKE SHORE WITH MOUNTAINS IN THE BACKGROUND. THE SCENE IS SET AT SQUAM LAKE IN CENTRAL NEW HAMPSHIRE, ON THE AFTERNOON OF A BRIGHT JUNE DAY. THIS KIND OF HABITAT IS PERFECT FOR DEER. THE OPEN WOODS ALLOW LIGHT TO REACH THE FOREST FLOOR SO THAT PLANTS AND SHRUBS CAN GROW WITHIN THE DEER'S REACH. SUCCULENT PLANTS GROW AT THE WATER'S EDGE, AND THE DEER ENJOY LYING IN THE SHALLOWS AND SWIMMING IN THE LAKE. THE BREEZES OF THE OPEN LAKE SHORE BLOW AWAY FLIES AND MOSQUITOES.

THE COMMON LOON is the water bird that startles summer visitors with its wild ringing cry. This large submarine-like bird is a strong diver, and uses its wings and feet for swimming under water after fish. Its range is eastern North America from Labrador to the Gulf of Mexico.

THE EASTERN CHIPMUNK is an industrious hoarder, gathering great quantities of fruits, seeds and nuts, which it carries in its capacious cheek pouches to its underground nest. During cold weather it hibernates in its burrow, occasionally nibbling on the food stored under its bed. It lives in the eastern United States and Canada.

THE DOWNY YELLOW LADY'S SLIPPER and the STEMLESS LADY'S SLIPPER (MOCCASIN FLOWER) are rare native orchids and *should not be picked*. The large pouch contains nectar which attracts insects, who pay for their meal by carrying fertilizing pollen from one flower to another.

THE PAINTED TRILLIUM and the NODDING TRILLIUM, JACK-IN-THE-PULPIT and BUNCHBERRY are other flowers on the *do not pick* list.

SQUAM LAKE lies in a lowland formed by the erosion of mountains made of soft rock by streams before glacial times, over two million years ago. The glaciers scraped and rounded the mountains still more. When the ice melted, it deposited masses of rocky debris that it had carried along with it. This dammed many of the valleys so that water could not drain out of them, and lakes were formed. The surrounding mountains are composed of more resistant rock that was not worn down as much by the streams and glaciers. The prominent Rattlesnake Mountains and Mount Morgan are made of such resistant rock. More information about the geology of central New Hampshire can be found in the Black Bear environment label.

SEE THE LABEL TO THE LEFT FOR INFORMATION ABOUT THE DEER.

Interim Label: Left of diorama

IT IS A JUNE AFTERNOON AT SQUAM LAKE, IN NEW HAMPSHIRE. THESE WHITETAIL DEER, A MOTHER AND HER TWO FAWNS, HAVE COME TO DRINK. THEY WILL SPEND MOST OF THE DAY BACK IN THE WOODS, RESTING QUIETLY, OUT OF SIGHT OF THEIR ENEMIES. IN A MOMENT,

THE SWIMMING LOON WILL DISAPPEAR UNDERWATER. THESE BLACK AND WHITE BIRDS ARE EXPERT UNDERWATER FISHERMEN.

THE DEER – Deer are plant eaters, not hunters. In New England, their chief enemies are people, dogs and coyotes. You could walk in the woods for hours and never see a deer, even if there are many around. WHY? A deer hears you, smells you and leaves, long before you get close. Its keen senses are the deer's best defense. Deer can run fast; about 35–40 miles per hour, but they tire quickly at that speed. Dogs run more slowly, but they can keep going. Often, dogs catch up with a deer when it becomes too tired to move on.

• Look at the deer. How do its long legs and large ears help it to live in its environment?

A hungry coyote might pass within a few feet of a fawn, and never notice it. WHY? These speckled fawns are too small to escape by running, but they have other defenses. They are born knowing how to lie as still as a stone. Their speckles make them hard to see. And newborn fawns have no deer odor at all.

The deer are in their tan summer coats. Their winter fur is different.

You can see and feel a deer's winter coat, at the activity station on your left.

Interim Label: Right of diorama

THE HABITAT – Squam Lake is surrounded by white pine trees (evergreens). There are also alders, wild cherry and other broadleafed trees. The forest floor is covered with early summer flowers.

• Look on your left for daisies, orange Indian paintbrush, and pink trillium. Look on your right, for the chipmunk sitting on a rock. It is surrounded by white bunchberry, pink lady's slipper, Indian paintbrush, striped Jack-in-the-pulpit and pink wild rose.

Final Label: Left of diorama
Whitetail Deer at Squam Lake

IT IS A JUNE AFTERNOON AT SQUAM LAKE, IN NEW HAMPSHIRE. THESE WHITETAIL DEER, A MOTHER AND HER TWO FAWNS, HAVE COME TO DRINK. THEY WILL SPEND MOST OF THE DAY BACK IN THE WOODS, RESTING QUIETLY, OUT OF SIGHT OF THEIR ENEMIES.

THE DEER — Deer are plant eaters, not hunters. In New England, their chief enemies are people, dogs and coyotes. You can walk in the woods for hours, and never see a deer, even if there are many around. WHY? A deer smells you, hears you and leaves, long before you get close. Its keen senses are the deer's best defense.

A hungry coyote might pass within a few feet of a fawn, and never notice it. WHY? These speckled fawns are too small to escape by running, but they have other defenses. They are born knowing how to lie as still as a stone. Their speckles make them hard to see. And newborn fawns have no deer odor at all.

• Look at the deer. How do its long legs and large ears help it to live in its environment? A deer's coat is tan in summer and brown-grey in winter. Naturalists refer to the summer coat as "red phase" and the winter coat as "brown phase."

OTHER ANIMALS — In a moment, the swimming loon will disappear under water. These black and white birds are expert underwater fishermen.

Final Label: Right of diorama

THE HABITAT — Squam Lake is surrounded by white pine trees and a variety of broadleafed trees. Near the shore, alders and wild cherry trees are growing in the moist soil. The forest floor is covered with early spring flowers. There is enough water and sunlight for many plants to grow here.

• Look on the left side of the diorama, for daisies, orange Indian paintbrush and pink trillium. Look to the right, for the chipmunk sitting on a rock. It is surrounded by white bunchberry, pink lady's slipper, Indian paintbrush, striped Jack-in-the-pulpit and pink wild rose.

Deer Audio Script

SOUND (birds, spring calls) Listen . . . It is almost summer at Squam Lake in central New Hampshire. The animals are active again, and the woods are bright with the color of new leaves and late spring wildflowers. Especially around the lakeshore, where sunlight and water are abundant, you can see daisies, orange and yellow hawkweed, ladyslippers, blue flag, white bunchberries and wild roses. You might, on this warm afternoon, notice the aroma of wild rose. Perhaps the breeze will bring a faint odor of deer.

SOUND (birds, green frog) The songs of the birds, the twang of the green frog, and the nighttime choruses of other frogs — all are aimed at attracting potential mates. Spring is mating season for all these creatures. Three whitetail deer, a doe and her two spotted fawns, have come to drink and browse the new growth along the shore. They spend most of the day resting quietly in the woods, hidden from their greatest enemies — people, domestic dogs and coyotes. Nighttime is safer: at dusk, the deer begin to move towards food and water.

SOUND (loon) The loon is alarmed. It is warning its mate of danger. Perhaps something is approaching their nest. These black and white water birds will not nest or live on a lake which has too many people. As New England's lakes and ponds become more congested, fewer and fewer of these beautiful birds can be seen. In many places, they are now only a memory.

6. Audience understanding of exhibit themes

An important goal of the modifications was to increase all visitors' understanding of the fundamental organizational concepts of the dioramas; that each diorama represents a typical New England environment (in fact, an actual place in New England), that these environments show diversity, and that the plants and animals in each diorama are typical of that environment and adapted to do well in that particular habitat.

a.   Connections between exhibits.

The general conceptual organization of the gallery was apparent to visitors before modifications; in the baseline data, 50 per cent of the respondents could connect at least two out of the three ideas associated with New England Life-zones, but only one answer mentioned all three aspects. In the final data, 33 per cent of the visitors interviewed could connect all three aspects. Both the observations and the interviews provide direct evidence of the impact of the new interactive components on the topic of exhibit themes. For example, when asked about a connection between the dioramas in the final interviews, 9 per cent of the respondents said that they 'all smelled'. In the notes from the observations, one woman said to a child, 'Each one has the smell of a habitat . . . where the animals live, and they got its smell'.

b.   Knowledge of adaptation.

Visitors were asked before and after exhibit changes whether they could give examples of animal adaptation. The responses changed dramatically after the exhibit included the additional components. This can be illustrated by the visitors' responses to a specific question concerning the moose and the beaver. Visitors were shown a picture of a moose and a beaver and asked, 'Can you think of any part of this animal or things about it which might make it good at living where it does or how it does?' Respondents were encouraged to give as many answers as they could. In the baseline interviews, more than half the visitors could give no response to this question. At the time of the final evaluation, all visitors could give at least one adaptive feature for these animals, and the range of different adaptations mentioned had increased from only 6 for the two animals in the baseline data to a total of 25 (Fig. 27.4).

The change in the knowledge about adaptation becomes especially clear when the kinds of responses that visitors gave during the various phases of the exhibit are compared. Table 27.5 provides this information. Visitors were shown pictures of the beaver and the moose and asked to name a specific adaptive feature of these animals after they had viewed the exhibit. In the baseline interviews, few visitors (under 10 per cent) could name any one feature, and the different adaptive features mentioned are small and encompass only the most obvious characteristics of these animals. After the modifications, a much larger percentage of visitors can think of adaptive features, but even more striking is the range of features that they suggest. It is evident that this longer list includes attributes that were noted through interaction with the beaver mount, from information on the recorded messages, or through other interactions in addition to reading the labels.

In the final evaluation, all the visitors who responded could name at least one adaptive feature for the beaver or the moose as compared to 89 per cent in the interim data; 88 per cent named more than two features for each, contrasted with only 32 per cent in the interim data.

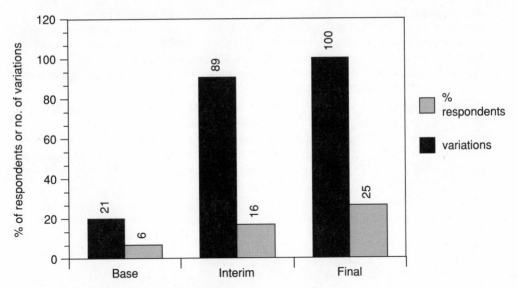

Fig. 27.4 Percentages of visitors who can name at least one adaptation feature for beaver and moose and number of different features cited

DISCUSSION

The modifications in the exhibits in the New England Lifezones Hall at the Boston Museum of Science have produced a significant alteration in visitor behaviour patterns. The time that visitors spend in the gallery has increased, the manner in which they interact with the exhibits has become more active, and they learn more from their visit to the exhibit. The quantitative data support these findings, but in many ways the qualitative are more revealing of the new feeling in the gallery.

The gallery has changed from a rather quiet, secluded place favoured by adults to a livelier hall populated by families and children. The noise level has increased, and the mood has altered. During the collection of baseline data, we observed many adult couples in the gallery who appeared to appreciate the relative seclusion and quiet of the gallery at least as much as the exhibits. This population does not appear as frequently after alteration. Museums may want to consider the potential negative impact of modifications on some audience segments before they remove all of the quieter galleries.

Before the changes, it was possible to observe many visitors as they walked through the gallery in traditional museum style, circling by the exhibits at the periphery of the room in clockwise or counterclockwise direction. After the modifications, the general visitation pattern appeared much more random. At any moment, the overall behaviour of visitors in the gallery seemed unsystematic. Some visitors went from diorama to diorama, others wandered across the room, and still others shuttled back and forth between particular sensory components.

However, when groups were tracked, it became clear that individuals followed purposeful paths. Just as adult couples, intent on reading labels, had been the predominant group before modifications, children who followed particular sensory modes became predominant after modifications. Children went from smell box to smell box, from earphone to earphone or from one hands-on activity station to the next. Analysis of the data suggests that children are making rational choices, indulging in preferred sensory learning modes (Gardner 1983), consistent with the general recognition that children's thoughts and actions are usually purposeful (Duckworth 1990; Hein 1988) when appropriate choices are available to them. This analysis suggests that the criticism often levelled at interactive exhibits – that they encourage aimless wandering from one exhibit to another – may need to be reexamined.

The data on attracting power are particularly rich in their implications. The addition of interpretive panels giving visitors the opportunity to learn about the dioramas using a wider range of senses has increased the attracting power of even the least popular dioramas. This suggests that traditional museum displays can be made interesting to a larger fraction of visitors with relatively minor modifications. The addition of hands-on

Table 27.5 Adaptive features mentioned for beaver and moose. An 'x' indicates a feature mentioned by at least one visitor. Per cent frequencies are given for features mentioned by more than 10 per cent of visitors

	Baseline		Interim		Final	
	No.	%	No.	%	No.	%
Beaver						
Teeth	x		x	71	x	82
Tail	x		x	43	x	84
Fur	x		x	25	x	41
Claws/paws			x	11	x	44
(Webbed) feet			x		x	22
Fat			x	11	x	
Colour			x		x	
Mouth			x			
Oil in fur					x	
Shape/body					x	
Nose					x	
Ears					x	
Membrane over eyes					x	
Soft					x	
Lungs					x	
Moose						
Antlers	x		x	39	x	66
Size	x		x	21	x	38
Hooves/feet	x		x	14	x	25
Fur			x	14	x	22
Long legs			x	11	x	22
Snout/nose			x		x	13
Fat			x		x	
Colour			x		x	
Ears					x	
Big heart					x	
Teeth					x	

components has added to the visitor time in the gallery; it has not detracted from the power of the dioramas to attract visitors. Visitors now stop both to look at the deer, moose, and bears and to peer in the microscope or to build-a-beast. The persistence of approximately 60 per cent as a maximum attracting power for all the dioramas, as well as for the other components, suggests a natural upper limit for exhibit components regardless of modifications.

This robust interest in traditional museum cases suggests that museums may wish to consider adding interpretive panels, materials, and activities to extant exhibits to allow for more physical and intellectual involvement by visitors, rather than eliminating the traditional cases in favour of only hands-on interactive exhibits. In some science museums, the actual artefacts are increasingly being replaced by videoscreens, models, and other components that make hands-on interaction easier for some visitors, but the new galleries lose the flavour of the original collections. These interactive galleries are often thin on actual museum objects. Also, videoscreens as an interactive component exclude blind visitors and, depending on placement, may not be accessible to wheelchair users. Our results suggest that an alternative and inexpensive strategy may be to preserve the more traditional cases and exhibits but to increase access by adding multisensory interpretive components.

Our questions to visitors concerning label use provided surprising results. When asked what they had gained from the exhibit, it became clear that visitors responded with information they had obtained from many sources: reading, listening, smelling, and touching. As educators and exhibit designers, we are conditioned to believe that conscious acquisition of information by visitors comes from written information. Our studies indicate that under the right circumstances, visitors are clearly able to synthesize information from many different sensory modalities into personal learning that they can articulate to an interviewer.

Redundant information provided by the variety of modalities was clearly of value for both the general public and special-needs groups. In addition, consistency of placement was noted as an important component leading to accessibility. During the interim modification phase as the placement of exhibit components changed, the gallery did not have the unified, consistent pattern finally achieved. The impact of this variation was noted especially with the handicapped visitors. For example, blind visitors simply would not find an earphone if they had discovered it at the left-hand side of one panel and it was placed at the right-hand side of the next panel they encountered. But all visitors responded in some way to this lack of consistency. If the second smell box they tried was not working, visitors would stop trying to use other smell boxes. The need for consistent basic design features and functioning exhibits is usually acknowledged, but the desire for interactive exhibits sometimes leads exhibit designers to disregard redundant labelling and mechanical consistency. This results in an increased physical and intellectual strain on visitors, making the exhibits less accessible.

A final point is the value of accessible exhibit design and content for all audiences. We think of making accommodations for people with special needs, but what we consistently saw is that these modifications constituted significant improvement in length of time spent and learning outcomes for *all* visitors. Multisensory learning opportunities not only provide a way to reach challenged audiences, but also provide an appropriate challenge for all visitors.

This paper first appeared in Curator 34(4) (1991), pp. 273–90.

NOTES

1 A full description of the exhibit modifications is contained in the final project report (Davidson 1991).
2 At the request of the Museum staff, the second set of observations was carried out on both school visitation days and nonschool days, although the original evaluation design had focused only on non-school visitors. Because schoolchildren were not a specific target audience for developing the new components, there is no comparable school visitation time in the baseline data. However, observation of school groups did help us to understand the patterns of this audience segment with the installation.

REFERENCES

Bloomer, R. (1987) Private communication.

Davidson, B. (1991) *New Dimensions for Traditional Dioramas; Multisensory Additions for Access, Interest and Learning*, Boston, MA: Museum of Science.

Duckworth, E. (1990) 'Museum visitors and the development of understanding', *Journal of Museum Education* 15(1): 4–6.

Disabilities Study Quarterly (1990) Special issue, 'Disability Demographics' 10(3).

Gardner, H. (1983) *Frames of Mind*, New York, NY: Basic Books.

Hein, G.E. (1988) 'How do children behave in museums?', *La Investigació de le'educator de museus*, Barcelona: Ajuntament de Barcelona (ICOM/CECA Conference Proceedings): 243–50.

28

A *picture* of *visitors* for exhibition developers

Sandra Bicknell and Peter Mann

The Interpretation Unit at the Science Museum, London, has used evaluation and visitor studies, both their own and those done elsewhere, to develop a model of how museum visitors use exhibitions. This paper summarizes the findings. Visitors (to the Science Museum) are described in four categories rather than one homogeneous group: experts, families, frequent 'museumers', and school students. Each group uses exhibitions in a different way.

INTRODUCTION

This paper is intended to provide the beginnings of a blueprint to help exhibition developers, in whatever role they may hold, to understand how visitors use exhibitions and exhibits. The picture which is painted is still a little fuzzy but some of the detail is clear.

THE ORIGINAL IDEA

The Science Museum in London, UK, is committed to the enhancement of the public understanding of science and to improving the accessibility of the Museum to its visitors. One of the ways we believe we can help achieve these aims is through the development of an idea one of us had when acting as project manager of a major redisplay. For this task, it was felt desirable for the project team to have an agreed-upon 'model of visitor behaviour' even if the model was wrong. There were two reasons for doing this. First, to encourage consistency within the team by providing a shared view which would help avoid endless arguments about undefined assumptions regarding our potential visitors. Second, should we wish actually to test such a model, it would provide a mutual starting point.

The model aimed to incorporate four main points:

- How visitors approach galleries as a whole. For example, do they want to envisage the gallery as a whole, or do they prefer a maze?
- How visitors approach the exhibits within a gallery. Do they read everything in sequence, or do they browse at random, only stopping to look at something that catches their eye?
- The quantity of information visitors require. Do visitors read anything at all, or will they read 400 words if it interests them?

- How the project team should view the visitors. Should they be seen as passive recipients of the information which is provided, or as active participants in the process of acquiring the information?

A literature search resulted in the construction of a model which suggested the following:

- Visitors do indeed appreciate a comprehensible structure to the exhibition as a whole, even if they don't follow it. They like to be able to orientate themselves within the exhibition.
- Few, if any, visitors will have the time, concentration, determination, or interest to look at everything in the exhibition, let alone read everything.
- Visitors browse through an exhibition looking for cues to make them stop.
- Most people spend only a short time at most of the exhibits they come across, and pass by having seen little to tempt them to stop. This is not a pejorative statement, nor is it assuming visitors are not taking anything in or not enjoying the experience.
- Perhaps most importantly, most people spend a much longer period looking at a small number of exhibits – the ones they actually stop at. It is at this point that the museum has the chance to put its ideas across to the visitor.

Based on these suggestions, the following guidelines for exhibition layout were developed:

- There should be an understandable logic to the arrangement of the exhibits, so that visitors can know where they are and can identify where they want to go next.
- Where there are groups of exhibits, the physical and conceptual boundaries of each group should be clear, as should the relationship between the groups.
- Within a group the links between exhibits should be clear. Each exhibit should have a consistent physical and textual structure so that each exhibit can be 'read' in the same way without having to learn a technique for each exhibit.
- Each exhibit and each group should have a bold title to be read from approximately five metres. The title should allow people to sum up the exhibit as they pass by, and decide whether they want to stop and spend their time there. Alternatively, the title should be intriguing or interrogating if its intention is specifically to draw people to it. These are the cues which are provided to allow them to decide whether they want to stop.
- Each exhibit and each group should have a piece of introductory text which briefly says why the exhibit or group is there and what the main theme is.
- Each object label should have the same structure so that they can all be 'read' in the same way. These labels should comprise a title to be read from approximately three metres, an introductory paragraph to say why the object has been included, and the remainder of the text to include other necessary information.

The model also had consequences for evaluation of the particular exhibition which was being created. Literature on the use of formative evaluation to improve attracting power and holding power seemed to be of little practical use and were felt to have the potential to be simplistic and misleading. Such indices did not address what would happen when such an exhibit is placed in a gallery of exhibits developed in a similar way. Would they simply be in competition with each other? Consequently it was decided to focus only on the attracting power and holding power of certain key exhibits where the intention was to attract and hold all visitors. This focus would be directed primarily toward the siting of key exhibits, and on formative evaluation to improve their attracting and holding powers relative to all the others in the exhibition.

In the main it was believed that the project team should concentrate on the use of formative evaluation to improve the comprehensibility of an exhibit so that:

- as visitors passed by they could decide, on the basis of the cues they were given, whether or not they wished to stop;
- once they decided to stop, the concepts, information, and relationships between the objects presented should be capable of being understood by the target audience;
- once they stopped they would be provided with the amount and level of information appropriate to the target audience;
- the target audience for a particular exhibit would include those visitors who stop to look at that exhibit. This is not meant to imply that such visitors are a sub-group of visitors. On the contrary the model assumes that all visitors will stop at one exhibit or another. Rather it means that the text for a particular exhibit could be targeted at those who stop at it and are in, for example, the top 10 per cent of time-spenders at that exhibit. This is perhaps a rather unusual idea and will be developed later.

Our criterion of success was taken from the work of Steve Griggs who recommends 'that an exhibit communicates its message if a visitor, on seeing the display, can *comprehend* the information without any misunderstanding or misconception about its conceptions and intention' (Griggs 1984; p. 416). It is then up to the visitor to decide whether he or she wants to learn or to forget the information with which they have been presented.

Unfortunately, since the project was not continued, the model was not developed further. However, a new project has provided an opportunity to resurrect the original model of visitor behaviour. This resurrection has involved updating the model to accommodate the evidence of internal evaluation work, more general visitor research, and the growing body of visitor studies literature.

DEVELOPING THE IDEA

The original model provided something practical and tangible that can be adapted for other project teams within the Science Museum. The four main areas addressed by the model were:

- how visitors will approach the gallery as a whole;
- how visitors approach the exhibits within the gallery;
- the quantity of information they require;
- the type of behavioural response (how should visitors be viewed).

The gallery as a whole

On the first day of the 1992 Visitor Studies Association conference Ross Loomis presented a précis of the findings of orientation studies. For the sake of brevity, please refer to chapter five of Loomis' (1987) book *Museum Visitor Evaluation: new tool for management*, which addresses this topic. Little will be added here except a note that there are advantages of stage setting and a coherent structure.

Exhibits within the gallery

In the original model it was felt appropriate to use John Falk's analogy of museum visitors being like people who are out window shopping – when something catches their eye they stop and look, and may eventually take away a purchase, i.e. take away ideas and information. Thus most people will spend a significant amount of time at a small number of exhibits at which they have decided to stop. It is this circumstance which makes possible the exchange of ideas and information by looking, listening, reading and discussing with party members (Falk, 1982). The work of Paulette McManus points out that a 'visitor reads up to twenty words in five seconds as he or she walks towards an exhibit, without an observer being aware that reading is taking place' (McManus 1987: 265). Visitors appear not to be reading but in fact they are scanning objects and text, looking for cues to help them to decide if they wish to stop and invest their time.

One of the ways to portray where visitors stop and invest their time is to translate the results from behavioural mapping into contour maps (see Fig. 28.1). The inference here is that few, if any, of the visitors look at everything in an exhibition. To misquote Abraham Lincoln:

> You can encourage some of the people to read/look all of the time, you can encourage all of the people to read/look some of the time, but you can't encourage all of the people to read/look all of the time.

Steve Bitgood has said; 'It is my opinion that at least 50 per cent of the visitors should read a label' (Bitgood 1987: 3). However, this can be unrealistic within the Science Museum. For example, the Land Transport gallery has 126 cases, 122 free-standing objects and 1,158 object labels. Even if the labels were only 50 words long, visitors would have to spend some four hours just reading the words (assuming a reading time of 250 words per minute). There are twenty further, equivalent gallery spaces in the Science Museum – some three and a half days' worth of continuous reading.

Based on available information, it can be said that any factor that involves visitors' time does not follow a normal distribution curve. Some form of exponential distribution seems more appropriate. This applies to time spent in the Museum, time spent in a gallery and time spent at an exhibit. For example, time spent by tracked visitors in exhibitions follows the pattern shown in Figure 28.2.

Much of this confirms work done by Margaret Menninger (1990) on 'survival curves'. However, these ideas can be taken even further. One of the Science Museum's evaluated exhibitions, a bicentennial celebration of the birth of Michael Faraday (see Fig. 28.1), provided some interesting data. If attention paid to the exhibits is plotted – be this text, objects, or interactives – it would appear we have yet another exponential decay (see Fig. 28.3). Breaking this down into the types of exhibits a very different pattern can be seen in Figure 28.4.

Frankly it is far from easy to explain this, since it appears that visitor attention to text and objects follows an exponential decay, but attention to interactives is linear. It is hoped that future evaluations carried out in the Science Museum will be able to follow this line of enquiry.

The examples given above serve to confirm the suggestion of the original model that few, if any, visitors will have the time, concentration, determination, or interest to look in depth at much of an exhibition. In general, visitors browse through an exhibition looking for cues to encourage them to stop and invest their limited time. Most people spend only a short time at most of the exhibits they come across.

Fig. 28.1 Contour map of what visitors paid attention to in the Faraday exhibition

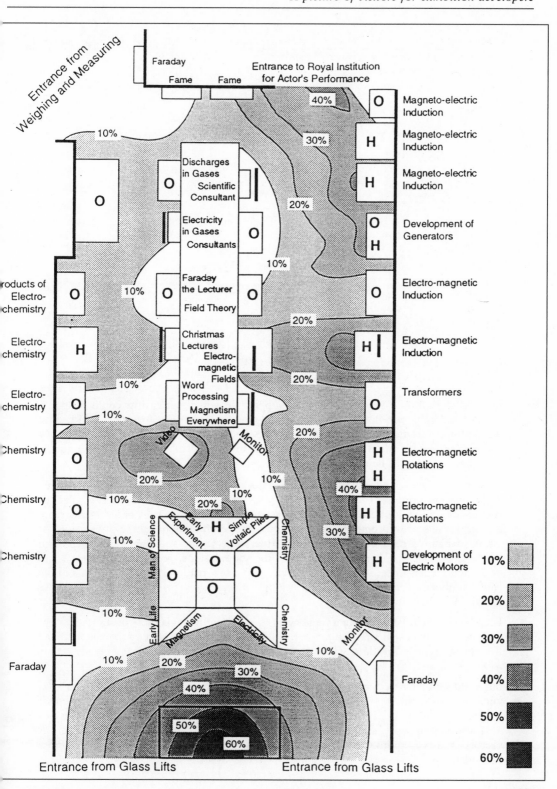

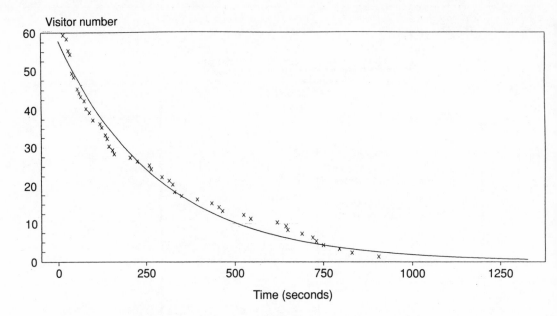

Fig. 28.2 'Survival curve' for visitor time in the Babbage exhibition with data point plot

Quantity of Information

Initially no published data were found to support the belief that visitors could be spending a considerable time looking at objects and reading labels they are interested in, since no researchers seemed to have observed or questioned visitors to ascertain the times they spent at those exhibits to which they devoted most of their time. It was therefore a hypothesis waiting to be tested.

This paper proposes an exponential model for visitors' investment of time in a label. The model encompasses the sort of label in widespread use in the Science Museum: title, summary paragraph and a paragraph of secondary information. In other words there are three levels of information. It is suggested that each label has three populations of visitors which correspond to these levels: title readers, title-and-summary readers and whole-label readers. There are of course other populations, perhaps the largest of all being non-readers. There are also those who perversely read only the beginning and the end! Combination of the three primary populations might produce results like those shown in Fig. 28.5

Each label should be seen as a unique event, and the individuals that constitute its population of readers will vary from label to label. In other words, it cannot be assumed that the whole-label readers will be the same people for each label.

This introduces a paradox: the model described here suggests the possibility of providing a substantial text for the small percentage who have accepted the cues to stop and invest their time in that exhibit, yet this substantial text may be the very cue that causes the majority of visitors not to invest any of their time in that exhibit. This is not an invitation to write a small book and call it a label. The evidence for numerous visitors studies is quite clear: increasing the number of words decreases the number of readers.

It is apparent that our model raises important issues which will need to be addressed by further research. However, it also provides a hypothesis which in principle is capable of being tested immediately.

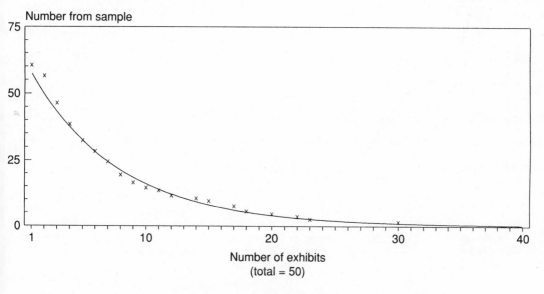

Fig. 28.3 Attention to exhibits: Faraday exhibition

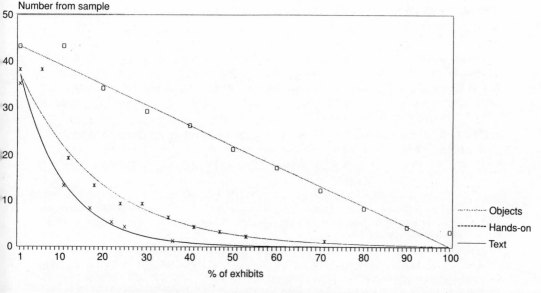

Fig. 28.4 Attention to exhibit types: Faraday exhibition

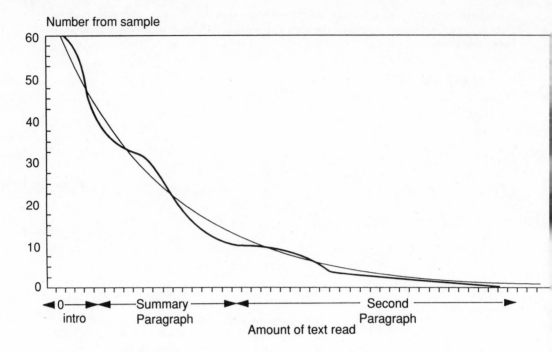

Number from sample

Fig. 28.5 Reading labels

Type of behavioural response

A major issue, and one that is all too easy to miss, is that attracting power and holding power imply that there is some unique characteristic which an object (or label) should possess in order to attract and hold all visitors. In reality, exhibit developers should consider the characteristics of the visitor, and not the objects. It is another manifestation of 'beauty lies in the eyes of the beholder'.

The fourth point of the model was initially phrased as 'the type of behavioural response'. This has been adapted to fit an area that, so far, has not been addressed. Looking at the Science Museum's visitors as a whole can be highly misleading and inappropriate. It works against the provision of an accurate picture because it obscures that fact that visitors are not a homogeneous group. It is therefore proposed the following categories can be used to describe the Science Museum's visitors:

- The 'buffs' – the experts who know the location of every rivet on the Spitfire. They are often male, usually adult, often solitary visitors, usually with a professional or leisure interest in the topic of a gallery. They invest large amounts of their time in very specific parts of a gallery.
- 'It's for the children' – usually families with children of ages four to fourteen, who implicitly or explicitly are a 'learning unit'. There may be two groups here: the focused learners and explorers and the 'we should do this for the children, but let's get it over and done with as quickly as possible'.
- 'I'm museuming' – often couples, often tourists, often older. Culture-vultures who know the international museum code, they tend to work their way through the museum systematically.
- School visits – in the UK these group visits are usually related to the national curriculum and range in age from 5 to 17.

Each of these groups is different, with different expectations, different reasons for visiting and, in general, different needs. What must be done next is to incorporate the needs of these groups into our model – or to ignore them if the targeting of the exhibition does not include a particular group.

CONCLUSIONS

It is believed that this paper presents the beginnings of a synthesis that can be of use to other exhibition developers. The model is an evolving one. There is a need to incorporate new findings, including the work of other visitor studies, and to test the validity of the above suggestions, as well.

The purpose of this paper is quite simply to help the authors to be more effective in the development of new interpretive projects. Our intent is to provide ourselves and our colleagues with a feel for the visitors who come to the Science Museum, come into the galleries, take part in programmes, attend lectures and so on. We want to provide a more tangible image than that ill-defined, nebulous term 'the general visitor'. We will continue to update this model and refine our understanding of our visitors. This paper is merely a beginning.

Note: A list of work completed to-date can be provided on request from Sandra Bicknell.

This paper first appeared in D. Thompson, A. Benefield, S. Bitgood, H. Shettel and R. Williams (eds) (1992) Visitor Studies: Theory, Research and Practice, Volume 5, Collected Papers from the 1992 Visitor Studies Conference (St. Louis, Missouri), *Jacksonville, Alabama: Visitor Studies Association.*

REFERENCES

Bitgood, S. C. (1987) *Knowing When Exhibit Labels Work: a standardised guide for evaluating and improving labels,* technical report 87–90, Jacksonville, AL: Center of Social Design.

Falk, J. H. (1982) 'The use of time as a measure of visitor behavior and exhibit effectiveness' *Journal of Museum Education Roundtable Reports* 7(4): 10–13.

Griggs, S. A. (1984) 'Evaluating exhibitions', in J. Thomson and D. Prince (eds) *The Manual of Curatorship,* London: Butterworth.

Loomis, R. J. (1987) *Museum Visitor Evaluation: new tool for management,* Nashville: Association for State and Local History.

McManus, P. M. (1987) 'It's the company you keep – the social determination of learning-related behavior in a science museum', *The International Journal of Museum Management and Curatorship* 6: 263–70.

Menninger, M. (1990) 'The analysis of time data in visitor research and evaluation studies', in S. C. Bitgood, A. Benefield, and D. Patterson (eds) *Visitor Studies: theory, research and practice, (3) Collected Papers of the Visitor Studies Conference,* Jacksonville, AL: Center for Social Design.

SUGGESTED READING

Cone, C. A. (1978) 'Space, time and family interaction – visitor behavior at the Science Museum of Minnesota', *Curator* 21(3): 245–58.

Heady, P. (1984) *Visiting Museums – A Report of a Survey of Visitors to the V & A, Science and National Railway Museums for the Office of Arts and Libraries,* London: HMSO.

McManus, P. M. (1987) *The Exploration of Space – A Review,* unpublished paper commissioned by A. Wilson, Education Department, Science Museum, London.

McManus, P. M. (1988) 'Good companions – more on the social determination of learning-related behavior in a science museum', *The International Journal of Museum Management and Curatorship* 7: 37–44.

Miles, R. S. (1985) *British Museum (Natural History) Department of Public Services Handbook,* unpublished document.

Stansfield, G. (1981) *Effective Interpretive Exhibitions,* Countryside Commission, Cheltenham: Countryside Commission.

29

Exhibit evaluation: taking account of human factors

Paul Alter and Rita Ward[1]

Human factors is a new applied science. It works with models of the human mind, how people learn, how they understand. The model can be used to predict the ways in which people interact with their surroundings. This article applies some key concepts to exhibition design and analysis.

Few things are more frustrating to a museum staff than discovering that the public doesn't get the 'picture' in a exhibition. What museums intend visitors to derive through labels, creative design, artefact association, audience interaction or sensory stimulation is not always perceived as intended. The problem is not just misperception. It is also miscommunication. Humans cannot transmit thoughts, emotions or opinions without some form of verbal, visual, or physical exchange. In our efforts to make an exhibit concept clear, we cannot expect the visitor to think the way the staff does.

Outside the United States, the term for human factors is 'ergonomics'. Both mean applying engineering disciplines and applied sciences in creating a design that works well in *human* terms (Rubinstein and Hersh 1984). The process is based on knowing a certain group of people – museum visitors – and a thorough analysis of the problem – communicating through an exhibit.

Human factors is relatively new as an applied science. Most recent advances come from cognitive psychology. An important aspect of this field is learning how people learn. While understanding the learning process is far from complete, certain concepts and guidelines are known from work already accomplished. A model in cognitive psychology (Card, Moran and Newell 1983) describes how the senses, short-term memory, and long-term memory interact. This interaction is key to learning, understanding, and remembering. The model can be used as a basis for understanding interaction and interpretation with an exhibit.

As a useful design aid, the tools of human factors can sometimes tell why people can't interpret the exhibit in the manner the museum staff has hoped for *before* the exhibit is complete. Museum professionals can learn how to communicate with their visitors by involving them in the process of creating an exhibit. Doing this calls for ways to analyse an exhibit and an exhibit-design approach that complements the analysis. The analysis technique is known as *thinking aloud* (Lewis, 1982). When combined with *formative evaluation* (Screven 1976, 1986; Griggs 1981), it can reveal problems and allow for changes in a controlled manner.

Over the last few decades, cognitive psychologists have been developing a model describing the processes of the human mind: the nature of these processes, how they work with the senses, and how people understand and remember. Polson (1986) describes a principled approach to human factors engineering. It is principled because the choices made in the human interface design are based on the model and the model is derived from what is known of the human mind, how people learn, and how they understand. When this model can be used to predict the interaction of people with their surroundings, it then becomes a useful exhibit-design aid. What follows is a brief overview of some key points in this research as they relate to exhibit design and analysis.

A MODEL OF THE MIND

'The Human Processing Model' is taken from the work of Card, Moran, and Newell (1983). The model shows three interactive pieces: (1) the *perceptual system*, (2) the *motor system*, and (3) the *cognitive system*. The perceptual system describes how information comes in through our senses, how it gets changed from raw input to the mind's internal representations, and where it is stored. The visual system is a key piece of the perceptual system, certainly from the perspective of exhibit design. It covers what information will be captured by the eye; whether movement, colour, or intensity will be detected; when the head will move to see something, and how long something will be viewed before the eye jumps to another angle.

Once information has been captured in the perceptual system, it gets translated and stored in special areas in short-term memory. The model describes the organization and the amount of information that can be stored and how long the information can be held before it decays and is replaced by something else. Information captured by the eye in the visual system is saved in the visual store and physically coded. For example, a number is represented by its curvature, length, colour, and other attributes but is not yet recognized by the mind as being a number. Information stays in the visual store briefly before being replaced by the next image, lasting anywhere from under a tenth of a second to a maximum of a full second.

Perception and understanding

Shortly after the physical representation appears in the visual store, a transformed and recognized image appears in short-term memory. If there is a great deal of information or if the information is seen only briefly, the image in the visual store rapidly fades and short-term memory gets filled before all is recognized and transferred. For example, if briefly shown a coloured list of numbers and letters, a person can select the contents in a certain area of the visual store or possibly all the same coloured items but cannot list the even-numbered digits or the digits versus the letters because the mind hasn't had a chance to figure out which are which. Short-term memory holds the intermediate steps of thinking and the translations of the perceptual system and can hold limited amounts of information. This is where the 'rule of seven' comes from – people can remember seven (plus or minus two) things easily.

Long-term memory is different. In the model, long-term memory holds an infinite amount of information. Effectively, nothing in this memory is ever erased. It is like a network of information. When something is remembered, or *activated*, other things related to it are also remembered. When something is 'forgotten', the path to that chunk of information is lost. Whether something will be remembered or not depends on the number of paths to it and the frequency of activation and whether similar chunks of information compete for activation.

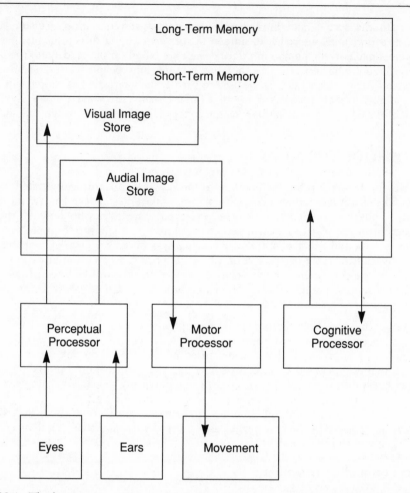

Fig. 29.1 The human processing model. Information comes in through the perceptual system and is saved in the visual or audial stores. The information is then transferred to short-term memory. Short-term memory is shown inside long-term memory since it is really activated chunks in long-term memory.

Short-term and long-term memory are closely related. Information in short-term memory activates items saved in long-term memory. If this doesn't occur, chances are whatever was in short-term memory gets replaced by something new. This, combined with the concept of 'chunking', allows more than seven items of information to be processed at one time. Chunking is one way the cognitive system relates information in short-term memory to information saved in long-term memory. Take the following two examples. Most people will have some trouble repeating these nine letters:

BACBCSCNB

However, they may easily recite a second list of the same letters arranged as follows, particularly if they are read aloud:

ABCCBSNBC

Effectively, three chunks of three letters each were activated, and depending on the familiarity, all three chunks may have been lumped together as one chunk. When this occurred, about three chunks in short-term memory activated untold amounts of long-term memory. However, the person viewing the letters must have already been familiar with ABC, CBS, and NBC.

This kind of chunking allows learning, understanding, and problem solving to occur. Some psychologists suggest that this partially explains the difference between a novice and an expert (Card, Moran and Newell, 1983). The novice stores individual facts in short-term memory. The expert can lump most of the facts as one chunk and also activate other chunks in long-term memory.

> But, if short-term can't hold all the information needed to solve the problem – either by directly storing the information in short-term memory or by chunking and activating information in long-term memory – and leave enough room in short-term memory for problem solving, the problem cannot be solved (Card, Moran and Newell 1983).

EXTERNAL MYTHS AND CONCEPTUAL MODELS

'Know thy user, for he is not thyself', counselled Rubinstein and Hersh (1984). Museum professionals are different from museum visitors. When planning an exhibit, the staff becomes connected with its work (Screven 1986). Individual pieces must be related in an overall system so that viewers understand the presentation, learn and interpret from labels and artefacts, follow a flow, and enjoy the experience. Subtle inconsistencies in colour schemes, visual distractions, or label presentations can detract in a large way. This isn't by accident. In developing an exhibit, the staff creates what Rubinstein and Hersh call the *external myth*. This is the staff's viewpoint and understanding of the exhibit. Elements of the myth include:

- *Items:* physical artefacts, objects, and props that make up the exhibit;
- *Terminology:* jargon specific to an exhibit topic, as in a science exhibit, but also the education level and reliance on assumed knowledge;
- *Ideas:* concepts behind the exhibit and the ideas the visitor is supposed to come away with;
- *Relationships:* how the pieces of the exhibit fit together to enhance each other and how the overall theme is conveyed;
- *Operations:* hands-on exhibits, controls, and sensing devices.

On one side of the exhibit are artefacts, labels, graphics, sounds, and even smells. This is the myth, the expression of the ideas, goals, themes, and concepts woven into the exhibit. The staff develops this external myth, and if the exhibit is a success, this external myth matches the viewer's understanding.

On the other side of the exhibit is the visitor. The visitor builds a *conceptual model* (Rubinstein and Hersh 1984) of what he sees. When the viewer generates this model, hypotheses about what is presented are created, and the viewer then attempts to verify them in the exhibit. The viewer probably isn't aware of it, but in fact it is a common method for learning and understanding at many levels. Conceptual models form the basis for expectations. If the person viewing the exhibit can easily form a model, possibly discarding several along the way, the exhibit is easy to understand. If the viewer needs a complex model, the exhibit will be confusing. Unless the staff can conceive, control, understand, and guide the conceptual model, it is likely to be vastly different from the staff's intentions.

Suppose the museum staff is developing an exhibit showing how people have entertained themselves at home through the decades. One part may show a period-room vignette of a log cabin with a fireplace, a lantern, a book on the mantel, and a whittling knife. The staff's external myth seems solid, particularly when viewed with the rest of the gallery, including supporting labels and exhibit title boards. Visitors, on the other hand, may have a completely different perspective. They might see an exhibit showing the development of home heating and lighting. At this point, their conceptual model bears little resemblance to the staff's external myth.

In the next room is a more modern setting: a VCR, a television and a compact disc player in a 1980s family room. The staff hopes the visitor will compare and contrast. But the viewer with the energy-development conceptual model will first need to discard the current model, adapt one that is closer to the facts presented, and prepare to test his hypotheses again.

Developing the external myth

The presence of an artefact may not be nearly as important as its relationships with the surroundings, the artefacts, and the overall sights, sounds, smells, movements, and appearance of the exhibit. The relationships developed by the staff become the external myth. If the viewer's conceptual model resembles the external myth, then the desired interactions and interpretations are more likely to occur. This is the heart of interpretive interactive exhibits: creating an environment wherein differing groups of people relate what they see to what they know, ending with an understanding and interpretation of the information that is intended. Creating a consistent and simple external myth is the job of the staff. It is through this that the viewer is influenced.

A multitude of design choices is available in exhibit designing – everything from what goes in the exhibit to what viewers should get out of it. This is the *design space*, initially huge. Anything that can be imagined is an option. As the design progresses, choices that begin to define and limit the design space are made.

Choices about the audience are also made. This may be the most important analysis step, leading to decisions that directly affect all others. Are there targeted age, educational, social, and ethnic backgrounds? How much do they already know? It is unlikely any one design will work perfectly with preschool children looking for an afternoon of entertainment and a historian beginning research on the topic of the exhibit. However, both groups may be typical visitors at the museum, and it is the staff's job to reach them. An external myth can be developed for several classes of visitors, so long as each group can create its own simple conceptual model. Certain guidelines should be followed:

1. Maintain a consistent myth

The external myth is typically a metaphor or analogy for something *like* what the viewer already knows. Taking advantage of common knowledge is essential to the interpretive process (Rubinstein and Hersh 1984). An example is using multiple labels aimed at differing age groups, each having its own consistent colour and design scheme to target the expected knowledge, interest, and interaction for each group. Visitors should rapidly learn which labels contain the information appropriate for them.

2. Limit the scope of the myth

The best designs are well bounded with limits the viewer can easily grasp. Although this may seem to contradict a design for several classes of viewers, it isn't true if each class of viewer develops its own conceptual model. One exhibit cannot possibly cover everything for the viewer, but interaction and interpretation are still reasonable expectations if they can grasp what is being presented and how it will occur.

3. Limit the states

How did the viewer get to this point in the exhibit and what are the options from here? Allowing easy entrance and exit from the middle of the exhibit (except for emergency purposes) is undesirable. If the viewer can walk from the middle of an arrowhead collection to Main Street, 1910, the staff's intended external myth probably won't be easily grasped. By the same token, make the states easily understood and visible. If the viewer accidentally makes a wrong turn, it should be obvious; otherwise, the previous conceptual model and the new external myth may become confused.

4. Minimize conceptual load

If a person cannot hold all the information needed for understanding something in short-term memory, the situation cannot be understood. Drawing upon probable prior knowledge, the visitor may have enhanced chances for chunking and, consequently, problem solving, learning, and remembering.

The cognitive devices available – sight, hearing, smell, touch, and taste – can easily be overloaded. When this occurs with sight, the viewer is effectively blinded to what is presented (Smith 1982). No matter how well a label is written, if the reader is expected to understand too many unfamiliar words, the brain shuts out the extra 'noise' in defence. This can be good or bad. If this blindness occurs while reading a label, the label might as well not be there. On the other hand, some exhibits are jam-packed with hundreds of artefacts explicitly overloading the senses and bring people back time and again because they 'always see something they didn't see before'. In fact, this may be exactly true. Note that there are no hard-and-fast rules for predicting or measuring the correct conceptual load. This is partially because not enough is known in this area but it is also a practical limitation. Formal measuring of this type is difficult, time consuming, and still well in the realm of experimental cognitive psychology. To summarize, the chances that the visitor will understand the external myth are *reduced* by the more new or unrelated information there is to be assimilated; the more inconsistencies there are in the design and presentation of the exhibit; and the more unfamiliar and unrelated to previous knowledge the topic is. The viewer's conceptual model can be so far removed from what is intended that the visitor is effectively blind to the exhibit. The result is a puzzled face and a stroll to the next gallery.

The following example helps demonstrate some of the concepts behind the cognitive model and its applications to exhibit design. In 1986, the Belmar Museum staff developed an exhibit exploring myths of the West through Hollywood westerns. The targeted audience included all ages. The exhibit illustrated western films over sixty years, using original film posters and film memorabilia. The myths – good guys, bad guys, codes of the West, sidekicks, damsels in distress, and dancing horses – were identified to visitors in the labels and guided tours. Posters were arranged in periods, starting from the early 1900s to the late 1970s.

After the exhibit opened and the tours began, it became obvious that children were not interested at all. They became bored within a few minutes. Actors like Gary Cooper, Randolph Scott, and even John Wayne were unknown to them. But they related so strongly to two mid-exhibit display cases containing such memorabilia as lunch boxes and bubble-gum cards that the tour immediately fell apart. The adults, on the other hand, found the exhibit fascinating. Labels were read, the exhibit concept understood, and memories of Saturday afternoons at the movies were exchanged with other people in the tour.

The model of the perceptual system fits nicely here. Long-term memory in adults was tapped as they recalled the old films. Experiences related by the network of long-term memory chunks were activated: popcorn, songs, the price of a ticket and even their own childhood. The children had few, if any, of these long-term memories to draw upon; all of the names, titles, and faces were new to them. Short-term memory was overloaded, and little learning or understanding took place. The lunch boxes and bubble-gum cards were familiar to them and held their interest. However, few goals of the exhibit were achieved since the myths of the West were not explored.

INFORMAL EVALUATION

Knowing how the human perceptual system works and some of its limitations is useful when beginning an exhibit design. However, a methodology is needed that can work with a team-oriented design approach taking advantage of the perceptual model. This is accomplished through two design techniques. The first is called formative evaluation (Screven 1976. 1986; Griggs 1981). The second uses an informal analysis method called 'thinking aloud', which enhances the evaluation steps of the formative process.

Building an exhibit involves many of the same features found in other user interfaces such as computers, automobiles, documents, and nuclear reactors. The user must be able to understand the surroundings and interact in an appropriate manner. Also, the external myth must come close to the conceptual model, and the limits of the perceptual system must be recognized and played to.

Formative evaluation lets the staff design, build, and test. This happens in a step-by-step and repeating process. The development cycle can be stopped at almost any point, and a complete exhibit exists. Screven's approach stresses exhibit observation and testing. To this end, he recommends several methods of testing. We recommend the additional use of thinking aloud. This has been a valuable analysis method in cognitive psychology for many years (Lewis and Simon 1982; Ericsson and Simon 1980; Newell and Simon 1972). When used carefully, it can help you understand why something is bad. Thinking aloud isn't particularly helpful for figuring out which pieces are good and for what reasons, but it does point to the problem areas.

Thinking aloud involves a couple of staff members and a few visitors. A staff member prompts a visitor to tell what he is experiencing while viewing an exhibit. Another staff member makes notes about what is said, where the visitor looks, expressions on his face, and even body language. The method uses one simple request: 'Tell me what you are thinking.' The visitor should never be prompted to interpret through specific questions or demands such as 'Do you see the relationship? . . . What does this mean? . . . Tell me how artefact A relates to artefact B. . . . Tell me what time period. . . . What do you like or dislike? . . .' Studies show that questions and requests such as these elicit false answers, since the visitor may be second guessing the staff (Newell and Simon 1972). And such leading questions stimulate the visitor to use short-term memory for problem solving, which competes with the limited space for exhibit interpretation.

When the thinking-aloud approach is properly used, responding can become almost second nature to the visitor without significantly adding to or detracting from the exhibit experience. But before using this method, the goals of the analysis and the backgrounds of the visitors should be listed. If a specific audience is to be tested, visitors will need screening. If specific aspects of the exhibit need analysis, the staff may need to direct and limit the interactions to specific areas. Limiting the scope can be important in reducing the quantity of information obtained to manageable amounts. Be prepared to stop the testing if it runs too long. Intervene or prompt only when the visitor stops talking or gets sidetracked.

Certain tools can be used to simplify and speed up the process. The drafting stage can be simplified through computer-aided design, making reiterative cycles less burdensome, time consuming, and costly. Tape recorders can relieve the recording burden, but transcribing the tapes can be expensive and time consuming. A good compromise is to record the testing, keep notes, and use the tapes later as a reference. Some groups have used video recorders focused on the viewer, but if two cameras can be used, one may focus on the visitor and one may 'look over the visitor's shoulder' at the exhibit. Care should be exercised, since some visitors will become camera shy while others will practise their acting abilities.

The purpose of formative evaluation is to find problems and rework them. The staff must take care to (1) control the time and resources allocated to evaluation and to say when enough is enough in a controlled manner, and (2) be aware of the visitors' sensibilities. The staff must not shoot the messenger. The visitors have been asked to relate their thoughts. Stress that the *exhibit* is being tested, *not* the visitors. After hours of listening, the responses can become frustrating. This, however, is precisely what needs to be heard. If the results are uncertain or confusing, sample more visitors. Four or five can give a 'gut feel' for what is happening. Ten visitors will give a more concrete view or confirm the confusion. Also don't try to explain why things are the way they are. Just collect their comments and move on. The visitors stop talking if you are defensive or if they think they will hurt your feelings.

CONCLUDING REMARKS: IF IT WERE EASY . . .

If it were easy, there would be no controversy over exhibit design. At one point or another, most museum professionals have come in contact with the process. Each has experiences and ideas to draw upon – or opinions and frustrations. The approach presented here is not intended to suggest that museum professionals have been inappropriately designing exhibits. Rather, it is suggested that we inject new ideas and methods into the design process, thereby changing the way museums teach and communicate with their visitors.

If it were possible to armchair-quarterback an exhibit and if the entire process were logical, someone would have long since come up with a blueprint for perfect exhibit planning and designing. But we all know that no matter how much effort is put into creating a good design, there will be times when the audience responds in unexpected ways.

The thinking-aloud approach combined with formative-evaluation methods can be of benefit to the museum profession. The two can enhance traditional methods of exhibit design and conducting museum surveys. Instead of blaming the visitor, the exhibit, or the staff, we can introduce the process into creating exhibits. By incorporating thoughts and reactions from museum visitors *while* creating the external myth, what the visitor sees and what the museum staff wants to be seen can come closer to one another.

This paper first appeared in Curator 31(3) (1988), pp. 167–77.

NOTE

1 Formerly Rita Alter.

REFERENCES

Card, S., Moran, T. and Newell, A. (1983) *The Psychology of Human-Computer Interaction,* Hillsdale, NJ: Lawrence Erlbaum Associates.

Ericsson, K. and Simon, H. (1980) 'Verbal reports as data', *Psychological Review* 87.

Griggs, S. (1981) 'Formative evaluation of exhibits at the British Museum (Natural History)', *Curator* 24(3): 189–201.

Lewis, C. (1982) 'Using the "thinking aloud" method in cognitive interface design', *IBM Research Report RC-9265,* Yorktown Heights, NY.

Newell, A. and Simon, H. (1972) *Human Problem Solving,* Englewood Cliffs, NJ: Prentice-Hall.

Polson, P. (1986) *Personal Communication,* Boulder, CO: University of Colorado.

Rubinstein, R., and Hersh, H. (1984) *The Human Factor,* Burlington, MA: Digital Press.

Screven, C. G. (1976). 'Exhibit evaluation – a goal-referenced approach', *Curator* 19(4): 271–90.

Screven, C. G. (1986) 'Exhibitions and information centers: some principles and approaches', *Curator* 29(2): 109–37.

Smith F. (1982) *Understanding Reading: A psycholinguistic analysis of reading and learning to read,* New York: Holt, Rinehart and Winston.

30

A beginner's guide to evaluation

Phil Bull

What is evaluation? What does it entail for exhibition producers? Front-end analysis, formative evaluation, and summative evaluation are each explained with an example.

The attitude of exhibition designers towards evaluation (and its professional practitioners) has traditionally been ambivalent. While recognizing the potential of evaluation to draw the attention of a design team to imperfections in their work, they have nonetheless tended to regard any adverse criticism as a slur upon their professional integrity. But suspicion of evaluators often stems from an ignorance of their function, their methods and their terminology. Professional evaluators have been accused of seeking to legitimize their prejudices behind a smokescreen of quasi-scientific jargon. This article attempts to provide a general introduction to the subject and to demystify some of its key concepts.

The evaluation of exhibitions usually falls into one of three categories:

> front-end analysis
> formative evaluation
> summative evaluation

These categories refer to when the evaluation takes place in relation to the design and construction of the exhibition. Generally speaking the earlier it takes place the more cost-effective it is likely to be.

Front-end analysis takes place during the pre-planning and planning stages. It is conducted with the intention of identifying potential problems before the exhibition goes into production. Strictly speaking, it cannot be classified as evaluation at all since it takes place before there is anything concrete to evaluate.

In an article in a recent issue of *Museum News*, Dr Giles Clarke of the British Museum (Natural History) describes how front-end analysis assisted in the planning of an exhibition on arthropods – a group of animals comprising insects, spiders, crustaceans and centipedes. Having decided that such an exhibition was necessary, the key question became 'How much do potential visitors know about arthropods already?' It is of paramount importance that the ideas and terminology of an exhibition should be neither so advanced as to confuse and alienate visitors nor so simplistic as to appear patronizing. A short multiple choice questionnaire was circulated to a representative sample of 145 visitors and its findings were helpful in determining the academic level at which the exhibition should be pitched. It was also considered necessary to assess the level of public enthusiasm for the subject and this was done by means of a series of four discussion groups in which visitors were invited to give their views on ideas for material to be included in the gallery. These discussions revealed that public attitudes towards arthropods tended to range from apathy to outright hostility. Rather than deterring the exhibition team from going ahead, this alerted the team to the need for an accessible, high profile exhibition which would stimulate and maintain visitors' enthusiasm. The Natural History Museum now conducts front-end analysis as a matter of routine before embarking upon any major new exhibition.

Formative evaluation takes place during the implementation of plans with the intention of providing directional guidance while work is in progress. Often it takes the form of 'developmental testing' which involves the testing of mock-ups of proposed exhibits on a random sample of museum visitors. Their reactions can provide valuable insights into the effectiveness of a particular exhibit in communicating its intended message. But developmental testing is restricted to assessing the impact of content rather than presentation since a crude mock-up will inevitably be less visually appealing than the finished exhibit. The Natural History Museum's Evaluation Coordinator, Jo Jarrett, has published a paper entitled 'Learning from the developmental testing of exhibits' in which she gives an account of a recent programme of developmental testing in the 'Inheritance and Variation' section of the museum's *Origin of Species* exhibition. It had become apparent that this particular section of the exhibition was failing to communicate its message clearly because it assumed too great a knowledge of the subject in visitors. A new set of exhibits were designed with the intention of explaining the concept of genetic mutation in layperson's terms and developmental testing was conducted on these.

The testing was done in two stages: a pilot stage to identify any major problems and a second stage to evaluate the amended mock-ups. At each stage the methodology was the same. Visitors were allowed to peruse the exhibits in their own time and were then given a semi-structured interview which was intended to establish how well they had understood the message being conveyed in each exhibit. Pilot testing revealed that one exhibit in particular was being misconstrued by an unacceptably large proportion of visitors. This exhibit, entitled 'Odd One Out', explained the effects of genetic mutation, using the Ancon breed of sheep as an example. Pilot testing identified a number of problems, the most serious of which was the tendency of visitors to interpret the exhibit too literally. Visitors construed the exhibit to be exclusively concerned with sheep-breeding and failed to realise that the principle of variation and mutation can be applied to any species of living organism. The exhibit also failed to rectify the commonly held belief amongst visitors that mutation is always a bad thing.

The findings of pilot testing led to the substitution of 'Odd One Out' with a new exhibit entitled 'Everybody Makes Mistakes' which provides an explanation of mutation without making reference to any particular species. The superiority of this new exhibit was well illustrated by the second stage of developmental testing. There was a substantial improvement in the proportion of visitors who were able to paraphrase the message. Developmental testing does not provide solutions to problems of ineffective communication but it can often draw the attention of the exhibition team to unsuccessful exhibits at mock up stage. This is important because the cost of making changes after an exhibition has been constructed are often prohibitive.

Summative evaluation takes place after an exhibition as been opened to the public, by which time it is usually too late to be thinking about alterations. Its purpose is to establish how successful an exhibition has been rather than to see how it could be improved or how it might have been done better in the first place. Just as a doctor might diagnose an illness without necessarily being able to cure it, summative evaluation might conclude that an exhibition has been a failure without being able to suggest how it might have been done better. Most summative evaluation takes the form of visitor surveys conducted by questionnaire. Surveys of this kind do not normally pose any complex methodological problems although there are certain golden rules to be obeyed when designing a questionnaire or obtaining a representative sample group. (See Miles *et al.* 1982: chapter 16.) Another form of summative evaluation is 'observational study'. This does not involve any direct contact with the visitor but simply entails observing visitors as they walk around the museum. Observational study can be very useful in gauging the attracting and holding power of each exhibit. But it can be fraught with methodological difficulties since it necessitates following visitors around. If visitors become aware that they are being 'spied upon' this may affect their behaviour. Where possible it is better to conduct observational study by means of closed circuit video cameras since these tend to be less obtrusive.

In the present economic climate with many budgets frozen or curtailed, there is a growing pre-occupation with cost-effective exhibitions. Against this scenario, the professional evaluator seems destined to become an increasingly integral member of any exhibition design team.

This paper first appeared in Environmental Interpretation *(July 1989), pp. 20–1.*

REFERENCES

Clarke, G. (1988) 'Front-end research: essential preparation in planning an exhibition', *Museum News* 43, Winter 1988/89.

Jarrett, J. E. (1986) 'Learning from the developmental testing of exhibits', *Curator* 29(4): 295–306.

Miles, R. S., Alt, M. B., Gosling, D. C., Lewis, B. N. and Tout, A. F. (1982) *The Design of Educational Exhibitions*, London: Unwin Hyman.

31

Empowering visitors: focus group interviews for art museums

Benjamin E. Braverman

Focus group interviews are discussed as a basis for theory building about what visitors do in art museums. Focus groups have specific characteristics that enable researchers to go beyond the familiar assumptions made by art curators about their audiences. A detailed analysis of the method and its potential is provided.

The term *empowered visitor* has been recently used in print by more than one museum professional (Stapp 1984; Williams 1985) to characterize those who are, as Williams (p. 122) stated 'likely to take an active role in telling us what they want and need'. Most art museum visitors readily express their reactions when approached by a researcher. Their attitudes are usually learned by anecdotes gathered in a gallery, exit interviews, or questionnaires. But they provide meaningful data *only* if specific research conditions are met. As individuals who purportedly communicate with their public, museum professionals need to acquire technical skills to gather data that reflect a range of reactions to given exhibitions. Evidence of this sense of responsibility is not found in the research literature dealing with art museums or in the attitudes of museum educators themselves (Zeller 1984, 1985; Eisner and Dobbs 1986).

All discussions, studies, and models that supposedly take into account the reactions of exhibition visitors are based on a single premise: the data on which theories are based are valid. How are we to know if this is the case? One looks in vain for traditional validity tests in the literature devoted to art museum visitors. None is to be found. There are two implicit assumptions behind this omission: (1) visitors' goals mirror those of curators; and (2) their goals are similarly defined and measured by experts who conduct learning studies.

To empower visitors, art museum professionals should develop theories on learning by a wide range of adult visitors. All information available in an exhibition space – not simply what art historians define as content – must be examined. At the basis of these theories *must* be valid data reflecting the motivations and attitudes of the visitors themselves. To make visitors' role a significant part of the art museum world, professionals must create situations in which visitors may express themselves in a way that reflects their own attitudes; a process far more structured than anecdote gathering.

Focus group interviews are suggested as the primary basis for theory building. These are participatory sessions in which visitors are encouraged to express their own perceptions concerning the subjects being studied. They are widely used in various social science disciplines as a springboard for both qualitative and quantitative studies (Calder 1977). I have conducted many such interviews for museums and market research firms. The research orientation presented here is the result of experience as head of the education department of the Minnesota Museum of Art and during doctoral study at the University of Minnesota. By focus group interview, I refer to an interview between a trained moderator and a group of six to twelve willing recruited participants. The composition of the group varies according to the needs of the art museum, but generally the participants do not know each other or at least have no working relationship.

This method of gathering data is used by art museums and has a reputation among many professionals for producing usable information. While there are no studies dealing with the extent to which focus group interviews are currently used, at least seven art museums are now using or have used them as a component in their programme evaluation. Yet there does not seem to be any methodological material dealing with focus group interviews. Art museums are unique civic institutions that present researchers with many difficulties that must be addressed to ensure the validity of their efforts.

First, participatory interviews are social situations that must be structured so that the vested professional goals and values do not distort the data being sought (Brenner 1981). Secondly, considerations must be given to psychological factors that set social research in art museums apart from that in other cultural institutions. As shown by Griggs and Hays-Jackson (1983), visitors' perceptions of art museums differ significantly from their perceptions of other museums. Their responses may reflect this perceived social distance between art and history or science-oriented museums. This distinction is ignored by most museum researchers, although it is not lost on the visitors themselves.

Given these necessary research conditions, the basic question remains: What sorts of visitor behaviour are important for the consideration of learning in an exhibit? Put another way, how should art museum researchers conceptualize exhibition outcomes for the leisure adult during the focus group interview?

> When museum education emphasizes teaching and verbal communication, it does a disservice to the museum as a learning environment
>
> (Hicks and Munley 1984: 59)

It is argued that most exhibition behaviour should be viewed within the concept of self-directed activities. Participation that is prompted by the demands of either profession or curriculum reflects, to a greater or lesser degree, singular behaviour. The task-oriented schemata of assigned students, art historians, or critics will structure exhibition behaviour in a manner reflecting that task. What of other learning behaviours, where goals are not as clearly defined? As Newsom and Silver (1978: 76) state: 'There is no definitive profile of the art museum audience. Only two things are certain about the self-selected, self-directed individuals who come to art museums on their own: one, they do so voluntarily, and two, no one can predict at what level of learning and sophistication they will be.

Researchers and art museum professionals seem to ignore both the range and complexity of learning that takes place in an exhibition. In fact, the desired outcomes of the exhibition experience, as expressed by visitors themselves, has not been documented. However, models purporting to structure the adult experience in the educational environment of the art museum have been published, for example, Mandel (1981). Representations of this nature employ the exhibition as an entry-level activity that will lead to progressively more structured and goal-oriented activities – docent tour, lecture, or seminar. This approach reflects the training, goals, and values of vested museum professionals. It is oriented toward the exhibition's content as defined by art historians, while ignoring the characteristics of most adult visitors.

Is the exhibition to be conceived of as merely an event that reflects or leads to class-room instruction? The study of visitor behaviour, exclusive of traditional educational goals, is of crucial significance for the art museum professional. While museums may offer formal educational programmes, the collection, conservation, and exhibition of art objects are what makes them unique institutions. The exhibition, then, must be seen as the primary vehicle by which the public is informed. Frequency data support the notion that exhibits attract most visitors. They have been characterized by Williams (1985: 119) as museums' best multipliers – they reach large numbers of visitors in the ideal manner. But what do the visitors learn? And why do they attend?

Attempts to classify visitor motivations have been made. Schouten (in Schouten, Guthrie and van Mensch 1983) has divided museum visitors into three general categories: scholarly visitors, visitors with specific interests, and visitors in search of recreation. He further contends that these categories are not exclusive but form a single continuum on which all adult visitors may be represented. One cannot fault this model in terms of description; however, like most museum research, it is two-dimensional. It has no attributes that may be expanded. Category names such as those employed by Schouten merely label the obvious; moreover, they provide no conceptual basis from which one may develop specific theories. Do adult visitors, other than scholars, have no cognitive goals, experiences, or attitudes that are meaningful for museum professionals?

Indeed, social science research suggests that visitors' nonacademic motivations are multidimensional. Penland (1977) cites data indicating that projects such as leisure art exhibition visits should be considered primarily inner-directed activities. Tough (1972) further contends that most informal adult learning begins with issues perceived to be meaningful in one's life, not because of a grand desire for a liberal education. Finally, Cross (1982) argues that almost every adult has more than one reason for engaging in informal learning activities; the average number of reasons rated either 'fairly' or 'very' important was 5.4. She points up the inappropriateness of attempting to discover a single reason for activities involving most adult learning.

> If we are truly committed to the idea that museums are more than passive repositories of objects and that museum learning is unique and important, we must study the special nature of learning on its own terms.
>
> (Hicks and Munley 1984)

After eliminating art-history-defined content-driven learning as the primary goal for most adults, how should art museum researchers approach the exhibition experience during the focus group interview? Most visitor learning in art exhibitions should be seen in terms of hedonic responses – those facets of visitor behaviour that relate to the multi-sensory and emotive aspects of one's experiences (Hirschman and Holbrook 1982). Multisensory means the receipt of experience in multiple sensory modalities, including visual data, sounds, and tactile impressions. In the art exhibition situation, visitor responses will be the result of more than one symbol system (Salomon 1979). These different symbol systems are to be seen in the art objects, the various forms of written information, and audio and/or video presentations. These systems interact with one another and elicit responses that do not necessarily relate to the semantic content of their messages. Having no assigned task to perform upon leaving the galleries, most visitors will participate in the exhibition in a manner reflecting their own notions of appreciation. These notions may be personal, but they may be articulated; see White (1985) for the relations between interview protocols and the dimensions of cognitive structure. For a discussion of interpretive cognition in art museums, see Braverman (1987).

Visitors view exhibits of art in situations that are, among other things, social in nature. Most attend in groups numbering from two to four. Most visits are made on weekends or admission-free days when the galleries are more than usually crowded (O'Hare 1975). On the other hand, some visitors attend when the exhibition is sparsely attended. Different visitors have different expectations and, consequently, different perceptions of the same exhibit (Fredericksen 1972; Cantor and Mischel 1982). The effect of various social situations is a significant component of the hedonic perspective. Such considerations place this form of culture consumption within the purview of what Lilla (1985) believes is a civic activity, that is, somewhere between purely private and purely public.

Another visitor response related to hedonic learning involves emotional arousal. According to Izard and Buechler (1980), emotions represent motivational phenomena with characteristic expressive and experiential components. The way in which visitors express these components should be made an integral part of the focus group interview. The arousal of emotions and the nature of that process will influence visitor decisions concerning future museum activities (Holbrook and Hirschman 1982). Although emotive responses have been studied, they have been narrowly defined as preferences for objects or instructional delivery systems, such as labels or panels (Lakota 1974). These effective variables reflect the activities and values of museum professionals rather than those of the public. The seeking of emotional arousal, while not addressed in museum literature, has been investigated in other forms of civic culture consumption; for example, dance, drama and music (Hirschman and Holbrook 1980).

Thus, employing the perspective of hedonic responses, exhibitions are viewed not only as the objective entities conceived by curators, but also as subjective symbols. During focus groups interviews, the museum researcher should be concerned with what the exhibition represents to most visitors, not merely as a vehicle for art historical content. A critical aspect of investigations will be the exhibition image; a key criterion will be viewer emotive response. This is opposed to a perspective that considers visitor responses exclusively in terms of semantic learning. It is emphasized that this proposed orientation does not replace traditional notions of art museum learning; rather, it seeks a new dimension of experience for the leisure adult visitor.

An approach of this nature would suggest reasons why visitors have formed their perceptions about the attributes of a given exhibition. As Kelley (1973: 107) defines it, 'Attribution theory is a theory about how people make causal explanations, about how they answer questions beginning with *why*'. During the focus group interview, this theory may be employed to structure the following process: (1) the nature of the information people employ when making causal inferences, and (2) how those inferences are used while making decisions about different exhibitions. For most visitors, art exhibition visits are discretionary activities. They make a choice on the basis of available information. Most surveys include an item or two intended to elicit the source of information: 'How did you learn of this exhibition?' Attribution theory continues from this point and focuses on a basic issue of communications. It asks, 'Why did you find this exhibition meaningful?' This approach emphasizes concepts such as category structures and inferential strategies that are employed by visitors to differentiate exhibitions (Pervin 1985).

Only the attributes to which an individual is attracted will guide his or her participation. Fennell (1980) asks, 'Where do the attributes come from?' Perceived attributes are significant when visitor expectations and their relationship to outcomes are being investigated. Fennell believes that expectations may be broken down into foci of relevant attributes. For art museums, these should include such hedonic responses as social or civic goals, intellectual aspirations, and emotional factors, as well as the content. These foci represent a range of perceived relevant attributes – one that does not remain constant across art exhibitions or individuals.

The entire range of visitors to an exhibition must be considered when characterizing responses. Focus group interviews do not represent a random sample of *all* visitors; consequently, they may be used to generate, not confirm, hypotheses about visitors. This point must be emphasized! See Rosenthal and Rosnow (1975) for an analysis of the psychological characteristics of subjects and the conditions in which they volunteer. While museum staff members may observe the process (ideally from behind a one-way mirror), they must be cautioned that the results are merely suggestive. Theories based on data gathered during such interviews should be used for further testing on a representative sample of the population.

Interviews are an invaluable source of visitor-driven data that will influence the results of a field study. Survey items used to test theories concerning visitor responses should incorporate the visitor's own descriptive language – in contrast to currently-used survey instruments that employ the vocabulary and conventions of art history or educational psychology. The resources required to develop such survey items have been shown to contribute to research validity. Studies have shown that in the development of a questionnaire, the pretest/revise process can detect questions that may be misleading or ambiguous (Hunt, Sparkman and Wilcox 1982). As Schuman and Scott (1987) state, the unexamined question, either open or closed, is not worth asking. Measurement errors generated by survey items that have not undergone rigorous testing are likely to be interrelated, further reducing the validity of the study (Bagozzi, 1980).

> Finally, it is difficult to translate research findings into information that can be used by museum professionals. Nevertheless, if museums are to be effective centers of informal learning they must have an objective means of evaluating their efforts and determining where improvements are needed.
>
> (Hicks and Munley 1984: 65)

One advantage of this research orientation is the collection of *valid* data that may be employed to compare visitor responses to different art exhibitions. Studies of exhibition outcomes currently found in the literature do not lend themselves to meta-evaluations. Therefore, continuity is lacking for developing theories that deal with a broad range of art exhibition content and outcomes.

Long-term research will provide museum professionals with the foundation necessary to increase the effectiveness of their strategic planning and audience-development efforts. As Banfield (1984: 202) has pointed out, the number of visitors has increased during the last three decades, but the proportion of them who are not well off and/or well educated has increased very little. This observation is supported by exhibition research. A market segmentation study of the *King Tut* exhibit found that visitors were not representative of a broadly based 'mass market' as had been touted to the funding community. Rather, most had a pattern of attending similar cultural events and were not first-time visitors (Robbins and Robbins 1979).

It appears, then, that relevant attributes of exhibitions attract people who are already predisposed to attend. However, this limited population has begun to shrink. Most museum visitors in the general population (40 per cent) do not attend every exhibition; rather, they attend only one or two a year (Hood 1981). Further, one may not assume that these occasional visits are to the same museum. According to a 1984 Harris poll, museum visits by occasional visitors have already begun to decline. These are individuals who presently represent between 50 to 55 per cent of all museum visitors. Competition for leisure time and cultural dollars between museums has been ignored in art museum visitor-research literature; Hood (1983) is the most notable exception. For a recent discussion of culture as commodity, see Kelly (1987).

As visitor perceptions of exhibition attributes are identified by the museum staff, they may be related to the characteristics of culture consumers in a given community. Data of this nature may be used to further educational goals; for example, communications based on perceived exhibition attributes should contribute positively to both attendance and programme participation. Such strategies have contributed to audience develop-ment programmes in the performing arts. Psychographic data form the basis of these strategies, in which the relationship between life styles and the consumption of culture is analysed. Such data structures are components of the Values and Life Styles (VALS) Data Base at the Stanford Research Institute and have been extensively documented by Mitchell (1983).

In summary, to reach the educational and research goals called for in *Museums for a New Century* (Hicks and Munley 1984), art museum professionals must test theories based on valid data by using reliable items that address a wide range of visitor responses over different exhibitions. The focus group interview was introduced in this paper as the primary means by which art museum visitors may express themselves in a manner that reflects their own attitudes, values, and goals. The ability to gather and use such data, that is, to empower the visitor, remains a primary task of our profession.

This paper first appeared in Curator 31(1) (1988), pp. 43–52.

REFERENCES

Bagozzi, R. P. (1980) *Causal Models in Marketing*, New York, NY: John Wiley.

Banfield, E. C. (1984) *The Democratic Muse*, New York, NY: Basic Books, Inc.

Braverman, B. E. (1987) 'Toward an instructional design model for art exhibitions', *The Journal of Aesthetic Education*.

Brenner, M. (1981) 'Problems in collecting social data: a review for the information researcher', *Social Science Information Studies* 1: 139–51.

Calder, B. (1977) 'Focus groups and the nature of qualitative marketing research', *Journal of Marketing Research* XIV: 353–64.

Cantor, N. and Mischel, W. (1982) 'A prototype analysis of psychological situations', *Cognitive Psychology* 14: 45–77.

Cross, K. P. (1982) *Adults as Learners*, San Francisco, CA: Jossey-Bass Publishers.

Eisner, E. W. and Dobbs, S. M. (1986) *The Uncertain Profession: Observations on the state of museum education in twenty American museums*, Los Angeles, CA: The Getty Center for Education in the Arts.

Fennell, G. (1980) 'Attitude, motivation, and marketing, or where do the attributes come from?', in R. Olshavsky (ed.) *Attitude Research Enters the 80s*, Eleventh Attitude Research Conference, Carlsbad, CA.

Frederiksen, N. (1972) 'Toward a taxonomy of situations', *American Psychologist* 27: 114–27.

Griggs, S. A. and Hays-Jackson, K (1983) 'Visitors' perception of cultural institutions', *Museum Journal* 2(3): 121–5.

Harris, L. (1984) 'Americans and the arts: a 1984 survey of public opinion conducted for Phillip Morris, Inc.' Study No. 831011, Louis Harris and Associates, Inc.

Hicks, E. C. and Munley, M. E. (1984) *Museums for a New Century*, Washington, DC: American Asso-ciation of Museums.

Hirschman, E. C. and Holbrook, M. B. (1980) *Proceedings of the Conference on Consumer Esthetics and Symbolic Consumption*, Ann Arbor, MI: Association for Consumer Research.

Hirschman, E. C. and Holbrook, M. B. (1982) 'Hedonic: consumption: emerging concepts, methods and propositions', *Journal of Marketing* 46: 92–101.

Holbrook, M. B. and Hirschman, E. C. (1982) 'The experiential aspects of consumption: consumer fantasies, feelings, and fun', *Journal of Consumer Research* 9: 132–40.

Hood, M. G. (1981) *Adult Attitudes Toward Leisure Choices in Relation to Museum Participation*, unpublished Ph.D. dissertation, Ohio State University.

Hood, M. G. (1983) 'Staying away, why people choose not to visit museums', *Museum News* 61(4): 50–7.

Hunt, S. D., Sparkman R. D. and Wilcox, J. (1982) 'The pretest in survey research: issues and preliminary findings', *Journal of Marketing Research* XIX: 269–73.

Izard, C. E. and Buechler, S. (1980) 'Aspects of consciousness and personality in terms of differential emotions theory', in R. Plutchick and H. Kellerman (eds) *Emotion: theory research and experience*, New York, NY: Academic Press.

Kelley, H. (1973) 'The process of causal attribution', *American Psychologist* 28: 107–28.

Kelly, R. F. (1987) 'Culture as commodity: the marketing of cultural objects and cultural experiences', in M. Wallendorf and P. Anderson (eds) *Advances in Consumer Research* XIV, Provo, UT: Association for Consumer Research.

Lakota, R. (1974) *The Efficacy of Three Visitor Learning Support Systems in Producing Cognitive and Affective Outcomes in an Art Museum*, unpublished Ph.D. dissertation, University of Wisconsin, Milwaukee.

Lilla, M. (1985) 'The museum in the city', *Journal of Aesthetic Education* 19(2): 79–92.

Mandel, R. (1981) 'Adult programming approaches', in Z. Collins (ed.) *Museum, Adults and the Humanities*, Washington, DC: American Association of Museums.

Mitchell, A. (1983) *The Professional Performing Arts: attendance patterns, preferences and motives*, Palo Alto, CA: SRI International.

Newsom, B. Y. and Silver, A. Z. (1978) *The Art Museum As Educator*, Berkeley, CA: University of California Press.

O'Hare, M. (1975) 'Why do people go to museums? – the effect of prices and hours on museum utilization', *Curator* 27(3): 134–46.

Penland, P. (1977) *Individual Self-Planned Learning in America*, Washington, DC: Office of Education, US Department of Health, Education, and Welfare.

Pervin, L. A. (1985) 'Personality: current controversies, issues, and directions', *Annual Review of Psychology* 36: 83–114.

Robbins, J. E. and Robbins, S. S. (1979) 'Segmentation for "Fine Arts" marketing: is King Tut classless as well as ageless', in N. Beckwith *et al.* (eds) *Educators' Conference Proceedings*, Chicago, IL: American Marketing Association.

Rosenthal, R. and Rosnow, R. L. (1975) *The Volunteer Subject*, New York, NY: John Wiley.

Salomon, G. (1979) *Interaction of Media, Cognition, and Learning*, San Francisco, CA: Jossey-Bass, Inc.

Schouten, F., Guthrie, M. and van Mensch, P. (1983) 'Exhibition design as an educational tool', *Reinwardt Studies in Museology*, 1, Leiden, The Netherlands: Reinwardt Academie.

Schuman, S. and Scott, J. (1987) 'Problems in the use of survey questions to measure public opinion', *Science* 236(4804) 22 May, 957–9.

Stapp, C. B. (1984) 'Defining museum literacy', *Museum Education Roundtable* 9(1): 3–4.

Tough, A. (1972) 'The adult's learning projects: a fresh approach to theory and practice in adult learning', *Research in Education Series*, 1, Toronto: Ontario Institute for Studies in Education.

White, R. T. (1985) 'Interview protocols and dimensions of cognitive structure', in A. L. Pines and L. H. T. West (eds) *Cognitive Structure and Conceptual Change*, New York, NY: Academic Press.

Williams, P. B. (1985) 'Educational excellence in art museums: an agenda for reform', *Journal of Aesthetic Education* 19(2): 105–24.

Zeller, T. (1984) 'Art museum educators: art historians, curators, or educators? A question of professional identity', *Curator* 27(2): 105–23.

Zeller, T. (1985) 'Art museum educators: who are they?', *Museum News* 63(5): 53–9.

32

Monitoring and evaluation: the techniques

G. Binks and D. Uzzell

A very practical outline of the strengths, weaknesses and likely costs of questionnaire surveys, in-depth interviews, structured interviews, and behavioural mapping.

Most of the techniques used are established techniques in the field of marketing, social survey and educational psychology, which are applied and modified to suit the particular situation about which the interpreter, interpretive planner or facility manager is concerned.

Regrettably there is not yet a British handbook of evaluation techniques for interpretation facilities and services. There are however useful guides to recreation site surveys and accounts of surveys and evaluation studies of individual interpretive media and facilities which are worth consulting. They offer valuable information, for example on planning and designing surveys, using questionnaires, observation, group and depth interviews and some deal with techniques of measuring learning and attitude change. Many of them include examples of questionnaires which provide a useful basis for devising your own.

It is possible with the help of some of the key references described on page 226 to devise, carry out and analyse your own survey. Alternatively you may decide to use an off-the-peg survey, some of which have been devised for museums, or you may decide to bring in outside help. It usually all depends on the size and complexity of the evaluation you wish to undertake and your budget. Market research companies, university and polytechnic marketing, tourism and social science and educational psychology departments and individual recreation and interpretation consultancy firms can usually offer tailor made surveys and evaluation packages on a consultancy basis. Many polytechnic and university departments have staff who are willing to advise you informally on aspects of your survey if you decide to do it yourself. Some may supply student help and some computer services departments also offer help with questionnaires, design and processing.

The sections below describe the main techniques, with their strengths, weaknesses and likely costs.

QUESTIONNAIRE SURVEYS

Strengths	*Weaknesses*	*Likely costs*
• Lots of experience around among people who have carried out questionnaire surveys in other nearby museums, visitor attractions, etc. You may be able to use, with minor modification, questionnaires they have designed – provided they answer the questions you want answered. Be careful! • Quite cost effective. You can produce a large number of questionnaires for the price of the print run. However, the more you produce, the more you will have to analyse. Also a larger sample may mean a more accurate sample. • Again easy to train people to give out questionnaires, or administer them.	• While there may be expertise available locally in the design and production of questionnaires, it doesn't mean that it's going to be good expertise! There are many badly designed questionnaires around. Poorly designed questionnaires give you inaccurate, unreliable and therefore useless results. Questionnaire design is a skill. • Large sample needed for reliable and representative results. • May require the use of computer to analyse results: see comments on structured interviews.	• Considerable staff time to plan, supervise, analyse. • Specialist advice as necessary £200–£300 per day. • Printing of questionnaires – depending on length and print run. • Off-the-shelf questionnaires e.g. DRS Museum Scan around £400 per 500 standard questionnaires printed and processed; or £2,000 for 3,000 questionnaires designed for your site, with analysis and customized report. • Interviewer's fees – ranging from student rates, staff time or professional interviewers. 20–40 questionnaires per interviewer per day depending on length. • Computer processing costs.

IN DEPTH INTERVIEWS (with a small sample of people)

Strengths	*Weaknesses*	*Likely costs*
• Detailed qualitative information, very revealing and 'true'. • Enables exploration of issues both guided and in response to respondents' concerns and agenda. • Useful for initial exploration of issues prior to a more representative survey. • Does not require sophisticated technology to analyse data, although there are advance computer programs which will, after content analysis, analyse the findings.	• Time consuming. • Typically only feasible with a small sample, therefore difficult to make representative. This may not matter – depends on purpose. • Needs skilled interviewer. • Difficulty of interpreting information – content analysis is typically used.	• Staff time to plan, supervise and, analyse. • Specialist advice (training of interviewers as necessary) £200–£300 + per day. • Skilled interviewers fees £100–£200 per day – maybe 4 interviews per day per interviewer. • Interviewers' travel costs if interviews are home based. • Costs of computer processing if appropriate.

STRUCTURED INTERVIEWS

Strengths
- Can deal with a larger sample than in-depth interviews.
- Allows respondents to elaborate their answers, perhaps unlike a questionnaire.
- Not too difficult to train interviewers.
- Can also be useful for initial exploration of issues prior to a more representative sample survey.
- Can use data in a qualitative or quantitative way.

Weaknesses
- Labour intensive and therefore expensive.
- Large sample needed, (like a questionnaire survey) if they are to be regarded as representative of a larger population.
- May require the use of computer to analyse results, with consequent necessary understanding of statistics and computer programs. There are now many 'off the shelf' computer programs available, but they still require an understanding of the statistical analyses, and the assumptions on which the statistics are based.

Likely costs
- Staff time to plan, supervise and analyse.
- Specialist advice £200–£300 per day.
- Printing costs of interview schedule/questionnaire.
- Interviewer fees ranging from student rates, £30–£50 per day to professional market research interviews, £50–£100 per day. 15–20 interviews per interviewer day.
- Computer processing.

BEHAVIOURAL MAPPING OR OBSERVATION

Strengths
- Direct measure of the public's behaviour. What the public say they do and what they really do are often two very different things. Enables you to see how they actually use your exhibition, country park etc.
- Useful complement to other techniques such as questionnaires or interviews, as it enables you to check or corroborate responses.
- Low technology – pencil and paper.
- Inexpensive.

Weaknesses
- Time consuming. Following or observing one person around an exhibition may take 30 minutes, therefore limited number can be completed in a day.
- Doesn't provide you with the visitor's account of what they were doing or why. You have to interpret their actions: in some cases it is not always clear what people are doing. They may spend 5 minutes looking at an exhibit – this could be because it is fascinating, or because they are having great difficulties understanding it.

Likely costs
- Staff time to plan, supervise and analyse.
- Specialist help if necessary.
- Observers' fees: student rates or equivalent staff time.
- Computer analysis as appropriate.

This paper first appeared in Environmental Interpretation *(July 1990), pp. 16–17.*

REFERENCES

Lee, T. R. and Uzzell, D. L. (1980) *The Educational Effectiveness of the Farm Open Day*, Countryside Commission for Scotland.

In a series of visitor surveys at Farm Open Days on Scotland, questionnaires were devised to elicit visitor attitudes and to establish the extent of attitude change as a result of what visitors had learnt or seen at the Farm Open Day. As with the Forestry Commission package this provides useful examples of sampling process, questions and analysis procedures.

Miles, R. S. *et al.* (1982) *The Design of Educational Exhibits*, London: George Allen and Unwin.

This book gives detailed guidance on the design and evaluation of educational exhibits based on the experience of designing exhibitions at the Natural History Museum. It is a manual of good practice and essential reading for anyone planning an exhibition however small. In particular it discusses techniques for formative evaluation – the testing of various approaches to presenting material before final choice of content and media, and of summative evaluation – the visitor response to the material and media which were used. It includes a useful explanation of sampling techniques.

Stansfield, G. (1981) *Effective Interpretive Exhibitions CCP 145*, Countryside Commission.

This booklet draws together the conclusions and recommendations for good practice which have emerged from a wide range of research into interpretive exhibitions in a range of museums and visitor centres in Europe and North America.

Tourism and Recreation Research Unit (1983) *Recreational Site Survey Manual: methods and techniques for conducting visitor surveys*, London: E. & F. N. Spon.

This manual provides comprehensive advice on survey planning, design and implementation at recreation sites. It covers sampling procedures; recruiting and training staff and administration of the survey, data preparation and analysis, as well as providing detailed guidance on mechanical methods of recording and counting visitors, observation methods and a range of questionnaire techniques.

Uzzell, D. L. and Lee, T. R. (1980) *Forestry Commission Visitor Centres – an evaluation package,* report to Forestry Commission, Edinburgh.

This report describes the evaluation package which was devised for the Forestry Commission to test the role of the Commission's visitor centres in attracting visitors, communicating with them, providing an enjoyable experience and encouraging them to explore the forest as a result. The package, designed to be administered by Forestry Commission staff, has four elements: a Visitor Centre interview using a questionnaire designed to elicit visitors' attitudes and opinions about the centre and particularly about the exhibition and their preferences for different media in use; a forest use questionnaire designed to elicit views of visitors using the forest, car parks and picnic areas about facilities their knowledge/use of the visitor centre (primarily to test the role of the visitor centre in encouraging people to explore the forest); a brief postal questionnaire for distribution in the visitor centre or in car parks and picnic sites, designed to elicit information retrospectively on visitors' activities and routes taken in the forest recorded by them on a map.

The purpose of the package is to provide relatively simple sets of interviews and observation techniques which can be administered by staff, and easily modified and updated over time.

The data are readily analysed on computer to provide tables showing frequency counts of the answers to each question and cross tabulations of answers to one question set against another.

Part 2
Learning theory and educational practice in museums

33

Museum education

Eilean Hooper-Greenhill

This paper acts an introduction to the second part of this volume. It outlines a brief history of museum education in Britain, discusses one way to develop object teaching, addresses issues pertinent to the management of an education department and describes a range of methodologies and examples of good practice. An extensive bibliography will enable further work.

INTRODUCTION

This chapter aims to provide a starting point in the construction of a philosophy of museum education, a philosophy which has partly emerged through a long tradition of thought and action concerned with learning and teaching with objects and specimens. The broad historical parameters of the practices of learning and teaching with objects will be outlined, although an analysis of discontinuities in these practices will not be addressed here.[1] This chapter is also written as a guide and a resource for further reading. There are, therefore, many references in the text, and an extensive bibliography.

Learning and teaching with objects has often entailed the collection of groups of related things, whether by individuals, groups, or by the state. Conversely, the existence of a collection of things has promoted and enabled the production of knowledge (Hooper-Greenhill 1992a). In some cases collections of objects have been assembled in order to shape consciousness in the context of ruling class control (Hooper-Greenhill 1980). In other cases a more democratic end has been paramount (Chadwick 1983). The construction of a world view through the choice of representative objects and their arrangement in space has been an enduring function for collections, although the world view so represented has varied with time, space, individual subjectivities and the context of knowing.

This chapter also aims to emphasize the importance of this long-undervalued area of museum work (Miers 1928; Markham 1938; Rosse 1963; Wright 1973; Eisner and Dobbs 1986), in such a way as to support those who are engaged in it or who are sympathetic towards it. It should not be forgotten that education is one of the prime functions of a museum and the reason for the existence of a museum. In the case of museums governed by charitable trusts there is a requirement in law to meet educational objectives. It should be stated very firmly at the outset that museums have clear responsibilities in their educational work both to the public (actual and potential) and to the educational workers within museums. It should also be noted that many museums fail on both counts. There is a pressing need both for more knowledge of who this public is (Hooper-Greenhill 1988b: 220) and for at least adequate resources and personnel to work in the museum on behalf of this public. The General Certificate of Secondary Education (GCSE) is one area of work for a specific user-group that has been emphasized recently (Anon 1987; Hale 1987: 22; Millar 1987; Museums Association 1987), as has the equivalent Standard Grade in Scotland (Lawn 1987), but this is just one area of need among many.

Curators and museum educators are often suspicious of each other. It has become clear that curators have been unaware of the training, skills, expertise, and experience of many educational personnel, despite (or perhaps because of) the fact that curators are likely to be the most under-trained section of the museum staff (Hale 1987). Other staff members, particularly the educators, are far more likely to have had specialist training. Curators tend to experience the use of 'their' objects as a threat, and in some cases complain about 'their' galleries being used by education staff who have not first approached them to discuss how this should be done. In turn, museum educators often experience curators as distant and unhelpful, and unaware of (and uninterested in) recent educational developments and requirements.

These difficulties are sometimes more pronounced in the larger departmental museums. In smaller museums, communications are likely to be much better, and curators and educators are likely to work more closely together and to share the same goals and objectives. The possibilities of using each other as resources is acknowledged, with the educator making suggestions as to appropriate topical themes for temporary exhibitions, and for relevant and interesting ways of communicating, and the curator helping the educator develop the necessary specialist knowledge about the collections and providing selected objects to be either handled, demonstrated or simply observed more closely than is possible in a display case. It must also be said that some museum educators are unaware of the 'museum' context within which they are required to work, and do not understand the curatorial concerns of their colleagues. There is no excuse for this, and it behoves both curators and educators to move more than half way towards each other in the joint objective of improving the museum experience for their publics. Clearly the overall work of the museum, both curatorial and educational will be greatly enhanced if various specialist staff members respect and allow for the expertise of others (Locke 1984).

Museum educationalists work to create relationships between the museum and its public. Problems may often emerge which stem from the dual functions of museums, to preserve and to display, to keep contained and to expose. Successful educational work articulates a combination of balances – first, a balance between the internal and external needs of the museum and its actual and potential audience, educational 'cover' for the entire museum collections as far as possible, and a response to curriculum needs; second, a balance of provision for different audiences, which includes all kinds of formal and informal educational groups, preschool, primary, secondary, tertiary, special education, open university, teacher trainers, teachers in-service, clubs, specialist groups, holiday groups, etc; and third, a balance of different forms and scales of provision both in the museum and in the community, which might include hour-long structured taught sessions, half-day discovery sessions, day-long drama-work, teachers' courses, loan services, written materials, film and video, lectures for adult groups, concerts, walks, or even a mobile museum.

THE HISTORY AND PHILOSOPHY OF MUSEUM EDUCATION

Museum education is centrally concerned with teaching from and learning with objects and specimens. Epistemological interest in the use of things has emerged in different and sometimes contradictory ways in the histories of teaching and learning in Europe, but enough evidence can be identified to suggest that museum education and object-teaching, if they have not been intimate bed-fellows, have at least gone hand-in-hand.

In the early Middle Ages, Thomas Aquinas stated that 'human cognition is stronger in regard to the *sensibilia*', and that 'it is natural to man to reach the *intelligibilia* through the *sensibilia* because all our knowledge has its beginnings in sense' (Yates 1966). By *sensibilia*, Aquinas is referring to 'sense impressions' or 'data' collected through the use of the senses, in other words the processes of human relationships to objects (Hooper-Greenhill 1988c). Later, Roger Bacon emphasized the *argumentum ex re* the observation of the things themselves rather than the exposition of doctrine (Heidegger 1951: 6).

During the Renaissance, knowing consisted of endless and circular references to all that had ever been written about a particular phenomenon, with no distinction made between that which had been observed from the real thing, that which had been written about it, and those myths and fables which surrounded it (Foucault 1970). Collections were compiled to represent the entire structure of knowledge, the theatre of the world (Kaufmann 1978; Laurencich-Minelli 1985).

As a reaction to the complexities of this, and as an attempt to cut away the endless proliferating words that had previously obscured the 'true' meaning of the thing itself, seventeenth-century philosophers and educationalists emphasized 'solid philosophy', the direct study of nature, and the rejection of all knowledge that could not be demonstrated through the study of objects (Hunter 1981). Francis Bacon was instrumental in promulgating this new approach to knowing, and Comenius applied Bacon's ideas to education: 'Instruction will succeed if the method follows the course of nature. It must begin with actual inspection, not with verbal description of things. What is actually seen remains faster in the memory than description a hundred times repeated. . . . It is good to use several senses in the understanding of one thing. . . . Things and words should be studied together. . . . The first education should be of the perceptions, then of the memory, then of the understanding, then of the judgement' (Calkins 1880). At least one museum (the Repository of the Royal Society) was established during the late seventeenth century specifically to enable this approach to learning at the scholarly level (Purver and Bowen 1960: 5; Ornstein 1938: 109; Hunter 1981: 65), while in 1660 'Mr John Tradescants, or the like houses or gardens, where rarities are kept' were recommended for the 'full improvement of children in their education' (MacGregor 1983: 23).

At the end of the eighteenth century, the Louvre in Paris was the first free public museum established as part of the state education system (Hudson 1987: 42). Cheap catalogues were produced, written from the point of view of the visitor rather than the curator (Hudson 1987: 186) and translated into several languages. The Louvre acted as the central museum in a country-wide network of museums which together were intended to partly enable the transformation of the still feudal peasant into a citizen of the Republic. For the first time, the Museum was constituted as an instrument of public education (Hooper-Greenhill 1988a). This had a great influence in Europe, with new major institutions being established, particularly in Germany. In Britain, the British Museum had emerged earlier, composed of three private cabinets, and the new museum retained the features of this earlier institutional model, with lip-service only paid to the needs and rights of the public. Indeed, the British Museum was celebrated as being 'like a family' as late as 1973 (Miller 1973: 17). Nonetheless, even in Britain, museums were seen during the nineteenth century as institutions with education and social objectives, along with libraries, public parks, and swimming pools (Hooper-Greenhill, 1991a).

During the nineteenth century, small collections, cabinets and museums were established in schools to furnish the required objects (Busse 1880: 423; Board of Education 1931: 17). Mechanics Institutes compiled small museums as an integral part of their educational work (Chadwick 1983: 50–3). Many museums were explicitly established with educational purposes. Early literary and philosophical societies at the beginning of the nineteenth century with their libraries and, later, museums, were among the media of dissemination of the radical ideas concerning the power of education to effect social change (Lawson and Silver 1973: 229). The Museums at South Kensington, originally the Museum of Science and the Museum of Art, were established to exhibit the progress of scientific discovery and the best of aesthetic design, for both educational and economic purposes.

The 'object-lesson' was a major feature of nineteenth-century schooling (Lawson and Silver 1973: 248) and its philosophical context is firmly set within the progressive, child-centred theories of Rousseau, Pestalozzi and Froebel, which in contemporary writing are placed in relation to the earlier ideas of Bacon and Comenius (Calkins 1880; Busse 1880). Although in the event much object-teaching may well have degenerated into rote learning, a process that was no doubt partly enabled by the production of endless methods textbooks, the initial aims of the object-lesson were imaginative and forward looking. The purposes of object-teaching were to develop all the child's faculties in the acquisition of knowledge, rather than to impart facts or information *per se* (Calkins 1880). This 'development of sense-perceptions', combined with reflection and judgement, was to lead to appropriate activity based on the existing knowledge and competencies of the child. In short, in some of these late-nineteenth-century discussions of the philosophy and principles of object-teaching we are looking, on the one hand, back towards the *sensibilia* of Aquinas, and on the other forwards towards the familiar child-centred progressive theories later to be crystallized by John Dewey (Dewey 1979), they underlie much of the most valuable educational work in schools, particularly primary schools, during this century.

What is learning with objects? How do you do it? As Aquinas and Comenius would recommend, learning and teaching with objects starts from sense-perceptions, from the use of all five senses to accumulate as much data as possible about the object(s) under analysis. This data is then discussed, related to previous information and experience, and compared with the perceptions of others. A synthesis of material demands the input of further information, and may promote research on the part of the teacher, the learner, or both together. Hypotheses and deductions as to use and meaning over time and through space may be constructed and tested. The meaning of things is not limited to one interpretation only. Individual interpretations may hold as much weight as scholarly ones, depending on the framework of reference used. Perceptions may be extended or changed through new input, either from other objects or other forms of information, including manuscripts, photographs, maps, letters, tapes, or through the perceptions of others.

Some objects stimulate or are discovered through practical activity, either in being recorded through drawing, writing, or photography, or through their use (or the simulation of this). Some objects stimulate interest and questioning through their oddness or attractiveness. Objects can be a lot more interesting both to teach with and to learn from than books. All objects require other sources of data to release their full information potential. Many objects lead learning into curious unpredictable paths, and most reveal the arbitrariness both of subject boundaries in the school and of collection classification schemes in the museum. Museums objects also lead to questions about the roles and functions of the museum, which in itself is a very important aspect of museum education. Although object-teaching is unfamiliar to many teachers, practice with an open mind and in a sympathetic environment soon brings expertise. Figures 33.1 to 33.5 (pp. 234–8) suggest one methodological process that works both in the museum and in the class-room, and suggest ways in which objects cross-relate to many areas of the curriculum. Experience will soon provide other ways of working (Durbin, Morris and Wilkinson 1990).The object-lesson at its best was, and is, intended to enable many different approaches to the learning of skills, including the training of the senses, the development of thinking, and the development of language (Busse 1880; Delahaye 1987). It underpins museum education today as it has done for a very long time.

The development of educational services in museums during the twentieth century has been sporadic and haphazard. It has followed no national plan, and specific instances have emerged as a response to local need (Hooper-Greenhill 1992b). Some outstanding practitioners can be identified (Harrison 1950, 1967; Winstanley 1966), but often the work done has gone unrecorded and unremarked. The pattern outlined by Carter (1984) can be traced through reference to the major contemporary reports (British Association for the Advancement of Science 1920; Miers 1928; Markham 1938; Rosse 1963). Bassett's useful bibliographic essay should also be consulted (Bassett 1984).

The two reports on museums in Scotland (Williams 1981; Miles 1986) are the most useful of the recent governmental reports on museums when it comes to thinking about museum education. Williams (1981) discusses museum education in the context of the communicative function of the museum, which it sees as a 'keystone in the conduct of the whole museum' (Williams 1981). It is further pointed out that 'the status and standard of a museum's education department are measures of that institution's commitment in the field of education'. The report goes on to deal with structural provision for education in the larger museums and stresses that education should have a properly constituted departmental structure in the same way as the other departments of the museum, with a head of department at Keeper level. Where there is the possibility to employ several staff these should represent a variety of expertise covering different subject areas and different age-related teaching experience. Strong links should be made with other departments, which include practical working together on such matters as the type of display, the 'storyline', or conceptual objectives of exhibitions, and the presentation and content of labels.

Miles (1986) deals with the matter of educational provision in the non-national museums and reiterates many of the points concerning the general educational responsibility of museums. The variety of educational work carried out by curators in museums without specialist staff is discussed.

It is clear that there are many choices to be made in deciding on the form and content of educational provision in the museum. As with other work areas of the museum, there is a need for a policy to articulate priorities in relation to objectives (Hooper-Greenhill 1991b). This must be drawn up after reviewing the differential weightings of the following elements – the objectives of the museum, the nature of its collections, the expertise of the staff, the existing pattern of public use, potential new patterns of use, the sources and availability of resources, relationships with the Local Education Authority, the location of the museum, and evaluative practices. In addition, and perhaps most importantly, the educational philosophy of the museum, department, or members of staff concerned (Hooper-Greenhill 1983, 1987a).

Some museums and museum authorities are now beginning to produce policy statements. This is recommended by the Museums & Galleries Commission (1991), the Audit Commission (1991) and the Museums Association (1991), as suggested by published guidelines and case studies (Hooper-Greenhill 1991b). Hertfordshire, a County Museum Authority, has produced a thoughtful and comprehensive document that reviews the current situation in the three main museums in the county, relates it to possible extended provision and proposes a two-stage development plan over five years. This kind of coherent thinking is vitally needed in this (as in all other) area of museum work. Policy statements for specific educational provision such as the production of materials for teachers, or the teaching of particular groups, for example, need to be written in the

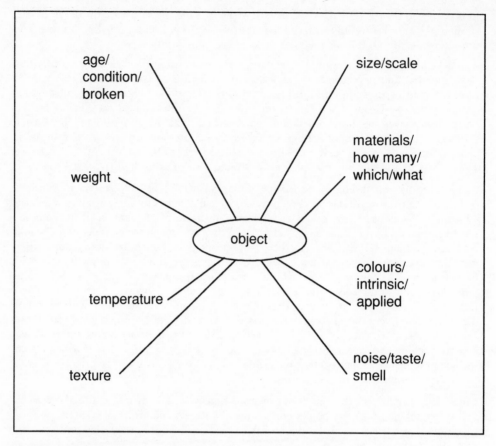

Fig. 33.1 Sensory exploration is one way to begin working with objects

context of the communicative objectives of the museum as a whole, including the display and exhibition policy, and other policies that relate to the qualitative experience of the visitors.

THE CURRENT SCENE

The recent Museums Association study (Prince and Higgins-McLoughlin 1987) suggests that less than 5 per cent of the total full-time staff (including security staff) are employed in each of either education, conservation or design work. Education staff make up a tiny percentage of the staff as a whole: 1.8 per cent in national museums, 3.6 per cent in Local Authority museums, and 2.1 per cent in independent and other museums. Carter (1984: 437) identified 362 professional museums posts in education in 154 museums. Volunteers are sometimes employed in educational work in museums, particularly in private-sector museums (Prince and Higgins-McLoughlin 1987: 103–5).

Full-time specialist education staff are employed in a number of different ways, with no overall national pattern of employment, remuneration or working practice. National museum education staff have up till now been employed as Civil Servants on

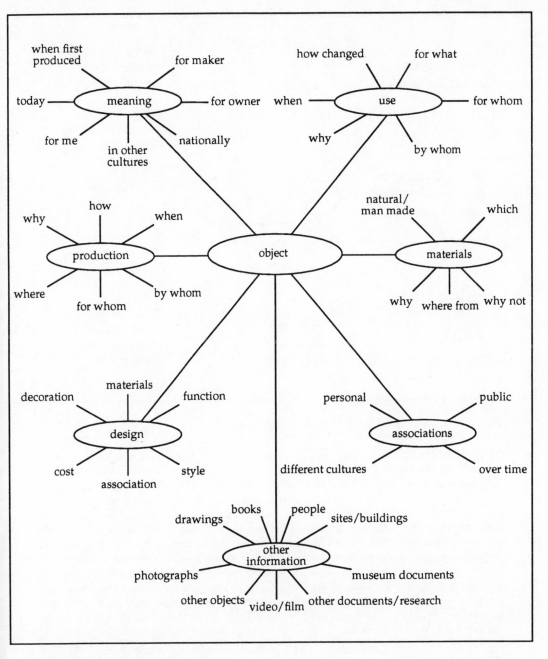

Fig. 33.2 Discussion and analysis

Civil Service pay scales along with the other museum staff. They work museum (Civil Service) hours with museum holidays. Education departments in the national museums generally take responsibility for the provision of service for all sections of the museum's clientèle.

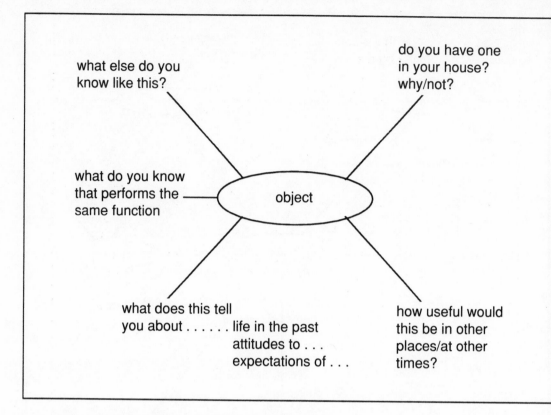

what else do you
know like this?

do you have one
in your house?
why/not?

what do you know
that performs the
same function

object

what does this tell
you about . . . . . . life in the past
attitudes to . . .
expectations of . . .

how useful would
this be in other
places/at other
times?

Fig. 33.3 Remembering, comparing and synthesizing

Until recently Local Authority museum education staff have been employed directly through the Museum Committee budget, or have been financed through the Education Committee budget to teach in the museum, or have been employed through a combination of monies from both these sources. In Leicester, for example, the Local Education Authority paid four-fifths of the salaries of the education staff, and the museum service paid the remainder. The staff were museum officers, but tend to work exclusively with schools and teachers. Work with adult groups is covered in the main by curatorial staff. In Birmingham, a secondment system is in operation, where teachers are employed directly by the Local Education Authority, working teachers' hours and with teachers' holidays, and pay scales, and are seconded to work in the museum, again working only with schools. Many different varieties of arrangement have evolved to meet local needs and possibilities (Bateman 1984). Section 11 (*Local Government Act 1966*) monies have been used to fund education posts in a handful of Local Authority museums. With the local management of schools and changes in the structures of local government, much is in flux at the moment.

A new form of educational provision has made its appearance and that is the use of sponsorship monies to pay for educational staff At the Barbican Art Gallery in London, British Petroleum PLC have sponsored an education officer to work for a period of three years. Dulwich Picture Gallery has acquired sponsorship to fund two one-day-a-week posts for specialist provision for two very particular areas of work. These are work with handicapped schools and work with deprived schools. At the Geffrye Museum in London the

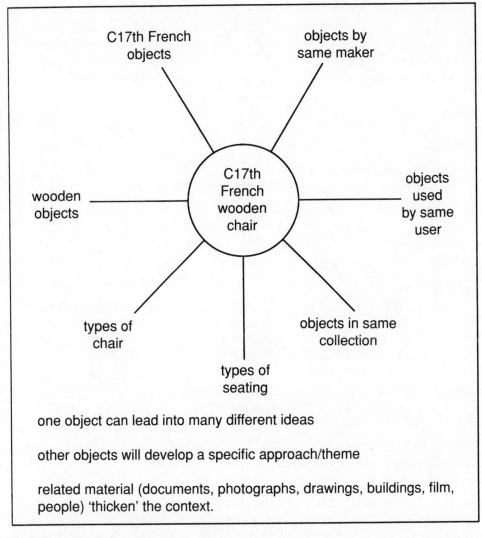

C17th French
objects

objects by
same maker

wooden
objects

C17th
French
wooden
chair

objects
used
by same
user

types of
chair

objects in same
collection

types of
seating

one object can lead into many different ideas

other objects will develop a specific approach/theme

related material (documents, photographs, drawings, buildings, film, people) 'thicken' the context.

Fig. 33.4 Objects can be multicontexted

excellent educational work carried out by the education staff has been supplemented by a local charitable foundation and industrial sponsorship. Although sponsorship may supplement existing educational provision in the short term, it is no substitute for permanently employed education staff.

The Museums Association study showed that approximately one-third of all museum visits are made by children, and given that some museums are unable to discriminate in their figures between adults and children, this figure could in fact be substantially higher (Prince and Higgins-McLoughlin 1987: 135). Although museum education is not only concerned with work with children, the mismatch between the percentage of child visits (30 per cent) and the percentage of education staff to provide for them (less than 5 per cent) is very striking. This is the kind of statistic that underlies the story one hears about a large national museum whose visitor figures were falling, but whose education

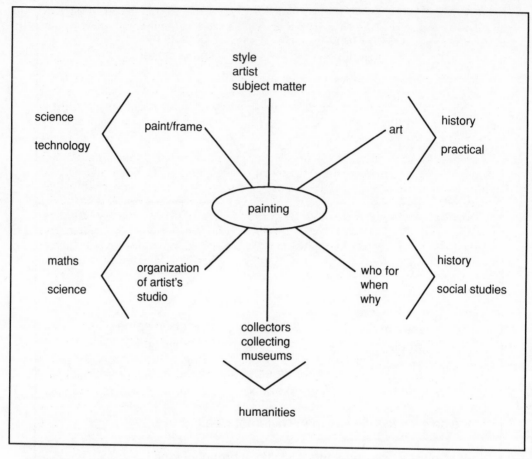

Fig. 33.5 Objects are cross-curricular

department was turning away customers because they were overstretched. Most museum education workers in large and small museums *are* overstretched. With museums looking desperately for ways to demonstrate their relevance to society in the late twentieth century, this is a thoroughly ludicrous situation, and one that must be changed in the very near future.

In the past, all but the national museums have largely depended on the Local Education Authority to provide either extra money or extra staff for educational provision. This has indeed been the recommendation of nearly all the Government reports. But it has not worked. There are very few education authorities that provide anywhere near the amount of educational provision that is needed. It is now time for Local Authority and independent museums to consider museum education staff as more central to the responsibility of the museum as a whole and to consider employing education staff from the museum staffing budget as the national museums do. This would be a radical change in policy, but would avoid many of the problems that occur when there are two sets of working conditions in one institution. With recommendations currently being made that every museum should provide an Education Officer (Anon 1987), perhaps new decisions over priority staffing need to be made? With new methods of allocating the LEA schools budget, following the *Educational Reform Act 1988*, it is possible that any monies previously used to support museum education may be withdrawn. This will force museums to develop new ways of funding the delivery of educational services.

In the appointment of staff it is strongly recommended that all museum Education Officers should have successful teaching experience behind them (Miles 1986) and that where possible this experience should span more than one age group. Museum education staff may work with all age groups from pre-school to postgraduate and adult students, and in the community with informal groups. A wide experience of communicating in different ways and at different levels is required.

The training available to museum education officers is, at present, limited (Hale 1987). The only full-time course is at the Department of Museum Studies, where an education option is offered alongside curatorial options on the one-year postgraduate course (Hooper-Greenhill 1985). The limited number of Government bursaries allocated to this course as a whole (13–15) which must be shared between all the different option groups, means that only a very small number are available for potential Education Officers. This course has been redesigned and offered on a modular basis, with at least two two-week modules of relevance to education and related staff. These are 'Museum education' and 'Communication'. These will form part of a full-time course of study but will also be available on an in-service basis.

The Ironbridge Institute offers courses on Heritage Interpretation, some of which are concerned with education and interpretation in the context of the heritage industry. The Museum Training Institute is developing standards of competence in museum education.

In some teacher-training courses there may be a museum-education component (Gooding 1985), with perhaps the best example of this being the Museums Option in the Post Graduate Certificate in Education (PGCE) course at the Institute of Education, University of London. This has been running for a good number of years and involves work within a museum education department in London which is related to the school-based teaching practice (Paine 1985). This is, however, designed more for the classroom teacher than for the museum teacher. The Inspectorate is currently encouraging the development of thinking among initial teacher trainers about how to use both museums and artefacts. Courses have been organized on a nationwide basis to encourage the permeation of the use of museums across the curriculum, and across the school-age range. Good practice in relation to the knowledge children should have of museums is described as follows: by the age of seven years children should be aware of museums, have visited at least one, and have handled artefacts; by the age of eleven children should have visited a variety of museums, understood their purposes, and have developed critical and discriminatory skills in relation to museums, have handled artefacts, and have undertaken sustained observation; by the age of sixteen pupils should understand all the services of museums, be fluent in the skills required to work with artefacts and specimens, know what can and cannot be learnt from museums and their objects, and be familiar with the appropriate recording techniques (Moffat 1988).

The specialist group concerned with museum education, the Group for Education in Museums (GEM),[2] offers valuable opportunities to meet colleagues, to discuss educational approaches, and to attend study sessions in museums. The annual conference has for some years taken the form of a study week. The Group produces a quarterly newsletter and an annual journal. The international committee of the International Council of Museums (ICOM) that covers museum education is the Committee for Education and Cultural Action (CECA). ICOM/CECA meet annually and publish *Education Annual* biannually.

The literature on museum education is mainly in the form of articles from journals, with very few books covering the topic, although two have recently been produced (Hooper-Greenhill 1991a; and Berry and Mayer 1989). GEM has produced a useful bibliography.

Museum education is currently being affected by wide social changes (Hooper-Greenhill 1991a), by changes in the structure and financing of museums, and by educational changes. The wider social changes include the fact that the leisure learning market is increasing, and was projected to increase from 5 to 10 per cent of total leisure spending by the end of the 1980s (Rodger 1987: 35). Although the emphasis is on learning, 'learning' here must not be equated with the old chalk-and-talk school-based learning of which so many adults have negative memories, but must be seen, and marketed, as participative, exploratory, activity-based, and informal (Hood 1983).

Changes in the structure and financing of museums include the move towards privatization and plural funding which is already identified in relation to the national museums, (Museum & Galleries Commission 1985: 9–11; *The Independent*, No. 458: 1) and which is on the not very distant horizon for Local Authority museums. Museums are now being referred to at Government level as the 'museums industry' (Luce 1988) and by marketing men as the 'museum business' (Rodger 1987). The 'heritage industry' is a £30 billion marketplace and the governing bodies of museums are rapidly trying to identify their market share. Educational work in museums is increasingly being scrutinized in this context, and arguments about qualitative experience, and about different levels of educational provision must be developed and strongly argued. It is also cautionary to note the analysis and condemnation of the 'history' as mere nostalgia, or, worse, as a useless past, manufactured at rapid speed by the heritage industry and by museums in order to capitalize on this new market (Horne 1984; Hewison 1987; Bennett 1988; West 1988). New forms of relationships between the institutional form, collections and people (both user-groups and workers) need to be actively developed (Hooper-Greenhill 1988b; Durrans 1988).

Educational changes which are affecting museum education include the new forms of exams, with an emphasis on resource-based learning, investigation, and modular courses, (Millar 1987; Lawson 1987; Museums Association 1987) and the National Curriculum. The stress on coursework, and the development of skills, concepts and understanding are leading to new opportunities for learning which will help to bring the museum and its resources into the front line (Goodhew n.d.). Museum education services are radically reviewing their practices in the light of these new possibilities and are finding new ways to make contacts in schools and to develop networks. In one example, having found ways to talk to potential users, the museum education staff designed provision that was jointly identified as necessary and relevant to the National Curriculum. This included teachers' courses on the study of artefacts, support material for museum visits including videos and 'self-service' selections of artefacts for handling, and document packs that related to the collections.

Current main emphases in educational provision in museums include a shift from direct teaching to the provision of resources and training for teachers; investigation of how best to provide for the National Curriculum, including making links and networks with examiners, coordinators, and classroom teachers; new publishing initiatives related to new developments in museum shops; consolidation and development of the specialist group; an emphasis on community outreach work (Nicholson 1985), and a growing concern for the museum as a really useful community resource (O'Neill 1987).

Current problems are almost entirely related to money and to governmental policies of self-sufficiency. On the one hand governmental action in reducing public expenditure is threatening jobs in some areas of the country, and on the other hand the squeeze on museum finance and the resultant search for new sources of revenue and the move towards a 'market-led' approach is being crassly interpreted in some museums as an emphasis on quantity rather than quality. Very few museums have carried out efficient visitor needs assessment as recommended by museum planners (Lord and Lord 1988: 176). Decisions are being made on visitor provision, emphasizing the visitor spend, in the time-honoured museum way, guesswork. Sensitive visitor analysis with clearly defined objectives such as that carried out at the National Portrait Gallery recently (Harvey 1987) reveals information that can support and direct both general visitor policies and specific educational provision. For example, at the National Portrait Gallery, London, nearly half of the visitors specified that one of their hobbies (or a secondary job) was painting (Harvey 1987: 10). This provides support and justification for the practical art sessions provided for adults at the gallery. It might even provide justification for restructuring and extending these sessions as a revenue-generating educational service. The development of a 'market-led' approach in the museum means researching the market, and building on the strengths of the qualitative work in which the museum is already experienced (Hooper-Greenhill 1988d). Too often this is being dealt with at management level in a way that disregards the experience, expertise, contacts and needs of the educationalists in the museum. This is clearly neither cost-effective nor good management.

The current scene in museum education presents a crossroads of change. Clear policies and well-founded educational convictions will be required to identify ways forward that do not compromise the genuine museum learning experience.

MANAGEMENT, STRUCTURE AND ORGANIZATION

An ideal structure for a museum education department is a Head of Department at Keeper level assisted by officers with a variety of different subject expertise in relation to the collections and different educational experience including primary, secondary, adult and outreach work. This is, in general only possible in the large departmental museums, and in many of the smaller museums, the work is done by one person. In some cases, staff work across a number of museums.

In the appointment of staff, the objectives of the museums are critical. At Sheffield and Dundee, for example, where outreach work in the community is a priority, officers with this kind of experience have been appointed. At Dundee, the appointment is linked to further training provision. Section 11 (*Local Government Act, 1966*) posts have been established in some Local Authority museums where multicultural work is a priority. These include Leicester, Bradford, Kirklees and Ipswich.

Clear communications are necessary both within the education department and within the museum. In all too many cases, there are large gaps in communication either within departments, or between education and curatorial workers. Clear delineations of responsibilities and tasks should be identified, and it should be clear how these interrelate within the department and the museum as a whole. Staff development should be considered and allowed for in the budget, including seminars and conferences, training or retraining to keep up with new educational methods and concerns both within the museum and in the educational world in general.

The educational work of the museum should have a clearly identified budget, which relates to the scale of the tasks identified and to the educational ambitions of the museum. Regular management meetings should be held, both within the department and with the other museum staff. These meetings should be used to review, evaluate (Hein 1982;

Otto 1979) and develop current practice and to identify priorities. Short- and long-term objectives should be set. A booking system should be in operation, and a detailed diary kept up to date. From this useful statistics as to the type of user, the frequency of use, and the areas of non-use can be generated, as can mailing lists. Specialist accommodation (Carter 1984: 439), often seen as a luxury, is necessary, as is at least access to a library, and to administrative support. Within a large departmental structure, a specific administrative office is necessary. Where the education work includes a loan service, drivers and design staff are required.

The educationalists of the museum should be used more in the planning and production of permanent and temporary displays (Locke 1984). This has been recommended for years by many reports (e. g. Williams 1981: 122), but few museums have adopted this as part of their policies. Where this has happened, qualitative changes have emerged in the interaction of visitors with artefacts. For example, at Nottingham Castle, where the Education Officer was heavily involved with the writing of the labels, visitors can be observed spending longer than usual in front of each painting, discussing aspects of the painting that the label has suggested, such as the changes the artist made in the painting.

Education staff should always be included in management meetings where decisions are made that affect their work. (How many education officers have gone to teach in a particular gallery only to discover it closed for redecoration for six weeks? And I for one have had a picture removed from the walls as I was actually talking about it, although that was in the days before I learnt to shout.) Planning committees for exhibitions should include education staff. In making decisions about which exhibitions to mount, the views of the education staff should be sought. If education programmes are expected to be arranged around these exhibitions, the timing of the school year must be considered. How many exhibitions with excellent educational potential are planned to neatly straddle the summer holidays, or the Christmas carol concert bonanza? With schools encouraged to use museums and their exhibitions far more in their teaching it makes sense to inquire widely into how exhibitions can relate to the National Curriculum, and to plan programmes of exhibitions that, for example, show how to use museums, or how to 'read' objects, or develop a group of related objects into many different syllabus areas (see Fig. 33.5). One example of an exhibition that explores museum as a process is *The Things That Time Forgot*, held at the Geffrye Museum in 1988.

In the relations outside the museum, lines of communication and networks of support to the Local Education Authority should be established and used. Other local and community groups can usefully be approached depending on the type of work that is identified as important. Multicultural work must be carried out in association with the various ethnic and religious groups, while work with special audiences such as the blind, will necessitate contact with the Royal National Institute for the Blind (RNIB) and local schools or day centres.

Networks can also be established between museums (Cox and Loftus 1979). Joint projects can exploit the relationships between collections. Museum Countywide Consultative Committees may act as vehicles for joint ventures.

Relationships with the press are necessary. Holiday projects, specially imaginative or innovative work, or large-scale ventures can all be used to promote the image of the museum both locally and nationally. Publishing should be considered. Longmans have developed a good relationship with museums and this seems likely to develop. Ironbridge has recently published a useful series of guidelines. Accounts of work done, including photographs, descriptions of activities, educational principles, and the uses of artefacts might be turned into a saleable product now that teachers are looking for ways to use museums. Now that museums are thinking about how to make themselves financially viable it must be said that museums hold vast resources and museum education staff are generally running very interesting projects which, if they were written up and well presented, would form interesting case studies. This is one way that sponsorship might be used, by paying for a temporary recorder and writer, and by paying for publishing costs.

METHODOLOGIES AND EXAMPLES

School services

The type of service for schools varies with almost each museum. It can include all or any of the following: direct teaching either in the museum or gallery itself, or in an adjoining room using demonstration and handling material, as at the National Gallery, the Horniman Museum (Mellors 1982), and Kelvingrove Art Gallery and Museum; the provision of resources for teachers and children, as at the British Museum (Reeve 1983) and the Natural History Museum, and the Weald and Downland Museum (Newbery 1987); the use of drama, as at Aberdeen Maritime Museum (Keatch 1987), Clarke Hall (Stevens 1981, 1987) and Suffolk (Fairclough 1980, 1982), or reconstruction (Phelan 1987); short-term displays can be mounted and used as a resource for a series of sessions for teachers and children, as at Leicester; and large-scale events are popular, if time consuming to organize. One or two museums have explored the possibilities of mobile museums which may tour schools or other venues (Porter 1982). Perhaps the best resourced and most well-known is the mobile museum in Liverpool (Rees 1981). Extended study is desirable where possible, but again can be time consuming if resources are limited. The GCSE in Museum Studies designed 10 years ago as a Certificate of Secondary Education (CSE) Mode 3 at the National Portrait Gallery provides a model (Cox and Loftus 1979; Morris 1985).

Almost all museums are now running courses for teachers which include museum or artefact teaching strategies. The *Journal of Education in Museums, Volume 6*, deals exclusively with this issue and includes general advice (Moffat 1985), accounts of work with science teachers (Sorsby 1985), art teachers (Paine 1985), advice on how to use historic buildings (Heath 1985), comparisons with work in America with initial teacher training (Gooding 1985), and some cautionary remarks about the usefulness of school visits (Pond 1985). Pond's work should be studied closely by museum educationalists as it is one of the few sustained investigations of the type of learning that is possible on museum visits (Pond 1983, 1984). He discusses some of the potential problems of depending on a Piagetian theory of cognitive development in planning learning experiences and outcomes in relation to the history subject area and suggests other theoretical models that might be more appropriate. These emphasize directed imagination, and the use of the emotions in learning. A useful counterpart to this work on young children and the learning and teaching of history is that of Blyth (1988).

Very young children have not often been provided for in museums, although the Bethnal Green Museum of Childhood and Norwich Castle Museum (Siliprandi 1987) are exceptions. Bristol Museum has recently run a day for children under 5 years of age in conjunction with Women Heritage and Museums (WHAM). This attracted a fair amount of publicity including a half-page spread in the *Guardian* and an interview on *Woman's Hour* (BBC Radio 4). Ironbridge Gorge Museum has begun a series of exploratory workshops with preschoolers and their teachers. This work is being recorded on video with the help of Shropshire Local Educational Authority, and is forming the basis for the production of guidelines for teachers of these groups. This is seen as the beginning of a long process that will proceed in a similar fashion through the other age ranges.

Primary-school children have in the past made up approximately two-thirds of the children provided for by educational departments. This pattern may alter as priorities and demands change with the introduction of new teaching methods in schools, which emphasize the analysis of evidence and the use of primary sources. The problem of reaching older students is reviewed by O'Connell and Alexander (1979) from Old Sturbridge Village in America. Many of their comments are very relevant to the British situation, and case studies of their work are available.

The structure of the school visit to the museum needs careful thought. Guidelines have been drawn up by individual museums, Area Museum Councils (e.g. Ambrose 1987) and by some Local Authorities. Preliminary visits by the teachers are desirable, wherever possible, as are jointly agreed objectives. Many teachers, at least when they first start to use museums, are not clear about what is possible, and so their objectives are often not completely formed. Courses explaining the potential of the museum can help here, as can discussions of the specific visit. Once the objectives and possibilities are defined, the visit to the museum can be placed within a course of study as a whole. This should include preparatory work at school, focusing on the knowledge required to best use the experience of the objects the children will experience. It should not include coaching on the specific objects and the rehearsing of apparently desired answers. The course of study might include visits to other institutions or sites, churches, record offices, historic buildings, or parks, for example. It is helpful for the museum officer to know this and often links and references can be made. Follow-up work stimulated by the museum visit should also form part of the course of study. Some follow-up work has been known to last many weeks, even a term on occasions where it is the museum as a set of processes that is the object of study (Hooper-Greenhill 1988d).

Teachers may well need support in planning the work at the museum, or even the course of study as a whole, and this might take the form of visits to schools, phone calls, teachers' courses, or notes or other written support. Where museums or historic houses are without any form of support in terms of staff, teachers' and children's handbooks can be prepared. English Heritage have produced some good models.[3] A long-term involvement with classroom and advisory teachers, schools, and, less often, individual children or students is more likely to lead to better learning outcomes.

Many museums have traditionally prepared worksheets for use during class visits. These can lead to either very good or very bad experiences. Bad worksheets are those which are not specifically geared to the needs and abilities of the group using them, direct attention to the label rather than the artefact, do not encourage thoughtful looking and use of observation, are too long, are limited to a 'see it, tick it' approach and, all in all, prevent rather than enable learning. Good worksheets are carefully planned, tried and tested in relation to specific objectives, are age-related, encourage deductive thinking, are theme or person based, are limited to a few key objects, often use drawings and illustrations in imaginative ways, enable follow-up discussion either at school or at the museum, and enable modifications by the teacher. Some worksheets are produced in 'suites' or series, with the same approach in each, which can be successful. Worksheets and their use are discussed by Jones and Ott (1983), Reeve (1983) and Fry (1987).

Loan services

Loan services to schools began at the end of the nineteenth century. Liverpool (1884), Sheffield (1891), and the Ancoats Art Museum in Manchester (Chadwick 1983) were among the first provincial museums to circulate material to schools, although the Victoria & Albert Museum had been loaning material to other museums and to art schools since

1864 (Whincop 1983). The newly founded Museums Association had as one of its first objectives in 1889 'the preparation of small educational loan collections for circulation to schools' (Rosse 1963: 288). Successive Government reports have encouraged loan services, particularly where distances between museums are great, but it is recognized that the burden of this work is high and that costs are heavy and, therefore, some assistance is required from the education authorities (Miles 1986). Loan services are suffering badly with the changes in Local Authority budgeting.

Several types of loan service can be identified: a loan service attached to the museum, and often receiving duplicate material from the main collections, as at Leicester (founded 1933); a loan service standing independently and purchasing its material, at least in the early days, with specific regard to the needs of schools, as in Derbyshire (founded 1936); a loan service attached to a museum, but with collections that have a broader scope, as at Oxfordshire; a loan service which includes original artefacts, but also performs the function of a large-scale resource centre, as at Wakefield; and a small-scale loan service, generally attached to a museum, but where the objects are only available by special arrangement, as at King's Lynn or Acton Scott. The larger scale loan services demand complex organization, and a great deal of time. In some museums where the loan service is extensive, and the staff numbers very limited, educational work may be limited to the administration of the loans for a considerable period each term. In general, the early and larger loan services tend to employ specific loan service officers and drivers to collect and deliver the material.

The early loan services held historical, archaeological or natural history material. Models and replicas have often been added since. Where original art work was included, this has sometimes, as in Derbyshire, had to be withdrawn owing to the increase in value of the material. Recently, loan services have begun to include material linked to specific ethnic groups to enable teachers to work with cross-cultural material. Some loan services include books, slides, or teachers' notes, although in some cases these are of some antiquity themselves.

Loan boxes vary in their construction and design but all must be light, strong, as easily carried as possible, and coded for their contents. Many boxes contain within them a method of display, so that the box becomes the pedestal for the artefact, for example, and the lid reverses to become a label. Most loan services provide a catalogue (Dundee, Leicester and Wakefield). Loan periods vary from 2 weeks to one term. Distribution is complex and ingenious schemes have been devised to keep track of up to 6,000 objects in the post. Now, many services are moving towards computerization.

The value of loan material in the classroom depends on the degree of skill of the teachers concerned. Good practice exists, but tends to be uncoordinated. A recent survey on the use of museum loan services carried out by the Department of Education and Science (Department of Education and Science 1987c) describes some projects and shows intelligent use of loan material in relation to reading, writing, mathematical, historical and art work. The loan material added to the quality of the school environment and provided effective stimuli for learning. However, much of the potential of the loan material was left unexplored. There were no curriculum guidelines in schools to guide teachers in their use of artefacts, to encourage teachers, or to share useful learning strategies and experiences.

Better links between schools and loan services are proposed in the Department of Education and Science report, including in-service or pre-entry courses on the use of loan material, and the effective identification and use of feedback from schools. Links between loan-service officers in museums to learn from each other are also suggested.

Adult education

There are very few museums that fully exploit their educational potential. While this is true in general it is more marked in the case of provision for adults. In the USA, adult education in museums is exciting, and possibilities are often exploited to the full (Gurian 1981). One example must suffice to illustrate the scope of possibilities. At Mystic Seaport, a museum complex of buildings on a river-side site (Carr 1986), 'adult education' includes the teaching of maritime skills (sailing, racing and boatbuilding) 'celestial navigation' (taught in the museum's planetarium), traditional wood-carving, weaving, and fireplace cookery. Both modern and traditional skills and techniques relating to the museum and its collections are taught on a regular and continuing basis to adult audiences. If a similar idea were adopted at the British Museum or the Victoria and Albert Museum, an enormous art school would be attached to the museum, with classes in stone-carving, wood-carving, ceramic work, tapestry, weaving, print-making of all kinds, painting, silverwork, glass-blowing, etc. This might be seen as extreme, but many museums across North America are taking exactly this approach, and with great success. Not only are visitors offered a new relationship with the collections, one aspect of the participatory experience we hear so much about, but these educational activities are also substantial income generators.

Webb (1986) points out that British and American museums use the governmental monies that they receive in very different ways. American museums use their initial income to generate more. The Metropolitan Museum of Art in New York received $20 million in grants in 1983, which generated $28 million in additional income. The British Museum and the National Gallery receiving a very similar base income generated £1.3 million, one-sixteenth as much. Now, Britain is not America, and the income received is no doubt committed in different ways. At present the national museums in Britain, for example, spend nearly 90 per cent of their income on salaries, which does not leave a lot to play with. In addition, not all of this generated income arises from educational programmes. Nonetheless, there are ideas here that we could think about. Webb goes on to say that, in general, American museums spend about 15 per cent of their income on education (not including display work). Given the vast unexplored educational potential of our museums that has been remarked on for the last 150 years, thought should be given to the possibility of practical classes in all kinds of activities for adults, on a paid basis.

Mystic Seaport runs annual research symposia in maritime history (autumn), Victorian life (spring), sea music (early summer), and conservation of artefacts (Carr 1986). The documentation of collections is made available for scholars and other visitors through oral and video tapes, written accounts, and drawings. The video tapes include the reissue of historic film for home consumption. The area of video production in relation to the work of museums and to the exploration of the collections is another enormous currently unexploited potential. Mystic Seaport expected to sell more than $200,000 worth of home video cassettes during 1987, and are looking into extending into new video technology, seeing this as a better way to publish, instead of in book form. The museum is collaborating with the National Geographic Society in the production of video programmes for transmission through cable television, and views this as a form of educational outreach. As the museum is a not-for-profit organization, the monies gained from these enterprises will be used to finance more educational ventures. These classes, symposia, and research publications are only one small part of the museum's educational enterprises. Extensive programmes for children are also provided, as is informal education for adults.

Adult education work in British museums includes both formal and informal provisions, such as lectures, concerts, readings and films. University museums often run programmes which are linked into university coursework. At the National Gallery in London, lectures are linked into Open University courses. Curators and educators are often involved talking both in the museum and elsewhere to specialist groups of all kinds. Lunchtime handling sessions for adults proved popular at the Museum of London, as have natural history handling and discovery sessions at Liverpool Museum. The National Museum of Wales has organized family walks (Sharpe and Howe 1982). A family room is offered during the holiday periods at the Natural History Museum, with objects to look at and things to do. Recently, experiments have been made with an 'art cart' in the galleries which provided both encouragement, expertise and materials for visitors to do a drawing of what they saw. The Royal Museum of Scotland provided a Discovery Room on an experimental basis for three weeks during the summer of 1987 which proved enormously popular. Interactive exhibits, generally concerned with principles of technology, have been installed in some museums, designed for both adults and children; Launch Pad at the Science Museum (Stevenson 1987), Green's Mill in Nottingham, and Liverpool Museum on Merseyside are examples. Their learning potential is always quoted as their main *raison d'être*, but this has been criticized as a naive approach, given the complexities of our current everyday involvement with science and technology (Shortland 1987).

In some cases adult education classes have been used to involve members in museum processes. A history class at Southampton resulted in new collections and new museum–visitor relationships (Jones and Major 1986). Some museums have been working with Help the Aged doing reminiscence work, using museums objects to stimulate discussion and recall for elderly people.

Some museums have concentrated on the involvement of ethnic groups that are currently underrepresented in museums (Nicholson 1985), although the problems of this work being perceived as tokenism and the resulting negative images of museums should not be ignored (Belgrave 1986).

Museums have long been interested in providing exhibitions that have catered for blind and partially sighted visitors. References to this kind of work can be traced back to the beginning of the century (Deas 1913) and recently interest has revived with several major national and provincial museums putting on handling exhibitions. This kind of provision, although to be encouraged, tends to be sporadic in any one institution, which makes the use of these exhibitions unpredictable (Coles 1983). More qualitative and regular work would be better, and pioneering work of the Adult Education Department of the University of Leicester is relevant here (Hartley, n.d.). Adult education classes where teacher and blind students work together to develop methods of working and learning through sculpture have shown what large educational and psychological gains can be made using artefacts and practical art work. These groups have always used museum handling exhibitions as sources, and have strongly developed ideas on the advantages and disadvantages of these kinds of exhibitions. Their experience in putting on their own exhibition in a museum exposed a vast communication gap between their own needs and priorities and those of the museum. If it were possible for museums to work much more closely with adult education classes such as those which had an exhibition component built into their aims, a much more profitable use of resources and expertise might be enabled, and misunderstandings might be avoided. The provision of tactile experiences on a regular basis in a part of the museum that is easy to negotiate would also be valuable. This would provide an opportunity to make contacts and establish networks which might lead to greater involvement.

The Carnegie United Kingdom Trust was instrumental in encouraging and financing a two-year study into the arts and disabled people, which resulted in two publications which every museum should have in their library (Attenborough 1985; Pearson 1985). These cover a wider span of provision, both in terms of institution and type of activity, thereby placing museums within the context of specialist provision as a whole.

SOME IDEAS FOR SMALL MUSEUMS

In many small museums staff act both as curators and education officers, often without educational training or experience, but often, too, with much goodwill. Possible links and ways of getting assistance and extra staff are comprehensively covered in Carter (1984). Certainly contact with the Local Education Authority, teachers' centres, advisory teachers and the local inspectorate are essential. Sponsorship may be a further way forward, although if this was to be tried, a longer rather than a shorter term sponsored appointment is likely to be more productive.

Some measures can be helpful to avoid the panic of failure of provision and the resulting knee-jerk responses: these include policies, strategies, and publicity.

A review of the existing needs and possibilities should be carried out, educational policies identified, ratified and implemented. Areas of future growth should be outlined so that the educational work which is possible is carried out within a clear analysis of where development could take place. This clear-sighted planning will pay off when unexpected opportunities present themselves.

Possible strategies of work include dividing the time available and alloting specified time (of the day, the week, the year) to educational work. Continuous haphazard demand from teachers can be limited by asking for letters rather than phone calls (with a pleasant answer-phone message to suggest a letter, while curatorial work is done).

Decisions must be made on the type of provision that is feasible; whether to teach, or to provide materials for teachers to teach the classes themselves, to do regular training sessions for teachers, to demonstrate and develop the educational possibilities, or more than one of these.

Various forms of provision should be thought about. Consider reviewing the possibilities of the museum together with advisory teachers for different subject or age-groups. Maybe some collaborative scheme could be devised. Perhaps an exploratory curriculum development project over a limited period of months might demonstrate the value and vast potential of the museum as an educational resource, and might lead on to further help or development. Most non-museum people seem very unaware of this enormous learning potential, and need to see it demonstrated in action before they can begin to understand it. The curriculum project for primary schools at the Horniman Museum provides a model which could be adopted (Mellors 1982; Hooper-Greenhill 1988d).

Teachers seem to ask most often for handling material. If it is possible to sort out some small collections of related objects or specimens that could be made available for handling, or demonstration by teacher or curator, or even close and sustained observation, these would probably be very popular. It would be possible to limit the availability of the collections to those teachers who had attended a short course of handling procedures. These could be held in the museum or teachers' centre after school for small numbers on a regular basis. Again, involvement with advisory teachers would be helpful. It would be possible to devise a work pattern for the curator that set aside, say four days of the week over a two to three week period during a four to six month period when handling groups were supervised. Most of the teaching work would be carried out by the teachers who had previously attended a training course where curatorial concerns and limits had been specified, and ideas for use had been exchanged between the teachers. These teachers' courses would need to be held some weeks before the handling sessions to enable the preparation work necessary in the schools to be both set up and carried out. A two-week period of four days in each week would enable sixteen groups (two each day) to visit the museum, and would produce a group of sixteen teachers trained to use at least those collections of objects. Although this seems small scale, it should result in a high standard of work, and in teachers who understood some aspects of the museum. A teacher–Friends group might evolve from such contacts which would provide a very solid base for changes in policy or for development in educational provision.

A further approach to the provision of handling material might be the development of loan kits. If it is kept to a small scale and teachers fetch and carry themselves, this might not be too overwhelming. At the Children's Museum of Boston, Mass., loan kits are only produced when sponsorship is available, and specific people can be appointed to carry out the research, identify and select the objects, design the packaging, and write the accompanying notes. This might be an idea to explore.

Written material can be useful, and not too time-consuming once it is produced. Consider writing notes on the use of the galleries, identifying possible themes that run through several galleries, or writing notes on specific objects on display so that teachers can choose their own way of using them. The writing style must be simple but succinct, and the presentation of the material must enable easy and fast assimilation. The use of diagrams, flowcharts, maps, illustrations, cartoons, notes, photographs, excerpts from related documents, and so on is more interesting and more useful than several closely written A4 pages. Just imagine settling down to read what you have produced after a day at school.

Consider asking teachers who use the museum to write short notes on how they approached it and what they did as preparation or follow-up work either at school or in other places. A teachers' handbook with half-a-dozen such case studies for your museum would be very helpful for other teachers who are generally very inventive and experienced in adapting material to suit their particular needs. 'Museums and the New Exams' (Goodhew n.d.) provides an example which could be adapted for use in one museum (or, if relevant, across several). 'The GCSE and Museums' (Ironbridge Gorge Museum 1987) (which in fact deals exclusively with Ironbridge Gorge Museum) provides a very elaborate model for just one museum. Simpler documents would also be useful. Visual records of the museum visit and its activities is also useful for in-service courses.

It may be possible to get sponsorship specifically for the production of written materials, either from local industry or charities, or from some of the larger firms that have sponsored museum publications over the last few years. The Local Education Authority, teachers' centre or local college may be able to help with production. Sometimes students can be available to produce some of the work, either from the Department of Museum Studies, University of Leicester, or from other institutions.

Once the educational strategy of the museum has been devised, a short document should be produced specifying what is possible and how to access it. This should be sent to all interested parties, including the Local Education Authority, and all its ramifications, schools, and libraries. It should also be available in the museum. If demand exceeds supply for the services that can be offered, this can be used as an argument for further help.

In most cases the Area Museum Service may be able to help. The Scottish Museums Council provides a model here, with their recently developed 'leisure learning' programme. The Scottish Museums Council have evolved a document that accompanies each of their travelling exhibitions which identifies a great variety of educational possibilities. These include detailed ideas for practical workshops, formal lectures, and films (useful and relevant ones listed), the names of experts and contact persons, and suggestions for community involvement. In the case of each suggestion, the estimated cost to the museum, the resources required. and other requirements are identified. The document provides a well-researched, comprehensive list of educational possibilities from which any curator hosting the exhibition can select. The Scottish Museums Council has appointed one member of staff with exclusive responsibility for this work and is now working with a number of museums on developing leisure learning programmes based on their permanent collections (Stewart 1988).

All in all, there are many ways that curators in small museums can provide a high-quality, if small-scale, service. In general it is probably better in the long run to aim for quality rather than quantity. Supplying a minimum for many teachers results in limited achievement, and does not provide a suitable base for solid growth. Working towards a qualitative educational experience, even for limited numbers, demonstrates what can be achieved with few resources and, therefore, also indicates what could be achieved with more, and enables in-depth contact and involvement which can be built upon.

THE GENERAL EDUCATIONAL RESPONSIBILITY OF THE MUSEUM

All too often education staff are doing qualitative work with different groups while the public front of the museum is boring, difficult, and neglected. Museums are becoming much more accountable very quickly indeed. Emphasis for the way forward is undoubtedly on the overall quality of experience for the museum visitor. The educational work of the museum should be part of a general communications policy. This should be planned, organized and evaluated.

Comfort services are essential, and museums are increasingly realizing that people need to eat, drink, rest and so on if they are to remain in the building for more than a short time. But after the provision of these basic facilities how should a communications policy be evolved? One of the most vital aspects is that of the museum displays (Gurian 1981; Patten 1982–1983). Educational staff are used to designing effective learning experiences of all kinds for all sorts of groups, and are used to working with and adapting often inadequate displays. Together, curators, designers and educators should develop a knowledge of the visitor and the potential visitor, and should develop a unified display policy that enables first time visitors to scan and browse and repeat visitors to look, to work, to participate in an in-depth way with the collections. Galleries should be varied to provide an initial introduction to the nonspecialist lay person, and then a more detailed, more in-depth approach for someone wanting something more specific (Cameron 1982).

The introductory galleries, or sections of the display, should assume a minimum level of knowledge, expertise and experience in the topic being introduced. The basic concepts behind the topic should be explained and demonstrated. The Bird Gallery at the Manchester Museum includes a case where it is shown by using specimens that birds have very light skeletons, that they do not all fly, and that they vary in size. A few very basic concepts are spelt out. This is not patronizing to the public. This acts as a warm-up to the topic, a way of shifting the mind from Egyptology or classical archaeology or whatever was previously being looked at. It works as a recall to people who have not thought about birds for some time, and it introduces basic concepts to those who have not been introduced to them before. A 'basic concept case' such as this could also be used to orient the viewer/reader to the approach to be adopted in the following cases and to introduce the styles of thinking which will be necessary. Are we to think like historians, or geologists? What sort of questions should we ask of the display as we view it? The current educational philosophy that lies behind the new educational approaches exemplified in the GCSE emphasizes the acquisition and use of skills, including the skills of thinking, i. e. organizing concepts, making comparisons, and detecting bias. Children are being encouraged to think like geographers, or mathematicians, and to recognize that these forms of knowing and thinking are not the same. Which do we use when in the museum? How do we know? The introductory case to the 'Lost Worlds' display in the New Walk Museum in Leicester introduces the geologist as a detective, gives examples of the kinds of 'clues' looked for, demonstrates the comparisons made between now and then, and points out the deductive method used by geologists to draw some comparisons. This case acts as the 'thought-model' for the rest of the exhibition.

In-depth displays can concentrate less on breadth of approach and more on depth of investigation. Examples might include interdisciplinary displays on specific themes, such as the exhibit on hairdressing that forms part of the Roman Life Gallery in the Yorkshire Museum, where different types of object are assembled to show different facets of the same topic; or the *About Face* exhibition at the Royal Museum of Scotland (summer 1988) where the topic of face decoration was explored across time, space and cultures, and related activities were organized by the education department for schools and in conjunction with local art schools and fashion courses.

Other approaches might include a multifaceted approach to one object, not presenting it in relation to its classified position within the museum collections, but looking much more broadly at who made it, when, why, who for, how it was used, how that use has changed, how the meaning of the object has changed as its context has changed. Contemporary cultural studies are beginning to explore the ideas of meaning within different discourses (Laclau and Mouffe 1987). Museums could take the intellectual lead here with their fantastic resources which demonstrate all too well how knowledge is constructed through different combinations of material things in different social, cultural and historic contexts (Hooper-Greenhill 1992a).

A museum communications policy should be based on the understanding that communication is only possible where shared codes are in operation. The museum code must not be isolated from the other codes that visitors are familiar with. Links must be made with what people know, understand and are comfortable with. Where, for example, archaeological fragments are on display, it cannot be assumed that the visitor can mentally complete the fragment and perceive the original artefact. Some help must be given, either by accompanying drawings (as on the labels in the Yorkshire Museum where the complete object in use is depicted) or by other means.

A communications policy should address the concept of 'the museum visitor' held by the staff of the museum. How are people conceptualized? As *tabula rasa* or as hypothesizing and meaning-making individuals? (Alt and Griggs 1984). How is the museum experience understood? Recent research shows that attention to the exhibit diminishes after about thirty-five minutes, regardless of type or attractiveness of exhibit (Falk 1985). A museum communications policy should pay attention to this 'concentration gap' and develop strategies that enable the lapse of concentration to occur naturally without feelings of guilt, inadequacy or boredom on the part of the visitor, and also strategies to enable a re-engagement with the displays. This means varying the museum spaces to create areas of mental relaxation, areas of high concentration, areas of sitting and listening or watching, areas of questioning or even self-testing in relation to content of near-by displays (Screven 1986), and so on. La Villette, the new science centre in Paris, provides an example of this kind of museum planning.

Research shows that museum visitors need to feel valued, appreciated, comfortable and at home (Hood 1983). A communications policy would start by evaluating the museum experience from the point of view of the visitor and would proceed to develop a complex, multifaceted, coordinated, planned set of objectives that would provide a qualitative overall experience for many different types of visitor with many different needs. Part of these objectives would be specific in-house provision for organized groups of all ages, part would concern outreach work in different parts of the community, part would be related to displays organized to present different forms of learning experiences, with the nature of each clearly spelt out, and part would be specifically concerned with publicity and marketing. The development of management skills to enable this form of qualitative provision for 'the museum visitor' should be regarded as a priority.

The days when 'museum education' meant parties of schoolchildren being dragged round the display cases are long gone. 'Museum education' is an infinitely more complex aspect of museum work, which is fast becoming one of the most necessary.

This paper first appeared in J. M. A. Thompson (ed.) (1992) Manual of Curatorship, *2nd edn, London: Butterworth, pp. 670–89.*

NOTES

1 Foucault (1970) outlines in detail the broad epistemological frameworks within which words and things have been related and meanings have been constituted. This is presented as subject to highly significant cultural shifts over time since the Renaissance. Laclau and Mouffe (1987) discuss the ways in which objects become meaningful through the discourses in which they are positioned. The writers together offer a theory of meaningful objects which celebrates proliferations of variously constituted meanings as opposed to an essentialist understanding of the 'truth' of objects.
2 The membership secretary is currently Jeni Harrison, The Old Manse of Lynturk, Muir of Fowlis, Alford, Aberdeenshire, AB33 8HS, Scotland.
3 These include *Osborne House – A Practical Handbook for Teachers*; *Life on a Royal Estate – A Document Pack for Osborne House*; and *The Tudors at Hampton Court Palace – A Pack for Teachers*.

FURTHER READING

Three free booklets have been produced by the Department of Museum Studies, University of Leicester, 105, Princess Road, East Leicester, LE1 7LG. These are available as long as stocks last.
Hooper-Greenhill, E. (ed.) (1989) *Initiatives in Museum Education*.
Hooper-Greenhill, E. (ed.) (1991) *Writing a Museum Education Policy*.
Hooper-Greenhill, E. (ed.) (1992) *Working in Museum and Gallery Education – 10 Career Experiences*.

REFERENCES

Alt, M. B. and Griggs, S. A. (1984), 'Psychology and the museum visitor' in J. M. A. Thompson (ed.)

Manual of Curatorship, London: Museum Association, Butterworth: 386–93.

Ambrose, T. (ed.) (1987) *Education in Museums: Museums in Education*, Edinburgh: Scottish Museums Council, HMSO.

Attenborough, R. (1985) *Arts and Disabled People*, London: Carnegie United Kingdom Trust.

Anon. (1987) 'Meeting the GCSE challenge', *North East Museum Service News* 16, Newcastle-upon-Tyne.

Bassett, D. A. (1984) 'Museums and education: a brief bibliographic essay', in J. M. A. Thompson (ed.) *Manual of Curatorship*, London: Museums Association, Butterworth: 448–59.

Bateman, J. (1984) 'The control and financing of museum education services in Britain', *Museums Journal* 84(2): 51–61.

Belgrave, R. (1986) 'Southampton's Caribbean Heritage: an analysis of the oral history project carried out by Southampton Museums 1983– 1984', *Archaeological 'Objectivity' in Interpretation* (3) World Archaeological Congress, 1–7 September, Southampton.

Bennett, T. (1988), 'Museums and the people', in R. Lumley (ed.) *The Museum Time Machine*, London: Comedia/Routledge: 63–86.

Berry, S. and Mayer, S. (eds) (1989) *Museum Education: Theory and Practice*, The National Art Association, USA.

Blyth, J. (1988) *Primary Bookshelf: History 5–9*, London: Hodder and Stoughton.

Board of Education (1931) *Museums and the Schools: Memorandum on the Possibility of Increased Co-operation between Public Museums and Public Educational Institutions Educational Pamphlets No. 87*, London: HMSO.

British Association for the Advancement of Science (1920) 'Final report of the Committee on museums in relation to education', *Report of the British Association for the Advancement of Science, 1920*, London: 267–80.

Busse, F. (1980) 'Object-teaching – principles and methods', *American Journal of Education* 30: 471–50.

Calkins, N. A. (1880) 'Object-teaching: its purpose and province', *Education*, Boston, USA, 1: 165–72.

Cameron, D. F. (1982) 'Museums and public access – the Glenbow approach', *International Journal of Museum Management and Curatorship* 1(3): 177–96.

Carr, J. R. (1986) 'Education everywhere for everyone at Mystic Seaport', *The American Museum Experience: In Search of Excellence*, Edinburgh: Scottish Museums Council: 41–58.

Carter, P. G. (1984) 'Educational services', in J. M. A. Thompson (ed.) *Manual of Curatorship*, London: Butterworth: 435–47.

Chadwick, A. (1983) 'Practical aids to nineteenth century self-help – the museums: private collections into public institutions', in M. D. Stephens and G. W. Roderick (eds) *Samuel Smiles and Nineteenth Century Self-help in Education*, Department of Adult Education, University of Nottingham: 47–69.

Coles, P. (1983) *Please Touch: An Evaluation of the Please Touch Exhibition at the British Museum, 31 March – 18 May*, Committee of Inquiry into the Arts and Disabled People Carnegie United Kingdom Trust.

Cox, A. and Loftus, J. (1979) 'Teaching through museums', *ILEA Contact, 11*: 9–10, London: Inner London Education Authority.

Deas, C. (1913) 'The showing of museums and art galleries to the blind', *Museums Journal* 13(3): 85–109.

Delahaye, M. (1987) 'Can children be taught how to think?', *The Listener*, 22 Oct: 14.

Department of Education and Science (1987a) 'Report by HM Inspectors on a survey of the use of museums made by some schools in the North West, carried out 17–21 June 1985', *HMI Report 20/87*, London: HMSO.

Department of Education and Science (1987b) 'Report by HM Inspectors on a survey of the use some schools in six local education authorities make of museum services, carried out June, 1986', *HMI Report 53/87*, London: HMSO.

Department of Education and Science (1987c) 'Report by HM Inspectors on a survey of how schools in five LEAs made use of museum loan services, carried out Spring 1987', *HMI Report 290/87*, London: HMSO.

Department of Education and Science (1987d) 'Report by HM Inspectors on a survey of the use some Oxfordshire schools and colleges make of museum services, carried out Sept–Nov 1986', *HMI Report 312/87*, London: HMSO.

Dewey, J. (1979) *Experience and Education*, London: Collier Macmillan.

Durbin, G. (1987) 'Practical courses for teachers', *Journal of Education in Museums* 8: 4–5.

Durbin, G., Morris, S. and Wilkinson, S. (1990) *A Teachers Guide to Learning from Objects*, English Heritage.

Durrans, B. (1988) 'The future of the other: changing cultures on display in ethnographic museums', in R. Lumley (ed.) *The Museum Time- Machine*, London: Comedia/Routledge: 144–69.

Ersner, E. W. and Dobbs, S. M. (1986) 'Museum education in twenty American art museums', *Museum News* 65(2): 42–9.

Falk, J. F. (1985) 'Predicting visitor behaviour', *Curator* 28(4): 249–57.

Foucault, M. (1970) *The Order of Things*, London: Tavistock.

Fry, H. (1987) 'Worksheets as museum learning devices', *Museums Journal* 86(4): 219–25.

Goodhew, E. (ed.) (n.d.) *Museums and the New Exams*, London: Area Museums Service for South Eastern England.

Goodhew, E. (ed.) (1989) *Museums and Primary Science*, London.

Gooding, J. (1985) 'How do you begin? Museum work with undergraduates and initial teachers training students in British and American Institutions', *Journal of Education in Museums* 6: 8–10.

Gurian, E. (1981) 'Adult learning at Children's Museum of Boston', in Z. Collins (ed.), *Museums, Adults and Humanities*, Washington, DC: American Association of Museums: 271–96.

Hale, J. (1987) *Museum Professional Training Career Structure*, Museums and Galleries Commission, London: HMSO.

Harrison, M. (1950) *Museum Adventure: the Story of the Geffrye Museum*, London: University of London.

Harrison, M. (1954) *Learning out of School: a Teachers' Guide to the Educational Use of Museums*, East Grinstead: Ward Locke Educational.

Harrison, M. (1967) *Changing Museums – Their Use and Misuse*, London: Longman.

Hartley, E. (n.d.) *Touch and See: Sculpture by and for the Visually Handicapped in Practice and Theory*, Leicester: University of Leicester, Department of Adult Education.

Harvey, B. (1987) *Visiting the National Portrait Gallery*, London: HMSO.

Heath, A. (1985) 'Training teachers to use historic buildings for educational purposes', *Journal of Education* 6: 28–31.

Heidegger, M. (1951) 'The age of the world view', *Measure* 2: 269–84.

Hein, G. E. (1982) 'Evaluation of museum programs and exhibits', in T. H. Hansen, K.-E. Anderson and P. Vestergaard (eds) *Museums and Education*, Denmark: Danish ICOM/CECA: 21–6.

Hewison, R. (1987) *The Heritage Industry*, London: Methuen.

Hood, M. (1983) 'Staying away – why people choose not to visit museums', *Museum News* 61(4): 50–7.

Hooper-Greenhill, E. (1980) 'The National Portrait Gallery: a case-study in cultural reproduction', M.A. thesis, London: University of London, Department of Sociology of Education, Institute of Education.

Hooper-Greenhill, E. (1983) 'Some basic principles and issues relating to museum education', *Museums Journal* 83(2/3): 127–30.

Hooper-Greenhill, E. (1985) 'Museum training at the University of Leicester', *Journal of Education in Museums* 6: 1–6.

Hooper-Greenhill, E. (1987a) 'Museums in education: towards the twenty-first century', in T. Ambrose (ed.) *Museums in Education: Education in Museums*, Edinburgh: Scottish Museums Council, HMSO: 39–52.

Hooper-Greenhill, E. (1987b) 'Knowledge in an open prison', *New Statesman* 13 Feb: 21–2.

Hooper-Greenhill, E. (1988a) 'The museum: the socio-historical articulations of knowledge and things', Ph. D. thesis, London: University of London, Department of the Sociology of Education, Institute of Education.

Hooper-Greenhill, E. (1988b) 'Counting visitors or visitors who count', in R. Lumley (ed.) *The Museum Time-Machine*, London and New York: Methuen/Routledge: 213–32.

Hooper-Greenhill, E. (1988c) 'The art of memory and learning in the museum: museum education and GCSE', *The International Journal of Museum Management and Curatorship*, June.

Hooper-Greenhill, E. (1988d) 'Museums in education: working with other organizations', *Working with Museums*, Edinburgh: Scottish Museums Council.

Hooper-Greenhill, E. (1989) *Initiatives in Museum Education*, Leicester: Department of Museum Studies, University of Leicester.

Hooper-Greenhill, E. (1991a) *Museum and Gallery Education*, Leicester: Leicester University Press.

Hooper-Greenhill, E. (1991b) *Writing a Museum Education Policy*, Leicester: Department of Museum Studies, University of Leicester.

Hooper-Greenhill, E. (1992a) *Museums and the Shaping of Knowledge*, London: Routledge.

Hooper-Greenhill, E. (1992b) *Working in Museum and Gallery Education: 10 Career Experiences*, Leicester Department of Museum Studies, University of Leicester.

Horne, D. (1984) *The Great Museum*, London: Pluto Press.

Hudson, K. (1987) *Museums of Influence*, Cambridge: Cambridge University Press.

Hunter, M. (1981) *Science and Society in Restoration England*, Cambridge: Cambridge University Press.

Ironbridge Gorge Museum (1987) *The GCSE and Museums: a Handbook for Teachers*, Telford: Ironbridge.

Jones, S. and Major, C. (1986) 'Reaching the public: oral history as a survival strategy for museums', *Oral History Journal* 14(2): 31–8.

Jones, L. S. and Ott, R. (1983) 'Self-study guides for school-age students', *Museum Studies Journal* 1(1): 37–45.

Kaufmann, T. D. (1978) 'Remarks on the collections of Rudolf II: the *Kunstkammer* and a form of *Representatia*', *Art Journal* 38: 22–8.

Keatch, S. (1987) 'Cloots, creels and claikin – drama on display', in T. Ambrose (ed.) *Education in Museums, Museums in Education*, Edinburgh: Scottish Museums Council: 77–84.

Laclau, E. and Mouffe, C. (1987) 'Post-Marxism without apologies', *New Left Review* 166: 79–106.

Laurencich-Minelli, L. (1985), 'Museography and ethnographical collections in Bologna during the sixteenth and seventeenth centuries', in O. Impey and A. MacGregor (eds) *The Origins of Museums*, Oxford: Clarendon Press.

Lawson, I. (1987) 'Standard grade and Scottish museums', *Museums Journal* 87(2): 110–12.

Lawson, J. and Silver, H. (1973) *A Social History of Education in England*, London: Methuen.

Locke, S. (1984) 'Relations between educational, curatorial, and administrative staff', in J. M. A. Thompson *Manual of Curatorship*, London: Butterworth: 482–8.

Lord, B. and Lord, G. D. (1988) 'The museum planning process', *Museums Journal* 87(4): 175–80.

Luce, R. (1988) Parliamentary reply to a question from Mr Tony Baldry on the future of museum training following the Hale Report, 17 March, *Office of Arts and Libraries Press Release 4047/107*, London.

MacGregor, A. (1983) *Tradescant's Rarities*, Oxford: Clarendon Press.

Markham, S. F. (1938) *A Report on the Museums and Art Galleries of the British Isles*, Dunfermline: Carnegie United Kingdom Trust.

Mellors, M. (1982) 'Horniman Museum and primary schools', *Journal of Education in Museums* 3: 19.

Miers, H. A. (1928) *A Report on the Public Museums of the British Isles*, Edinburgh: Carnegie United Kingdom Trust.

Miles, H. (1986) *Museums in Scotland*, London: Museums and Galleries Commission, HMSO.

Millar, S. (1987) 'An opportunity to be grasped', *Museums Journal* 87(2): 104–7.

Miller, E. (1973) *That Noble Cabinet*, London: André Deutsch.

Moffat, H. (1985) 'A joint enterprise', *Journal of Education in Museums* 6: 20–3.

Moffat, H. (1988) 'Museums and schools', *Museums Bulletin*, 28(3) 97–8.

Morris, S. (1985) '"Museum Studies" – a mode three CSE course at the National Portrait Gallery', *Journal of Education in Museums* 6: 37–40.

Museums & Galleries Commission (1985) *Report 1984–85*, London: Museums & Galleries Commission.

Museums & Galleries Commission (1987) *Report 1986–87*, London: Museums & Galleries Commission.

Museums & Galleries Commission (1991) *Local Authorities and Museums – report by a working party, 1991*, London: HMSO.

Museums Association (1987) 'GCSE and museums', *Museum Journals* 87(1).

Museums Association (1991) *A National Strategy for Museums – Museums Association Annual Report, 1990–1991*.

National Audit Commission (1991) *The Road to Wigan Pier? Managing Local Authority Museums and Art Galleries*, London: HMSO.

Newbery, E. (1987) 'Something for all the family', *Journal of Education in Museums* 8: 9–10.

Nicholson, J. (1985) 'The museum and the Indian community: findings and orientation of the Leicestershire Museums Service', *Museum Ethnographers Newsletter* 19: 3–14.

O'Connell, P. and Alexander, M. (1979) 'Reaching the high school audience', *Museum News* 58(2): 50–6.

O'Neill, M. (1987) 'Quantity vs quality or what is a community museum anyway', *Scottish Museum News*, Spring: 5–7.

Ornstein, M. (1938) *The Role of Scientific Societies in the Seventeenth Century*, Chicago, IL: University of Chicago Press.

Otto, J. (1979) 'Learning about "neat stuff": one approach to evaluation', *Museum News* 58(2): 38–45.

Paine, S. (1985) 'The art classroom in the training of art and design teachers', *Journal of Education in Museums* 6: 15–19.

Patten, L. H. (1982–83), 'Education by design', *ICOM Education* 10: 6–7.

Pearson, A. (1985) *Arts for Everyone*, Edinburgh: Carnegie United Kingdom Trust and Centre on Environment for the Handicapped.

Phelan, B. (1987) 'The Sussex time-machine', *Journal of Education in Museums* 8: 11–12.

Pond, M. (1983) 'School history visits and Piagetian theory', *Teaching History* 37: 3–6.

Pond, M. (1984) 'Recreating a trip to York in Victorian times', *Teaching History* 39: 12–16.

Pond, M. (1985) 'The usefulness of school visits – a study', *Journal of Education in Museums* 6: 32–6.

Porter, J. (1982) 'Mobile exhibition services in Great Britain: a survey of their practice and potential', *Museums Journal* 82(3): 135–8.

Prince, D. R. and Higgins-McLoughlin, B. (1987) *Museums UK: The Findings of the Museums Database Project*, London: Museums Association.

Purver, M. and Bowen, E. J. (1960) *The Beginning of the Royal Society*, Oxford: Clarendon Press.

Rees, P. (1981) 'A mobile for the teacher', *Journal of Education in Museums* 2: 26–9.

Reeve, J. (1983) 'Museum materials for teachers', in N. Hall (ed.) *Writing and Designing Interpretive Materials for Teachers*, Conference papers, Manchester Polytechnic, Manchester.

Rodger, L. (1987) 'Museums in education: seizing the market opportunities', in T. Ambrose (ed.) *Education in Museums, Museums in Education*, Edinburgh: Scottish Museums Council: 27–38.

Rosse, Earl of (1963) *Survey of Provincial Museums and Galleries*, London: Standing Commission on Museums and Galleries, HMSO.

Screven, C. G. (1986) 'Exhibitions and information centres: some principles and approaches', *Curator* 29(2): 109–37.

Sharpe, T. and Howe, S. R. (1982) 'Family expeditions – the museum outdoors', *Museums Journal* 82(3): 143–7.

Shortland, M. (1987) 'No business like show business', *Nature* 328: 213–14.

Siliprandi, K. (1987) 'Playgroups and museums', *Journal of Education in Museums* 8: 13–14.

Sorsby, B. (1985) 'Teaching science teachers to use museums', *Journal of Education* 6: 24–7.

Stevens, T. (1981) 'Dramatic approaches to museum education', *Journal of Education in Museums* 2: 30–3.

Stevens, T. (1987) 'Change: a constant theme', *Journal of Education in Museums* 8: 15–17.

Stevenson, J. (1987) 'The philosophy behind Launchpad', *Journal of Education in Museums* 8: 18–20.

Stewart, D. (1988) 'Leisure learning programme – update', *Scottish Museum News*, Summer: 2–3.

Webb, C. D. (1986) 'Museum in search of income', in T. Ambrose (ed.) in *The American Museums Experience: in Search of Excellence*, Edinburgh: Scottish Museums Council, HMSO: 75–80.

West, B. (1988) 'The marking of the English working past: a critical view of the Ironbridge Gorge Museum', in R. Lumley (ed.) *The Museum Time-Machine*, London: Comedia/Routledge: 36–62.

Whincop, A. (1983) 'Loan services in Great Britain – historical and philosophical account', unpublished paper, available from the Department of Museum Studies, University of Leicester, Leicester.

Williams, A. (1981) *A Heritage for Scotland – Scotland's National Museums and Galleries: The Next 25 Years*, Glasgow: HMSO.

Winstanley, B. (1966) *Children and Museums*, London: Blackwell.

Wright, C. W. (1973) *Provincial Museums and Galleries*, London: Department of Education and Science, HMSO.

Wright, P. (1985) *On Living in an Old Country*, London: Verso.

Yates, F. (1966) *The Art of Memory*, London: Routledge and Kegan Paul.

BIBLIOGRAPHY

Booth, J. H. and Krockover, G. H. (1982) *Creative Museum Methods and Educational Techniques*, Springfield, IL: Charles C. Thomas.

Chadwick, A. and Hooper-Greenhill, E. (1985) 'Volunteers in museums and galleries: a discussion of some of the issues', *Museums Journal* 84(4): 177–8.

Cheetham, F. W. (ed.) (1967) *Museum School Services* London: Museums Association.

Collins, Z. (1981) *Museums, Adults and the Humanities*, Washington, DC: American Association of Museums.

Coulter, S. (1987) 'Cables of communication', *Journal of Education in Museum* 8: 2–3.

Council for Museums and Galleries in Scotland (1981) *Museum Education in Scotland: A Directory*, Edinburgh: Scottish Education Department, HMSO.

Department of Education and Science (1971) *Museums in Education*, (*Education Survey 12*) London: HMSO.

Department of Education and Science (1986) 'Report by HM Inspectors on a survey of the use some Hertfordshire schools make of museum services, carried out 1–4 July 1985', *HMI Report 40/86*, London: HMSO.

Fairclough, J. (1980) 'Heveningham Hall midsummer 1790: a Suffolk schools project', *Museums Journal* 80(1): 8–9.

Fairclough, J. (1982) 'Heveningham and after', *Journal of Education in Museums* 3: 3–4.

Grinder, A. L. and McCoy, E. S. (1985) *The Good Guide, a Sourcebook for Interpreters: Docents and Tour-guides*, Scotsdale, AZ: Ironwood Press.

Harrison, M. (1942) 'Thoughts on the function of museums in education', *Museums Journal* 42(3): 53.

Hooper-Greenhill, E. (1982) 'Some aspects of a sociology of museums', *Museums Journal* 82(2): 69–70.

Hooper-Greenhill, E. (1985) 'Art gallery audiences and class constraints', *Bullet*: 5–8.

Hooper-Greenhill, E. (1987) 'Museum education comes of age', *Journal of Education in Museums* 8: 6–8.

Hooper-Greenhill, E. (1991) *Museums and Gallery Education*, Leicester: Leicester University Press.

Kavanagh, G. (1988) 'The first world war and its implications for education in British Museums', *History of Education* 17(2): 163–76.

Marr, A. (1988) 'Museums and galleries face hiving off plan', *The Independent*, 15 March.

Nichols, S. K. (ed.) (1984) *Museum Education Anthology: 1973–1983; Perspectives on Informal Learning, a Decade of Roundtable Reports*, Washington, DC: American Association of Museums.

Schools Council (1972) *Pterodactyls and Old Lace: Museums in Education*, London: Evans/Methuen Educational.

Scottish Museums Council (1985) *Museums are for People*, Edinburgh: Scottish Museums Council, HMSO.

Simpson, M. (1987) 'Multi-cultural education and the role of the museum', *Journal of Education in Museums* 7: 1–6.

Sorsby, B. D. and Horne, S. D. (1980) 'The readability of museum labels', *Museums Journal* 80(3): 157–9.

Standing Committee for Museum Services in Hertfordshire (1987) *Museum Education in Hertfordshire: A Development Plan*, Hertfordshire Museums.

Vygotsky, L. S. (1933) 'Play and its role in the mental development of the child', in J. S. Bruner, A. Jolly and K. Sylva (eds) *Play: Its Role in Development and Evolution*, Harmondsworth: Penguin: 537–54.

34

The past, the present and the future: museum education from the 1790s to the 1990s

Eilean Hooper-Greenhill

An overview of the history and development of museum education in Britain. The need for a policy for museum education is discussed. Further information on the need for policies, with detailed advice and case studies can be found in E. Hooper-Greenhill (ed.) (1991) Writing a Museum Education Policy.

At the end of the twentieth century, it is appropriate both to look back on the past and forward to the future.[1]

EDUCATION: THE PRIMARY FUNCTION OF MUSEUMS

Looking back two hundred years, we see the birth of the public museum. The Louvre, in 1792, formed an integral part of the newly democratic state, an essential element in governmental efforts to educate the French people as citizens. The educational role of the museum was carried out in a variety of ways: through thematic and labelled displays, through inexpensive catalogues, and through gallery teaching. The museum became a place to learn, to browse, to meet friends, to talk, to paint and to enjoy exhibitions and events. This museum demonstrated, for the first time, both the immense power of museums to appeal to a vast public, and the enormous inherent educational potential of museums.

This educational potential was a driving force behind the establishment of many museums, particularly, in Britain, the Victoria and Albert Museum. In the 1850s museums were, without question, institutions for public education. Some institutions performed this function better than others, with the work of the museums of Mechanics Institutes being of particular significance. A general consensus insisted on education as a primary function.

THE ESTABLISHMENT OF SCHOOL VISITS

As museums were established by civic authorities and by Literary and Philosophical societies, schools began to make use of them. By the end of the nineteenth century, some aspects of the educational role of museums were becoming formalized. In 1895, in England, through the efforts of Thomas Horsfall and the Committee of Manchester Art Gallery, the day school code was modified to allow visits of school children to museums and galleries to count as valid school attendances.

At the same time, loan services were becoming established and links were being made with education committees and teachers. In relation to school visits, the problem of who actually taught in museums and who paid for this provision has been an issue since the early years. In the early 1900s there was considerable debate as to who was suitably qualified to teach in museums. School teachers felt that curators who knew about the objects should teach, while curators felt that they were not trained as teachers and had other duties that left them little time. Various solutions were arrived at in different museums. This debate over provision and funding has never been entirely resolved and is today a particularly acute problem in local authority museums.

THE EDUCATIONAL ROLE DIMINISHED

At the beginning of the twentieth century, organized provision for visitors other than school groups was limited. As the new century began, the Victorian values that celebrated museums as institutions for educational self-help were already dying, to be replaced by less altruistic attitudes. The self-evident nature of museums for education was lost as curators struggled to establish museums as places where important objects were collected and cared for.

As the century progressed, holistic approaches to the museum as an educational institution in its own right were superseded by piecemeal arrangements for different audience segments, with a concentration on school groups. Soon, 'museum education' was understood to mean children's activities and provision for schools. As all the offficial reports from the 1920s onwards lamented, the main communicative role of museums was not considered. Museum education became a separate sub-specialization in many museums, with different categories of staff, and different objectives and values from the rest of the institution.

EDUCATION EXPANDED AND REVITALIZED

At the end of the twentieth century, a new approach to museums and galleries repositions museum education in a new way, and many new initiatives have emerged.[2] Over the last twenty years, and particularly over the last five, the communicative roles of museums have been explored. These explorations have included discovery galleries. interactive exhibits and new relationships to new audiences.

The new developments in museum communication have been carried out equally by education and by curatorial staff. However, efforts to find new ways of communication with publics have often come about because of individual conviction rather than as a result of planned policies and management. Often, too, education and curatorial staff have been pursuing the same goals without working together. A whole museum approach has not been in evidence, except in a very few cases. The time has now come when these disparate strands must be pulled together. How can relationships be made between, on the one hand, schools provision which must take account of new curricular structures and new funding arrangements, and the provision for a more demanding and active public who want to be involved in dynamic experiences in museums and galleries rather than to be passive viewers? How can scarce resources be maximized at a time when new measures of accountability are being developed for museums and galleries,[3] and when demands seem to increase and diversify daily?

MUSEUM EDUCATION AND COMMUNICATION POLICIES

The new report from the Museums and Galleries Commission[4] recommends (recommendation 47) that all museums should produce education policies based on guidelines that have recently been formulated.[5]

In drawing up a policy for museum education, it will quickly become apparent that a whole museum policy for communication is required. This policy for museum or gallery communication must in turn be informed by the mission statement of the museum. The mission statement of the museum or gallery will, in fact, guide the formulation of policies in all area of practice, including communication, collection management and museum, management (see Figs 34.1 and 34.2)

The development of a communications policy and communication strategies and action plans will enable the identification and implementation of a comprehensive and coherent approach to the many and varied communicative roles of museums and galleries. As the pressure increases for museums to relate more efficiently to their publics it will become necessary to develop new strategies for communication management. The need for coherence across the whole institution to design, marketing, exhibition planning, outreach work, and provision for schools will generate new project management systems, and new understandings of the relationships between these activities. The role that museum education staff will play in these new strategies will vary from institution to institution, depending on the local structures and funding arrangements, the personalities of the individuals concerned, and management approaches. Nonetheless, however the role of museum education staff is defined, it will be essential to understand this role within a framework of museum communication in general.

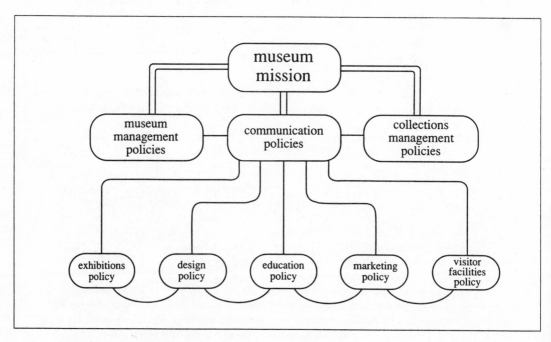

Fig. 34.1   A museum education policy is one of the communications policies

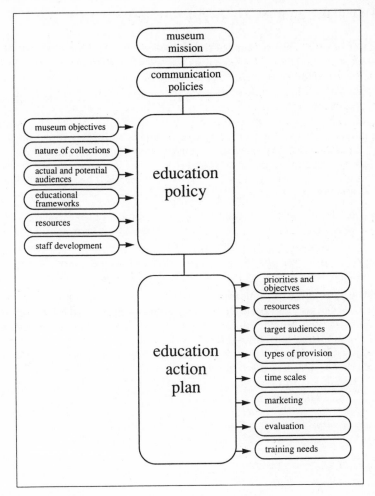

Fig. 34.2 The museum education action plan is developed following the identification of the museum education policy

In drawing up the policy for education in the museum or gallery, therefore, the knotty problem of the definition of 'museum education' will have to be faced. Does this refer to the entire public face of the museum, or only to provision for organized groups? In all too many museums, 'museum education' is still conceptualized as working with school and adult parties, and the consideration of effectiveness of displays, publications and other communicative methods is not addressed. It is of extreme significance that the new guidelines, supported by the Museums and Galleries Commission and funded by the Office of Arts and Libraries, insist on education as a whole museum issue, with a general remit that relates to all aspects of the museum's work.

Conceptually, museum education is now in a position to develop and expand, and to take up a new and strong position in relation to the needs of the various museum publics. A new attention to developing the experience of the museum visitor can be articulated around the contribution of museum education.

MUSEUM EDUCATION AS AUDIENCE ADVOCACY

How can this be done? The concept of the 'audience advocate' has been developed at the National Museum of American History, as part of a more effective system for the management of the development of the experience of the visitor. The audience advocate has the function both within the institution in general, and within the exhibition team in particular, to review events from the point of view of the visitor and potential visitor. The audience advocate helps to improve the general experience of the museum including facilities for physical comfort; the spatial and intellectual orientation; the varieties of pace, style and communicative approaches of successive displays within the building; and the interface between the museum staff and the public. The audience advocate identifies those sections of the potential audience that are not involved because the experience the institution offers does not relate to their specific needs.

A further role for the audience advocate is the management of the evaluation of the experience that museums, galleries and sites can offer. This covers preliminary front-end analysis including audience research, formative evaluation into the effectiveness of communication methods, and summative research to identify how far the exhibition or event has achieved its goals.

The challenge for museum education in the next decade is the development of the management of the visitor experience in all its complex aspects. Many of the methods are still in their infancy in Britain, and in many museums some of the ideas discussed above will seem like fantasies. But museums will only survive through delivering opportunities that are enjoyable, valuable, unique and easy to access, and, also, related to specific target groups. The recent report on the future of Independent museums[6] placed them very firmly within a cut-throat competitive leisure market. The lessons of the report do in fact speak to us all.

This paper first appeared in Journal of Education in Museums *12 (1991), pp. 1–3.*

REFERENCES

1 The ideas in this paper are drawn from the final chapter of Hooper-Greenhill, E. (1991) *Museum and Gallery Education*, Leicester: Leicester University Press.
2 Hooper-Greenhill, E. (ed.) (1989) *Initiatives in Museum Education*, Leicester: Department of Museum Studies, University of Leicester.
3 The National Audit Commission (1991) *The Road to Wigan Pier? Managing Local Authority Museums and Art Galleries*, London: HMSO.
4 Museums & Galleries Commission (1991) *Local Authorities and Museums*, London: HMSO.
5 Hooper-Greenhill, E. (ed.) (1991) *Writing a Museum Education Policy*, Leicester: Department of Museum Studies, University of Leicester.
6 Middleton, V. (1991) *New Visions for Independent Museums*, Association of Independent Museums.

35

Museum multicultural education for young learners

Joseph H. Suina

Multicultural education underpins all education work, including museum education. Symbolic, iconic and enactive learning modes are described, with museums being identified as rich with iconic and enactive learning opportunities. Through their objects museums can provide the knowledge and stimulate the thinking skills, social and academic skills, and values and attitudes that can help achieve society's goal for multicultural living.

Multicultural education has been defined in numerous ways by various groups and individuals for the past twenty years.[1] Some definitions reflect the perspectives of specific disciplines such as psychology, anthropology, and sociology. Others represent the views of professional organizations and accrediting agencies that are concerned with what teachers need to teach and what students need to learn for effective participation in the multiple realities of life. An example of this is the statement on multicultural education issued by the American Association of Colleges for Teacher Education.[2] Still other definitions have been developed and adopted by educators within schools and school districts across the country.

Most teachers recognize the multiple realities that exist within the population of each school and, in many cases, within each classroom. They are also very aware of the demands that society places on them for preparing students for the world in immediate and long-range terms. These demands mean students must learn to communicate and interact with people from a wide range of cultural backgrounds. Thus multicultural education is first of all a process through which individuals develop ways of perceiving, evaluating and behaving within cultural systems unlike their own.[3] Second, multicultural education requires a consideration of the forces that exert powerful influences within local, national, and global settings. These forces will affect priorities and direction in education at all dimensions.

In the final analysis multicultural education is education for all students in what is reality today – a multicultural society. What classroom teachers and museum educators ultimately do depends upon their point of view and their knowledge and ability to provide positive crosscultural experiences and attitudes for their students.

Museums possess a tremendous potential for the development and encouragement of the goals of multicultural education. By their nature and function, museums confront the multiple dimensions of human cultures across time and space. For schools, museums serve as places where people collect, display, and share fragments of the world in which we live. Many focus on nonhuman topics, such as desert ecology, and many more focus on people from different cultures or at least on a part of their life. This slice of culture may be the world of work, or inventions over the years, or a famous artist. Museums are filled with a wealth of real things and replicas of people, places, processes, and events. Most important, museums are places for teaching and learning.

G. W. Maxim describes learning experiences for young students through three modes of contact with the material to be learned.[4] One is through the symbolic mode. The symbolic mode is by far the most prevalent in elementary schools, and it almost always takes the written form. Yet, while literacy is much valued in our society, experts tell us that the symbolic mode is highly abstract and too advanced for many elementary school-age pupils. Their concrete stage of cognitive development may not permit sufficient comprehension of the material even if the word symbols are recognized. The limited experience of most young children further limits the use of the symbolic mode.

The second type of contact is what Maxim refers to as the iconic mode. This mode involves 'imagery' or the use of representations of the actual through physical models, films, and other means. Student-made dioramas or scenes from a unit of study are examples that can be found in classrooms. Pioneer life might be presented by means of a small-scale but lifelike model of a frontier town. Iconic material need not, however, be to scale; the important thing is that it illustrates in realistic form what is being taught. Students may have an opportunity to interact with iconic material through some kind of hands-on experience, but most often they experience it through the medium of film.

The enactive mode is the third form of learning experience. It is learning through the use of authentic items, events, ideas, and people. This form is only rarely used in classrooms, but it does occur when, for example, a community resource person is brought in to do a demonstration or students are taken on a field trip to observe a process. Because the enactive form requires planning, coordination, and possible fees, learners are not often exposed to the 'real thing'.

Yet the iconic and enactive modes are the most successful because younger learners learn best by doing and 'just messing around' with materials and ideas, by experiencing through touching, hearing, seeing, smelling, and tasting. Firsthand interaction with learning materials tantalizes senses not usually exercised in symbolic school experiences. At best, textbooks provide facts and information about names, dates, places, and events, but models and authentic experiences 'breathe life' into the print on the page.

At the same time, museums are incredibly rich with iconic and enactive learning opportunities. They furnish firsthand experiences and allow for learning by discovery. One museum, for example, offers a 'Try-out Tools Kit' of materials from a prehistoric culture. Through their objects museums can provide the knowledge and stimulate the thinking skills, social and academic skills, and values and attitudes that can help achieve society's goals for multicultural living.

While all the kinds of learning that museums foster are important, their promotion of knowledge, values, and attitudes are most essential in the achievement of positive multiculturalism. Since museums frequently present different cultures at various points in time, their contribution to greater understanding and appreciation of different lifeways can be invaluable. Many museums state that their goal is to enhance the visitors' ability to understand, appreciate, and respect the cultures they feature. This goal can be accomplished through responsible and sensitive teaching practices in collecting, exhibiting, and explaining artefacts and ideas.

In museum education, as in any education, the educators are the critical variable. It is they who make the goals of acceptance, appreciation, and respect attainable. As teachers, they provide the inspiration for others to adopt pluralism as a positive goal to strive for.

The critical variable that begins with the teacher requires constant self-scrutiny.[5] Museum educators, like everyone else, have developed their share of biases and prejudices. Educators are often reluctant to admit that they harbour feelings and attitudes that relegate lesser status to certain groups. Like most people, they tend to think of prejudice and racism as blatant expressions of hatred toward those who are different. Since most educators do not perceive themselves as blatant discriminators, they might see themselves as free of prejudice. Yet their 'colour-blind' approach may be nothing more than a veneer of acceptance over true feelings, just below the surface, that remain unexamined and so ready to come into play. Dealing with these biases begins with individual awareness. Once the biases have been recognized, action can be taken to correct prejudices and to develop more suitable attitudes and behaviours.

It is important to recognize that the perception of the culturally different almost always involves some degree of ethnocentrism. The perceiver's own culture naturally tends to be the standard against which others are measured and quite unconsciously accorded superior status.[6] The danger is that such measurement tends to obstruct understanding. Museum educators come into contact with schoolchildren who hold varying degrees of ethnocentrism, and the educators cannot be held responsible for that. They do have to assume responsibility, however, for the impression they leave with the schoolchildren.

It is extremely important that museum educators do not encourage the natural tendency toward ethnocentrism through insensitive dissemination of information. Instead, they should provide a context for the cultures they present, explaining the circumstances of time, place, and situation the people of the culture faced.

For many visitors both young and old, the museum may be the only 'educational' contact they have had with another culture. The impression they get from the museum will persist in future encounters, be they casual conversation about the culture or face-to-face associations with the people and their descendants.

Proper presentation of a culture begins with a sound preparation for working with young people and a thorough knowledge about the culture to be shared. The knowledge should be accurate, up to date, and deep enough to cover what is significant for young learners. The presentation should allow the learners to understand people in terms of universal concerns as well as differing responses. Detailed information helps educators present individual artefacts in broad context. Projectile points, for example, can be presented as important food-gathering tools as well as viable weapons for use against the enemy. Recognizing similar needs and cross-cultural concerns provides a framework within which young learners can achieve understanding and empathy.[7] It is also an effective means for combating stereotypes, which develop by identifying those who are different through only a few isolated, salient features.

Knowledge also provides a basis with which to model respect for the culture. It is very important, for example, to know and respect a culture's prescribed practice for disposal of the dead. Some cultures believe that the spirit of the dead resides in the remains and will never be at rest until the remains are properly placed in the final resting site. Violating mores like these denigrates museums and those who run them. And insensitivity propagates insensitivity. On this issue of human remains, one Asian-American woman remarked, 'Anglos have no sense of right and wrong, and that's just the way they are!' The victim culture will not be the only one to react with disdain on such matters. Many informed groups outside a culture have protested insensitive treatment of one group by another.

265

In situations where it is permissible to share skeletal remains, the sharing should always be with the utmost respect and dignity. An example of a serious breach of respect occurred in a display of the remains of a prehistoric woman at a much-visited museum. The museum staff renamed her Esther. No doubt the idea was that the name would affectionately personalize the woman, but in reality the name encouraged her to become the brunt of modern-day humour among the museum employees. This humour, thought to be clever, was shared, to the delight of museum visitors. One day Esther was adorned with a tourist hat and sunglasses and a cute notation at her side. After a while she became just a joke.

Callous, inhumane treatment of people and cultures should not be condoned, especially by those charged with the task of developing respect and appreciation for world cultures. Consider that none of us would want to have our remains or those of our loved ones on public display, much less be the brunt of jokes no matter how innocent the intent. Second, such treatment not only violates common decency across cultures but repulses many people. But most tragically, it sends a clear message to schoolchildren that it is perfectly acceptable to treat other human beings in this manner as long as they are not a member of one's immediate concern.

Religion is an area that is highly susceptible to misinterpretation and ridicule, particularly religions that are not Judeo-Christian. A religion that is not fully understood may appear to be 'odd' or superstitious. That does not mean, however, that it cannot serve its people or that those who practise it are simpleminded pagans. When shamans are discussed, for example, they are often confused with witch doctors, magicians, and medicine men. Even when the term 'medicine man' is correctly applied, it is often thought to suggest primitivism that closes off understanding. Yet the unexplained cannot be explained through scientific reasoning or modern-day religion. The truth of the matter is that many modern-day religions do not fare much better in their explanations of the metaphysical, resorting to faith as the catchall justification through which the unexplained becomes acceptable.

Some cultures have artefacts that are regarded as highly sensitive and even forbidden because of their deep religious significance. That is, the artefact and the meaning it holds are not to be shared with nonmembers of the culture. In some cases they are not to be shared with members who are not yet privileged: children who have not reached a predetermined stage of maturity or adults who have not been initiated.

While this meaning may seem like nothing more than information and so legitimate for sharing by the general public, museum educators need to take care that nonprivileged members of the culture are not exposed to the meaning. It is not always possible to honour a specific taboo, yet museum educators, particularly when they take a travelling display to a classroom, need to be alert to the composition of the student audience. One example of a forbidden artefact is the kachina doll or model of the Pueblo Indian spirit in the South-west. Kachinas are considered highly sacred and should be respected accordingly. To the people of the Pueblo culture, museum displays or programmes using kachinas violate the taboo that the dolls should not be seen in any form outside the ceremonial context. To them such a display or sharing is as sacrilegious as permitting children to play with a holy communion host would be to Roman Catholics. In both instances the artefacts were intended to be shared only under well-defined conditions. Some cultures represented in museums no longer exist, but there are others whose members maintain traditions, and issues regarding the display and treatment of their artefacts are increasingly sensitive.

There are other taboos of a less severe nature that still need to be acknowledged if not adhered to, especially if it is known that the cultural group will be affected in a personal way. Telling and reading stories designated for seasonal use are examples. One culture may have stories for winter use only. If possible, those should be read in winter only, and the seasonal associations should be explained. Such action is a lesson in respect for all cultures. In this way, children develop the caring and sensitivity that are essential to the values and attitudes of positive multicultural education.

In summary, museums offer young learners experiences that are highly desirable for their developmental level and have the potential to involve multiple senses in a discovery learning format. The content of this museum learning is often the culture of a people. Thus museum educators are in an excellent position to develop ideas and attitudes critical to the success of young learners in understanding and ultimately participating in our multicultural world.

This paper first appeared in Journal of Museum Education *15(1) (1990), pp. 12–15.*

NOTES

1 Sleeter, C. E. and Grant, C. A. (1987) 'An analysis of multicultural education in the United States', *Harvard Educational Review* 57(4): 421–40; Hernandez, Hilda (1989) *Multicultural Education: A Teacher's Guide to Content and Process*, Columbus, Ohio: Merrill.
2 American Association of Colleges for Teacher Education (1972–3) *AACTA Statement on Multicultural Education*, Washington, DC: AACTA.
3 Ramsey, P. G. (1982) 'Multicultural education in early childhood', *Young Children* 37(2): 13–24.
4 Maxim, G. W. (1987) *Social Studies and the Elementary School Child*, Columbus, Ohio: Merrill: 267–8.
5 Gold, M. J., Grant, C. A. and Rivlin, H. N. (1977) *In Praise of Diversity: A Resource Book for Multicultural Education*, Washington, DC: Teacher Corps, Association of Teacher Educators.
6 Ramsey, P. G. (1987) *Teaching and Learning in a Diverse World: Multicultural Education for Young Children*, New York: Teachers College Press.
7 Moyer, J. E. and Engelbrecht, Guillermina (1977) 'Multicultural education: where do we begin?' *Childhood Education* 53 (March): 241–4.

36

Children, teenagers and adults in museums: a developmental perspective

Nina Jensen

A developmental perspective based on the work of Jean Piaget and Erik Erikson is used to describe the different needs of children, teenagers and adults in museum learning. Common to all is the tenet that our perceptions are based on our individual and unique histories and experiences. None the less, there are broad similarities in the ways in which people of different life-stages view the world. Knowledge of these can help with programme planning.

This article is based on the panel 'Museum Audiences: The Educator's Perspective', presented at the 1981 AAM Annual Meeting. The panelists, museum educators who have applied developmental theory to their work with museum audiences, were Peggy Cole, director of the Fieldston Lower School, Riverdale, NY, and formerly on the faculty of the Bank Street College of Education, New York, NY who spoke on elementary school children; Kathryne Andrews, manager of School and Youth Services at the Brooklyn Museum, Brooklyn, NY, who spoke on teenagers; Adrienne Horn, museum consultant in adult education and programme coordinator for the Center for Museum Studies, John F. Kennedy University, San Francisco, Calif., who spoke on adults; and Theodore Katz, chief of the Division of Education at the Philadelphia Museum of Art, Philadelphia, Pa., who spoke on creativity and motivation. The panel was cochaired by Nina Jensen, acting director of the Museum Education Program at the Bank Street College of Education, and Susan Reichman, former director of the programme. This article has been a collaborative effort of the panelists and was edited by Nina Jensen.

Museum programmes must relate to the life experiences of the audiences they seek to motivate and engage. As museum staff members come to understand their audiences in greater depth, they can create programmes more directly relevant to them.

Traditionally, museum audiences have been considered demographically – by age, ethnicity, occupation, and so forth. There is, however, another perspective – that of developmental theory. The term 'development' refers to the sequential changes in circumstance and perspective that all people experience over time. Loosely linked to chronological age, developmental growth is organized in distinct stages or eras through which all people pass, pushed by a combination of physiological maturation and increased understandings, abilities and knowledge. Developmental theorists whose work has important implications for museum programming include Jean Piaget and Erik Erikson. While their ideas have played a crucial role in shaping current educational theories in schools, their impact has been much less widely felt in museums.

An important tenet of developmental psychology is that all experiences are a unique function of our individual past. Since everyone has a different history and a different way of looking at the world, no two individuals, even of the same age, family or socio-economic background, have identical perceptions. On the other hand, our experiences also have some important elements of commonality. There are broad descriptors of how infants are different from 5-year-olds, 5-year-olds from 20-year-olds and 20-year-olds from 50-year-olds. These descriptors are useful to educators.

This article will examine the characteristics of three major age groups – elementary school children, teenagers and adults – and their implications for museum programming. Issues of creativity and motivation that cut across developmental lines will also be considered.

ELEMENTARY SCHOOL CHILDREN

Because the experiences of adults in museums are qualitatively different from those of children, it is often difficult for adults to understand the museum visit from the perspective of the child. An important idea from developmental psychology, with implications for children's programming in museums is that children bring their own experiences and conceptions of the world with them. These conceptions determine how they receive what is presented to them and what they will learn from it. For example, Michael, an 8-year-old intensely interested in the Middle Ages, was taken to see the armour at the Metropolitan Museum of Art. A week later he asked if people had metal in the Middle Ages. When reminded about the armour he had seen in the museum, he replied, 'Yes, but what does that have to do with the Middle Ages?'

This question suggests that children have only the vaguest ideas about how an object gets into a museum and why it is there and even what a museum is. It illustrates how our life experiences limit our ability to understand objects in the context of a museum. It also suggests the errors in adults' assumptions about what children experience. Despite his interest and background Michael did not understand that the objects in a museum come from another historical period. He has been in the world only eight years, and the armour has been there a lot longer. His experience tells him that something old is dirty, whereas the armour at the Metropolitan is polished and shiny – attributes he associates with new things. Michael's confusion illustrates a phenomenon described by Jean Piaget – that perception is shaped and limited by experience.

Another important idea from developmental psychology is that interaction is the most powerful mode of learning. Interaction is the opposite of passivity. We do not simply bring experiences to the world, nor do we perceive what is there in pure form. We impose our experiences on the world, be it an object or another person. In terms of Kantian epistemology, the basis of Piagetian theory, 'The mind gives the law to nature'. Knowledge is acquired in a continuous process of accommodating prior expectations and beliefs to new realities learned through interactive experiences.

Learning involves conflict between a person's conception of reality and new encounters with the real. This conflict or dissonance leads to what Piaget calls 'accommodation'. Children (and adults also) are constantly restructuring their ideas about the world as new information is received. This dynamic process between the learner and his or her experiences is basic to what happens in museums.

Words are confusing to children who do not have experiences to back them up. Piagetian theory suggests that ideas are formed first, words second – not the other way around. But words have a special seduction for children because their language acquisition is at an all-time high. Most children who have heard Peter Rabbit stories have chamomile tea in their vocabulary, but their ideas of what it is are often confused, even humorous, because they have no experience with it. One can find out about chamomile tea only by drinking it; it has a particular colour, smell and taste. Because children can recite words by rote without understanding their meanings, they may seem to known more than they do. Learning moves from the concrete to the abstract more slowly that many educators care to admit. Because their thinking is so concrete, children often are confused about what is real and what is representational. They can become frightened by images of things; the distinction between reality and fantasy is not always clear. A costumed mannequin in the Brooklyn Museum's eighteenth-century period rooms magically came to life for a fourth grader as he exclaimed, 'Look! I saw her move!'

Elementary school children have trouble dealing with the past because their understanding of time periods is incomplete. Since many museum programmes and collections require an understanding of the context of historical periods, and since most children have not got this understanding worked out yet, they make the most amazing connections between things that have no relationship. For example, a group of 10-year-olds had just completed a detailed study of how Christopher Columbus had preserved food during his voyage to the New World. They had learned that the food was hung over the side of the ship to dry in the air. When the teacher asked the children what the sailors used for containers, some children thought they used baggies.

Children experience a sense of powerlessness in museums, as they do in many aspects of their lives. Unlike other age groups, they are rarely in museums by free choice. For the most part adults tell children what to do; adults have control, while children wish that they did. By offering children choices during museum visits, such as allowing them to choose a work of art on which to focus, educators can give them some feeling of power and command over their museum experience.

In addition, museum programmes for children should focus on only a few objects of interest to them and present ideas about those objects that are graspable and relevant. Otherwise the artifacts in museums will be for children like so many other things in their lives – simply there, without explanation and outside their control. A selective and limited focus will foster in children a sense of mastery and command in a potentially strange and overwhelming setting and will increase the chances of their really understanding the ideas behind the words and objects to which they are introduced.

TEENAGERS

Developmental theory plays an important role in understanding the museum experiences of teenagers as well as children. These experiences are necessarily modified by the cultural setting in which teenagers find themselves, a setting shaped by their families, their peers and the larger aspects of American society in the late twentieth century. The reasons teenagers visit museums less often than younger children or adults are suggested by a study of teenagers and museums done at the Brooklyn Museum.[1] The teen years are a volatile point in emotional development. Teenagers are especially sensitive to condescension, and museum staff who act in patronizing ways merely confirm their opinion that museums are 'not for them'. Preoccupied with their own independence and coming separation from their families, they often reject museum visits because of their close association with family values.

Teenagers are, physically speaking, adults. Capable of giving birth or carrying a gun to war, they are, at the same time, financially and intellectually dependent on their families. They live with the continual contradiction that while they have the capacity to be on their own, apart from their families, most in fact do live at home. Required to comply with family viewpoints and roles in exchange for financial support, teenagers often feel conflicts of allegiance.

It is in their groups that teenagers develop a sense of themselves as individuals. Thus, for most teenagers a vital aspect of their school life is social as well as academic. Museums are also viewed as places in which to socialize with friends. In fact, visiting museums without friends holds little interest for them. Over two-thirds of the teenagers interviewed in the Brooklyn Museum study were significantly more interested in museum visits when they could attend with friends.

Because nonacademic clubs and interest groups are voluntary, they serve important social needs for teenagers. Groups play a very large role in teenagers' lives, and teenagers devote enormous amounts of time to them. In seeking teenage audiences, museums might productively turn to these groups, both within and beyond the school setting. Teenagers for the Brooklyn Museum study, for instance, came from voluntarily attended youth and community groups. Interest groups can be formed by the museum itself. In conjunction with an exhibition of documentary photographs, the Brooklyn Museum invited photography students from several high schools to create their own exhibition. One of the most important aspects of the programme was simply the opportunity for these teenagers to meet and talk shop with peers from other schools.

Today's teenagers have a practical outlook on life. School is often perceived as a means to an end – getting into college and getting a good job in the face of high unemployment and economic instability. The Brooklyn Museum study found teenagers to be singularly lacking in curiosity and without access to an aesthetic, humanistic or historical framework to help them appreciate the objects a museum. Their life experience is necessarily narrow. Museum educators are thus challenged to present programmes that focus on universal human experiences and that teach the tools or frames with which to think and perceive. We need to help teenagers understand, for instance, that art and history can connect them to the thoughts and feelings of others. As they learn how artists have expressed feelings about power, conflict, war, justice and love, they may be helped to understand these and other issues in relationship to their own lives.

Despite their lack of curiosity, teenagers have the capacity to be imaginative and thoughtful and to extend themselves into the lives of others. They need opportunities for self-expression and creative learning. When asked what they did like about museums, teenagers in the study stated that museums gave them opportunities to 'have conversations about important issues' and to 'absorb ideas about other cultures into our own thoughts'. One 16-year-old girl commented that 'seeing a painting is like reading a poem'.

Perhaps most of all, teenagers want and need opportunities to learn in ways that support their self-esteem and growing independence. Having developed the ability to think at least somewhat analytically and abstractly, they need to know that their ideas will be listened to and respected in the museum setting.

ADULTS

Over the years attention to human growth, learning and development has focused on childhood and adolescence. Recent changes in our society and its values, however,

271

together with an ageing population, have created a greater awareness of learning and development in adult life.

Adult learning is different from that of children. Malcolm Knowles, a scholar widely respected in the field of adult education, has explained the characteristics of adult learners that make them different.[2] To children experience is external, something that happens to them; to adults personal experience has defined their individual identity. Because adults have a richer foundation of experience than children, new material they learn takes on heightened meaning as it relates to past experiences. For example, because middle-aged and older people have a personal sense of history – they have lived through events – they relate to history in a way that few youngsters can. Adults see how various social problems have recurred during their lifetime; they see vital movements and issues with an insight that children cannot have.

For children, learning tends to be teacher directed; children learn what is taught by parents and teachers. Adults, on the other hand, are independent learners and search for education programmes that answer their own questions instead of those of someone else. They seek learning experiences related to their changing roles as workers, parents, spouses and leisure time users. Adults enroll in classes or participate in programmes related to their personal interests or to acquire skills and understandings that will help them answer immediate questions. Children, by contrast, view education as something to be used in the future. For adults education is an independent and personal choice. Since they take responsibility for their own learning, they expect excellence in education programmes.

While adult learning ability may remain relatively stable throughout adult life, there is still substantial growth and development. The popular conception of adulthood as a time of little change over the course of many years has been challenged by the findings of developmental psychology. Knowles points out that adults have a 'readiness to learn' which, at its peak, presents a ' teachable moment'. Just as a child cannot walk until he has crawled and his leg muscles are strong enough, so adults, too, have their phases of growth, development and teachable moments. The development of adults, however, is not primarily physiological; it is related to their changing social roles.

Adults experience developing patterns of interest as they move through the life cycle. Generally speaking, vocational and family life are the primary concerns of young adults (ages 18–35) as they seek to establish themselves in work and at home. In middle adult-hood (ages 35–55) these concerns decrease in favour of interests in health and civic and social activities. As they near retirement adults become occupied with interpreting culture and life with the health problems of advancing age.

The unique perspectives of adulthood have implications for museum programme themes and topics. Themes from the humanities can be of particular interest to adults who, because of their own experiences, may identify personally with the subjects presented. The Toledo Museum of Art's programme 'The New American Scene' examined various aspects of the life-styles and art of contemporary American society. Some natural history museums have used the humanities to link their collections with life-related issues. The Carnegie Museum of Natural History in Pittsburgh has used the theme 'Becoming Human' to explain the influence of biological and cultural forces on the processes of human development.[3] Relating museum programmes and collections to the broad threads of human experience is one means of bringing objects to life in a way that is emotionally stimulating and meaningful to a broad spectrum of adult audiences.

In considering the stages of adult development, it is important to recognize that the adult population is not homogeneous. Obviously many variables, such as occupation, sex, social class, income level, educational background and ethnicity, further define adult groups. In programming for its exhibition *Manifestations of Shiva*, the Seattle Art Museum appealed to adults with various interests and at different stages of their lives. Elements of the programme, which dealt with the culture of India – its music, literature, history, religions, art and daily life – were adapted to different segments of the public, such as families, senior citizens and scholars. Museums can conduct 'needs assessments' in order to determine what programmes are of interest to their potential adult audiences.

Regardless of the motivation – the particular reason for the 'teachable moment' – it is important for museums to capitalize on the readiness of adults to learn. Adults bring their own expectations, goals and experiences to museums, and museum programmes should recognize and accommodate them.

PROGRAMMING FOR CHILDREN, TEENAGERS AND ADULTS

Accepting the implications of developmental theory as it pertains to potential partici-pants in museum programmes, we face the challenge of providing rich encounters for diverse audiences from our equally diverse collections. Is the ultimate implication of developmental theory that there should be separate exhibitions or programmes for separate audiences? Can a single programme reach all three groups?

This is what the Division of Education of the Philadelphia Museum of Art set out to discover through a programme entitled 'Art as a Reflection of Human Concerns'.[4] As the basic goal was to produce a programme that would make possible significant and interest-ing experiences for visitors of all ages, the subject had to be broad. Seven themes were selected – family, humour, religion, ageing, death, birth and love – each to be considered for a period of one month. Topics focused on the vital importance of these themes, not only in subject matter but as inspiration for human creativity. Consideration of developmental theory helped staff members to design specific activities introducing the monthly theme to various age groups. Gallery talks, films, workshops, concerts, plays and lectures were planned and presented specifically for children, teenagers, adults and family groups. These related the monthly theme to selected objects from the museum's collections. Information sheets as guides to independent study were available as well as other handout material that visitors could pick up around the museum each month. Staff members developed these 'pick-me-ups', each of which presented a brief, humanistic interpretation of a work of art selected from the collection.

For elementary school children, programmes combined education with entertainment so children would want to participate instead of feeling their visit was one more activity forced upon them by adults. During the Family month children viewed such films as *The Red Balloon* and *The Golden Fish*; during Humour, they participated in a live mime presentation. Peter Pan came to life in a performance during the month on Ageing. Even the programme concerning Death – a theme that might be expected only to frighten youngsters – became an enjoyable learning experience through an afternoon of story-telling and folk songs.

For teenagers, preeminently concerned with asserting their own identities and indepen-dence, programmes were designed to consider what the world looks like when coloured by the strong private visions of artists. Teen activities were not structured around group sessions with their atmosphere of authority. Instead young people were given printed programme material and directed to the galleries on their own. One programme appealed to their interest in personal identity by asking them to match self-portraits in the galleries with written passages either by or about the portrait subjects. The 'detective work' aspect of the activity further appealed to their sense of challenge and gamesmanship.

For adults, programmes aimed to cut across divisions of social class, cultural interests and race. Lectures by visiting scholars on topics such as 'Are Pictures to be Smashed or Worshipped?' 'Ageing: East and West' and 'Family: Fragmented or Whole?' further reinforced programme themes, as did gallery talks like 'Humour in Oriental Art' and 'Ageing and Agelessness in the Painting of Thomas Eakins'. *Beauty and the Beast*, *The Clowns* and *Ulysses* were among the films shown during the course of the programme. A visitor survey administered at these programmes confirmed that most people attended because of their interest in the topics rather than in specific speakers or works of art. Because topics such as birth, family, ageing and death speak directly to the developmental concerns of all adults, the programme successfully attracted a large and diverse new audience. Over half those attending the programmes were not museum members, and significant numbers were not regular museum goers. Variations in age, sex, race and level of education were much greater in those attending these programmes than in more traditional museum offerings.

William James said,

> Every new experience must be disposed of under some old head. The great point is to find the head which has to be least altered to take it in. . . . The great maxim in pedagogy is to knit every new piece of knowledge on to a preexisting curiosity – i.e., to assimilate its matter in some way to what is already known![5]

An important implication of developmental theory as it pertains to museum programmes is that the museum environment must reward the individual's attention. The enjoyment of, and learning from, museum collections will vary according to the individual's perception and learning abilities. We must know our audiences, their interests and their abilities, in order to offer programmes and exhibitions with which they will identify. We must respect the value of initial 'engaging' activities; from the immediately attractive and easily accessible, visitors can proceed to consideration of the content of collections in more sophisticated and subtle forms. With attention to developmental theories, exhibitions and programmes can be designed to reveal the richness of museum collections not only as ends and objects of study, but also as beginnings, subjects for wonder and exploration, insights into one's own identity and potential.

NOTES

1 Andrews, Kathryne and Asia, Carolyn (1979) 'Teenagers' attitudes about art museums', *Curator* 23: 229. This article is a report on a study, funded by the National Endowment for the Humanities, on the interests and needs of Brooklyn's teenagers and the development of museum programmes.
2 Knowles, Malcolm S., (1977) *The Modern Practice of Adult Education*, 8th edn, New York: Association Press.
3 The programmes developed by the Toledo Museum of Art and the Carnegie Museum of Natural History are described in detail in Zipporah W. Collins (ed.) (1981) *Museums, Adults and the Humanities: A Guide for Educational Programming*, Washington, DC: American Association of Museums: 177–97, 211–18.
4 'Art as a reflection of human concerns' is described in detail in ibid.: 236–56.
5 Quoted in William James (1966) *Psychology: Briefer Course*, New York: Collier Books: 332–3.

37

Teaching with collections

Lynn Plourde

A classroom teacher with specific skills in language teaching outlines how she used a collection of teddy bears with 6-year olds. The description of the initial methods are supplemented by other ideas on ways to use collections. The ideas suggested show how objects are of value in working with young children. The methods are transferable from the classroom to the museum. Equally, they could be adapted for hints for follow-up work after a museum visit.

How well I remember that unruly first grade. I went into their classroom once a week for an hour to teach listening and speaking activities – and oh how I dreaded it. Children constantly fought with each other, several regularly threw temper tantrums, and three or four were *always* out of their seats. I was dreading that day's activity with the class. But instead, a miracle happened – the children were angels. They sat quietly, listened eagerly and then asked stimulating questions. What was the activity that caused this major transformation? It was the use of collections!

COLLECTIONS IN THE CLASSROOM

On that particular day I brought in my collection of teddy bears. I told each bear's name, where the bear came from, and any special features about the bear. The children loved hearing about Gregory the little Scottish bear with the plaid bow, and the bride bear complete with veil and garter, named MiMi after its French owner. The children learned to tell the difference between handmade and manufactured bears (the joints on the bears, how facial features were attached, the type of stitching). They learned new vocabulary words about the bears and their garments: knickers, patchwork, ascot, childproof, suspenders, miniature. And they learned some history about the teddy bear (whom it was named after, when it originated).

After speaking for 15 minutes about my collection of teddy bears, I gave each child a chance to hold the bears and ask questions. Then we voted: Which is your favourite teddy bear? I asked each person to have a *reason* for selecting a favourite bear 'Just because' wasn't reason enough. A child had to have a reason such as 'The Santa bear is my favourite because he is the only one to wind up and play music. And Christmas music puts me in a good mood.'

By this point the children seemed to have a good concept of a collection. They knew that a collection is more than a matter of having many similar objects. You should become a mini-expert on those objects.

Next I randomly divided the group into smaller groups of three to five children. In their groups, they were asked to reach a joint decision about what they would collect as a group during the next two weeks. Reaching group consensus was hard. These six-year-olds needed guidelines on how to make a decision. For example, I explained that it wasn't fair to collect expensive items that some children might not be able to afford. If a group could not come to agreement on what to collect, they they simply used the good old American method of voting. I also suggested a number of possible collectibles to groups unable to generate their own ideas.

rocks
baseball cards
types of cloth
magazines
kinds of paper
insects
stamps
stickers
flowers
stuffed animals

Children left that day knowing what they were going to collect and with the following note for their parents:

Dear Parent,

Your child is learning about collections in school. He/she is part of a group that will be collecting . . . . during the next two weeks.

You can help your child by encouraging him/her to find as many objects as possible to add to the collection. At the end of two weeks, your child will be able to bring home whatever he/she has added to the collection. Your child may then want to keep adding to this collection on his/her own.

Thanks for your cooperation.

Over the next two weeks, the children's collections steadily grew. Each group had a special box or shelf in the room for storing its collection. Children eagerly told others about ongoing additions to collections and asked questions about each other's items.

At the end of the two weeks, each group gave a 5- to 10-minute oral presentation about its collection. Each group was anxious for a turn, but nonetheless children listened intently to other groups. Children learned not only by collecting themselves, but through the collections of others as well.

MORE WAYS TO USE COLLECTIONS

A visiting collector

Invite another adult into your class to share a collection. This is a wonderful opportunity to include parents, grandparents, older siblings, older children in the school, and other community people in the educational programme you provide. Many adults and older children collect things that they would be eager to 'show off' to your students. It doesn't matter what they collect – I've seen students fascinated by collections of decoys, music boxes, wind chimes, and hats. You could even have a different collector visit your class each month.

Similarities – differences contest

Divide the class into two teams. Using any collection, select two objects from it. Show these two objects to the class. One team must then jointly brainstorm to think of as many similarities as possible between the two objects. The other team must brainstorm differences. See which group has the longest list. Continue with two other objects if you have time, encouraging children to come up with more similarities and differences each time.

Sorting collections

Have several 'touchable' collections such as buttons or writing utensils available at centres in your room. Invite children to sort the collections into as many different groups as possible. For example, in a button collection, students might sort buttons into groups based on their size, colour, number of holes, material, purpose, and so on.

Which one?

Have the whole class bring in a specific type of object, such as toy cars. Set up the collection of toy cars in front of the class. Then give each child a turn to describe one car and ask the others to guess which one she or he described. For example, a child might say, 'I'm thinking of a car that is made out of metal and plastic, is medium-sized, and has decals on both sides. Which car am I thinking of?'

Imaginary collections

Once children have had an opportunity to collect real objects, let them try their skills with imaginary collections. You might share one with them first. Here's my imaginary collection. Remember that since it's imaginary I can create whatever my brain can dream up. Here's my imaginary collection of Talking Insects:

Mushy Mosquito

This mosquito is always saying mushy things like when she bites you and says 'You've got the best blood in the whole world, darling'.

Silly Spider

He loves to tell jokes.

Angry Ant

He's always angry. For a little thing, he can speak in a very loud angry voice.

Then ask children to create their own imaginary collections. Remind them to give names to all the things in their collections. As each girl or boy finishes, have them find a partner to tell about the imaginary collection and to hear about the partner's collection.

OTHER BENEFITS

Besides the obvious benefits of teaching with collections (developing vocabulary skills, questioning skills, oral presentation skills), children will learn some other, more subtle skills. They will take pride in their own collections and readily see that collections are 'special' to others too. The young children I've worked with are very careful when handling another's collection. They truly *respect* each other's work.

Some children have begun to collect objects seriously after beginning a collection in class. Two years later when they see me, they eagerly talk about their still expanding collection. These children may be developing a lifelong hobby. And isn't that what education is all about – lifelong learning?

38

Improving worksheets
Gail Durbin

Many people dislike worksheets, arguing that they result in limited experiences which focus on filling in the sheet rather than anything more productive. However, if well-designed and carefully piloted, worksheets can structure a museum visit in terms of space used, time spent, knowledge gained and objects looked at, all of which are essential.

This article discusses how to plan and write good worksheets. It discusses the various issues involved including practicalities, questioning techniques, skills involved in completing the sheet, and relationship with the curriculum. A useful annotated bibliography is included.

It is very easy to pick holes in worksheets and it is a very skilled task to design good ones. The purpose of this article is not to rehearse the arguments for and against worksheets; this has been covered elsewhere (Fry 1987). I start from the premise that worksheets are one of many methods of interpreting museum collections. Large numbers of teachers use and feel comfortable with worksheets so it is worth spending time assessing them critically and look for ways of making them more effective.

This article suggests five areas to consider when assessing a worksheet. These are:

Practicalities
Questioning techniques
Variety
Developing a sense of the whole
Curriculum context

PRACTICALITIES

There are a host of minor things that can stop a worksheet being effective. These are obvious to those with experience but pitfalls for the unprepared. It would be wise to examine worksheets for the following:

- Are a large number of children going to be focused on one small space or item at once? Can the sheet be designed so that children can be spread round the space more evenly to avoid the frustration of not being able to see?
- What else might stop the child seeing the object referred to? Are the cases too high? Is there a reflection on the glass at child height?
- Is it clear where the answer is to be found? Name the room, gallery or case as

appropriate. Give clear instructions when children have to move to another location.

- Is it clear what kind of answer is expected? Say if notes are wanted rather than continuous text. Children with little experience of the worksheet approach will find it easier if you provide a box for a drawing to be done in or dotted lines for a written answer. If you are expecting several answers then numbered spaces are a useful hint to children to keep looking.
- Look at the level of vocabulary and the length of the text. Does it suit the age and ability range aimed at? Keep sentences short and vocabulary simple. The difficulty of coping with a strange place, a clipboard and the general excitement may well depress a child's reading level.

QUESTIONING TECHNIQUES

The nature of the questions asked are at the heart of the success of a worksheet and it is worth spending time analysing them. Here are some questions on *Goldilocks and the Three Bears*:

1 How many bears are there in the story?
2 What is porridge?
3 How would you have felt if you were Baby Bear?
4 Should Goldilocks be punished for breaking the chair?
5 Who went into the house where the three bears lived?
6 What happened first in the story?
7 What happened first after Baby Bear's chair broke?
8 Do you think the three bears will lock their door the next time they leave their house?
9 Is this story like another bear story you've read?
10 Are all little girls like Goldilocks?

Some of these questions require simple recall of the story and low level thinking (nos. 1, 5, 6, 7), some require opinion and higher level thinking (nos. 3, 4, 8, 9, 10) and one (no. 2) requires previous knowledge, for no amount of careful listening to the story will provide any more information than the fact that porridge is edible and can be the wrong temperature!

An effective worksheet will probably require both low and high level thinking but it is generally easier to think of low level questions. Devising more stretching ones take time and practice. However, you will find that small adjustments to the phrasing of a question can change its nature. 'How many bears are there in the story?' could become, for example, 'Is the number of bears in the story significant?'

Questions that require only a yes/no answer can generally be upgraded to become more interesting. Similarly questions that require counting are useful only if the information is needed to answer a further question. Avoid questions that require guessing. Make the activity more precise by either asking for an estimate or an opinion.

In *The Good Guide: A Sourcebook for Interpreters, Docents and Tour Guides* Alison Grinder and Sue McCoy outline a four-level question classification. The types they identify are:

Memory questions
Convergent questions

Divergent questions
Judgemental questions

Memory questions

These questions seek a single right answer. They are the narrowest type of question requiring the lowest level of thinking. They require facts, precise recall, recognition, descriptions of previously obtained factual knowledge or observation. The answer may often be supplied in one word. The question may begin with:

'How many . . . '
'What is the . . . '
'Name the . . . '
'Which one . . . '

Convergent questions

These seek the most appropriate answer or the best answer. They focus on specifics and on what is already known or perceived. They may require explanations, comparisons or interrelationships. A higher level of thinking is required than for the memory questions. The questions may be phased as:

'What does . . . do?'
'How is this . . . like that one?'
'How do . . . and . . . differ?'

Divergent questions

These questions allow for more than one possible right answer. They demand imaginative thinking, and require the formulation of a hypothesis and the ability to use knowledge to solve problems.

Prediction, inference and reconstruction may be needed. The questions may be phrased as:

'What if . . . '
'How many ways . . . '
'Imagine that . . . '

Judgemental questions

These provide personal and possibly unique answers. They require choice and evaluation and demand the formulation of an opinion, value or belief. A view may have to be justified and evidence be assembled to defend a position. Criteria may need to be applied or standards of judgement developed. This is the broadest type of question requiring the highest level of thinking. The questions may be phrased as:

'What do you think about . . . '
'Do you agree that . . . '
'What is your reaction to . . . '
'Which do you think . . . and why?'

Applied to an exhibit displaying a pair of hair powdering bellows the classification might produce the following questions. A progressively more taxing worksheet could be designed by selecting questions from each level.

Memory

What is this?
What is it made from?

Convergent

What was the purpose of this object?
How did these bellows work?

Divergent

How could the design of these bellows be improved?
What does this object tell us about the society that produced it?

Judgemental

Do you think it is important to spend public money preserving items like these?

Do you think this would be more appropriately displayed as a work of art, as an example of craftsmanship or as a social history object?

Good questions for worksheets are not just stimulating ones, they have to be appropriate too. The whole point of going to a site or museum is to learn from physical things and the questions should direct attention towards the object not the label. It is, of course, often easier to frame a question on the label because it is likely to provide specific facts and figures. Asking questions about the object requires an understanding of the potential of artefacts to reveal information about the societies that made, used and preserved them. The main emphasis of the work should be on observation not reading.

Consider how far previous knowledge is essential to completing the sheet. On one level the success and the sophistication of the task accomplished in the museum will depend on the child's previous knowledge and preparation. A child who has an understanding of historical sources and their range will be better placed to make an assessment of a specific object or display. But there are other types of question requiring previous knowledge that should be avoided. 'Who built Hampton Court?' cannot be answered by observation of the building. You either know the answer or you don't. 'What year was Hampton Court built?' presents similar problems. If a question can be better answered away from the site in the comfort of the school library then omit it. Examine your worksheets carefully for these kind of question as they creep in almost unnoticed.

Questions need to be unambiguous and it is helpful to have only one question in a sentence. One technique for achieving greater clarity is to start the question with a verb in the imperative as this is an instant pointer to the action required e.g., 'List the differences between X and Y' rather than 'What differences are there between X and Y?'. Other suitable verbs might be draw, discuss, explain or estimate.

GCSE has made teachers more aware of the questions they ask. The desire to encourage children to show what they can do and the need to differentiate levels of attainment has sharpened practice and will have a beneficial effect on worksheet design.

VARIETY

A well constructed worksheet will be varied in content and approach. Where appropriate you may want to provide variety through games or exercises such wordsearches, crosswords, joining matching pairs, annotating, completing sentences or drawings, underlining, sequencing or spotting similarities or differences.

Call on as many different skills as possible not just verbal ones. Drawing should play an important part at all ages. Since observation is at the root of work in museums an activity that slows a child up and keeps the eye engaged will be valuable. It is also important to learn that there are other ways of conveying information than through the written word and that drawing for recording is a different sort of activity from drawing as art. You might ask simply for an object to be recorded or you might set a task that required selection such as asking for a drawing of something the child found beautiful or details of decorative style.

Mathematical skills can be brought into play. Measuring and estimating are useful ways of recording buildings and room layouts and give a good opportunity for reinforcing classroom skills. Dealing with scale and devising methods of working out weights and volumes all have a place. Children could, for example, work out how far a housemaid walked to provide hot washing water for all or what volume of water had to be carried to fill a slipper bath.

The design of a worksheet will also provide variety and should motivate. Good layout and interesting lettering sets high standards of expectation. Illustrations may be appropriate where they are central to the activity but beware of using them simply as space fillers or of letting them discourage children's own efforts.

DEVELOPING A SENSE OF THE WHOLE

One of the great dangers with worksheets is that you learn to design practical and varied activities directed through well framed questions and yet the children still only end up with a collection of disparate facts and ideas. The thought process behind the worksheet may be more obvious to the writer than to the student. Try writing down the answers to your own worksheet and see if they retain any sort of coherence.

This problem can be dealt with in a number of ways. Firstly there needs to be a reason for collecting the information that is as clear to the children as it is to the teacher. It is important that the need to know has been created and that the children have to apply their new knowledge in some way.

The children may need to do research in order to make an accurate model or put on a play. They may be trying to find out what kind of person lived in that room or worked at that place. They might be trying to see whether a television play on medieval life was accurate. They could be looking for the strengths and weaknesses of archaeological evidence. This can be made clear at the outset and then the questions on the worksheet guide them to the displays to use and the information they need. They become a form of guided note-making and the ultimate aim will be for children to generate their own questions and recording method.

An alternative approach is problem solving in role outlined by Barbara Roberts (1988). By giving children a problem to look at through a specific pair of eyes the questionnaire approach becomes redundant. Instead the worksheet sets the problem and can be used for recording the solution. With care it is possible to allow the children to establish their own criteria through discussion so that much of the work of thinking is shifted from the teacher to the child. The article did not give many examples so here are a few designed for use at Osborne House on the Isle of Wight but easily transferable to other sites and circumstances.

> You are a stage designer working on a play based on a murder in a country house. You have decided to base your work on Osborne. You still need a scene for a party and a scene for a plot to be hatched. Choose the most appropriate spots and make some sketches of the architecture and the furniture to help you when you return to your studio.

> You are the curator and you have been told that the load on the floor is too great. Which pieces of furniture are you going to put into store? You are anxious not to spoil the atmosphere of the house for visitors.

> *Next*'s new household range has been enormously successful. They have asked you to design a range of frames and mirrors based on Victorian designs. You have decided to use Osborne for your inspiration. Make some sketches. Which three designs are you going to recommend?

> You are researching the pictures for a book on conservation. You still need examples of things that have and have not been protected from light, touch and general wear. Can Osborne provide you with any suitable illustration?

CURRICULUM CONTEXT

Although this section comes last in this article it should come first in the mind of the teacher who should have a very clear idea of why the visit is being made and how it fits in with the curriculum.

Some sites refuse to provide any written material at all saying that the only effective material is that written by the teacher in the context of the topic and approach being followed. Ideally written material should come from a discussion between the teacher and the museum education department where the teacher's knowledge of their class and the curriculum can be married to the museum educator's knowledge of the collection and specialization in wringing ideas and information from apparently mute objects. There may, however, be pressures of time and there is still a value in the experienced museum teacher creating some more general teaching material. These may be used as they stand by the hurried or unconfident teacher or adapted by the more experienced one. Worksheets will benefit from being tied to one or more specific National Curriculum attainment targets.

There is no such thing as the perfect worksheet. Fashions and educational ideas change but constant critical appraisal can improve practice.

This paper first appeared in Journal of Education in Museums *10 (1989), pp. 25–30.*

FURTHER READING

Davis, H. B. (1980) 'Kids have the answers: do you have the questions?', *Instructor* 90: 64–6, 68.
    Suggests ways of converting low-level thinking questions into higher level thinking ones. The source of the questions on Goldilocks.

Fry, H. (1987) 'Worksheets as museum learning devices', *Museums Journal* 86(4): 219–25. A survey of changing attitudes to worksheets with a positive tone and a helpful bibliography.

Grinder, A.L. and McCoy, E. S. (1985)*The Good Guide: A Sourcebook for Interpreters, Docents and Tour Guides*, Arizona: Ironwood Press. The section on questioning strategies has been drawn on heavily for this article.

Hall, N. (ed.) (1984) *Writing and Designing Interpretive Material for Children*, Design for Learning and Centre for Environmental Interpretation, Manchester Polytechnic. Includes written material with AVs and audio-tours.

Jones, L. S. and Ott, R. W. (1983) 'Self-study guides for school-age students', *Museum Studies Journal* 1(1): 36–42. Survey with examples of practice both sides of the Atlantic.

Lauritzen, E. M. (1982) 'The preparation of worksheets', 43–6 in T. H. Hansen, K. E. Anderson and P. Vestergaard (eds) *Museums and Education,* Copenhagen: Danish ICOM/CECA: 43–6. Suggested procedure.

McManus, P. (1985) 'Worksheet-induced behaviour in the British Museum (Natural History)', *Journal of Biological Education* 19(3): 23–42. Study of conversation between groups filling in worksheets. A warning.

O'Connell, P. S. (1984) 'Decentralizing interpretation: developing museum education with and for schools', *Roundtable Reports* 9(1): 17–22. Designing material in collaboration with teachers,

Roberts, B. (1988) 'How do you clean a chandelier?' *Journal of Education in Museums* 9: 9–11. Introduces problem solving activities in role.

39

Museumgoers: life-styles and learning characteristics

Charles F. Gunther

What research is available to help understand why adults come to museums and what they learn there? This article describes psychographic and market research, and discusses the learning style of adults according to life stage and individual preferences.

The needs of adult learners within the museum are identified and suggestions made as to what provision would be appropriate.

> *This museum is a lot more than pretty pictures on the wall.*
> *This is a hall of ideas!*
>
> Michael Morgenstern,
> *sculptor and former factory worker*

The author of the epigraph tells us as much about his needs as an adult as it does about the museum. In attempting to analyse these needs, researchers have acquired a great deal of general information about adults, their leisure-time activities, and their values, lifestyles, and learning characteristics. Moreover, visitor studies in museums have shown us who our adult visitors are and how they behave. Community studies have also revealed who the *potential* visitors are and how to bring them into the museum.

While this research assists us in meeting the learning expectations of adults, the really creative opportunities and choices about the museum experience and its programmes fall to adult educators, either within the museum or in university continuing education programmes. This chapter examines some of the available data explaining how and why people use museums, and it explores the role that learning plays in attracting people to museums and in enhancing the museum experience. The final section deals with applying this information, not only to the museum environment and programmes but to cooperative efforts with continuing education programmes.

ADULTS: LEISURE TIME, VALUES, AND LIFESTYLES

Adults who come to the museum will of course vary, but the ideal visitor comes initially because the museum offers a new experience and a chance to be around other people. If this visitor has a good time, he or she will most likely return. Thus, the crux of the issue is determining what 'having a good time' means for different segments of the population and ways in which that knowledge can be applied to enhance the museum experience.

In researching her doctoral dissertation, 'Adults Attitudes toward Leisure Choices in Relation to Museum Participation', Marilyn G. Hood found five attributes of pleasurable or satisfying leisure experiences, based on literature in the fields of leisure science, sociology and marketing:

- the opportunity to learn
- social interaction
- the challenge of new experiences
- participating actively
- feeling comfortable in one's surroundings[1]

In conducting community research in the Toledo metropolitan area, Hood identified a sixth condition that had received minor attention in the literature; doing something worthwhile, or performing some service for other people while engaging in leisure activities. This last attribute emerged from focus groups in a community where over 1,000 volunteers were contributing some 8,300 hours of their time annually to the museum.

This research indicates that a leisure experience must be seen as package of good and bad moments, with total worth to the individual balanced against the total cost (travel, time, mental saturation fatigue, cost, etc.). Studies of theatre and symphony attendance show that the decision to participate is based on the likelihood of liking the particular programme, understanding what is going on, enjoyment of the event by one's companions, and attending a stimulating event.[2] A recent University of Chicago study talks about 'the problem of providing fertile enough conditions so that viewers might encounter works of art with interest, confidence, and the anticipation of a positive and enjoyable experience'.[3]

Both family and friendship groups list social interaction as a prime reason for participation in cultural events. In the Toledo community study, the most important leisure factors for occasional visitors were found to be opportunities for social interaction with family and friends, feeling comfortable in one's surroundings, and active participation. Beaches, parks, and zoos are recreation places not only because of the activities that occur there or because of their physical environments, but because of the social meanings attributed to them by the people who go there.[4] The socialization process, or transmission from parents and reference groups of values, attitudes, skills, social norms, tastes, and expectations that may predispose a person toward certain future actions or lifestyles, also proved to be a major motivating factor for participation in leisure activities.[5]

The Values and Lifestyles programmes (VALS), begun in 1978 by the marketing research firm SRI International, has focused on behavioural analysis, with an emphasis on the individual as consumer. With attention to theories of human motivation, such as Abraham Maslow's needs hierarchy, SRI has developed a typology for American consumer behaviour that identifies nine different market segments.[6]

	% of population
Need-Driven	<u>11</u>
Survivors	4
Sustainers	7
Outer-Directed	<u>67</u>
Belongers	38
Emulators	21
Achievers	8

Inner-Directed	<u>20</u>
I-Am-Me's	3
Experientials	5
Societally Conscious	12
Integrated	<u>2</u>

In 1983, the Association of College, University, and Community Arts Administrators, Inc. (ACUCAA), contracted with SRI to study the most affluent and generally sophisticated 40 per cent of Americans in relation to attendance at performing arts events. This research, which focused on only four of the VALS market segments, provides very useful information about those adults most likely to visit museums and participate in museum-continuing education programmes:

Achievers Strongly outer-directed, middle-aged, prosperous, self-assured leaders and builders of the traditional American dream, the least well educated of these four VALS groups. 'Arts and music are important in my life' – 11 per cent strongly agree; 15.44 per cent mostly agree.

Experientials Youthful, tend to be single females seeking direct experience, artistic, intensely oriented toward people and inner growth. Many are employed part-time. 'Arts and music are important in my life' – 31.1 per cent agree; 17.0 per cent mostly agree.

Societally Conscious Mission-oriented, mostly married, excellently educated, self-aware, liberal, having wide-ranging interests, reasonably affluent, inner-directed. See themselves as middle- or upper-class. 'Art and music are important in my life' – 24.6 per cent strongly agree; 24.6 per cent mostly agree.

Integrated Psychologically mature, balanced, flexible, having an excellent education; often concerned with 'the big picture'. 'Art and music are important in my life' – 11.4 per cent agree; 18.2 per cent mostly agree.[7]

In general, adults attend concerts and performances to be entertained, or to see a particular show, performer, or group. More specifically, *achievers* are motivated by external reasons, such as sociability and business, while *societally conscious* persons are largely inner-oriented. They attend in order to be moved or to fulfil themselves. *Experientials* value these events as social celebrations. SRI concluded that persons in the categories of *integrated* and *achievers* appear to be users of the performing arts, rather than enjoyers. They detected a hint that these adults attend out of obligation rather than pleasure.

The upscale consumers who form the core of performing arts patrons had extensive exposure to the arts as children. An early background in the arts seemed more important for music than for theatre or dance. To be active as an artist, however, seemed unrelated to attendance. In general, those surveyed by SRI had positive feelings about the arts, which they generally regarded as pleasurable, creative, fun, inspiring, and educational. These adults were most likely to be involved in the arts and were potential future marketing targets.

In the SRI study for ACUCAA, Arnold Mitchell observes that individuals are not fixed at one level but may move to another level that brings with it a whole new set of values rearranging, redefining, and extending those of the previous stage.[8] So an individual's totality consists of layers of spheres of values 'like the layers of an onion'. The more developed a person is, the more levels she/he has moved through, the more complex her/his value-based reactions.

More recently, the National Association for Senior Living Industries commissioned SRI International to conduct studies similar to the VALS programme, but focused on older Americans. Pretesting of the Lifestyles and Values of Older Adults Survey questionnaire revealed that older adults are uncomfortable with such age-based terms *senior citizen*, *retiree*, and *golden years*.[9] Rather, products and services intended for the older market are best sold as gateways to personal growth and development. To older people, the value of a discretionary product or service is determined by its potential for consequential experiences or its capacity to serve as a gateway to other pleasurable experiences.

ADULTS AS LEARNERS

Museum visitors represent a full range of educational levels and learning styles. However, most are well educated: they have high-level occupations and high incomes. Many are young professionals who also enjoy being outdoors and active. They tend to be involved in the community and participate in various cultural events.

In the museum, some of these adults appear to wander aimlessly but want to be left alone; others seek out information. Their enjoyment of any given gallery or object will be more intense if past experience has given them some relevant knowledge or insight. In fact, they will seek out those areas that reinforce current preferences and knowledge, and will avoid areas foreign to them. If you tried to reach all these adults through a lecture tour, the majority would not learn as well as the 25 per cent who thrive on this format.

Over the past twenty-five years, theories about adult education (often called *andragogy*, as opposed to *pedagogy*, the teaching of children) have blossomed and now provide a rich resource for educators who are developing museum programmes. Perhaps the most widely known and accepted theories have been developed by Malcolm S. Knowles, who identified these major characteristics of a learners:

1 They are highly independent and self-directed in their choices of learning opportunities. Further, they teach themselves much of what they learn.
2 Their backgrounds and experiences provide rich resources for learning.
3 Phases of social development often motivate their choices of learning activities (young parent, upward-moving professional, retiree, etc.).
4 They choose learning opportunities that address a specific problem or that permit the information or skill to be used immediately.[10]

To recognize and capitalize on the characteristics of adult learners, Knowles and others recommend designing learning experiences in a climate of openness and respect, with mutual collaboration to identify what adults want and need to learn. Adults enjoy planning and carrying out their own learning exercises, and they need to be involved in evaluating their progress toward self-chosen goals. Adults, says Knowles, define who they are in terms of past experience. Failure to recognize the experiences of an adult learner is equivalent to rejecting the adult as a person.

Adults choose development tasks that increasingly move them toward social and occupational role competence. Readiness to learn and teachable moments peak when a learning opportunity is coordinated with a recognition of the need to know. The young parent enrolls himself and his child in a museum family workshop because he wants to transmit his own cultural values. A mother with grown children signs up for a photography class because she finds herself with more time to develop her own interests. A retired couple attends a weekly series on Japan because they have more opportunity to travel, while the business executive comes because of new contacts with Japanese counterparts.

Addressing the need for immediate application of knowledge and skills requires a strong emphasis on the concept of students learning rather than teachers teaching. Practical, hands-on experiences that result in an end product and gallery activities that require using new information to make additional discoveries, have proven to be highly successful with adults. In an article called 'Why Adults Learn in Different Ways', Mary Jane Even notes that learning is private while teaching is public, and she stresses the need to use many examples, techniques, and approaches. She observes that each individual learns in a unique manner due to 'personal life experiences, neurological brain responses, style preferences, personality dimensions, resultant interests, predispositions to select topics and approaches to work to life, and to processes which generate individual interest and need'.[11]

Individual learning styles have been the focus of research by Bernice McCarthy, who has combined her teaching experience with analysis of twentieth-century learning theory to identity four basic types of learners. Variations in learning styles describe those educational conditions under which adults are most likely to learn and where their comfort level will be high. To some degree, these learning styles explain what sorts of experiences adults are looking for in a museum. A brief summary of McCarthy's descriptors follows.

The 4Mat system of teaching–learning styles

Type One Learners
Perceive information concretely and process it reflectively. Learn by listening and sharing ideas. Like discussions. Excel in viewing direct experience from many perspectives. Value insight thinking. When visiting museum, they are seeking personal meaning. Favorite question: 'Why?'

Type Two Learners
Perceive information abstractly and process it reflectively. Like facts and details. Need to know what the experts think. Critique information and collect data. Are uncomfortable with the subjective. When visiting a museum, they will read all the labels looking for facts. Favorite question: 'What?'

Type Three Learners
Perceive information abstractly and process it actively. Are pragmatists who apply common sense. Are skills oriented. Need to know how things are put together. Seek information which is useful. When visiting a museum, they want to know how artists create and how objects evolve. Favorite question: 'How does it work?'

Type Four Learners
Perceive information concretely and process it actively. Learn by trial and error. Believe in self-discovery. Like variety and are enthusiastic about new experiences. Like to get involved. They would tend to take museum classes where they can experiment with new material and different ideas. Favorite question: 'If?'[12]

McCarthy observes that all four learning styles are equally valid and are usually found equally present in the typical group of adult learners. Museums must recognize that visitors are approaching the experience of viewing their collections from different points of view. If learning is directed toward only one type of learner, the others are not receiving the message.

ADULTS AS MUSEUM VISITORS

Some adults visit museums frequently, while others come only for a special reason, such as an exhibition opening or social event. Frequent visitors may comprise as much as 50 per cent of a museum's annual attendance.

One segment of adult visitors, often seen in family groups, seem to be truly uncomfortable in museums. If children are with them, the adults tend to act as disciplinarians. In observations of parents at several New York City museums, Deborah P. Benton noted they were often unprepared for the role of teacher, and frequently misinterpreted the museum and its meanings. Few of these people allowed their children to set the pace or to interact with exhibits. Rather, the majority of parents directed both their children's behaviour and their attention, eliminating much of the magic of encounter possible in a museum.[13] For such a group, visiting the museum is not a pleasant, rewarding experience. They feel obliged to bring their children to the museum, but it is a foreign environment that is difficult to decode.

By contrast with this group, some older visitors will visit the museum in pairs and find it immensely enjoyable now that life's other cares and responsibilities are behind them. While some older visitors feel animosity toward museums, many are fascinated by ideas, and the museum satisfies this craving. This need for ideas and challenges is not exclusive to older adults; young professionals seek similar experiences, often to balance their highly technical weekday world.

Childhood experiences in museums were found by Hood to be a factor in enjoyment of museums later in life. She cites several sources, including Paul DiMaggio, Michael Useem, and Paula Brown, who pointed out that arts appreciation is primarily developed through training. Understanding most works of art requires familiarity and some background information. This kind of orientation usually takes place through family and school socialization and is most likely to be available to upper-education, upper-income, upper-occupation families.[14]

Hood observed that adults are likely to choose leisure activities that are valued by those people important to them. Several researchers noted that the same leisure activity may be an outlet for different interests as one moves through the life cycle. Hood's research in Toledo showed that influence of family life-cycle stage on leisure decisions was less important than the age of the adult decision-maker.[15]

The six attributes of leisure participation described earlier correlate with Hood's identification of three types of museum visitors: frequent participants, occasional participants, and nonparticipants. Each audience perceives benefits of a museum visit in a distinctive way.[16] *Frequent participants* are the minority of the present museum audience, but they account for a large proportion of the annual attendance. While representing only about 14 per cent of the Toledo metropolitan area population, they made up 40 to 50 per cent of the annual attendance at the museum. Frequent visitors believe that art museums embody all six of the important attributes for pleasurable and satisfying leisure experiences cited by Hood. Three of these attributes are of utmost importance to them: the opportunity to learn, the challenge of new experiences, and the achievement of something worthwhile during leisure time. They are empathetic with museum values, understand the language of art and the museum code, and are familiar with the social norms of participation in museums.

Their adult involvement with museums usually was a conscious choice made from a wide exposure to cultural organizations and activities from childhood. These people do not mind visiting a museum alone and may even relish the chance to explore at their own pace. Because they visit museums so frequently that they feel at home, the comfort factor is no longer a consideration for them. Making the best use of leisure time is important. They believe that visiting a museum is a worthwhile activity, providing feelings of accomplishment and expanding horizons. These feelings are closely linked to volunteer involvement. Volunteers know the staff, know all the inside news about what is happening and will happen. At a museum, volunteers enjoy leisure activity that is of service to others and yet personally stimulating.

Frequent participants are less likely to have parental responsibilities than are the other two groups. Since they are less involved with family responsibilities, they are freer to make individual plans. If they are new to the community, they may not yet have established a circle of friends. If they have had pleasurable experiences in museums elsewhere, newcomers to a city are likely to seek a local museum as a focus for their intellectual and cultural life. For frequent visitors, the benefits of museum participation consistently outweigh the price of a visit.[17]

Occasional participants in art museums go once or twice a year. Though they do visit museums, they more closely resemble the non-participants than they do frequent visitors in their values, attitudes, and expectations. Because occasional visitors often do not feel comfortable in a museum – or are even intimidated by the building and by exhibitions they do not quite understand – they do not return frequently.

Young adults and parents of young children are interested in social interaction and entertainment activities, but are usually least interested in learning opportunities and doing something worthwhile in leisure time. The social interaction provided by a support group, such as family, friends, or organized clubs, is important because it offers a transition into the less-familiar environment of the museum and validates their being in this setting.

Occasional participants are more likely to be high school educated and strongly family-oriented. The very recognition by occasional visitors that a museum offers learning opportunities may be a negative element, for their leisure is equated with relaxation, which is associated with interacting socially and informally with a close family or friendship group. Occasional participants are most likely to find a museum visit worthwhile when a special event or exhibition occurs at the museum or when they are entertaining out-of-town guests.[18]

Nonparticipants in art museums are nearly the opposite of frequent visitors in their values, attitudes, and life-styles. Of the three groups, they least value the six leisure attributes identified by Hood. Minimally interested in learning and the challenge of new experiences, they are most interested in social interaction and entertainment activities.

Most are high school educated individuals whose socialization from childhood has not emphasized cultural experiences. Since they may have had negative experiences with formal education and no socialization to prepare them to read the museum code, museum visits are studious, exacting experiences rather than the casual, relaxed diversion they seek in leisure time. Nonparticipants feel that museums are useful for teaching children, but they find no reason for adults to visit a museum. The attributes they value are minimally present in museums. Consequently, they seek and find rewarding experiences elsewhere.

It is important, however, *not* to dismiss nonparticipants as apathetic or unintelligent. These adults are active persons who find great satisfaction outside of museums. Home and family responsibilities restrict leisure time, in many cases because both parents have to work. At middle age, they not only have responsibilities for their children but often for ageing parents. As devoted do-it-yourselfers, they gain great satisfaction from making home improvements and from other activities that permit them to use their hands. When leisure time is available, they seek family-centred experiences.[19]

Additional insights into the reasons why adults come to museums and also into the ways museums can meet their expectations are provided in Ross J. Loomis's book *Museum Visitor Evaluation: new tool for management*. In one of the most useful surveys summarized in the book, participants in a nationwide Canadian survey were interviewed at home and completed a follow-up mail-in questionnaire the 1970s. The study suggested that the decision not to visit a museum was influenced less by negative images than by problems of accessibility and lack of communication. Admission fees were less of a barrier than lack of information about the museum and problems in gaining access. Three of the researchers of this study concluded that efforts to increase museum attendance should be concentrated on those who already attend.[20] Hood confirmed this point in her Toledo research, emphasizing that occasional visitors offer the greatest opportunity for museums to develop new audiences.

The Canadian National Survey went on to say that museums can and should improve communication, be more accessible, and inform people about the kinds of experiences provided. A lack of public information about the museum results in no expectations at all. Moreover, hindrances in travelling to and from the museum or problems in gaining access increase visitors' fatigue and colour their final recollection of the visit.

TOLEDO SURVEYS

Surveying audience perceptions can be done on a modest scale using small discussion groups. In 1986, I questioned a group of adults who had taken studio or art history classes at the Toledo Museum of Art. They agreed that the most appealing aspects of attending classes at the museum were the nonthreatening atmosphere, the quality of instruction, and the personal attention they received. The museum environment was considered very important, and anything that detracted from that environment lessened the total experience.

Such detractions could occur before or after the actual experience in the museum, such as an impolite entrance guard or a parking problem. It could even be a diminished sense of ownership because children and university students were using the same instructional space. However, the atmosphere was positively reinforced by the socializing that took place in the classroom and the 'halo' effect of having access to great works of art. Basically, these adults felt that they were improving themselves through worthwhile activities in a pleasant and important setting.

As a follow-up, a questionnaire was sent in 1987 to 250 adults who had taken studio or art history classes or workshops at the Toledo Museum. Four questions were asked, in hopes of learning more about adult attitudes and expectations regarding the museum. Seventy-eight questionnaires, or 31 per cent, were returned.

The first question, asking why the student had taken a course at the museum, established that nearly every respondent listed one of Hood's conditions for a satisfying use of leisure time. Seventy-four per cent, however, also mentioned reasons such as the opportunity to learn, self-fulfilment, a chance to produce artworks, the reputation of instructors, or personal growth. Seventy per cent had participated in other activities at the museum.

When asked what they considered unique about visiting the museum, 31 per cent mentioned the quality of the collection, while another 25 per cent described the environment, using such words as 'escape' or 'entering another world'. The widest range of answers came in response to the question 'What is the most meaningful experience you have had at the Toledo Museum of Art?' Taking classes was the most common answer, given by 41 per cent of those responding. We obtained similar responses from surveys of an Elderhostel group in 1987.

The results of these informal Toledo surveys are not particularly surprising. Generally, they confirm the findings of the more professional researchers cited in this essay. Perhaps of greater importance, surveys have helped us establish a stronger rapport with a segment of our audience, showing these patrons that the museum cares about their interests and needs.

Moreover, the responses on these surveys describing what is unique about visiting a museum and most meaningful experiences in museums relate to research conducted by University of Chicago behavioural scientist Mihalyi Czikszentmihalyi. He has studied activities and the enjoyment of objects that 'give a sense of transcendent harmony'.[21] He describes enjoyment as 'the flow condition in which one acts with total involvement and excludes the pressing concerns of everyday life'.[22] Clearly it is this flow condition that many who enjoy museums have come to anticipate and expect.

In their unpublished reported submitted to the J. Paul Getty Trust, 'The art of seeing: toward an interpretive psychology of the aesthetic encounter', Czikszentmihalyi and Rick E. Robinson elaborate:

> When philosophers describe the aesthetic experience, and psychologists describe the flow, they are talking about essentially the same state of mind. What this in turn means is that human beings enjoy experience that is more clear and focused than ordinary experience is. When this state of consciousness occurs within an aesthetic context – in response to music, painting, and so on – we call it an aesthetic experience. In other contexts – in sports, in hobbies, in challenging work and social interactions – we call it a flow experience.[23]

Many of my recommendations for meeting the learning expectations of adults in museums and of adults in continuing education who would use museums as a resource are based on that specific expectation. A myriad of other adult needs have been raised throughout this essay; none of them should be ignored. Indeed, in satisfying those more practical needs, museums may greatly enhance the act of perception and potential for flow.

MEETING THE LEARNING EXPECTATIONS OF ADULTS

'The primary skill one needs to unlock the magic of things is that of seeing them objectively and subjectively at the same time, thus joining the nature of the perceiving subject with the nature of the object'.[24] All this research on leisure needs, values, life-styles, and learning characteristics has provided insight into 'the nature of the perceiving subject'. Based on those insights, the recommendations below are logical. Some are directed at museums themselves; others are for those continuing educators who might like to use museums as a resource.

Everyone on the museum staff is an educator

Because the totality of the museum visit is what visitors remember, every person they encounter teaches them what a museum is. For occasional or nonparticipant visitors, initial encounters are crucial. Car park attendants, cloakroom assistants, information desk volunteers, security officers, and a host of others must be sensitive to their potential for winning over adults as frequent visitors. Even municipal and state governments can have an impact if the museum is difficult to find because of inadequate signs or if public parking is not available. (How lucky we were in Toledo when state and city officials agreed to post highway and street signs directing visitors to the *El Greco of Toledo* exhibition in 1982!)

Help adults to decode the museum environment

Be sure that signs and floor plans are easy for occasional visitors to understand. Try mock-ups with visitors before permanent signs are printed. Continuing education programmes might offer a workshop on decoding the museum for those upwardly mobile VALS groups who want to begin visiting museums. It could be a course on language, symbols, and objects. We take for granted that everyone understands that museums require umbrellas or large parcels to be deposited, that many museums are closed on Mondays but open at weekends, that touching is not permitted, and that gallery arrangements have a certain logic. Museum staff are mistaken if they assume that adult visitors will know exactly what everything on an object label refers to. (Many of us have overheard visitors wondering if the accession number is the price.)

Such seemingly obvious museum information as the difference between an original print and a photographic reproduction could save first-time visitors from asking embarrassing questions. I am not suggesting that such information is the real meat of a museum visit; but understanding these things raises one's comfort level and clears the way for the optimum museum experience.

Learning and fun are not mutually exclusive

Combining a traditional learning activity (tour, lecture, film) with a social activity (refreshment) is an obvious way to satisfy people. If you can enlist volunteers or frequent visitors to act as hosts and make sure people meet one another, you could win a whole new crowd of frequent visitors for future educational offerings. Offer more opportunities and programmes that incorporate the three attributes that occasional visitors value, so there will be more incentive for them to come (social interaction, active participation, and comfort in area surroundings).

Less is more, if you can do it

Blockbuster exhibitions and attendance figures notwithstanding, our programme participants tell us often how much they appreciate personal attention and opportunities for interaction with speakers, instructors, and other participants. One solution to the numbers game is to offer popular events more than once. We always invite audience members to come up and meet speakers after lectures, and many do so, if only to thank them. Even during the *El Greco* exhibition, visitors commented that they felt they received personal attention from our volunteers and staff. Amenities such as frequent resting places, easy-to-locate lavatories and drinking fountains, food service, gift shops, and comfortable lecture rooms all indicate personal concern. The frequent visitor who has experienced all of this constitutes a high-percentage of our attendance figures. Blockbuster visitors seldom return.

Museums should consider the distinct advantage of the 'un-blockbuster' exhibition. In 1987, the Toledo Museum of Art participated in an exchange with the State Hermitage in Leningrad, which presented one painting by Rembrandt from Leningrad and twenty-two Rembrandt etchings. Visitors described an optimum aesthetic experience that focused their attention in an atmosphere that encouraged contemplation. They seemed to be challenged to *look* rather than press on to another painting.

Avoid canned presentations

All of the information on adult learning characteristics underscores the need to be flexible. The speaker or docent who acknowledges that audience members may have some background or experience related to the subject, may have learning goals slightly different from the presenter, may choose other learning opportunities quickly if this one proves unfulfilling, has won over the audience at the outset. Beyond acknowledging these factors in theory, the speaker must be able to respond flexibly to circumstances that may develop during the presentation.

Overall, the museum and its continuing education staff must demand this kind of sensitivity to audiences. It is not satisfactory to bring in reputed scholars who put people to sleep. For several years, the museum education staff at Toledo has sought recommendations from people who have heard a scholar speak before inviting him to lecture at the museum. Our success rate with our audiences has been much higher as a result.

Use new technologies to win new audiences

In Toledo, we are sadly behind many museums that have begun to incorporate new technologies into their educational offerings. The possibilities are broad and are expanding almost daily. Hood has noted the potential for museum education through techniques such as 'the linking of TV sets with computers or telephones for information delivery, video cassette recorders and players, high quality home satellite reception, culture-only channels on pay TV, low-power TV to serve specific audiences, and greater targeting of audiences by network TV as its percentage of viewing time declines'.[25] Museums must not fail to exploit these opportunities.

Offer a balanced curriculum for different types of learning

I have already made suggestions to help nonvisitors take their first steps into a museum. For occasional and frequent visitors, educators must be sensitive to those who are self-directed and need only an opportunity to visit a museum, as well as to those who are looking for formal instruction to fill in the gaps in their background.

The different learning styles identified by Bernice McCarthy emphasize the need for a variety of programmes to attract adults. For example, art museums can use a range of techniques, including lectures, demonstrations, films, videos, discussion groups and studio experiences. Other possibilities include more humanities presentations, such as discussions of social history, performance events, or experiences with food, costume, or theatre. Universities provide rich resources for these types of programmes in museums.

Go with the flow

Finally, I would like to return to the opening quotation of this chapter: 'This is a hall of ideas!'[26] This statement reflects what Czikszentmihalyi finds in his research, namely, that the optimum museum experience is one of transcendence, of flow, that many call an aesthetic experience. After we have helped visitors become comfortable in the museum, after we have socialized with them, given them personal attention, and then given them an outstanding educational presentation in a controlled, distraction-free environment, what we really hope will happen is that they have a flow experience. We hope their focused attention will provide an experience in which their intelligence and feelings will become one, and this challenge will be their joy.

As educators, we might begin by sharing these factors with our clients. In our courses and workshops, we must give them not only information about our collections but also clues on how to evaluate those objects. Authors such as Rudolph Arnheim, Harry Broudy, and E. B. Feldman have given us plenty of ideas for teaching visual analysis. We need to use those ideas, and then go one step further and ask people simply to look at the objects. And then look a little longer. And then just a few seconds more to be sure nothing was missed.

The challenge for educators is that once this is done, new skills will be needed on an even higher level. Then we as educators will realize that the learning expectations of adults in our museums will never end. Our challenge is to know our audience, to raise their expectations continually, and to make their excitement our flow.

This paper first appeared in J. W. Solinger (ed.) (1989) Museums and Universities: New Paths for Continuing Education, *Phoenix, AZ: American Council on Education.*

NOTES

1 Hood, Marilyn G. (1981) 'Adult attitudes toward leisure choices in relation to museum participation' Ph.D. Diss., Ohio State University; Ann Arbor: University Microfilms International, cat. no. 8121802, 3. I am very grateful to Dr Hood, who has not only shaped our staff's understanding of what we know and what we ought to know about our audiences, but has also offered valuable advice about the contents of this article.
2 Ibid. 24.
3 Czikszentmihalyi, Mihalyi and Robinson, Rick E. (1987) 'The art of seeing: toward an interpretive psychology of the aesthetic experience', University of Chicago, report submitted to J. Paul Getty Trust: 108.
4 Ibid. 26.
5 Ibid. 356.
6 Mitchell, Arnold (1984) *The Professional Performing Arts: Attendance Patterns, Preferences, and Motives*, Madison, WI: Association of College University and Community Arts Administrators, Inc. 8.
7 Ibid. 13–16.
8 Ibid. 18.
9 Wolfe, David, B. (1987) 'The ageless market', *American Demographics* 9, July: 29.
10 Knowles, Malcolm S. (1978) *The Adult Learner: A Neglected Species,* Houston: Gulf: 184–5.
11 Even, Mary Jane (1987) 'Why adults learn in different ways', *Lifelong Learning* 10 June: 25.
12 McCarthy, Bernice (1986) *The 4Mat System: Teaching Learning Styles Using Right/Left Mode Techniques,* Barrington, IL: Excel, Inc: 3–6.
13 Hood: 31.
14 Ibid. 28.
15 Ibid. 284.
16 Ibid. 282.
17 Ibid. 296–8.
18 Ibid. 298–300.
19 Ibid. 300–4.
20 Loomis, Ross J. (1987) *Museum Visitor Evaluation: New Tool for Management,* Nashville: American Association for State and Local History: 125 .
21 Czikszentmihalyi, Mihalyi and Rochberg-Halton, Eugene (1981) *The Meaning of Things: Domestic Symbols and the Self,* Cambridge: Cambridge University Press: 244.
22 Ibid.
23 Czikszentmihalyi and Robinson: 10.
24 Czikszentmihalyi and Rochberg-Halton: 246.
25 Hood, Marilyn G. (1981) 'Adult attitudes', report of a study done at the Toledo Museum of Art, based on the author's dissertation: 33.
26 Morgenstern, Michael (1987) *Artists Talk About Art*, public lecture at the Toledo Museum of Art, 22 February.

40

Passionate and purposeful: adult learning communities

Luke Baldwin, Sharlene Cochrane, Constance Counts, John Dolomore, Martha McKenna and Barbara Vacarr

The diversity of adult experiences and learning needs is strengthened by involvement in a learning community, whether this is a professional group, a workshop or internship. Participation and active engagement, related to relevant life-stage needs enable reflection, evaluation and the application of learning.

Many museums need to develop targeted provision for a range of adult audiences: equally, many are already engaged in working with volunteers, work-placements or internships, or other forms of training provision. This article offers useful concepts in understanding the ways in which adults learn which is relevant to many different situations.

A key concept in educating adults is the idea of a 'learning community'. Adults often learn most effectively in groups that they join by choice, groups characterized by discussion, interaction, and collaboration and in which participants both receive and provide academic and social support. Such groups value the individual; at the same time they require that the learner communicates and reflects within the group. These groups might be work partnerships, professional organizations, workshops, seminars, or internships. At Lesley College Graduate School a faculty group called the Collaborative on Adult Research and Practice is one such learning community. Our shared reflections and analyses of developmental theory and our own teaching have served as a model of the process through which adults learn effectively, and we have collaborated on this article.

THE NATURE OF ADULT DEVELOPMENT

Adult learning is characterized by diversity. Adults bring a great variety of life experiences to learning communities, and their cultural backgrounds, interests, and passions generate the questions that help determine the shape and course of their learning. Adult development theorists concur that adulthood is marked by emerging challenges and opportunities for growth. Human development is a lifelong process that goes beyond the maturational competencies and understandings of adolescence. Views of self, relationships, and place in the world evolve into old age.

Contrary to earlier theories of human development that concentrated on childhood and adolescence, a life cycle perspective on development sees continued transitions and change as essential elements of adult growth as well. Recent research indicates that adults' lives are patterned in predictable sequences of growth, adaptation, and transformation.[1] The psychologist Daniel Levinson calls these predictable sequences 'seasons':

There is the idea of seasons: a series of periods or stages within the life cycle. The process is not simple, continuous, unchanging flow. There are qualitatively different seasons, each having its own distinctive character.[2]

Certain key issues and tasks are associated with each life stage. There is, however, a great deal of individual and contextual variation in how themes, stages, phases, or events characterize particular journeys through adulthood. Not all people deal with life events in the same way, and individuals vary considerably along the developmental continuum – even within the same relative positions.

The transitions of adulthood can be described as 'decisive turning points' that carry the potential for 'intrapersonal integration'. In transition, adults rework prior learning, reformulate their identity, and reaffirm or renegotiate previous resolutions.[3] This period of vulnerability provides opportunities to challenge old assumptions, reach deeper understandings, seek new balances, and create new life meanings.

Earlier life experiences that were characterized by a need to work and produce in order to satisfy external authorities are transformed by adults' strong drive toward competence and achievement. The Harvard psychologist Robert Kegan describes the central transition in adult development as moving from an 'interpersonal' stance to an 'institutional' stance.[4] Adult learners make a transition to a culture of self-authorship as they become engaged in a learning community.

Many adults enter learning communities with the assumption that the ideas and opinions of others are what constitute knowledge, and learners tend to seek 'truths' from those whom they perceive as experts. This tendency is exemplified in the following comments made by an adult who had recently returned to college to complete her undergraduate degree:

> The teacher asked the question: 'What is the meaning of evil?' For the next three hours I had to sit and listen to all my classmates talk and waste time talking about what they thought evil was. It was so boring . . . but the worst part was that the teacher never gave us the answer.[5]

Development moves from a strict reliance on an absolute authority, through an understanding that truth is relative, to a conceptualization that knowledge is constructed. This movement is characteristic of the transition described by William Perry, in which exclusive reliance on external authority as the 'source of truth' is rejected.[6] As adults enlarge their understandings of the world, they tend to move from a dualistic to a multiple, contextual view in which they may begin to see themselves as the creators of knowledge. The developmental position one inhabits affects the view of self in relation to the world. Transitions that are marked by a process of questioning, evaluating, experiencing, and ultimately synthesizing diminish the importance of external authority, and through this process adults take ownership of their own learning. The comments of another returning adult student clarify this shift. She describes becoming an active participant in the process of her own growth:

> Things have opened up for me, and I'm much more sure about what I want to do. When I first came back to school I felt like it was just something I had to do, to finish. But now I really feel invested in what I'm doing, and I have so many things that I want to check out.[7]

This sense of direction is the beginning of self as knower, out of which grows an informed and more powerful personal voice.

Although this phase of development may be qualitatively different for men and women, when procedures for knowing are integrated with a more committed personal voice adults are on the verge of constructing knowledge. Four psychologists explain the process:

> Once Knowers assume the general relativity of knowledge, that their frame of reference matters, and that they can construct frames of reference, they feel responsible for examining, questioning, and developing the systems they will use for constructing knowledge.[8]

At this point in the cycle of development adults have greater tolerance for ambiguity, and questions become more important than answers. They seek to determine criteria for learning, framed and tempered through an understanding that truth is contextually relative. Adults' capacity to construct knowledge is enhanced when communication with others facilitates a connection between the self and the wider community of learners.

THE PROCESS OF ADULT DEVELOPMENT

Our understanding of adult development and our experience in successfully educating adult students have led us to understand our work as a three-step process: purposeful engagement in the content of the experience; reflection, evaluation, and analysis (as individuals and as a group); and the application of new learning to concrete situations. Slightly different versions of this construct have been suggested by John Dewey and David Kolb as models for solving problems or illustrating learning styles. Throughout these processes, adults are both passionate and purposeful. And that blend enlivens learning communities and contributes to the building of personal and intellectual support systems.

Diversity and active engagement

Although group participation and interaction are critical elements in our model, learning communities need to be flexible and multidimensional, encouraging and building on the diversity within the group. Differences in experience, culture, learning styles, and gender may serve to complement each other. Extremely diverse groups tend to generate many options for solving problems, examining content, or testing and applying theories. When adults share their strengths in those areas, the results can be both powerful and lasting. A dreamer and a mechanic make an impressive pair of inventors. In addition, adults have a complex network of experiences through which they carry themes, questions, and interests that give their search for knowledge intensity and imagination. The community must allow the opportunity to engage material in different ways, nurturing different types of expression and activity that capitalize on a wide range of passions and styles of learning. Opportunities may include independent study and research, small groups for discussion or study, presentations for large groups, site visits, fieldwork, case study development or analysis, written or visual tasks, and movement between quiet reading and candid conversation. In guiding these types of activities, effective facilitators initiate dialogue among members of the learning community to identify shared and unique experiences, knowledge, expertise, and passions about the subject.

The educator may propose goals and activities for reaching them, but through this initial dialogue the learning community may respond to such plans and offer suggestions for making adjustments or modifications. The educator in such a setting is not the 'expert dispensing truths' but the resource person and facilitator, adapting activities, helping to connect content with individual passions, and shaping experience that can provide meaningful learning within the set amount of time for the experience. This approach applies whether the learning situation is a semester course, a daylong workshop, or a two-hour museum visit. While the depth of learning may vary, learning communities are created whenever a group engages in a process of learning that interactively draws from the knowledge and experience of the participants.

The ways educators accomplish this learning again need to be varied, weaving individual interests into the exploration of content. Participants may prepare special projects or presentations, develop research teams, arrange debates, and so on. Invariably, by guiding individuals within the learning community in pursuing their own passions, important questions about the content emerge – in forms more meaningful and critical than educators often expect. This dynamic process of socially constructing new forms of knowledge through the learning community promotes both individual and collective growth and serves to empower adults as learners.

Reflection and evaluation

A critical aspect of educational experiences for adults is the need for reflection and evaluation of new learning. Educators must provide time and space in every learning experience for participants to reflect on the experience and evaluate its meaning in their lives. In our experience as adult educators, we have found this stage to be the most creative of the learning experience and the one most likely to be overlooked without careful planning. Effective educators facilitate this stage within learning communities by encouraging participants to share their reflections and insights with their peers in every new learning activity. This process requires learners to integrate new learning with past experiences, creating meaning for the present and looking toward expanding on the experience in the future. Participants should reflect critically on new experiences and have the opportunity to challenge information or beliefs set forth based on their own knowledge or experience in the field. The personal authority that adult learners bring to educational activities must be acknowledged and respected by educators. Finally, as learners respond to each other's comments, comparing insights and possible meanings of the experience, collaboration is enhanced and learners have the opportunity to expand their range of possible meanings of the experience and learn to value various points of view. All participants should have the chance to express their ideas and listen to others as the learning community constructs its own meanings and values particular attributes of the learning activity.

APPLICATION AND FURTHER INQUIRY

Without a context in which to test their new knowledge, adults run the risk of viewing learning as being separate from personal experience. Ideally, in order to ensure integration of knowledge, adults should have a forum for applying new insights and formulating new interactions. Such interactions offer adults opportunities not only to apply theory but to construct new theories based on subsequent experiences. This dynamic process of knowing and doing provides a vital connection in learning experiences.

Adult learning communities offer a variety of ways for adults to implement their new knowledge. Through practice, work experiences, and internships, adults act on what they have learned. Action projects provide a means for learners to try out their ideas through solving problems, collaborating with others to refine concepts, and reacting to changes. This kind of learning allows adults to modify ideas and assumptions by testing their validity or usefulness in the field. Theoretical concepts often represent ideals that do not fit everyday situations, and adults become constructors of knowledge by modifying and shaping theories to conform to their own experiences. In essence, the field becomes the laboratory. As adults continually apply and adapt what they have studied in learning communities, they become more aware of their own learning processes. This awareness ultimately results in a strong foundation from which adults build knowledge based on a broad range of interaction and integration.

A FINAL NOTE

The Collaborative on Adult Research and Practice formed at Lesley College to study adult development has experienced this shift between interaction and integration. Through collaborative efforts in small study groups, we compiled and assembled this article, and this task has served as an action project that has allowed us to reflect on our experiences in the group and to apply the knowledge we have gained. The final product also incorporates our hands-on learning as teachers. The examination and articulation of our own learning processes and practices yielded new insights that enhanced our understanding of how adults develop and learn. It became clear that a view of development as a linear path in which adults grow to construct knowledge within a community of learners was not sufficient. Our experience informs our belief that entrance into a learning community becomes an integral part of the developmental process and facilitates growth to more complex and integrative epistemological positions. As our awareness of this phenomenon has continued to grow, our new knowledge has infused our teaching, leading to new interactions with our students, which we have then brought back and discussed with our collaborative group. That circle continues, inspiring our own research and practice and enlivening the academic experiences of our students.

This paper first appeared in Journal of Museum Education *15(1) (1990), pp. 7–9.*

NOTES

1 Weathersby, Rita, Preszler, Rita and Tarule, Jill Matuck (1980) *Adult Development: Implications for Higher Education*, American Association for Higher Education-ERIC/Higher Education Research Report 4, Washington, D.C.: American Association for High Education: 2.
2 Levinson, Daniel (1978) *The Seasons of a Man's Life*, New York: Alfred A. Knopf: 6.
3 Weathersby, Preszler and Tarule, *Adult Development*: 22.
4 Kegan, Robert (1982) *The Evolving Self*, Cambridge, Mass.: Harvard University Press.
5 Quoted in Barbara Vacarr (1989) 'Peer mentoring and epistemological development of adults', paper presented at the annual international meeting of the Mentoring Association, Kalamazoo, Michigan, May: 4.
6 Perry, William G. (1970) *Forms of Intellectual and Ethical Development in the College Years*, New York: Holt, Rinehart & Winston.
7 Quoted in Vacarr, 'Peer mentoring and epistemological development': 6.
8 Belenky, M. F., Clinchy, B. M., Goldberger, N. R. and Tarule, J. M. (1986) *Women's Ways of Knowing*, New York: Basic Books: 138–9.

FURTHER READING

Adams, Frank (1975) *Unearthing Seeds of Fire: The Idea of Highlander*, Winston-Salem, N.C.: Blair.
Brookfield, Stephen D. (1986) *Understanding and Facilitating Adult Learning*, San Francisco: Jossey-Bass.
Daloz, Laurent A. (1986) *Effective Teaching and Mentoring: Realizing the Transformational Power of Adult Learning*, San Francisco: Jossey-Bass.
Dewey, John (1916) *Democracy and Education*, New York: Macmillan.
Freire, Paolo (1973) *Education for Critical Consciousness*, New York: Seabury Press.
Kegan, Robert (1982) *The Evolving Self*, Cambridge, Mass.: Harvard University Press.
Kolb, David (1984) *Experiential Learning*, Englewood Cliffs, N.J.: Prentice Hall.

41

Whose museum is it anyway? Museum education and the community

Jocelyn Dodd

Museums are slowly changing to meet the needs of their communities, and along with this change goes a shift in the skills used and roles played by museum education staff. As museums become more consumer-oriented, so collecting, display and education policies must evolve to meet new challenges.

Like many museum education professionals, my invaluable pre-museum experience was teaching. But is museum education about teaching any more? In the past, museum education has concentrated primarily on formal education, structured curriculum-led school parties, student teachers, teachers' planning sessions, INSET courses and museum loans. How many of us have done endless sessions on 'the Victorians', for an albeit enthusiastic junior school audience? Perhaps we have the government to thank for a few more decades of that, now it is laid down in the History National Curriculum. But we do so much more as well – family fun days, holiday playscheme events, reminiscence sessions. though these tend to be extras, in addition to formal education. We live in a time of change and challenge: increased accountability, local management of schools, poll tax capping and the recession have decimated some services. It has forced many to rethink, reorganize, refund, question and justify their positions. It has necessitated a radical rethink of the role, function, practices and outcomes of museum education.

What, I think, lies at the heart of the matter is the question 'whose museum is it anyway?' How can we begin to define what we do in terms of education unless we know who we are educating? Some, perhaps still too many, curators would have us think that museums were for that select little gathering of highly motivated, highly informed, white, middle-class intellectuals with a passion for eighteenth-century ceramics. There are signs that those days of intellectual elitism at last are beginning to wither.

Why then have we, as educators, concentrated on an often equally small section of our museums' clientele? In the case of Nottingham museums only about 10 per cent of our visitors are in formal educational groups. Perhaps a different agenda was set for me from that of many colleagues. Nottingham museums are City Council funded, with no grant or financial support from the LEA. Actually being called an education officer can stir wrath in councillors. Why should they be funding something which is the function of the LEA? (Before long, we may all be wondering what LEAs were anyway!) But education is not just about schools; it is about lifelong learning. Of course it is about children, but equally about adolescents and about adults. Do they suddenly stop learning when they leave formal educational establishments? What then of the community which, as tax payers, are the financial providers of the service? How much are they considered? Or are they just another neglected user group or potential group? Do museums actually serve the needs of the community at all?

How do we even begin to define 'the community' – as a society it defies the confines of a restricted definition. It is, in an all encompassing sense, people between 'the cradle and the grave', mother and toddler groups, the elderly, youth groups, partially-sighted people, groups from specific cultural communities, groups from women's refuges. Many are disadvantaged, lack confidence, and lack any sense of feeling that museums have anything to do with their lives. Perhaps what we are defining is the 'rights of the public'. We certainly live in a rapidly changing society, with more active old people than ever before. Only one in five households is a traditional nuclear family. More people live alone than ever before and are looking for interactive social opportunities. Rising unemployment has left huge numbers of people with seemingly endless spare time. Many communities are now multicultural, multilingual, multiethnic and multifaith. As communities change, so do our museums' potential audiences. Are our thinking and our provision evolving to keep pace with these new challenges?

The process of first meeting the community, and then working with it, requires many skills different from those traditionally used in formal museum education. Such skills are less concerned with systematic learning, but much more about negotiating, networking and confidence building. To meet these new needs, we need staff with different skills and knowledge, and experience of working with community groups is essential. The vocabulary and networks are different from formal education, and teaching ability may in future become just one of several skills we will be looking for.

Our curatorial colleagues have sometimes led the way with good practice of community collaborations. For example, a project at Springburn Museum influenced and shaped the whole museum from its instigation. From collecting to exhibitions, the creation and ownership of the museum lay within the community. In Glasgow, the community at large made a huge impact in a major city project with the People's Palace. Does this sense of ownership by community only lie with local authority museums? I think not; Springburn is a trust museum. The Bass Museum in Burton on Trent is a company museum, yet strongly reflects the ethos and involvement of its local Burton community. What these projects all have in common is a social history basis, perhaps the most comfortable and most obvious bedfellows of museum collections and community involvement. The challenge for us, as educators, lies in making all collections accessible to the community at large, from fine art to natural history, decorative art to archaeology.

The process of introducing community groups to museums is not about high levels of educational achievement. Rather it is concerned with negotiating, confidence building and providing opportunities. It is about empowering community groups to realize that museums are as much for them as for the social elite, and that they too can have access to them culturally, physically, and intellectually. It can be a political process, with repercussions for the status quo within museums. As new groups gain confidence, they will begin to question the institutions – why they collect what they do, what their displays are like, how 'relevant' they are, what facilities and provision they make for the community at large, even the fundamental role of the museum. How often do museums really address the question, 'why are we here?'

The impetus for change may come from a small encounter, like a Sikh community group in Nottingham, previously nonmuseum goers, who were outraged to see ceremonial Sikh swords displayed alongside those used in battle. This incident resulted in a whole Sikh project being undertaken and the investigation of a community showcase and huge curatorial involvement. It brought into question why the only Sikh collections the museum had were 'ethnographic', and may culminate in a change in collecting policies to reflect the cultural diversity of Nottingham's population as a whole. A more customer-led museum service is slowly evolving in place of the traditional object-led, curatorially biased service of the past. Objects are still of prime importance – museums wouldn't exist without them – but which objects are displayed, how they are interpreted, and for whom, is of the essence.

A fundamental change is taking place in the relationship between the public and museums; a change towards a collaboration of joint interest, joint views, feelings and sensitivities. This calls for new skills on the part of museum educators, but it means a fundamental redefining of research, too. No longer will exhibition and display research be just about the museum content, but about the social content of user groups as well. It will question whether we can continue to produce general museum displays aimed at 'the public'. How often do we, as educationalists, make remedial use of exhibitions and displays aimed at some undefined audience, quite inappropriate for our specified groups? How often are exhibitions selective in their audience, actually aimed at children or specific groups of adults? We need to be bold in defining exhibition objectives with specific audiences in mind, aiming to create inspirational museums rather than didactic exhibitions. Perhaps now, as educationalists, we are forced to address the questions we should have faced long ago. When most museum education services were set up, it was to meet demands from schools. We have developed very effective strategies for dealing with these. We have increased the popularity of museums, with excellent handling sessions and terrific loan materials, but meanwhile museum displays have remained static and traditional. Often, as museum educators, we were put in a ghetto separate and remote from the fundamental planning of the museum. We did not insist that curators developed a new skill base in order to create displays which met the needs of the users. Now we need to take up a joint challenge of meeting the needs of the community, while redefining the nature of curatorship. Building up their collections is as much a product of the museums' relationship with their communities as any outreach work.

Museum educators' involvement with the community began with educators diversifying and working with groups outside the formal education sector. Some museums have appointed community outreach officers, but provision is still patchy and the area is as yet largely unformed. The process of enabling and empowering the community forces a radical rethink of the role and purpose of museums and their relationship with the community. This may lead to a redefining of curatorship and the role of museum education. But if we are committed to 'life-long education' for the community, we must commit ourselves to a central role in the creation of those newly-shaped museums.

This paper first appeared in Journal of Education in Museums *13 (1992), pp. 31–2.*

42

Evaluation of museum programmes and exhibits
George E. Hein

The need for evaluation of programmes and exhibits is discussed, along with an outline of main theoretical approaches, indicating what the epistemological antecedents of these approaches are.

A practical approach is described which offers a useful methodology that is successful in the evaluation of museum education programmes. This relies on the collection of a wide range of data that enables a holistic picture to be obtained. Evaluation should be part of the on-going work of the education section, and an evaluation plan should form part of the museum education policy.

THE NEED FOR EVALUATION

During the last twenty years, museum staffs have become increasingly self-critical and self-inquiring about their programmes and their *raisons-d'être*. A number of factors have contributed to this self-examination. Most important has been the worsening world-wide economic situation. After a period of prosperity following the Second World War, an era of growth, rebuilding and renewal, museums, like other institutions, have had to ask some hard questions about priorities, programmes, audiences, and operating styles. There is clearly not enough money (and consequently insufficient staff and support services) to do everything that might be desired. So questions arise as to which activities are most essential, or most benefitial to the museum and to society.

As a result of the economic crisis, pressure on museums has increased to perform a variety of functions. As schools face cuts in staff, especially in the 'cultural' or 'humanities' areas, they turn to museums and other institutions to provide educational experiences in these areas for their pupils. Museums are asked to make up for discontinued art programmes, decreased material resources, and even for cuts in the science teaching previously carried out in the schools.

This pressure to provide services to the education community also forces museum staffs to question the activities of museums: which are useful, which help children to grow and learn, which efficiently use the museum resources? At the same time, museum audiences are growing. One result of the post-war expansion and prosperity and especially of post-war social changes, is that a much wider segment of the public makes use of public institutions, especially museums. New museums have opened, old ones have expanded, and larger numbers of individuals from a broader spectrum of the population visit them. This pressure of numbers on the institutions also raises questions about the efficient use and best distribution of resources.

Finally, the museum world is becoming increasingly professional. The inspired amateurs and government employees who staffed museums in the past are being replaced by people trained specifically for museum work, many of whom are making a life-time commitment to museum work, and even to museum education. This professionalization brings with it the desire to develop a cumulative review of practice, to document instances, to build on former experience: to establish a profession of museum work and museum education with accepted professional standards and shared procedures.

All these factors – economic constraints, increased museum use, and professionalization – create pressure on museum personnel to look more carefully at their priorities and programmes. The kinds of questions that are raised about museum programmes are of two types. First is a set of concerns about what actually happens in museum programmes: what occurs, when children come to a programme, when classes view an exhibit, when the public wanders through the halls? Second is a need to determine if the things that happen are what was intended. Do visitors really learn more about the origins of humanity, do children begin to understand the baroque style, did the museum provide a replication of a 'hands-on' experience in family life of two centuries ago?

Both these types of questions are basic questions of *evaluation studies* – a careful documentation of what a programme is, and examination to see if it meets its objectives. In short, the increased pressures for 'accountability' in museums – both from external economic factors and internal forces leading to increased professionalization – result in greater need for evaluation activities.

THE RANGE OF EVALUATION

The increased need for evaluation in museums is not unique. Other institutions and professions have felt similar pressures in recent years. The spectacular rise in health care facilities (and the rapidly escalating costs!), the expansion of the criminal justice system, and (in the United States) the introduction of Federal funds into the education system starting after the passing of the Elementary and Secondary Education Act in the mid-1960s, have brought with them the need, and often the statutory requirement, for more evaluation.

At the same time, and partly in response to this need, the evaluation field has gone through a dramatic period of growth. This expansion can be seen in the establishment of professional societies of evaluators, the rapid increase in publications devoted to evaluation work and the development, by professional committees, of standards for evaluation. However, the most important change in the evaluation enterprise during this time has not been its considerable growth in size, but the widening of conceptual approaches to evaluation. As professionals have needed to look carefully at a very broad range of programmes and activities they have recognized that systematic inquiry into what happens in the world, how things occur and whether they take place as planned or intended, requires a wide range of approaches and methods.

Before this period of growth, formal evaluation work was confined largely (but not exclusively) to education in schools and was dominated by a scientific approach which took as its model the epistemology and style of the physical, laboratory sciences. Evaluation work was primarily an offshoot from educational psychology, a profession dominated by this quantitative, laboratory-based model. The best known achievement of this type of evaluation is the now ubiquitous standardized test and the most common method is that of pre-/post-test experimental design.

More recently, a new range of evaluation strategies has been developed. Although these strategies use a variety of means, they share an approach which has a different epistemological base from the traditional 'experimental' model. They look to the field-based sciences – ethnography, anthropology and sociology – for their basic theory and rationale. Characteristically, these newer evaluation methods stress documentation, observation and in-depth interviews, and result in case studies and 'thick' descriptions of practice. They tend to be qualitative rather than quantitative in method and result in primarily narrative reports.

These two general approaches to evaluation have been repeatedly characterized in recent years, and their values and shortcomings discussed in the literature.[1, 2, 3] As the museum world has begun to examine itself more carefully, and more systematically, a variety of evaluation strategies are used. The more traditional evaluation mode, based on careful specification of desired outcomes and clear efforts to approximate controlled situations, is exemplified by the work of Shettel[4] and Screven,[5] among others. Anthropological and ethnographic approaches to studying museums have been used by a group in Berkeley,[6] while more strictly evaluative studies based on observation and interviews have been carried out, among others, by Wolf,[7] and my colleague Brenda Engel and myself.[8] I will describe our own approach to evaluation in a later section. First I want to make some generalizations about all evaluations.

SOME TRUTHS ABOUT EVALUATION WORK

1. All forms of evaluation can be useful. The styles of evaluation available may appear to be so different that they are contradictory, but each can be of use in certain situations. Each represents a different approach to knowledge, and each provides data and leads to conclusions. The choice of the form of evaluation that will be carried out depends on the problem that is being addressed, the audience to whom the work is directed, and the professional and personal inclinations of the people involved. That does not make one form 'right' and the other 'wrong'. Each must be assessed on its own merits and within its own frame of reference.

2. Under appropriate conditions any form of evaluation can address questions related both to what occurs and what the outcomes are, although the traditional form of evaluation is usually associated more with measuring predetermined objectives, while the field-based methods are better at providing descriptive information and documenting unanticipated outcomes. If both sorts of questions are of interest, it is important that museum professionals stipulate their needs and see to it that the evaluation addresses their concerns.

3. No matter what the form of evaluation chosen, it is crucial that museum programme staff be involved in the evaluation. There is a mistaken assumption that evaluation, like plumbing or accounting, is an activity carried out in isolation from other activities by outside experts. Most of us do call on professionals to repair the water pipes and leave the methodology completely up to them. But, many of us at institutions have learned that it is essential to work with financial experts in order to get an accounting system that meets our needs. It is even more important to work with evaluators because, unlike accounting, there is no standard system that can be applied in the absence of input from programme staff. Evaluation studies are useful only to the extent that professional staff are involved in every phase from planning to data collection and analysis. There is no such thing as evaluation in the absence of goals. These goals should be determined by the people who intend to use the information.

4. Evaluation activities should be an ongoing part of the programme itself. They should be carried out concurrently with the activities, not initiated after the programme or exhibit is only a memory for the participants. We and other evaluators are often asked to evaluate a programme after it is almost ended or already completed. This makes more work for everyone, leaves the conclusions nebulous at best, and drastically limits the usefulness of the whole process. An evaluation that occurs while a programme is going on has the following advantages over a retrospective evaluation:

a. it forces participants to look at what they are doing in a formal and reflective way while they are doing it;
b. it permits ongoing modification and correction of components that are not working well, or permits changes in later phases based on earlier experiences;
c. it maximizes the use of normal programme components (records, interviews, observations, participants' products) as part of the evaluation, making it possible to carry out the evaluation with a minimum additional burden to anyone.

5. In the preceding paragraphs I have argued that evaluation is contextual: it happens in a setting. It is an applied task performed in the service of some larger organizational framework. There is no 'pure' science of evaluation independent of its purposes within the context of the institution that carries it out. Another way to say this is to point out that evaluation is political. The kind of questions asked, the sort of information determined to be useful, the means used to gather data, and the way the information is organized and presented will depend on the social views of those who carry out and direct the evaluation. This in no way diminishes the value of evaluation work. It is simply important to remember to ask why any particular study is carried out, what the authors' or sponsors' intentions are, and how the study is to be used.

The above point is only an extension of a more general point about museums. Exhibitions and educational programmes inevitably and necessarily illustrate some social/political point of view. We call them 'neutral' when from *our* point of view they reflect the prevailing socio-political norm. They appear to us apolitical when we cannot even imagine an alternative viewpoint.

PRACTICAL EVALUATION WORK

For the last six years, my colleague Brenda Engel and I have carried out hundreds of evaluation studies for museums and other cultural institutions. Many of these evaluations were of educational programmes developed as part of the effort to bring about racial integration in Massachusetts schools by involving cultural institutions with schools. In our work we have looked at programmes that include younger and older children, that take place in schools, museums or other settings, that are intensive (all day for a week or two) and extensive (once a week for an hour over a long period), that include children who know each other previously and those who don't, as well as programmes that include teachers, parents, and others. Much of our work has been of necessity quite limited: the funds available for evaluation are often only a small fraction of the total budget, and they are usually the first to be cut when, as happens so often, the programme is forced to carry on with a smaller than anticipated appropriation. In the course of this work, we have developed a careful, systematic approach that allows us to meet at least some of the needs of evaluation. We have described this work elsewhere in more detail.[8] What I wish to do here is to outline the essentials of our method, and to draw some conclusions from it for evaluation work in general.

We have found that it is absolutely essential that we meet with programme staff and

309

hear, directly, their description of the programme: what they intend to have happen, and what they expect the outcomes to be. Written descriptions found in proposals or funding requests are usually inadequate and often out of date by the time a programme actually gets underway. At this meeting we match programme intentions and expected outcomes with means for collecting data. There are many possible sources for evaluation information including programme products and activities. The enclosed table (Table 42.1) lists a wide range of data sources that we have found useful. The match of programme issues or interests (whatever is important to the people who are responsible for the programme) with means for collecting data is done graphically in the form of a matrix, so that we can see what means will address each particular issue.

Table 42.1 General matrix and list of possible sources of data

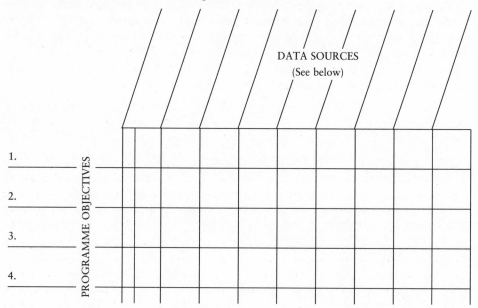

Sources of Data:

Logs and Journals
– personal journals
– records of meetings
– records of class activities
– journal from trip

Reports
– meeting notes
– staff evaluation form
– children's evaluation

Curriculum
– lesson plans
– description of activities

– resource book
– outline
– bibliography of resources
– slide/tape show

Observations
– in class
– on a trip
– of meetings

Interviews
– teachers
– museum staff
– administrators
– children (single or in groups)

Student Products
– pictures
– written work
– objects
– photos of products
– tests
– record of field trip

Other Products
– photos of trip
– children's interview

When we make up this matrix, we make sure that for any issue that we intend to investigate we have more than one means for collecting data. For example, if we are interested in programme impact on children, we may interview programme staff, the children, and their teachers, and look at some of the work produced by the children. If we are concerned with administrative cooperation, we may not only interview the people concerned, but look at meetings notes and a log of telephone calls or other correspondence.

After determining what data will be gathered, we decide on a schedule for these tasks and distribute responsibility for carrying them out among the programme staff and ourselves. Since much of the information comes from the ordinary activities of the programme (meeting notes, participants' products, curriculum produced, etc.) some portion of the documentation is always carried out by the staff. This has several advantages: it keeps down the cost of the evaluation, it provides a way for the staff to remain involved in the evaluation, and it takes much of the mystery out of the summary report written at the end. Our conclusions are based on the data that have been collected openly and is available to all the programme participants. No matter what other information we gather, at least one personal visit to the programme is essential to us if we are to write a report of our findings. There is no substitute for first-hand experience of a programme.

We have come to some generalizations from doing this work many times:

1. Unless we have worked together previously, our initial meeting with museum staff members to define the issues to be addressed in the evaluation is usually difficult and threatening for the staff. But it is also the most important part of the process. It is simply very hard to sit down with an outsider and describe in detail just what is going to happen in a programme, to justify the activities, to explain how the activities are related to the proposed outcomes, and to commit oneself to the kind of evidence that would constitute satisfactory results. But, this first step is crucial. It both provides the basic working contract for our relationship and helps everyone understand what is going to happen.

2. If we have taken the trouble to meet at the beginning of the programme and define issues important to the staff, we have never failed to obtain data that are relevant to the expressed concerns. Although the mountains of information which come in as the programme progresses often at first appear shapeless and vague, the data always contain information relevant to the questions that were addressed, after the data are organized and analysed.

3. It is as important to look at and to define what actually happens in a programme as it is to define what the expected results of a programme are going to be. Often just the fact that children from two different schools came together for two hours once a week for eight weeks is as important an achievement as that they learned something about different cultures. We have documented many instances where the trials and difficulties in simply carrying out a programme provided a strong endorsement of the activity. In other instances, documentation of the factors which prevented the programme staff from performing the activities they intended provided important information for the institution. In any case, the extent to which expected results were achieved must be examined in the context of what actually occurred, as well as in relation to what was proposed.

4. Inevitably, the evaluation process helps programme staff to think about what they are doing and to plan for the future. We find that the considerable interaction we have with programme staff during the course of a programme often encourages modification of the programme, either for the current sessions or for some future time.

5. The data invariably allow us to make generalizations that were not anticipated at the beginning of the evaluation. Whether it is communication between administrators and, staff, problems with transportation, the physical condition of the galleries, or some other factor which had not occurred to any of us at the beginning, we always find something which is illuminated by the evaluation process, and for which the evaluation provides the solid data for addressing the issue. Even in cases where the deficiency or problem is obvious to all, the evaluation sometimes provides the documentation that is needed to convince a higher administrator that the issue is serious.

CONCLUSION

Thoughtful and careful museum professionals recognize the need to document their work and to ask serious and systematic questions about what they are doing. Many already carry out such inquiries as part of their daily activities.

In this paper I have argued that evaluation work should be an integral component of any museum education programme. By making evaluation a part of the activity itself, it can be carried out with a minimum of additional effort and can provide useful information to improve future activities. Appropriate evaluation styles exist to match the philosophical inclination of the programme staff and specific methods exist for any kind of programme.

A formal evaluation plan can help to strengthen museum education work. If it is carried out with the help of an independent consultant, this professional can provide a fresh perspective on the museum's work.

This paper first appeared in Museum Education *(1982) Copenhagen: Danish ICOM/CECA, pp. 21–6.*

REFERENCES

1 Guba, E. (1978) *Towards a Methodology of Naturalistic Inquiry in Educational Evaluation*, Los Angeles: Center for the Study of Evaluation.
2 Mitroff, I. I. and Kilman, R. H. (1978) *Methodological Approaches to Social Science*, San Francisco: Jossey-Bass.
3 Hein, G. E. (1979) 'Evaluation in open education: emergence of qualitative methodology', in S. Meisels (ed.) *Special Education and Development*, Baltimore: University Park Press.
4 Shettel, H. H., Butcher, M., *et al.* (1968) *Strategies for Determining Exhibit Effectiveness*, Final Report: AIR E95–4168FR, ED 026718 ERIC Document Reproduction Service.
5 Screven, C. G. (1976) 'Exhibit evaluations: a goal referenced approach', *Curator* 19: 271–39.
6 Laetsch, W. M. *et al.* (n.d.) *Naturalistic Studies of Children and Family Groups in Science Centers*, unpublished manuscript, Berkeley, CA: Lawrence Hall of Science.
7 Wolf, R. L. (1980) 'A naturalistic view of evaluation', *Museum News* 58, July/August: 39–45.
8 Engel, B. S. and Hein, G. E. (1981) 'Qualitative evaluation of cultural institution/school education programs', in S. N. Lehman and K. Inge (eds) *Museum School-Partnerships: Plans and Programs*, Washington, DC: Center for Museum Education.

43

Small scale evaluation

Tim Badman

This paper describes a specific evaluation project in a historical setting. The objectives of the programme to be evaluated were clarified in terms of messages to be conveyed and the feelings that staff hoped visitors would have. A change in attitude to the historical theme was hoped for and this formed the subject of the evaluation. The methods used, which involved questionnaires used on site, the results and the lessons learnt are discussed.

Quarry Bank Mill is owned by the National Trust and run by the Quarry Bank Mill Trust with the purpose of interpreting the development of the factory system at the end of the eighteenth century. The Apprentice House aims to contribute to this theme by giving a glimpse of domestic apprentice life in the 1830s. The approach taken combines living history with an informal guided tour. The general public are accompanied around the house by costumed demonstrators, who aim to maintain an informal atmosphere in the group – visitors are encouraged to pick up and touch artefacts, to question and to chat. The emphasis is on learning through experience rather than taking in large amounts of historical fact.

AIMS AND OBJECTIVES

The first thing to be clear about in an evaluation is exactly what is to be evaluated. This means knowing definite objectives for the interpretation: 'What are we trying to say or do? These should hopefully be written down in some sort of plan or statement, but if not then it will be necessary to sit down and clarify them. This is an important exercise in its own right. At the Apprentice House the aims of the interpretation divide into two categories which can be termed *messages* and *visitor experience*.

Messages

The messages basically revolve around creating empathy with the apprentices and portraying the institutional way of life in the Apprentice House. Within this framework a series of specific factors were identified. Examples included:

- awareness of the lack of individuality of the apprentices
- awareness of the strict routine of apprentice life

Visitor experience

Visitor experience relates to the feelings which staff at the House hoped that visitors would have about the interpretation itself. Specific objectives included:

- feeling entertained and at ease
- feeling the house had an atmosphere of activity
- feeling that the portrayal of apprentice life was honest

At the Apprentice House the principal aim of the survey was to assess attitude change and a questionnaire survey was decided upon as the appropriate method. The detailed work of designing the questionnaire needed to take into account a number of external factors. The main one of these related to time. It is essential that any questionnaire is not too long. People are normally very happy to take time to answer questions but this can quickly become an imposition. The nature of the site may also impose constraints. At the Apprentice House most people arrived for their tour between five and ten minutes before it began – giving a maximum possible time for each interview. It is also useful at this stage to have an idea about the number of results required. This will reflect the amount of time available for data collection. Collecting data is hard work and time consuming, a reasonable expectation for a questionnaire survey is twenty results per person per day.

SAMPLE SIZE

A certain number of results are needed before data can be considered to be reasonably representative of any group of visitors. This is essential for the definite results which can be produced by statistical analysis. There are several techniques for estimating sample size, but a useful rule of thumb is that at least fifty results are needed for each *group* of data (e.g. 50 results before the visit, 50 results after). This is particularly important if you plan to analyse results according to different types of visitor. Detailed information about visitors may be irrelevant if you are planning to collect a small data set.

For the Apprentice House the finished questionnaire consisted of three sections. The first two aimed to gain basic information about the visitors themselves and about visitor attitudes to apprentice life. These were asked to visitors both before and after visiting the House. Interviewing can 'sensitize' people and affect the way they experience and react to interpretation. It was important, therefore, that people asked before were not interviewed afterwards. The third section of the questionnaire gained information about the visitor experience on the tour and was only asked to visitors who had already visited the House.

Trying to assess attitudes to apprentices presented difficulties; how do you measure empathy? The approach taken was that used by Lee and Uzzell in their work on assessing Farm Open Days. A series of fourteen statements were devised to tap into the attitudes which the interpretation tries to address, for example 'The millowner exploited the apprentices' and 'Apprenticeship gave poor people a chance to improve their lot'. Visitors were asked to grade these on a numbered scale according to how much they agreed or disagreed with them. Giving numerical values to opinions in this way permits detailed statistical analysis. This analysis can seem quite daunting, but the maths is fairly straightforward and the results are worth the effort.

CONCLUSIONS

So what can result from evaluation? At the Apprentice House the basic conclusions showed that the interpretation was broadly meeting its objectives. The 'graded statement' technique worked and showed a clear difference in attitudes before and after. Changed reactions were observed for nine out of the fourteen statements, and six cases were statistically significant. The survey also showed that most of the aims set for visitor experience were being met. These results have been useful in encouraging staff and giving confidence in the approach that has been taken. The process of the survey itself has also focused the minds of staff on exactly what the interpretation is trying to achieve. The report also highlighted one area of weakness. A number of visitors didn't feel that the house had an atmosphere of 1830s activity. This was something which staff had expected might be the case. Thought is now being given to this aspect of the interpretation.

The total amount of time spent on the project amounted to about ten person days and almost half of this was spent collecting data. This provided about 100 responses. In some cases, a way of reducing the time involved is to use questionnaires or survey forms which can be taken away by visitors and filled in independently. This removes the time consuming data collection stage but is not appropriate in all cases. An alternative, as was the case with this project, is to work with students. This sort of project can be useful to the site, reducing staff input to a supervisory or liaison role, and make a complete and fulfilling piece of work for the student. Possible places to approach about conducting a student survey include educational establishments which run courses in subjects such as tourism, countryside management, or leisure management .

This paper first appeared in Environmental Interpretation *(July 1990), pp. 20–1.*

REFERENCE

Lee, T. R. and Uzzell, D. L. (1980) *The Educational Effectiveness of the Farm Open Day*, Countryside Commission for Scotland.

44

Pupils' perceptions of museum education sessions

Marilyn Ingle

The museum education service was at a point of change and in order to make informed decisions about the way forward decided to survey the opinions of a range of children of different ages to discover their thoughts after experiencing a visit involving the handling of objects.

The post-visit survey and its results are discussed in detail, with notes made on how changes have been made to the services offered.

The interpretation of museum collections for pupils offers much scope for museum educators. Rarely have the opinions of pupils been sought about their perceptions of museum education services. It seemed appropriate to canvass pupils' opinions about a museum education service which had diversified and developed in response to the educational changes of the 1980s. This article is based on research for an MA thesis for the University of York.[1]

THE MUSEUM EDUCATION SERVICE

The survey was restricted to the museum education sessions which took place in York Castle Museum. The education service, funded to work with the schools and colleges of North Yorkshire County Council, has many regular visitors. Large collections of military, textile and social history exhibits are displayed in two former eighteenth-century prison buildings constructed in the bailey of a medieval castle. The museum education department provides a service to interpret the museum's site and collections through object-based learning. Visitor pressure limits teaching sessions in the galleries, therefore the museum education sessions tend to take place in the education room. Teachers are requested to make preliminary visits to plan their pupils' sessions at the museum.

DESIGN OF THE SURVEY

An opportunity sample was taken of pupils visiting York Castle Museum Education Service during a five-week period from the middle of February until late March 1986. Unfortunately, the sample provided an age imbalance compared with the mean use for the education service. There were far more infant pupils (19.5 per cent of the total sample), and fewer secondary pupils, (16.5 per cent of the total sample). However, age imbalance is not unusual over a half-term period. The sample had a reasonable spread of day and half-day visits.

On their return to school, the pupils were asked to complete questionnaires about the museum visits. Seven hundred and thirty-two pupils (an 80.5 per cent response rate) from thirty-four classes returned questionnaires. A brief survey sheet was given to each teacher for completion. See Fig. 44.1 for the questions which the teachers were asked.

The sample provided classes which were frequent, infrequent or new users of the Education Service. History, science and textiles were the main subjects associated with the visits. All the teachers had helped to plan the museum education sessions for their pupils, so that the museum visits were extensions of the work in school.

As the pupils were aged from 4 to 18 years, the questionnaires had to be reasonably brief and easy to understand. The questions had been refined in a pilot survey. Most questions were open-ended which provided problems in categorizing the information. For greater reliability, the pupils' responses were coded into minor groups of reasons, which were later placed into broader categories of reasons.

The questionnaires, printed on coloured paper, were designed to be attractive to children. The questions, listed in Fig. 44.2, were spread over three sides of A4 paper to provide sufficient space for pupils' handwriting. There was evidence that some of the younger primary pupils found the questionnaires too long as the response rate declined to 69.8 per cent for the last question. There was little evidence of teachers influencing the questionnaires' completion. For pupils spending a full day with the education service, an additional sheet was included about specific activities. Pupils were asked to comment about their likes and dislikes of wearing costume, using drama, trying skills of the past and making models and pictures.

FINDINGS

Pupils liked to handle objects

The educational literature emphasizes the advantages of handling objects, yet many museum professionals have strong reservations about touching artefacts. All the pupils in the survey had had the opportunities to handle objects. It was hoped that useful insights into the pupils' opinions about handling objects would come from the replies to the open-ended questions of 'What did you like doing?' and 'Which object interested you the most?'.

Of the categories of activities liked by pupils, 32.9 per cent liked touching and using objects. One 14-year-old pupil wrote: 'I liked how we were given objects. Being able to touch them was better than just looking at them through glass or at displays you can't touch'. The other categories of activities were looking at objects (28.0 per cent), recording objects (22.5 per cent) and past skills or drama (16.5 per cent). Pupils did not have the same activities, although all had had the opportunity to look at and touch objects. Therefore the percentages needed to be interpreted with caution; for example of those who had experienced drama, 37.2 per cent had listed it as the favourite activity.

The secondary pupils studying history or textiles, were more likely to prefer the activity of handling objects than primary pupils. An 18-year-old's comment was: 'I prefer to be able to handle the garments, to see the construction and be able to measure the garment as I think this gives a greater realization of the sort of people who wore them and the extremes they went to fit into them, I like this activity because it makes drawing the garments a lot easier as seams, darts etc. are very clear.'

Teachers' survey sheet

Date of the questionnaires' completion

Was this the first subject lesson after the visit?
Yes or No

Date of the museum visit

Theme of the museum visit

Please name the school subject associated with the visit

Does the museum visit form an integral part of the pupils' current work?
Yes or No

With which subject theme is the museum visit linked?

Since September 1985, how many times has this class visited the Education Service?

Fig. 44.1 Teachers' survey sheet

For the activities of touching and using objects, all pupils were much more likely to give historical reasons. The appearance and qualities of the objects were important to those who wrote about liking to touch the objects.

In response to the question 'Which object interested you the most?' 44.1 per cent had liked the less spectacular objects which they had handled in the education room. One-third of primary pupils and three-quarters of secondary pupils chose education room objects. Objects touched had appeal even if they were not as impressive as those displayed in the galleries.

Less than a fifth of the pupils chose as their favourite object one which was behind glass in the galleries, usually dolls and doll's houses. There was a tendency for infant pupils to select large gallery objects such as the hansom cab, gypsy caravan, fire-engines, sweet shop and automaton clock.

Two-fifths of the pupils liked the gallery objects due to the appearance and qualities of the objects, whereas a quarter of pupils liked the education room objects for the same reason. Another quarter of pupils chose education room objects because they liked the involvement of being able to touch the objects in the education room. A 6-year-old boy, from the class where pupils worked the mechanism of the deadfall mousetrap, liked the mousetrap: 'Because every mouse likes cheese they go for the cheese the rope goes up and the hard piece of wood goes down splat – one squashed mouse.'

Pupils were more likely to give historical and comparative reasons for liking objects which they had touched in the education room. 'The wheel of life was like a television', wrote one 8-year-old boy.

The pupils' questionnaire

First page
Your age. Boy or girl?

What did you like doing?

Why did you like doing these things?

Second page
Which object interested you the most?

Why were you interested?

Since your visit, have you wanted to learn more about this object?

If your answer is yes, what are you going to do?

Third page
What did you like doing the least?

Why did you dislike this?

What do you think you came to learn about at the Castle Museum?

Has your Castle Museum visit helped you to understand the way people lived in the past?

If your answer is yes, how has the visit helped?

Fig. 44.2 The pupils' questionnaire

The choice of favourite objects may have been affected by the length of time which had elapsed before the completion of the questionnaires at school. Of the primary pupils who completed the questionnaires on the same day, 24.0 per cent selected objects which had been handled; whereas for those given the questionnaires to complete four or more days after the museum visit, the number who selected objects which had been handled rose to 49.0 per cent.

The pupils' opinions have been useful in selecting objects for the handling collection. As pupils had liked the opportunities to touch and work objects, more thought has been given to collecting objects with the potential for varied sensory experiences. The findings suggested that certain activities could be more relevant depending on the teachers' purpose; so touching objects would be a suitable activity if the intention was to focus the pupils' attention on historical and comparative understanding.

Pupils enjoyed wearing costume

A tenth of the 732 pupils had chosen wearing costume as the favourite activity, though only a half of the sample had had the opportunity to wear costume. A 10-year-old considered a soldier's uniform was 'heavy and prickly.' Pupils, used to modern standards of comfort and cloth textures were unable to cope with the fit, style and discomfort of armour, uniform and civilian clothing.

Although much of the costume was reproduction, 27.1 per cent gave historical reasons for why they liked wearing costume, like this 10-year-old boy. 'Because somebody had worn it in the seventeenth century in a battle and I felt as if I was going back in time.'

Costume seemed to provide a tangible link with the past; as Radcliffe suggested: 'Instead of looking at stationary, inanimate objects and wondering about their place in history, visitors develop a greater perspective on the past. They can see the drape of fabric or the hindrance of a too-tight sleeve and watch living people in action.'[2]

A 13-year old girl's comment was: 'Because you could see people try them on, and even you could try them on, it made it a lot more interesting than seeing a dummy dressed up. You could see the problems they had and experience them for yourself.'

Despite the difficulties of resourcing reproduction costume, the pupils highlighted the value of wearing costume. Perhaps, when trying on costume, more consideration should be given to explaining about the discomfort due to fit, fabrics and styles of historical costume.

PARTICIPATIVE EXPERIENCES WERE ENJOYABLE

Due to the teachers' planning, the opportunity to try former skills and drama was restricted to 45.2 per cent of the 732 pupils. All were primary pupils. Only one child out of the 47 pupils who experienced drama considered that the visit had not helped in her understanding of the past. For one class, on a series of visits, the favoured activity was taking part in the dramatic sessions, rather than the more recent activities of touching, recording and former skills. One 10-year-old wrote: 'It really made me feel like a Victorian girl in a Victorian street, which was great because I haven't been one before.'

More than half of the pupils gave reasons for liking the activities because of the personal involvement, with the second group of reasons being fun. Less than 6 per cent gave historical reasons for liking to learn former skills. 'I like turning the dolly peg round and I liked scrubbing on the rubbing board,' wrote one 6-year old girl.

However, there were pupils who disliked taking part in participatory activities. Reasons given were associations, skills needed, repetitive tasks and discomfort. Some dislikes were inevitable and formed part of the experience as for this 7-year-old boy. 'I don't like cold water and I hate having a bath.' Writing with a quill pen had posed problems for a 10-year-old girl: 'I thought it was easy to write with and it was not. It kept dripping all over the paper.'

In teaching skills of the past, it seems necessary to offer a balance of different former skills, whilst considering their possible unpleasant associations and the historical purposes for teaching the skills. If to have fun and pleasure through former skills and drama will increase motivation to learn as O'Connell and Alexander suggested,[3] then these activities are of educational value. However, care should be taken to prevent the learning experiences from being too shallow.

Regular visitors preferred participatory experiences

Regular and infrequent users of the museum education service appeared to have different requirements. For first-time visitors, it was found that more than half the pupils selected gallery objects and more than half the pupils chose looking as the favourite activity. By contrast, 'We can touch things and we like doing things rather than being told things,' wrote a 9-year-old boy from a school which made regular visits.

Since the survey, first-time visitors to the museum have been allowed more opportunity to browse in selected galleries. Secondary pupils have been given more practical activities because the regular visitors favoured this form of museum education experience.

Pupils intended to learn more

Two-thirds of the half-day visitors intended to learn more about their favourite objects, supporting the idea that museum visits are good for the motivation of pupils. However, more primary (72.3 per cent), than secondary (49.1 per cent) pupils intended to learn more about their favourite objects. Some secondary pupils considered the knowledge they had gained about their objects was finite. With increasing age, pupils were more likely to seek further information in libraries and museums.

Museum education visits promoted interests in further visits to museums. The pupils were not asked specifically if they intended to visit museums. Most of the 17.3 per cent of pupils, who intended to return to museums to learn more about their favourite object, named the York Castle Museum. However, most pupils were not thinking of museums as resources for further learning about objects.

Vary the recording experiences

The findings provided a considerable number, 19.8 per cent, who liked drawing and writing and a slightly lower percentage who disliked drawing and writing. 'It was fun. I met a real artist in Kirkgate. He helped me,' wrote an 8-year-old boy, whereas an 18-year-old disliked: 'Drawing in the museum when visitors are wandering round. Because these people are more interested in what you are doing rather than what is on show. Seats at the back of a room are better as visitors are unable to notice what you are doing'.

Since the survey, methods of recording have included the use of the computer and attempts have been made to diversify recording techniques. Older pupils have been made more aware of the purpose of recording in relation to their school work.

Differences in responses according to pupils' ages

The problems of understanding time language, mentioned by Vukelich,[4] were apparent in the pupils' responses, especially the vagueness of those pupils under eight years of age. In general terms, four-fifths of all pupils recognized the historical link and if the pupils were studying history, a higher number thought the visits had helped in their understanding of the past. A 9-year-old boy wrote: 'It has put a picture in my mind what it would be like to live 100 years ago.'

Secondary pupils liked tactile opportunities. Preferences for looking declined with age, fewer fourth-year juniors preferred looking to first-year juniors. There was evidence of the problems of working in a large building with young children. One tenth of primary pupils complained about climbing steps or walking long distances in the museum.

Different responses of boys and girls

Very few gender preferences existed. Twelve primary pupils, all below the age of nine years, expressed dislikes because the activities or objects were thought to be more appropriate for the other sex. One 4-year-old wrote: 'I didn like the girls toys girls toys are not fo boys.'

There was a tendency for boys and girls to select different objects, and the differences were most noticeable for gallery objects rather than the education room objects which would have been touched. In the galleries, the most popular exclusively male exhibits were the fire-engines, compared with dolls and doll's houses for the girls. However, where children had handled exhibits, fewer objects were chosen exclusively by one sex, perhaps because there had been the opportunity to find out more about the objects.

Further research would be useful taking subjects traditionally associated with one sex, such as warfare; for from the class of 10- and 11-year-olds where both military and domestic aspects were studied by both sexes, boys tended to ignore the domestic aspects, though only one girl failed to mention military objects for either the preferred activity or object. Although the favourite object was the close helmet because it had so many parts which moved, one 11-year-old girl put the military and domestic objects into relative importance: 'I liked trying on the helmets and best of all I liked looking at the embroidery patterns that the seventeenth-century girls sewed. I enjoyed trying on the helmets because I knew that people had actually maybe died or got injured in that helmet. I enjoyed the embroidery patterns because it fascinated me how they sewed things that small, and how the sewing had secret messages behind the pictures.'

Pupils should understand the purposes for the museum visit

Compared with school classrooms, museum galleries and education rooms contain a wealth of images and objects unrelated to pupils' current studies. Beer had found that more than half the displays in museums were likely to be ignored by visitors.[5] Problems in focusing attention to promote effective learning in the museum had been noted by Chase.[6]

In the York Castle Museum survey, it was found that there were noticeable differences in the pupils' responses where more than half the class were unclear about why they had been brought. When teachers and pupils were not sharing the same purposes for the visits, pupils expressed more dissatisfaction, preferred looking generally and were more attracted to objects and galleries irrelevant to the teachers' themes for the visits.

Clearly, at the start of each museum lesson, it is important to reinforce the links between the museum education sessions and the pupils' current work in school. During teachers' preliminary visits and on information sheets for teachers, it seems wise to inform teachers of the benefits of pupils and teachers sharing common purposes for the museum visits.

CONCLUSION

From the limited information a survey supplies, useful insights were obtained for developing the education service. In discussions with curatorial and conservation colleagues, pupils' opinions have been used to justify the provision of high quality objects for the handling collection and for continued access to the reserve collections. At teachers' meetings and courses, knowledge of pupils' opinions has been useful in planning pupils' museum sessions: in particular, making sure the pupils are aware of the purposes of the museum visits.

More research concerning the needs of frequent visitors and the pupils' views of museums as learning institutions would be useful. On this survey's very limited evidence most pupils were not aware of the potential for learning in museums.

All ages of pupils confirmed the benefits of museums education provision which stressed tactile practical experiences. Relatively few dislikes were expressed. The museum visits had been positive, enjoyable experiences which had helped the pupils' understanding of the topics being studied.

The advantages of a museum education visit were summed up by a 10-year-old girl: 'I liked handling, touching, and trying on things better than looking round the museum. I liked especially trying clothes on, because you can't normally touch things and try things on when you go to a museum with your parents and it gives you an idea of what it was like then when the things were used.'

This paper first appeared in Journal for Education in Museums *11 (1990), pp. 5–8.*

REFERENCES

1 Ingle, M. G. (1988) 'Pupils' perceptions of museum education sessions planned by their teachers and the museum education officer', unpublished MA thesis, University of York.
2 Radcliffe, P. M. (1987) 'Period dress projects: considerations for administrators', *Curator* 30(3): 193–8.
3 O'Connell, P. S. and Alexander, M. (1979) 'Reaching the High School audience', *Museum News* 58(2): 50–6.
4 Vukelich, R, (1984) 'Time language for interpreting history collections to children', *Museum Studies Journal* 1(4): 42–50.
5 Beer, V. 'Great expectations: do museums know what visitors are doing?', *Curator* 30(3): 206–15.
6 Chase, R. A. (1975) 'Museums as learning environments', *Museum News* 54(1): 37–43.

45

Education: at the heart of museums

Eilean Hooper-Greenhill

Education has moved from a marginalized addition to one of the central functions of museums in the last fifteen years as museums have become more democratic, more cus-tomer-oriented and more aware of the needs of their visitors. In Britain, the move has been accelerated in recent times because of various factors external to the museum. Recession, new management approaches, and the contract culture have taken their toll of museums, including education staff, but the new consumer-oriented philosophy does open up possibilities for the reconceptualization and development of the educational role of museums. In fact, without this major internal shift, museums will be poorly placed to exist into the next century.

Museums and galleries are becoming more professional, and one of the areas in which this is most noticeable is the area that we might loosely term 'museum education'. There are some interesting consequences. Firstly, the professionalization of 'museum educa-tion' demands that we define what we mean by this expression, and secondly, having defined it, we need to establish the means to deliver it.

In Britain at the present time, museum education is in turmoil. Structures of delivery, which relate intimately to definitions of meaning, are being or have been overturned, and new ways of both understanding museum education and carrying it out (or as we say in the new management-speak, delivering it) are being sought. To take an example close to home, in Leicestershire the museum education team which consisted of seventeen people in 1990 was reduced to two by April 1993. In 1990 there was a separate department of museum education which covered schools provision and a large and historic loan service; now the two remaining staff members are 'integrated' into the main museum staff structure and the loan service has been much reduced (Schadla-Hall 1993).

In another example, since the introduction of the National Curriculum, at the British Museum school visits have increased by 400 per cent (Reeves, pers. comm.) and a new £10 million education centre is being planned. At Coventry Museum, in the West Midlands, following a very radical restructuring the Education Officer has been appointed in charge of a new division of Interpretation and Visitor Services, which will manage all front house activities, including exhibitions, events, education, marketing, site management and trading.

What is happening to museum education? Do we know what it is and who should do it any more? Why are these changes, which range from the extremely destructive and demoralizing to the very encouraging, taking place? What is going on?

The answers to these questions are revealing. They indicate that a massive change is taking place in the way that museums are to be understood. This change provides a climate for museum education that could be more positive than anything we have seen up till now.

NEW CONTEXTS FOR MUSEUM EDUCATION

Today in Britain there are new contexts for museum education. One important factor is the major change in attitude to visitors that is taking place in museums. Where has this come from and why? Another vital aspect is the Education Reform Act 1988. What effects has this had on museums and galleries? We can identify both positive and negative features in the current context of museum education in Britain. We are at a time that requires a radical redefinition of museum education, both on our parts as museum educators and on the part of our colleagues, curators and managers in museums.

Two years ago, when presenting the publication *Writing a Museum Education Policy* (Hooper-Greenhill 1991) at the Museums Association Annual Conference, Nigel Pittman, then Head of the Museums and Galleries Division of the central government Office of Arts and Libraries, remarked that the booklet should not really be necessary at all. The booklet urges that the museum education policy should reflect the policy of the museum as a whole. Nigel Pittman wanted to go much further than this, and in fact turn this idea on its head. 'The policy of any museum' he stated, 'should *be* an education policy' (Pittman 1991: 22).

When I first began to work in museums in the mid-1970s, such a statement would have been impossible. Museum education at that time was still frequently accepted in museums on sufferance. Staff structures reflected scholarly expertise, with departments based on object classifications and subject knowledge (Fig. 45.1).

I worked in national museums, especially the Tate and National Portrait Galleries, where museum education had been virtually in abeyance since before the First World War. In the national museums, which are funded through central government, education staff were (and still are) employed as civil servants on the same terms and conditions as the other museum staff. 'Education services' included provision for schools and all other educational institutions, holiday activities, and lectures and conferences for adults. There was a limited involvement in exhibition planning.

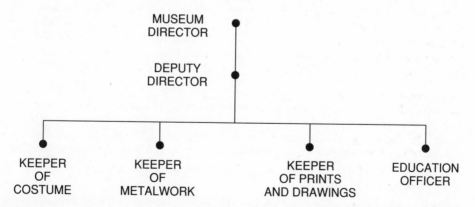

Fig. 45.1 Typical staff structure of national museums in the 1970s and 1980s, showing the relationship of education to curatorial posts

In local authority museums things were very different. At the local level, with museums funded through local government committees, museums thought about education almost exclusively in relation to schools, and argued that if they had a duty to schools, in order to discharge this duty a partnership was necessary with the Local Education Authority (LEA). Few museums saw education as their own responsibility. Where links were made with LEAs, relationships were established that ranged from teachers employed on teachers' terms and conditions (by the LEA) but seconded to the museum, to funding being given directly from the LEA to the museum's budget for the employment of museum education officers on the same terms and conditions as the other museum staff (Fig. 45.2). There were many variations on this basic pattern. No national picture emerged and we were left with a plethora of fairly unstable local agreements. There were a number of problems here: museum education staff worked only with schools (on the whole) and not with other constituencies such as adults, or local communities); as contractual conditions such as hours, holidays and salaries were different for teachers and curators, unified staff structures were frequently impossible, and this was often reflected in a mutual lack of understanding and sympathy; education could be (and sometimes was) seen as something separate from and less important than the main responsibilities of the museum.

During the 1970s and into the early 1980s many curators and other museum staff were suspicious of education and did not understand either the teaching methods or the inherent values and objectives. Since these distant days the context for museums and museum education have changed considerably, especially recently. In the UK we are just emerging from the deepest recession since the 1930s, and the market philosophy of the Thatcher years has penetrated even the most socially remote institutions, including museums. The contract culture, the introduction of performance measures, the sharp cutting of arts funding, the sudden push to self-reliance, and the development of new management and marketing strategies have led to great changes in UK museums. The situation is particularly acute in the non-national museums, and a sharply differentiated picture emerges.

Where effective management structures have been put in place rapidly, where the local government climate has been supportive, and where individual managers have been hard-working, effective, creative, and intelligent, museums have managed against difficult

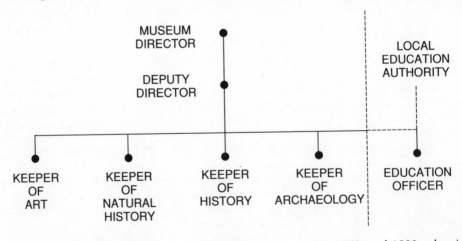

Fig. 45.2 Typical staff structure of local authority museums in 1970s and 1980s, showing the relationship of education to curatorial posts

odds to hold their own, cuts and closures have been minimized and in some cases significant gains have been achieved. Where management has been weak, local government officials have failed to support the museum, and museum senior staff have not understood the political situation, budgets have been cut, posts have been lost, and museums have been closed.

The situation for museums in general has therefore been extremely unstable and inhospitable in the last few years. Watching my colleagues struggle, I have been able to observe extreme change. On the one hand existing museum patterns, practices and values have been all but destroyed, but on the other hand museums have been shaken out of their long-standing complacency and they have had to become more aware of their social use and the needs of their customers. A succession of official reports have emphasized the uselessness of collections and accompanying scholarship without a social outcome (Audit Commission 1991; Museums and Galleries Commission 1991; National Audit Office 1993).

What has been the context for museum education in particular?

In 1988 the Education Reform Act came into force. This introduced the National Curriculum and among other things the Local Management of Schools (LMS). The Education Reform Act did not mention and did not consider museums and galleries at all, but it has had considerable effects on the museum world. As you might expect, some of these are positive, while others are more challenging.

The National Curriculum went through lengthy development processes, with plenty of opportunity for consultation at all stages. The processes were monitored closely by the HMI (Her Majesty's Inspector) responsible for museum education, and by GEM (Group for Education in Museums), who organized a system for reading and responding to the draft curriculum documents, using the acronym DAPOS, which stood for documents, archives, photographs, objects and sites. Curriculum documents were scanned for references to all of these, and suggestions were made as to where such references might be strengthened or introduced. In the case of art, a museum education officer worked as part of the curriculum development working party. As a result of all this hard work, some of the curriculum documents specifically refer to the use of museums, galleries or artefacts and it is not difficult to show how museums and galleries are relevant to other subject areas. As a result, school use has increased enormously: many museums are considering national curriculum use when mounting displays, and many curators are familiar with the broad outlines of the national curriculum.

This has all been very positive. The Local Management of Schools, however, has created problems. Under LMS, the money that is given to local government by central government specifically for spending on schools now has to be devolved to each school to spend as they wish. The limited amount of money that can be retained centrally by the LEA is severely proscribed and in a great many (although not all) cases, there are no longer any monies available for funding museum education staff. Some museum education staff have lost their jobs, as in Leicestershire as we have already seen. In Manchester, a city-wide museum education team has been broken up, with some of the individuals concerned being found other jobs within the LEA, two being kept on by the art gallery concerned with a temporary cushion of funds from the LEA for a few months, and one, officially retired from the LEA, being retained by an independent museum as Education Manager, but at a much lower salary than was paid by the LEA.

Where LEA funding has ceased for museum education delivery, a range of events have occurred. In some museums, the central museum budget has taken over funding of museum education, but in a time of decreasing budgets this has sometimes meant that other posts have had to go. In several cases, education, alone of all museum functions, has had to go into the market-place and earn its keep. One solution that seems to be spreading is the employment of an education manager by the museum, who organizes the training of unemployed/retired teachers to work as a supply team for the museum, to be called on as required, and paid for by the schools or the other groups who use them.

These processes of finding new ways to deliver museum education have brought educational issues to the fore in a way that is entirely new in museums. And big decisions are having to be made about the management of museum education.

THE MANAGEMENT OF 'MUSEUM EDUCATION'

When it became clear a few years ago that the future for museum education was becoming increasingly uncertain a great deal of encouragement was given to the development of museum education policies. The argument was that if the future was uncertain, at least if we knew what we were doing and why, it might be easier to support and sustain it. The development of policies for museum education opened up many vital issues.

In the process of policy development, which is lengthy and if genuine, needs to involve museum management at all levels, and constituent groups/customers, it quickly becomes evident that what is being called into question is the identity or nature of the museum itself.

To quote from Nigel Pittman again:

> In the past, too many museums – and worse still, art galleries – have been content to put objects on display in a way that encourages appreciation of them from a purely aesthetic point of view. The message for the future has to be that this isn't good enough. Too often galleries have been planned by curators and designers who fail to see the need for communication. If 'education' in its broadest sense was considered, it was as an afterthought, frequently too late to alter the planning or design. Planning an education policy should help with that, but what is really needed is recognition that education is a key component of every museum's *raison d'être*.
>
> (Pittman 1991)

These words marked the recognition that education should step out of its ghetto and step forward to claim its inheritance – parity with the collecting and conserving role of museums, and an understanding that collecting and conserving are means to an end, which is communication with the museum's users.

And this is indeed happening. Museums are developing new philosophies in relation to their visitors. These new philosophies require new ways of working, and new ways of thinking. Visitors (actual and potential) are understood to be people with particular and varying characteristics, with their own opinions about things, and with something to say about the museum and its products. New expressions are to be heard in the basements of museums, and are to be read in forward planning documents, such as research and evaluation, consultation and collaboration, users and their needs.

The new philosophies are being brought into effect through moves from enlightened managers (some few from educational backgrounds) and from new team approaches to exhibitions and projects. The education officer is being asked to develop new skills and sometimes to take on new management roles. There is the potential for what have always been the traditional concerns of the education officer to move to the centre stage of museums.

Part of the explanation for museums with these new values lies in the great cultural shift we have experienced in Britain since the emergence of Thatcherism. We have moved from the post-war political consensus over social welfare provision and concern for the quality of life with the state playing a major role in service provision, to an emphasis on the freedom of the individual to make choices within the market-place and a reliance on the private and voluntary sector for provision. Part of this ideology has meant the 'rolling back' of the state at both local and national level, with consequent cuts in the services (including museums) offered.

The management and measurement of provision through public and private sectors is now to be organized within a 'value-for-money' (VFM) framework. Museums, like other organizations, use their resources to purchase inputs (buildings, collections, expertise) in order to provide outputs or services (exhibitions, educational programmes, publications) which customers demand. The VFM framework examines a museum from the point of view of the relationship between its resource inputs and its service outputs, while seeking to establish whether or not the service outputs that are being provided are those which are valued by the various constituencies of the museum (which might include its visitors, other users, potential visitors and users, the governing body, and professional colleagues).

The VFM framework is based on three fundamental elements – the Three Es: economy, efficiency, and effectiveness (Fig. 45.3).

Economy is concerned with minimizing the cost of resources used, while being mindful of the quality of the inputs. Economy is about spending less.

Efficiency is concerned with the relationship between the output of goods, services or other results and the resources used to produce them. How far is a maximum output achieved for a given input, or minimum input used for a given output? Efficiency is about spending well.

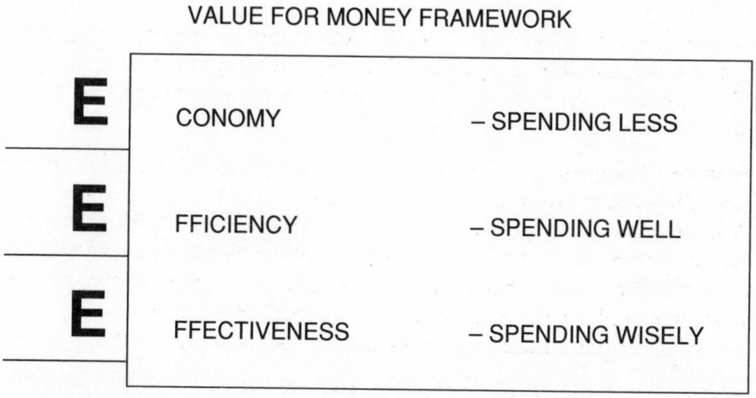

VALUE FOR MONEY FRAMEWORK

E CONOMY	– SPENDING LESS
E FFICIENCY	– SPENDING WELL
E FFECTIVENESS	– SPENDING WISELY

Fig. 45.3 The VFM framework

Effectiveness is concerned with the relationship between the intended results and the actual results of the projects, programmes and services. How successfully do the outputs of goods and services achieve policy objectives. Effectiveness is about spending wisely (Jackson 1991).

The value-for-money framework has been developed in the UK by the National Audit Office (which is responsible for ensuring the maximization of central government expenditure), and the Audit Commission for England and Wales (which has a similar function for local government public expenditure). Indeed both of these bodies have recently reviewed the performance of both local and national museums (Audit Commission 1991; National Audit Office 1993).

A museum that is structured in relation to the VFM framework is a museum that has undergone a major internal restructuring process. The restructuring entails a shift in internal organization from staff and resource divisions based on scholarly and collection-related expertise (see Fig. 45.2) to staff and resource divisions based on inputs and outputs (see Figs. 45.4 and 45.5).

A museum that is structured in relation to inputs and outputs has a bi-partite division, which inputs identified as collections, data about collections, the expertise of staff and other people, buildings, budgets and so on. The outputs include educational programmes, exhibitions, events, conservation for the future, a cultural environment, opportunities for entertainment and so on (Fig. 45.4). To ensure a balance between inputs and outputs it is logical to split the museum staff and budgets equally between the two divisions: half of the museum's effort will maintain and ensure continued inputs, and half will deliver relevant outputs (Fig. 45.5).

I am indebted to my colleague Alf Hatton at Coventry City Museum Service in the West Midlands for sharing with me his vision of the new museum service. He has designed a way of managing the several museums in the city to relate to the need to work within a VFM framework (see Fig. 45.6). This is all very new, and it is only recently that the

	MUSEUM
INPUTS	**OUTPUTS**
COLLECTIONS	EDUCATION
DATA	SCHOLARSHIP
STAFF/PEOPLE	ENTERTAINMENT
BUILDINGS	CONSERVATION FOR FUTURE
MONEY	CULTURE
OTHER RESOURCES	

Fig. 45.4 An input/output model of museum functions

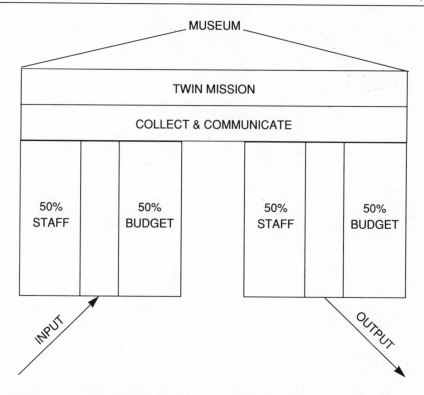

Fig. 45.5 A simple straightforward mission and division of functions and resources

former Education Officer had been appointed to manage the new division of Interpretation and Visitor Services.

Here we see education truly moving to the heart of the museum: the broad educational role of the museum has parity with the collection function. As Alf Hatton puts it 'There is a simple mission – to collect and to communicate, and the staff and budget will be split into these two divisions' (Hatton 1993).

What does the Interpretation and Visitor Services Division look like? At present it still reflects the old job titles that have been merged to form the division (see Fig. 45.6). As time goes on the description of the division will develop to reflect the need to identify and measure outputs and might look something like Fig. 45.7.

The objectives of managers within the VFM framework are to maximize value added. What this means is first, making sure that there is an effective balance between inputs and outputs, and second ensuring that the outputs are in fact valued. Who is to judge the value of a museum's outputs? The consumers. What this means is that the views of the museum's audiences must be discovered and brought into the managerial decisions concerning service levels, mixes and qualities (Jackson 1991). Implicit in the VFM framework is the commitment to evaluate by collecting data that shows who wants the service and how specifically they value the service. Do teachers, for example really want the exhibitions and educational programmes that the museum is producing? Why and how do we know?

The forward plans for Coventry Museum Service detail the systematic collection of data relating to outputs. One example of how this will work in the next few months is the

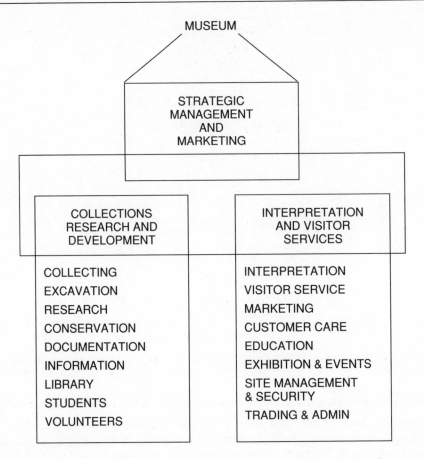

Fig. 45.6 Functional map for the restructuring of the City Museum Service, Coventry, UK

evaluation of the experience of children and teachers visiting an exhibition designed especially for children aged 7 to 11 years. This will entail talking to teachers about their objectives for visits to the exhibition and reviewing the children's products (drawings, poetry, creative writing) and experiences in the exhibition.

I find this notion of customer-centred management very exciting. It seems to me that museum education has been built on exactly these customer-centred values. Few education officers have designed their services without consulting their users, without evaluating and piloting their programmes, and without assessing and modifying their products in response to their customers. The VFM framework asks the whole museum to work in this way.

It is ironic that it has taken the philosophy of the market-place and individual choice to shake museums out of their old complacency. Museums are only just now beginning to discover what it means to think about their users, and are only now developing new structures and new methods that will enable them to become responsive and in tune with their audiences.

We have looked at the new contexts for the development of customer-centred museums, and reviewed one way of establishing internal structures to achieve this. (There are other ways in which this can be done; see Locke 1995.) What would a customer-centred museum actually be doing?

```
┌─────────────────────────────┐
│       INTERPRETATION        │
│        AND VISITOR          │
│         SERVICES            │
├─────────────────────────────┤
│   PERMANENT DISPLAYS        │
│                             │
│   TEMPORARY EXHIBITIONS     │
│                             │
│   EDUCATION & OUTREACH      │
│                             │
│   MARKET RESEARCH &         │
│   EVALUATION                │
│                             │
│   VISITOR FACILITIES        │
│                             │
│   TRADING                   │
│                             │
│   ADMINISTRATION            │
│                             │
│   SITE MANAGEMENT &         │
│   SECURITY                  │
└─────────────────────────────┘
```

Fig. 45.7 Development of interpretation and visitor services, the ouput side of the bi-partite division

A customer-centred museum would have a number of features that we can identify:

1. It would know its actual and potential audience, and would understand the diversity, needs, likes of the various different groups concerned. It would have carried out a needs assessment, researched its actual visitors, and talked to those who were not visiting to identify the barriers to full participation (Harvey 1987; Susie Fisher Group 1990; MacDonald 1995). The results of this research would be based in management decision-making processes.
2. It would have built up long-lasting and secure relationships with groups from many sections of the community, and this would be reflected in its trustee board/committee, which would be representative of men and women, the main ethnic groups that lived within its catchment area, and people with special needs.
3. It would understand museum communication and education theory, including a range of approaches to evaluation, and would apply these ideas in the development of its programmes and exhibitions (Hooper-Greenhill 1994).
4. It would understand its audiences in terms of different segments with specific needs and interests and would review its outputs on their terms (Millard 1992).
5. It would be aware of and implement the various standards and guidelines that have been developed in this area, such as *Standard Practices Handbook* (Alberta Museum Association 1990); *Excellence and Equity – Education and the Public Dimension of Museums* (American Association of Museums 1992); *Guidelines on Disability for Museums and Galleries in the United Kingdom* (Museums and Galleries Commission 1992); *Quality of Service in Museums and Galleries: Customer Care in Museums – Guidelines on Implementation* (Museums & Galleries Commission 1993).

333

CONCLUSION

Many museums are currently involved in rethinking their way forward for the future. The way forward will inevitably be hand-in-hand with those people who value what museums do. The more people are involved, the more of them that there are and the more enthusiastic they feel, the rosier the future will be. This cannot be achieved without education – at the heart of museums.

This paper was the keynote paper to the conference Pathways to Partnerships, *organized by the Museum Education Association of Australia and the Museum of Education Association of New Zealand, Melbourne, September 1993.*

REFERENCES

Alberta Museums Association (1990) *Standard Practices Handbook*, Alberta, Canada.

American Association of Museums (1992) *Excellence and Equity – Education and the Public Dimension of Museums*, Washington, DC: American Association of Museums.

Audit Commission (1991) *The Road to Wigan Pier? Managing Local Authority Museums and Art Galleries*, The Audit Commission for Local Authorities and the National Health Service in England and Wales, London: HMSO.

Coxall, H. (1991) 'How language means: an alternative view of museums text', in G. Kavanagh (ed.) *Museum Languages: Objects and Texts*, Leicester, London and New York: Leicester University Press.

Ekarv, M. (1986/7) 'Combating redundancy – writing texts for exhibitions', *Exhibitions in Sweden* 27/28: 1–7.

Harvey, B. (1987) *Visting the National Portrait Gallery*, London: Office of Public Censuses and Surveys/ HMSO.

Hatton, A. (1993) 'Education at the core of the museum', paper to the Museums Association seminar *Museum Education in Crisis*, 18 May, London.

Hooper-Greenhill, E. (1994) *Museums and their Visitors,* London: Routledge.

Hooper-Greenhill, E. (ed.) (1991) *Writing a Museum Education Policy*, Leicester: Department of Museum Studies, University of Leicester.

Jackson, P. (1991) 'Performance indicators: promises and pitfalls', in S. Pearce (ed.) *Museum Economics and the Community*, London: Athlone Press: 41–64.

Locke, S. (1995) 'A manager discusses museum communication', in E. Hooper-Greenhill (ed.) *Museum: Media: Message*, London: Routledge.

MacDonald, S. (1995) 'Getting the message: planning a responsive service', in E. Hooper-Greenhill (ed.) *Museum: Media: Message,* London: Routledge.

Millard, J. (1992) 'Art history for all the family', *Museums Journal* 92(2): 32–3.

Museums and Galleries Commission (1991) *Local Authorities and Museums – a Report by a Working Party*, London: Museums and Galleries Commission.

Museum & Galleries Commission (1992) *Guidelines on Disability from Museums and Galleries in the United Kingdom*, London: Museums and Galleries Commission.

Museums & Galleries Commission (1993) *Quality of Service in Museums and Galleries: Customer Care in Museums – Guidelines on Implementation*, London: Museums and Galleries Commission.

National Audit Office (1993) *Department of National Heritage, National Museums and Galleries: Quality of Service to the Public*, London: HMSO.

Pittman, N. (1991) 'Writing a museum education policy – introductory remarks', *Group for Education in Museums Newsletter* 43, Autumn: 22–4.

Schadla-Hall, T. (1993) 'The current situation in Leicestershire', paper to the Museums Association seminar *Museum Education in Crisis*, 18 May, London.

Susie Fisher Group (1990) *Bringing History and the Arts to a New Audience: Qualitative Research for the London Borough of Croydon*, London: The Susie Fisher Group.

FURTHER READING

Ambrose, T. (ed.) (1987) *Education in Museums: Museums in Education*, Edinburgh: Scottish Museums Council and HMSO.

Berry, N. and Mayer, S. (1989) *Museum Education – History, Theory and Practice,* Virginia, USA: the National Art Education Association.

Collins, Z. (1981) *Museums, Adults and the Humanities: a Guide for Educational Programming,* Washington, DC: American Association of Museums.

Communications Design Team, Royal Ontario Museum (1976) *Communicating with the Museum Visitor,* Toronto, Canada: Royal Ontario Museum.

Falk, J. and Dierking, L. (1992) *The Museum Experience,* Washington, DC: Whalesback Books.

Hooper-Greenhill, E. (1991) *Museum and Gallery Education,* Leicester: Leicester University Press.

Hooper-Greenhill, E. (1994) *Museums and their Visitors,* London: Routledge.

Hooper-Greenhill, E. (ed.) (1989) *Initiatives in Museum Education,* Leicester: Department of Museum Studies, University of Leicester.

Hooper-Greenhill, E. (ed.) (1991) *Writing a Museum Education Policy,* Leicester: Department of Museum Studies, University of Leicester.

Hooper-Greenhill, E. (ed.) (1992) *Working in Museum and Gallery Education – 10 Career Experiences,* Leicester: Department of Museum Studies, University of Leicester.

Loomis, R. (1987) *Museum Visitor Evaluation – a New Tool for Management,* Nashville, Tennessee: American Association for State and Local History.

Museum Education Roundtable (1992) *Patterns in Practice: Selections from the Journal of Museum Education,* Washington, DC: Museum Education Roundtable.

Newsom, B. Y. and Silver, A. Z. (1978) *The Art Museum as Educator,* Berkeley, Los Angeles and London: University of California Press.

Nichols, K. (ed.) (1984) *Museum Education Anthology 1973–1983,* Washington, DC: Museum Education Roundtable.

Serrell, B. (ed.) (1990) *What Research Says about Learning in Science Museums,* Association of Science Technology Centres, USA.

Index